F. (Friedrich) Hassaurek

The Secret of the Andes

A Romance

F. (Friedrich) Hassaurek

The Secret of the Andes
A Romance

ISBN/EAN: 9783744673792

Printed in Europe, USA, Canada, Australia, Japan

Cover: Foto ©Thomas Meinert / pixelio.de

More available books at **www.hansebooks.com**

THE SECRET OF THE ANDES:

A ROMANCE.

By F. HASSAUREK,

Author of "Four Years among Spanish Americans," etc.

CINCINNATI:
ROBERT CLARKE & CO.
1879.

F. HASSAUREK.
1879.

STEREOTYPED BY CAMPBELL & CO., CIN., O.

THE SECRET OF THE ANDES.

BOOK I.
DREAMS.

Que es la vida? Un frenesi.
Que es la vida? Una illusion,
Una sombra, una ficcion
Y el mayor bien es pequeño;
Que toda la vida es sueño
Y los sueños sueño son.
   CALDERON DE LA BARCA, *La vida es Sueño.*

BOOK I.

DREAMS.

CHAPTER I.

STORM CLOUDS.

It was in the spring of 1592. The city of Quito, in the Spanish Viceroyalty of Peru, in South America, was trembling with excitement. Angry crowds of wildly gesticulating men, of high and low degree, filled the public squares and blockaded the streets. Defiant exclamations, such as "*Down with the Alcabala! Death to the Chapetones!*" (natives of Spain), were heard in every direction. A new member of the Royal Audience, the supreme judicial and executive tribunal of the Province, had just arrived from Spain. He had brought official confirmation of the report that a great and crying breach of faith was contemplated by the Home Government. The crushing tax called *Alcabala* was to be introduced in the Viceroyalty of Peru! And yet, by an express stipulation of the Royal grant to Don Francisco Pizarro, the conqueror, Peru was to be exempted from the imposition of the Alcabala for one hundred years, which term had not yet expired, and would not expire during the lifetime of this generation.

The people of Quito were impoverished and in debt. Their fathers had been disappointed of their golden expectations. The men of Benalcazar had founded the city in the vain hope of discovering, sooner or later, the hidden treasure of Atahualpa and Rumiñagui. To that *ignis fatuus* they had sacrificed the lives of thousands of unfortunate Indians. For that unattainable object the first settlers had impoverished themselves by long and fruitless explorations, and by the neglect of more useful and legitimate pursuits. Now, coined money had become almost a curiosity among them. Their business transactions were reduced to a most primitive system of barter and exchange. Could such a people afford to pay a tax of four or more per cent. on all sales—a tax which was levied and re-levied on the same article as often as it changed hands, until it reached its final consumer? Impossible! Death in battle was preferable to slow starvation. The Alcabala must not be collected. Resistance—forcible resistance—was the general cry. It was taken up eagerly by hundreds of old soldiers who had served in the civil wars of the conquerors, and of whom many who had fought on the losing side were left penniless, and ready to engage in any brawl that promised rapine and booty.

It was about an hour after sunset, when two young gentlemen, of the highest nobility, on their way to the Plaza of San Francisco, elbowed themselves through the throngs of indignant and excited men. The one was Don Julio de Carrera, perhaps the best liked young cavalier of Quito, modest, affable, refined, a lover of books in an age of barbarism, honest and honorable. Beloved, although penniless, his father having died in poverty, the young man depended on the liberality of an uncle, a childless bachelor, and, next to the Marquis de Solando, the richest man of the whole province. The other was Carrera's intimate friend, Don Roberto Sanchez, an impulsive, highspirited, frank, and dashing youth, the son of Don Alonzo Sanchez, who was an influential member of the Cabildo, or Municipal Council of Quito, famous for his eloquence, and known as one of the boldest and most determined opponents of the contemplated introduction of the Alcabala.

The two young gentlemen arrested their steps before the mansion of the Marquis de Solando, where they in-

tended to spend the evening. The great wealth of the
Marquis and the extraordinary attractions of his daughter,
Dolores, had given him the leading position in the society
of Quito. His daily evening receptions (*tertulias*) were
attended by a larger circle than those at any other house.
This evening, too, a very numerous company was assembled
when the two young cavaliers entered the *salon*. The ladies of the house excepted, the party consisted exclusively
of gentlemen, who eagerly discussed the all-absorbing
topic of the day. The Marquis, a thorough loyalist, advocated submission. The Señor Alonzo Sanchez, the
father of young Roberto, who had just entered, spoke en-
ergetically in favor of resistance, and was warmly supported by most of the gentlemen present. High words
passed, and the discussion threatened to become loud and
angry, when it was interrupted by a new visitor, whose
presence and official character forbade its renewal. This
newcomer was the Count Joaquin de Valverde, a young
officer of the best blue blood of Spain, who had been sent
by the Viceroy of Peru to command the Spanish arquebusiers and other regular troops stationed at Quito, and to
instruct the native militia. The young nobleman had
come to America to recuperate his broken fortunes, but as
he stood high in the favor of the all-mighty Viceroy, the
Count's future was considered secured, and the mothers of
marriageable daughters looked upon him as one of the
highest prizes attainable in the matrimonial lottery. This
prize, however, it was generally believed, would fall to the
lot of Dolores Solando, for whose favor Count Valverde
had but two prominent rivals, the Señor Don Julio de
Carrera, and the Señor Don Manuel Paredes, who was
among the visitors in the room, and will presently be introduced to the reader.

CHAPTER II.

THE MYSTERIOUS QUEEN.

"I hope I shall be the first," said Doña Dolores to Count Valverde, after the customary exchange of salutations, " to tell your Excellency the news of the great adventure our friend, the Señor Carrera, has met with."

"I shall be delighted to hear it," said the Count, not at all edified by the prospect of hearing an adventure discussed of which he was not himself the hero.

"Your Excellency must know that the Señor Carrera is fond of solitary rambles. He is a poet, Señor Count, and we all admire his verses. He loves to explore the lonely recesses of Mount Pichincha; and there he met with his wonderful adventure. He came upon a maiden radiant with beauty, an apparition from Fairy Land. He has been in love with her ever since, and the ladies of Quito are dying with jealousy. The maiden, of course, was unknown to him, and, what makes his adventure more mysterious, she was an Indian."

"An Indian?"

"Yes, Señor Count, an Indian of exquisite beauty, majesty, and grace. He had come upon her suddenly, near the entrance of a ravine. He stood before her struck dumb with admiration. Still, we suspect he would have recovered his faculty of speech. We are even inclined to believe that he would, upon the spot, have made a declaration of love, had not the wonderful creature suddenly and most capriciously and unaccountably disappeared."

"Disappeared?"

"Yes, Señor Count, disappeared, vanished into nothingness, sailed away in a cloud, or sunk into the center of the earth. Was it not provoking? The belt of Señor Carrera's sword broke at the most inconvenient moment, and caused that bloody weapon to drop to the ground. He stooped to pick it up, and when he looked up again the apparition was gone. There was no trace of her anywhere. There was no bush, no tree, no rock in the ravine behind which she might have hidden herself, and yet she was gone, vanished into air, as I said. What does your Excellency think of it?"

"I hope," said the Count, "it was not one of Señor Carrera's poetic fancies, inspired by—"

"No, Señor Count," interrupted Dolores, "there is proof positive and tangible of the reality of the apparition—a dagger found by his Grace on the very spot where the maiden had stood. We have made him produce the *corpus delicti*. There it is."

"This is Moorish steel," said the Count, examining the weapon with the eye of a *connoisseur*, "of excellent temper and approved fashion. How could it fall into the hands of an Indian?"

"Ah! this is the very complication of the mystery, Señor Count," rejoined Dolores, who loved to address herself to the representative of real, genuine, old-country nobility. "We have come to the conclusion that that wonderful Indian must either be a witch or the mysterious Shyri Queen of Quito, of whom we have heard so much and seen nothing."

"She may be both," added the Señora Catita, the aunt of Dolores, who sat beside her on the sofa.

"To my shame, I must confess to your Ladyships," answered the Count, "not to have heard of this Shyri Queen."

"Your Excellency has not resided with us long enough," resumed Dolores, "to become familiar with our Indian traditions. The Shyri Queen is supposed to be a granddaughter of Atahualpa, the Inca, secretly brought up in the family of some great cacique, or among the unsubdued Indians of our oriental provinces, so as to prevent her from being seized by the authorities. The Indians of the ancient empire of Quito recognize and revere that mythical queen as their rightful sovereign. At her command they would rise in rebellion; at her command they would kill us all, and burn our houses if they could. Her mere name, whether she be a myth or a reality, is a threat to the peace and security of these provinces."

"And why do they call her the Shyri Queen, if your Ladyships will allow me?"

"Her ancestors, the ancient kings of Quito, were called Shyris. Their kingdom was overthrown by the Peruvian Incas about forty years before the arrival of the Spaniards. The last Shyri was slain in battle. His only child, a daughter, was taken for a wife by the victorious Inca, and thus became the mother of Atahualpa. But it is not the mysterious Indian Queen or Princess, it is her dowry, Señor Count, in which we are principally and intensely interested. If there is such a being as the Shyri Queen, and I have no doubt of it, although no white man or woman has ever seen her, she possesses the secret of the hidden treasure of Atahualpa, for which our gentlemen have been searching in vain during three generations. What a grand discovery it would be, if her disappearance where the Señor Carrera had seen her, should indicate the presence of a subterranean passage, through which the treasure might be reached. Come, Señor Sanchez, you are learned in history, and can speak from a knowledge of the chronicles of the Cabildo, give his Excellency an account of what is known of the origin and character of that treasure."

"Let me beg of your Grace," insisted the Count.

"O, please do!" shouted the company; and all leaned

forward eagerly to listen to an authoritative statement of the great problem of their lives, the one great object of their aspirations. They all had heard the story before. They had listened to it many a time. They were familiar with all its details; but they never grew tired of listening to it again. They could not hear it often enough. They drank in every word, as it fell from the lips of the venerable Alcalde.

CHAPTER III.

EVIDENCE.

"Your Excellency is, of course, familiar," began Señor Sanchez, the Father, "with the circumstances of the original conquest of Peru. Atahualpa was a prisoner in the hands of Don Francisco Pizarro at Cajamarca, and being a man of natural shrewdness, the Inca could not fail to observe the great greed of our people for gold, and the thought struck him that through this he might gain his liberty. Hence he proposed that, as his ransom, he would fill the room in which they kept him, as high as his arms could reach, with vessels and ornaments of gold and silver. To bring these treasures together, orders were sent to all parts of the empire to rifle the palaces and temples of their precious contents and send them to Cajamarca. These orders were obeyed everywhere except here in Quito. And yet here, where the great Inca, Huyanacapac, Atahualpa's father, had spent the last thirty years of his prosperous reign, immense treasures had been accumulated. But a usurper had seized the reins of government here, and refused to comply with the royal mandate. This usurper was Rumiñagui, a name which, in the Quichua language, means "The eye or face of stone." He was a great general, who had been with Atahualpa when the poor Inca was taken prisoner by the cunning stratagem of Don Francisco Pizarro. Rumiñagui was in command of the army stationed at Cajamarca; but without attempting to strike a blow for his master, he retreated to this province, with the intent of making himself the King or Shyri of Quito. He seized the royal treasures and the Virgins of the Sun, killed all the wives, sisters, brothers, cousins, and other relatives of Atahualpa, and considered himself secure in his usurpation, in view of the small number of foreign invaders by whom the Inca had allowed himself to be entrapped. Rumiñagui offered a desperate and very skillful resistance to the Spanish troops that were sent against him; but when he found that these invaders were irresistible, and that all his efforts were unavailing, he killed the Virgins of the Sun so that they should not fall into the hands of the Spaniards, and he hid or buried the great treasure of Quito somewhere in the mountains. To this present day nobody has discovered where, although the search has been incessant. Rumiñagui was captured and put to the rack; but an Indian never reveals a secret of his race. He died without opening his lips. Hundreds of his captains and followers were tortured until they expired; but either they did not know the secret or they would not reveal it. And so our men of high and low degree are still delving and burrowing in the earth; but thus far to no avail. We know that the treasure existed—hundreds of Indian eye-witnesses admitted that. We know that it must be hidden somewhere, but we are unable to find it."

A long pause followed, during which each of the company seemed to be pondering over the great secret and dreaming the dream of its discovery. The silence was at last broken by the Count.

"I must trouble your Grace with a question. I heard,

while in Lima, that the scepter of the Incas could not descend to a female, and yet their Ladyships speak of a Shyri Queen as the successor of Atahualpa."

"Your Excellency is right as to the law of Peru, which several hundred years ago was also the law of the kingdom of Quito; but it was changed by the eleventh Shyri, who had no sons, brothers, or nephews, but an only daughter by the name of Toa, to whom he was fondly devoted. In order to secure her succession, he made a new law, which received the sanction of all the great nobles of the realm. It stipulated that upon the extinction of the male line, the Shyri's daughter should succeed her father and reign jointly with the husband of her own free and untrammeled choice. The husband whom the old Shyri recommended to his daughter Toa, was Duchicela, eldest son of Cundurazu, King of Parruhá, a kingdom extending from Riobamba to Paita and the coast. By this marriage the two crowns were united, and the house of Duchicela was thus placed upon the throne of Quito. The mysterious granddaughter of Atahualpa, if she does exist, may confer the Indian kingdom of Quito in a similar manner by the free bestowal of her hand."

"And she might," interrupted Dolores, "bestow it on his Grace, the Señor de Carrera, the only cavalier to whom, thus far, she seems to have shown herself. How would your Grace fancy the title of Don Julio I of the house of Carrera and Duchicela, Shyri-Inca of Quito and Purruhá?"

A burst of laughter rewarded this pleasantry, while Carrera blushed and looked uneasy. Some of the gentlemen seemed inclined to elaborate the suggestion; but Dolores was too prudent to allow it, and turned the conversation back into its original channel.

"Your Excellency must not believe that we Creoles invent all these wonderful stories. The Indians firmly believe in the existence of their Shyri Queen, and I can only say I share their belief. Let me furnish your Excellency with a living witness of my faith. There is my nurse, Mama Santos, an Indian of high nobility. She is a granddaughter of Cozopangui, who was governor of Quito under Atahualpa and Rumiñagui. Call her, Raimundo. She will tell your Lordships what she has told me a hundred times, no more, no less. She will betray no secret of her race, if she knows any, but she will bear testimony to the reality of the Shyri Queen."

Mama Santos, who now made her appearance, and at the command of Dolores took her station behind the sofa, was a woman of uncertain age, like all Indian women after they have passed their teens. Her features had probably been beautiful once, but her beauty had faded. Her eyes were still attractive, and bore an expression of sadness and resignation. Her bearing was full of deference, but self-possessed, dignified, and indicative of quiet determination.

"Mama Santos! These gentlemen wish to take a glass of wine with thee in honor of the royal house of Atahualpa-Duchicela. Raimundo! A goblet for Mama Santos! Fill the glasses of these gentlemen!"

Mama Santos bowed impassively, and taking her glass, she said: "Your Lordships honor me by your kindness. May your Lordships live many years!"

"Thy good health, Mama Santos," said Carrera, "and honor to the memory of thy ancient kings."

"Mama Santos," continued Dolores, "wilt thou tell these gentlemen who would now be entitled to wear the royal diadem of the Shyris, if this country did not belong to our Lord, the King of Spain?"

"The Lady Toa Duchicela is the successor of Atahualpa, Niñita* Doloritas."

"Who is the Lady Toa Duchicela?" resumed Dolores.

"She is the granddaughter of Atahualpa."

---

* An endearing, and yet respectful diminutive.

"Hast thou ever seen her?"

"No!"

"How dost thou know, then, that she lives?"

"How does Niñita know that King Philip II lives? Niñita has never seen him."

"Bravo! bravo!" exclaimed the Marquis. "Well said, Mama Santos."

"But there is a gentleman here, Mamita," answered Dolores, "who has seen him. This is the count Valverde, Mamita, a gentleman from Spain, who has seen His Majesty very often."

"I am your Lordship's servant," said Santos, with a graceful bow.

"Where is the Shyri Toa now, Mamita?" asked Dolores.

"I do not know, Niña."

"Wouldst thou know her if thou shouldst see her?"

"I can not tell, Niña."

"Suppose a common Indian should pretend to be the Shyri Toa."

"No Indian woman would do that, Niña."

"Suppose the Shyri Toa should die, how wouldst thou know it?"

"I should soon know it, Niña."

"But how?"

"How would Niña Doloritas learn of the death of His Majesty of Spain. Somebody would tell her. Somebody would tell me that the Shyri Toa was dead."

"Is she married?"

"No, Niña."

"Not married! Señor Don Julio de Carrera! Take heed of this important statement. The Shyri Toa is still at liberty to bestow upon your Grace her hand and kingly title. Many thanks, Mamita Santos. We shall not detain thee any longer."

Mama Santos returned her glass to the servant, bowed to the company, and withdrew. At this moment the clock of San Francisco struck ten. A horn was sounded in the street; every one in the room became silent, and the voice of the watchman was heard to sing:

> "Ave Maria, Santisima!
> Las diez han dado,
> Noche clara y serena,
> Viva el Rey de España!"*

"The stay-bell!" exclaimed all the gentlemen.

"We have taken no heed of the flight of time," said Señor Sanchez. "How embarrassing. I had no idea it was so late."

"You are my prisoners, gentlemen," said the Marquis, "and I shall keep you under arrest till morning."

CHAPTER IV.

GAMBLING.

After the ringing of the stay-bell (*toque de la queda*) the use of the streets was forbidden by municipal ordinance to the inhabitants of Quito and other Peruvian towns. Heavy penalties awaited the transgressor. If armed, his arms were to be taken from him; if unarmed, he was to be put in the stocks for a number of days. A third repetition of the offense was to be visited with banishment. The turbulence of the original conquerors, their frequent insurrections and civil wars, and the violence and licentiousness of the soldiers of fortune who had participated in these commotions, made it necessary to enforce such regulations, with great severity, against persons of all ranks, and especially against those who enjoyed the high privilege of bearing arms. Hence when visitors had lingered at the

---

*Ave Maria, most holy. The clock has struck ten. The night is calm and clear. Long live the King of Spain.

houses of their friends until it was too late to go home, it became a duty of hospitality to provide them with accommodations for the night.

This duty the Marquis most attentively complied with. His house was one of the largest at Quito, and might have accommodated double the number of guests; but the gentlemen present, after a graceful recognition of the kindness and liberality of their noble host, soon relinquished the thought of retiring to bed-rooms, but crowded around the card-table, which in those times possessed the same irresistible fascination for Spanish-Americans that it exerts nowadays. Even the ladies, with the exception of the Marchioness, who, being an invalid, soon excused herself and withdrew, took part in the exciting pastime. Carrera alone, for a while, contented himself with the part of a looker-on. He had vainly attempted to address a few words privately to Dolores, who skillfully eluded him and divided her attentions with becoming impartiality. The young gentleman, disappointed in his attempts, then drew his friend, Roberto Sanchez, into one of the deep window-embrasures to ask him for a loan of money. "I hardly dare to ask thee for an additional favor," he said, "but how can I exclude myself? If I lose, it may be some time before I can repay thee. I want but a trifle to keep up appearances. Still, do not inconvenience thyself, unless thou art fully able to help me out."

"Most assuredly," answered Roberto, "I shall help thee out to the best of my ability. But beware of that villain, Paredes. He and that Spanish Count must be watched closely. I should not trust either of them, unless I could keep my eyes on them steadily."

The game had commenced, first moderately, but soon increasing in intensity and passion, until it had completely riveted the attention of the players to the exclusion of everything else. So much has been said and written on the theory of luck, that it would be fruitless labor to add to the literature of the subject. Why some men will alway lose, while others will nearly always win, is one of the problems that are doomed to remain unsolved. Poor Carrera was one of those who almost always lost. For some time he held his own that evening, but at last the tide set in against him, until the loan from Sanchez was nearly exhausted. Then came a brief run of luck, but it was cut short by his turn to take the bank. His rivals, the Spanish Count and Manuel Paredes, now played strongly against the banker, and when his turn closed, he was involved in a heavy debt to Paredes, and had but a few pieces left to continue the hopeless struggle.

The ladies withdrew unnoticed, and the game went on. A collation was served at one o'clock which was rapidly taken. The Marquis and nearly all his guests, with the exception of the Spanish Count and the Senor Manuel Paredes, lost heavily. To these two the battle for the spoils seemed to be confined, and was waged with continually fluctuating success. As to Carrera, it was a repetition of his old experience; hope deferred, anger, mortification, cautious timidity alternating with the imprudence and recklessness of despair, silent self-reproaches, and bitter remorse, coupled with vows to abstain forever afterward often made, and broken as often as they are made, and a sinking heart while he forced a sickly smile on his lips, and endeavored to appear composed. His hands and feet were cold, while his head was burning. Deeper and deeper he became involved in debt to Paredes, vainly hoping that his luck would change at last. And so the game was kept up until daylight broke upon the scene, and chocolate was served to the exhausted players.

When Carrera left the house of the Marquis, he owed a hundred and fifty ducats to Paredes in addition to his debt to Sanchez the younger, a formidable sum of money in those days.

Haggard, pale, wearied, crushed, he threw himself upon

his couch, and tossed about restlessly; but sleep would not come to his relief and silence the voice of remorse. The cards still danced before his eyes, and the monotonous exclamations of the players reverberated in his ears. Had he but conquered his false shame, and refused to play! Had he but stopped after the loan of Sanchez was exhausted. The question, "How shall I pay these debts?" again and again arose before his mind, and his racked imagination suggested no solution. Would he have to tell his uncle? Must he appear before that stern and austere man and accuse himself of reckless profligacy? His uncle was a devoutly religious man. The convents entertained high expectations of rich endowments from him. Would he not devote his fortune to works of faith and charity rather than bestow it on the spendthrift who had no idea of the value of wealth or of the difficulties of its acquisition.

And now, the physical effects of dissipation added misery to Carrera's mental agony. His head throbbed and ached, and shivering he covered himself with additional blankets, and lay waking, fretting, despairing, disgusted with himself and the world, while the busy hum of life had revived in the streets, and the glaring rays of the equatorial sun broke through his windows.

CHAPTER V.

A BARREN DISCOVERY.

The day was far advanced, when Carrera rose from his bed. He summoned his Indian servant, and ordered him to bring his breakfast.

"How pale you look, Master," said the boy. "Is your Lordship sick?"

"I am not aware of it."

"Yes, Master, your Lordship looks very pale. Your eyes are dim. Your step is uncertain. If you are sick, Master, you had better consult Mama Rucu; she will make your Lordship well."

"Dost thou think so, Mariano?"

"Yes, Master," replied the boy. "I know it. When the plague ravaged the country a few years ago, she saved every one who came to her, while all those who took the medicines of your white leeches, died. She cured me, Master, when my own mother had given me up."

When the Lord had abandoned Saul, his despair prompted him to consult the witch of Endor.

"*Flectere, si nequeo superos, Acheronta movebo.*" Not those basking in the sunshine of prosperity, but those around whom the clouds of adversity gather, will seek aid or advice from the powers of darkness. The card-player, especially, is naturally prone to superstition. It was customary in those times to consult Moorish Astrologers, fortune-tellers, and Indian sorcerers. The Church fulminated its censures against these practices, but even the Church was powerless against the weaknesses of the human mind, as it had been powerless against its vanities.

Mama Rucu, the great Indian sorceress, whom pries's and nobles had consulted in sickness and distress, and whose immunity rested on her real or supposed knowledge of the secrets of all the leading families of Quito, would she be able to help him? Probably not. How should she? And yet, why should he not try? Even if she gave him no satisfaction, he would lose nothing by the experiment. He still could fall back on his last and only resort, the dreaded confession to his uncle. But she might give him a charm to soften that stern man. Yes, he would consult the old witch; and, this resolution once arrived at, he determined to carry it out immediately. He also determined to avoid his friends, as much as possible, until he had seen his uncle and obtained the means from him to pay his debts of honor. And then he would forever renounce gambling. Why should he play? Was he not a lover of books? Did they not look sadly at him from their shelves, reproaching him with having neglected their delightful companionship of late? No, he would return to his silent friends again, and remain faithful to them hereafter. He snatched his *Horace* from the shelves, and, opening the book at random, he alighted on that well-known ode, which had steadied the minds of so many before him, and would be comfort and solace to yet unborn thousands: "*Æquam rebus in arduis servare mentem,*" etc.

His servant had opened the window, and the bright, bracing, sunny air of Quito, revived his drooping spirits. The freshness and vigor of youth returned and filled him with new hope. He left his house, and, avoiding the main streets, he soon reached the rear of the acclivity of San Juan, and passing the villa and gardens of Don Manuel Paredes, he began the ascent of one of the mountain spurs which rock-crowned Pichincha sends forth into the plain of Quito. He was not far from the scene of his adventure with the mysterious Indian maiden, when, to his utter astonishment and surprise, he heard the usual quietness of this lonely neighborhood broken by the sound of loud and angry voices.

Let us precede him.

Manuel Paredes had eagerly listened to the narratives and surmises of Dolores and Sanchez the night before. There was, evidently, some subterranean hiding-place in the ravine where Carrera's maiden had disappeared. The supposition that the Inca treasure might be buried there was not at all improbable. If the girl whom Carrera had seen was Toa Duchicela, the mysterious Shyri Queen, it was also probable that she knew the secret. Manuel Paredes was a man of action. Books and poetry were nothing to him. He dealt in the realities of life, and his main and only object was to promote the interests of Manuel Paredes. He determined to investigate the mystery. He had obtained, from Carrera, an accurate description of the locality, which was very near his own summer-house. He would make excavations. He would sink shafts in every direction, and if there was a subterranean passage in or under that ravine, he was determined to discover it. He summoned his *Mayordomo* and four of his Indian farm-laborers with spades and crow-bars, and ordered them to follow him. But he was not without a competitor. Just when he was about to leave his garden-villa, on the hill, Count Valverde made his appearance.

"I have come," said the Spaniard, "to ask your Grace to take me to the place the Señor Carrera described to your Grace last night. If a treasure is to be found there, I want to search for it, and I ask your Grace to join in the search. If your Grace is willing to investigate the matter, I can order my sappers and miners to work for us systematically."

Paredes was not at all pleased. What he intended to do he wanted to do for himself, and not for, or with another. Yet, the Commander of the royal garrison at Quito, and the *protegé* of the Viceroy of Peru, was not a personage whom it would be profitable to offend. He would submit to his company in the day time, but he would secretly continue the search at night. The chances of the Count should not be even, if Manuel Peredes could help it. So he consented, and the party proceeded to the place.

Foot by foot the soil was probed with spade and crowbar, Paredes testing one side of the ravine and the Count the other, while the Indians, puzzled and bewildered, did as they were ordered. The search had not proceeded more than a few rods from the entrance of the ravine, when the crow-bar, in the hands of the Mayordomo, struck a hard substance in the hill-side, and a hollow sound accompanied the blow. The Mayordomo uttered an exclamation of surprise. A repetition of the blow produced the same result.

"I have struck a hard substance," said the Steward, "which is not a rock." And tearing up the sod with the bar, he laid bare a dark and smooth surface which had the appearance of bronze.

"It is bronze!" shrieked Paredes. "Come with your shovels and clear away the earth."

The vegetation covering that particular spot was scarce and the earth dry. It readily yielded to spade and shovel and exposed a plate of bronze of about four feet in length and two feet in width.

"Santa Maria!" exclaimed the Count; "this is a discovery."

"This seems to be a door or a lid covering an aperture!" said the Steward. "Listen how hollow it sounds!"

"Force it open!" said Paredes. The plate seemed to be imbedded slantingly in the side of the ravine. The Steward viewed it carefully, touched it with his bar inch by inch, and finally stemmed his foot against it, when to the astonishment of everybody the upper part suddenly gave way, and, sinking to a flat level with the base, opened a dark passage into the mountain side. The excitement of the men at this discovery knew no bounds. Pale, trembling with eager anticipation, with bated breaths and palpitating hearts, they stared into the darkness of the aperture. Suddenly a shrill, hoarse laugh interrupted the breathless silence. Instinctively white men and Indians shrank back in terror and looked about to see from whom the grating sound had come. They did not have to look long. It was right above them. Just upon the brink of the ravine, on the side in which the opening had been discovered, and almost perpendicularly above it, stood a figure which sent a shudder through Count Valverde's frame. It was a woman; at least she wore the garments of a woman, but her face, shriveled with age, would not have betrayed her sex. Her hair was short, thick, and white. Her countenance was that of a mummy, only her eyes, wildly rolling and shooting the fiercest glances, showed that her face was alive, terribly alive. She rested her left side on a crutch; in her right hand she held a stick, which helped to support her tottering form.

The four Indians, on beholding her, at once uncovered, and bowed their heads, and stood in reverential silence. It was Mama Rucu, the Indian witch, the prophetess, the medicine woman, the last of the great sorceresses of her race. Again she gave a laugh, short and shrill, and arousing in the awe-stricken breasts of those who beheld her all the superstitious fears of the sixteenth century.

Three times she raised the heavy stick in her right hand, and then exclaimed in Quichua, her shrill voice reverberating from the mountains:

"Pachacamac! Pachacamac! Be thou the witness of the truth of my words! The spirits of the mountains speak! The spirits of the volcano are aroused! You seek what you have not lost. You seek what you shall never find. You are disturbing the repose of the vanquished and the dead. There must be a victim! One of you shall be the victim! One of you shall be stricken from the land of the living for this profanation of the mysteries of Pichincha. Who shall it be? I hear the voice of the spirit and shall announce the coming judgment. He who passes first through the sacred gate you have opened, shall die before the rains of winter descend again upon the plains of Aña-Quito. He shall die, not surrounded by friends and mourners, but he shall die a horrible death in the hands of infuriated enemies, and biting fire shall lick the skin from his flesh and the flesh from his bones. Hear it, ye mountains! Hear it, ye men of Quito! Hear it, Viracochas! Pachacamac the great is my witness!"

And, as if the mountains had understood it, the rumbling

thunder of Cotopaxi, so frequently heard at Quito, broke forth at this very moment, increasing the terror of her listeners. Count Valverde had not understood a word of what she had said, but he stood rooted to the spot, and could not avert his gaze from her terrible features. Everybody stood aghast, as if bound by some fearful spell. Again the old woman waved her stick three times, and then hobbled away slowly, laughing and muttering to herself as she went. Paredes was the first to recover his self-possession, and, with a forced laugh, said to his Indians: "The good old woman is getting crazy. It is all stuff and nonsense."

"What did she say?" said the Count.

"Oh, nothing!" replied Paredes. "It was nothing but wild and incoherent talk. She wanted to frighten us from the work we have begun, but her threats are powerless against Christians, who believe in the Savior and His Holy Mother!" And, with these words, he crossed himself, devoutly pronouncing the formula. The Count and the Steward followed his example. The Indians still stood motionless.

"And now, Andres!" Paredes said to one of his Indians, in Quichua, "thou art the smallest of us, and canst easily squeeze through this hole. Go in and see what it is."

"No, amo mio!"* answered the Indian. "A thousand pardons, amo, but I shall not go!"

"What!" thundered Paredes, "the villain refuses to obey my command?"

"Mercy, amo mio, for God's sake, mercy!"

"Mercy in hell, you scoundrel!" shrieked Paredes. "I am the master, and I command thee to go into this opening, and see what there is inside. Don Tomas, make the villain go!"

The steward approached the Indian, who shrank back in terror.

---

*Amo means master.

"Do not be a fool, man!" continued Paredes. "No harm shall come to thee. We shall all follow thee. I shall follow thee myself, if thou art afraid, and hold thee up, so that thou shalt not drop into a precipice."

At this moment Carrera made his appearance on the other side of the ravine, just opposite the elevation where the old witch had stood, and looked upon the scene beneath him with eager astonishment.

The Indian dropped on his knees and implored his master for mercy. But the Steward seized him on one side and Paredes on the other, and thus attempted to drag him to the dreaded opening. Suddenly the poor fellow threw himself on the ground, and with tears streaming down his face, declared that he could not and would not go.

"This thing has gone too far!" said Paredes, pale with rage. "If I tolerate such insubordination from any of my Indians, I shall soon have to till my lands in person. We shall have to provide against a repetition of such mutiny. Mayordomo, take this fellow back to the villa, tie him to a post, and let him taste five hundred lashes, well laid on and well counted."

"And what is the cause, Don Manuel?" asked Carrera, whose presence had not been noticed by anybody, "of such exceptional severity?"

"You here, Don Julio?" replied Paredes, gruffly. "I have always claimed and exercised the right to manage my Indians in my own way, and without any interference"—

"There is no necessity for any irritation, Don Manuel. I have just arrived here. I do not know what has happened. I only hear that your Grace is about to inflict a most cruel punishment on a helpless Indian, and I do your Grace the justice to suppose that you have given the order in the heat of passion. I am sure, Don Manuel, you would regret its execution. It might kill the man."

"If I kill my Indians, Don Julio, this is *my* affair, and

although I honor the motive of your interference, I can not tolerate it. This Indian belongs to me."

"But the Señor Paredes must be aware of the fact that the Indians are not slaves; that they are vassals of the crown, to which they pay tribute, and that your Grace has no right to treat them in such a barbarous manner, unworthy of your gentility and standing in society."

"Señor Carrera, I have spoken. I do not wish to quarrel with you, as I have an account to settle with your juvenile friend, Roberto Sanchez, and I believe in one thing at a time. I must repeat, therefore, that your interference is inadmissible. This Indian belongs to me, and I shall punish him for his outrageous insubordination."

"But what has he done?"

"No matter what he has done. It concerns me, not you. Mayordomo, take him away."

"Señor Paredes, you are about to violate the laws of the King, and, worse than that, you are violating the laws of religion and humanity. How much is this Indian worth to you?"

"Does your Grace want to buy him?"

"I would, if you would sell him to me."

"He is not for sale, Don Julio; and even if he were, you are without money to make the purchase. Your Grace seems to have forgotten that you owe me a hundred and fifty ducats. You had better pay your old debts before you contract new ones."

"This is a very ungentlemanly reminder, Don Manuel. Every cent I owe you will be paid. You know I can not do it to-day; but it shall be done in less than a week. In the meantime, I shall not stand by and allow you to commit a plain violation of the law. If I can not prevent it in a friendly manner, I must resort to other means. Will you do me the favor to come out of the ravine, or do you prefer that I should come down to you." With these words, Carrera drew his sword.

"As you please!" answered Paredes, drawing his.

"One moment, gentlemen!" exclaimed the Count.

"No interference, Señor Count," said Paredes. "Your Excellency knows the Viceroyal orders forbidding peacemakers to interfere on such occasions. Does your Excellency wish to violate the law?"

"Indeed, not," replied the Count. "But I wish to say a word to you in private," and approaching Paredes, he whispered: "Give in, Don Manuel, your Grace knows that he is right. I admit that such punishments are very frequently inflicted by masters upon their Indians, but it is done in violation of law, and it might get your Grace into trouble. The Viceroy is determined to protect the Indians against what he calls excessive cruelty, and if your Grace gives way to your passion, you place yourself at the mercy of any enemy who may choose to instigate a prosecution."

"But how can I give way to threats? It would be cowardice to yield."

"Fight him, if you must, but consent to the pardon of the Indian first. Your Grace can punish him at any other time."

Paredes yielded to this advice, and coming out of the the ravine, he said to Carrera: "I am at your Lordship's disposal. But before we begin, I wish to say that owing to the advice and request of Count Valverde, I have concluded to pardon this Indian. I have not done it for your sake, Julio de Carrera, because I never yield to threats. And to show your Grace that your challenge has not influenced my determination in the least, I shall now respond to it as becomes a gentleman." And with these words he threw himself into position. "Be on your guard, Don Julio!"

The Indians sent up a wail.

"One word, Don Manuel," said Carrera. "As the object of my interference has been attained, I should grasp your hand and thank you for your noble self-restraint, rather than meet you as an enemy."

"Well said, Don Julio!" exclaimed the Count. "Take his hand, Colonel Paredes."

"Señor Carrera has challenged me to fight," replied Paredes. "If I do not hold him to his challenge, he will claim that I have acted under compulsion with reference to that Indian."

"You are mistaken, Don Manuel. I pledge you my word of honor that I shall never refer to this unpleasant occurrence. I have always looked upon you as a friend, and if our friendship shall terminate, it will be your fault, not mine. I am ready to proceed; but as I may have been the aggressor, I offer you my hand before I strike. Will you take it?"

"Embrace, gentlemen, embrace," urged the Count.

"You are always amiable, Don Julio," said Paredes. I accept your hand, and shall forget what has happened." Thus saying, he approached Carrera, and the two embraced with all the appearance of cordiality, but both of them well aware that there was no love lost between them, and that the slightest breeze would fan into a fresh blaze the half-smothered fire of hate.

"And now, Don Manuel," said the Count, "I shall encourage these Indians a little. They want encouragement more than lashes. I do not understand the Quichua language, and do not know what the old witch has said to them; but I can see that she has appealed to their superstitions. Let me show them the folly of their fears;" and thus saying, he entered the opening. And again, by a wonderful coincidence, Cotopaxi sent forth its roaring thunder, while the terrified Indians vainly exclaimed: "Stay, Señor, do not go! It is death and destruction."

A smile of grim satisfaction distorted the features of Paredes, but disappeared as quickly as it had come.

Count Valverde returned after a few moments of painful

suspense. "It is the entrance," he said, "to a subterranean passage, which widens as it lengthens. But it is too dark to see; light up a torch."

"But this time, Señor Count," said Paredes, after having lit the torch, "your Excellency will allow me to lead the way. You, men, may follow us."

The fears of the Indians had disappeared. The curse of Mama Ruca attached only to the first man who should pass through the opening. The Count, in their eyes, had knowingly offered himself as the victim, and so they had nothing to fear. Hence, they willingly obeyed their master's command. The Mayordomo and Carrera, who had also descended into the ravine, entered last. And again the thunder of Cotopaxi reverberated from the mountains.

The subterranean passage expanded after a few steps. It became high enough to allow the men to walk erect. Cautiously, they threw the light of the torch on the path before them, lighting up every foot of ground and of the earth-walls around them as they proceeded. Suddenly the noise of rushing waters struck their ears. At the same time the ground disappeared before their feet. They had reached the brink of a precipice. The passage was intersected by a deep ravine, of considerable width, through which a mountain torrent rushed into deeper and darker abysses with noisy rapidity. They bent over the brink, and looked down into the chasm. They could see the water below them, and feel the spray on their cheeks, but the light of their torch was too dim to enable them to form an estimate of the chasm's depth. One thing was clear, there was no way to descend into it. The passage in which they found themselves, terminated abruptly, and there were no steps or projections in the steep rocky bank by the aid of which a descent might have been attempted. Moreover, the rapidity of the torrent would not allow them a foot-hold, even if they should let themselves down by means of ropes and ladders. Thus far their discovery seemed to have proved a barren one. They tested the sides of the passage with their spades and daggers. They plowed up the ground under their feet; but the soil was hard and rocky, and defied their instruments. Other torches were lit, and the digging and boring continued for over an hour, without the slightest result. No side-passage leading out of the corridor which enclosed them could be found. Again and again the subterranean ravine was inspected, but it was of no avail. Tired and disappointed, they abandoned the ungrateful task.

"Don Tomas," whispered Paredes to his Mayordomo, "take these Indians out and forbid them under threats of death to disclose to any living soul, but especially to any white man, what we have seen here to-day." And after the Mayordomo had taken the Indians out of the dark passage, Paredes addressed his companions: "Now, gentlemen, we may stop for to-day. We have found nothing, but this is no proof that we shall find nothing hereafter. We must come back and give this hole a thorough overhauling. For the present, however, we may come to one conclusion. Let us keep this matter secret. If we tell of it, the whole town will be here to-morrow, and we shall be cheated out of the possible fruits of our discovery. There is no danger that Mama Rucu will tell. These Indians never reveal anything. And as to my own Indians, I vouch for them. To-morrow, or whenever it may suit your pleasure, we may come back again. And, in order to avoid suspicion, it will be well for us to appear among our friends and acquaintances in the forenoon. We can meet here in the afternoon. I shall send one of my Indians to you, Señor Count, for some of your mining tools, but I should not advise the introduction of any new parties, even in a subordinate capacity. Are your Lordships agreed?"

The Count and Carrera consented, and the party left the passage. Before they stepped into the open air, Paredes stopped to examine the door. It was a simple plate of bronze, upon which the turf had been so carefully arranged as to hide the plate completely on the outside. The plate was inserted into a groove of masonry-work at the base, so contrived that it fell back into its original position as soon as it was lifted from the ground. The turf which hid it must have been of one piece, for it had not only concealed it, but it completely fitted in with the surrounding vegetation. The plate, when covering the aperture, stood in a position slanting slightly toward the mountain, so as to retain the sod on it. It was altogether an admirable, yet simple piece of workmanship, highly creditable to the ingenuity of its Indian inventors.

Paredes carefully replaced the plate, and, with the aid of Carrera, covered it with the original sod, filling up the interstices produced by the Mayordomo's iron bar with earth and vegetation. The Indians silently looked on, waiting for orders.

Count Valverde turned to the Mayordomo while the two noblemen were at work covering up the entrance, and, slipping a gold piece into his hand, asked him:

"What did that old woman say?"

"Why should your Excellency care to know?"

"But I want to know it, man. It must have been something terrible; for why should that Indian have braved the wrath of his master rather than enter the passage? Tell me the whole of it."

"I dislike to obey your Excellency. Your Excellency might be sorry for it."

"Thou doublest my curiosity. Give me a full translation."

The Mayordomo reluctantly complied with Valverde's command, and slowly and hesitatingly reproduced in Spanish the terrible curse of the old woman.

The Count's face turned white as he listened. Cold perspiration started from his forehead, and his stout heart sank as the man proceeded. Silently he followed the party on their way home, and to their attempts to draw him into conversation he returned but short and inappropriate answers. Silently he descended the hill with them on their return to the city, and soon left them, after a short exchange of civilities. What was it that made this brave man shrink within himself and seek the privacy of his chamber? What made him sit for hours that night, gazing into vacancy, his head resting on his hands? He did not notice the fleeting hours and the approach of darkness. He did not notice the entrance of his servant with lights, and it was late at night before he aroused himself from his lethargy, prostrated himself before a wooden crucifix suspended over his bed, and sent up a long, fervent prayer.

Was it the remembrance of some occurrence in his past life, that had thrown him into this unusual revery? We shall know in time.

CHAPTER VI.

THE FOOL.

CARRERA was ashamed to tell his companions that he had been on his way to Mama Rucu's cottage when he fell in with their exploring party; but as he could not have assigned a suitable excuse for leaving them on the mountain, he returned to the city with them, concluding to postpone his visit to the Indian sorceress to the following day.

Carrera's wealthy uncle was the possessor of several houses in the city of Quito, one of which he had placed at the disposal of his nephew. At the door of this mansion the young gentleman was welcomed in a mysterious manner by his servant, Mariano.

" What is it, Mariano? Who is that queer figure in the doorway?"

" Mariano looked around cautiously, and then laying

his fingers to his lips, he said: It is *El Loco* (the Fool); he brings a message for your Grace."

"A message for me? From whom—and who is *El Loco*?"

"Does not your Grace remember him? He is Mama Rucu's *Yanacona* (servant or slave)."

"A message for me from Mama Rucu!" said Carrera, surprised. "Well, we shall hear her messenger." And thus saying, he entered the doorway, which, passing the great staircase, led into one of the court-yards (*pateos*), common to all the houses of Quito.

He beheld a queer figure. It was that of a little man, almost a dwarf, of uncertain age, with a real or feigned expression of mental aberration on his face, relieved by occasional flashes of cunning shrewdness. The man was dressed miserably—almost in rags. His head was very large. His face was ugly but not repulsive. His feet, of course, were bare. His arms were fleshless, but bony and muscular. His chest and the upper part of his body betokened great strength, and seemed to have developed at the expense of his legs. He wore a tattered hat, which he politely doffed at the approach of the nobleman, to whom he bowed with a good-natured grin. There was fierceness in his eyes, although their regular expression was that of dreamy abstraction. Carrera remembered to have seen the man before, but he had never taken special notice of him. He also remembered that the imp had been pointed out to him as a harmless lunatic, who was allowed to roam the streets, an object of indifference or contemptuous pity, and would starve if it were not for the support and protection of Mama Rucu. Some looked upon him as the familiar spirit of the old witch, but the general belief was that he was too foolish to be of any service to her, other than that of a common menial.

"Good evening to your Grace," said the Fool, for he seemed to be known by no other name, slowly turning his tattered hat in his hands. "May your Grace live many years. My mistress sends her regards to my Lord. My mistress hopes that my Lord and all his family are in the enjoyment of good health, and that my Lord has passed a good night."

"It is well," interrupted Carrera. "Spare thy compliments and tell me what thy mistress wants of me."

"My mistress wishes to know," said the man slowly, "why your Grace has not come. My mistress has been waiting for my Lord these last two hours."

Carrera stood aghast. How could Mama Rucu know that he had intended to visit her? He fixed a sharp, piercing glance on his servant, Mariano, who received it as unconcerned as if it were not intended for him.

"My mistress is still waiting for his Lordship," continued the Fool.

"Why, man," said Carrera, "I do not understand thee."

"Your Lordship's Fool can speak the language of the *Viracochas* (the white men) if Your Lordship should prefer." The conversation thus far had been in Quichua.

"I understand thy Inca language well enough," answered Carrera, "but I do not understand why thy mistress should have waited for me, and what thy mistress can want of me."

"I am my mistress' servant," replied the Fool." "I carry her messages. I know nothing of the business of my mistress."

"Well, give my regards to thy mistress, and tell her that I shall see her tomorrow."

"But my mistress waits for your Lordship now," said the man, nodding and grinning.

"It is too late now, I might not be back before the ringing of the night-bell."

"But your Grace will not come back at all to-night. Your Grace will pass the night at the house of my mistress."

"Man, they rightly call thee a fool. *I* spend the night at Mama Rucu's cottage! What dost thou mean?

"I am a fool," the Indian rejoined meekly. I am your Lordship's fool, and the servant of my mistress. Your Grace, I hope, is not afraid of Mama Rucu."

"But how can I stay there over night? It is unheard of!"

"And will remain unheard of! Your Lordship's visit to Mama Rucu will not be known to any living soul, except Mariano. To-morrow morning your Lordship will return to this house, hale and hearty, and a much wiser man."

"Thou art bold, my boy!"

"I am a fool, my Lord."

Carrera stood irresolute. The invitation was so extraordinary and preposterous that he was undecided whether to laugh or to get angry. And yet how could Mama Rucu have divined his intention to visit her! It was strange—like a weird romance. His meditation was interrupted by Mariano, who now approached the group, hat in hand.

"Will your Grace allow me a word—"

"Certainly, my boy!"

"I have served your Lordship honestly and faithfully!"

"I have no complaint to make, Mariano."

"Your Grace has been the very best of masters to me, and I love your Lordship—"

"I believe it, Mariano. I should have said, 'I know it!'"

"Then allow your faithful servant to say but one word: Your Lordship can trust yourself blindly to Mama Rucu."

Carrera made no reply.

"It is the first time that Mama Rucu has sent such a message to any living Viracocha, lady or gentleman. Mama Rucu seems to entertain a regard for your Lordship, which she entertains for no other gentleman of Quito. Others seek her, while she has sent for your Grace. She refuses so many, and she invites my master. For the Virgin's sake, go, *amo;* no harm will come to you."

"But if it should become known"—

"The Fool is right; it will never be known. Your

Lordship can trust me, and as to Mama Rucu, her word is sacred."

"But if she is a witch"—

"Master, I am a Christian, like your Grace, and think the new faith more powerful than the faith of my fathers; but as a Christian, I can tell your Grace that Mama Rucu, heathen as she may be at heart, has done more good to her fellow-beings than all your lawyers, doctors, and monks will ever do. Go, Master!"

"Well, then," said Carrera, who, whatever his religious scruples may have been, was too proud to allow his servant to suspect him of fear, "bring my cloak and my mother's cross and rosary. I shall fasten it to my belt, and defy whatever of witchcraft there may be in the cottage."

Mariano was delighted, and hurried up the staircase to comply with his master's orders.

"And now the Fool will beg your Lordship to listen to him again!" said the messenger. "The streets are crowded by mobs; it will be dark in a minute, and we might be detained. If your Lordship will follow me, I shall lead your Grace through lanes and byways. Your Grace will please to keep an eye on your Fool. If the Fool slackens his pace, Your Lordship will do the same. If the Fool hastens, your Grace will please to hasten likewise. Is his Lordship ready?"

"I am! Lead on! Good night, Mariano!"

"The Holy Virgin bless you, Master!" said Mariano; and after Carrera had left, he pressed his arms to his breast and muttered with a sigh: "Great Sun! Great Pachacamac! Let Mama Rucu's undertaking thrive, whatever it may be!"

CHAPTER VII.

MAMA RUCU.

It was a clear, beautiful night. The rainy season was over. The rays of the moon played tenderly on the snowy robes of Mt. Antisana in the east. The quietness of the mountain solitude, where Mama Rucu's cottage stood, was interrupted only by occasional detonations from Mt. Cotopaxi. The great volcano had been active of late, and had filled the public mind with apprehensions of new eruptions and earthquakes. Clouds of smoke, too, were issuing from the crater of Pichincha, while the city of Quito quietly slumbered, as it were, in the lap of its dangerous neighbor.

The cottage of the old Indian woman stood in the entrance of a ravine, which partly hid it from the outside view. It was built of *adobe*, like most of the Indian huts, although larger in size than others. It had no windows, but only a door, which gave it light and air, and served as a chimney when fires had to be built inside, and the smoke could not escape sufficiently through the breaks of the thatched roof. On a bench of adobes in front of the hut sat the old witch when Carrera approached, with her hands resting on her staff and her head leaning on her hands. She sat motionless and silent, and had no word of welcome for her visitor.

"Here we are, Master," said the Fool. "I shall leave you for the present. I shall not be far off, if your Grace should want me."

"Good evening, Mama Rucu!" said Carrera, who could not entirely conquer a certain superstitious awe when he found himself alone in this secluded place with one whom public opinion designated as the greatest sorceress of the kingdom of Quito.

Mama Rucu slowly raised her head, looked at him for a few moments, and then, with a strange tone of kindness, said:

"Thou hast made me wait a long time."

"How could I know, Mother, that you were waiting for me?"

"Didst thou not intend to come here early in the day?"

"How do you know that, Mamita? Had Mariano informed you?"

The old woman uttered a contemptuous laugh: "Mariano! Do I want Mariano to teach me what I know? My eyes are dim with age, but they can see farther and deeper than thine will ever see. I knew thou wouldst come. It was so ordained by a power unknown to you of the new faith. Thy tarrying on the way was unnecessary. Seeking for treasure! Ha, ha, ha! A vain attempt! That treasure exists, my son. I can tell thee that it exists, but no Viracocha shall see it until its rightful owner shall show it to him. You might as well attempt to level Mt. Pichincha into the valley of Chillo, as to discover that secret. It is the secret of our race, and our race will keep it until we choose to reveal it. Wouldst thou see thy good friend Paredes? Return to the spot where you met this afternoon. Thou wilt find him there in the bowels of the earth with torches and spades probing every inch of ground and finding nothing. To-morrow his occupation will be gone. To-morrow the passage will be closed and no trace of it will ever be discovered."

Carrera was lost in astonishment. He did not know what to make of this woman, and the belief in her witchcraft grew firmly upon his mind.

"I have confidence in thee, my son. Thou art better than thy race, although I fear thou art weaker than thy inferiors. Thou hast acted well on many occasions. Think not that our race is ungrateful or undiscerning. Stupid, torpid, brutal my people may appear; but there is a fire within them which, let the proper time arrive, will burst forth into devouring flames. Look thou at yon volcano. It sleepeth! Peace and quietness reign in the valley; an inoffensive cloud of smoke and vapors curls up from the mouth of the crater; in it and around it everything is in repose. Yet, let Pachacamac but give the word, and roaring thunders will strike terror to the human heart; flames will burst forth from the crater; a rain of ashes will darken the air; rocks and pumice-stone will be thrown in every direction, and the destructive earthquake will shake the land, burying cities, swallowing rivers, rending mountains asunder, and creating dreary lakes where flourishing villages had stood. Such is our race. We are the children of Pichincha, Cotopaxi and Sara Urcu, hiding the thunderbolts of Death under the snowy robe of Peace!"

The old woman relapsed into her revery, and a long pause followed, during which Carrera stood irresolute, uncertain whether to remain or to go. At last she continued: "I speak to thee, my son, as I have not spoken to any living Viracocha. I have confidence in thee. Thou art better than the others. Thy heart is pure and good; and a great future awaits thee. But it must be carved out by thyself. Listen! The Viracochas are the conquerors. We, of the Shyri race, are the conquered. The two races are enemies. But Pachacamac in his infinite goodness, sometimes allows men and women to be born who may be the harbingers of peace, and put an end to the deadly feud by divine conciliation. If I mistake not, some such doctrine is taught by the priests of the new faith. But thy race belie it by their actions. I have heard the white men preach the law of love, while they hunted down, racked, burned, and enslaved my people. Their love is death. But there are times when Pachacamac creates men and women who can change sadness into joy, hatred into love, war into peace. These men, like Manco of Peru, and Duchicela of Purrubá may become the benefactors of their race, if they accept the mission which God has assigned to them. A great mission has been reserved for thee, my son. Whether thou wilt accept it or not, I can not tell. The future has not yet been fully revealed to me. I fear thou wilt shrink from the dangers and struggles of the task. I confide in thy goodness, but not in thy resolution. Still it is meet that I should disclose to thee what will await thee in either case."

"I do not understand you, Mamita."

"Thou shalt not understand me, at present. The time has not yet come to reveal what Pachacamac, or Christ, as thy race call Him, expects of thee. What hast thou come for? To consult me about little trivial things! About thy self-inflicted misfortunes, thy losses at the gaming table, thy troubles with thine uncle, thy foolish longing for a girl who is unworthy of thee! Ha, ha, ha! Dost thou think that I would bother with these trifles? Dost thou imagine that for such I should have waited here by the hour, straining my old eyes to discern the great future, and preparing the wonderful potion, which, for the time being, will make thy vision as clear as mine? Foolish boy! I pity thee. I love thee for thy kindness to my people; but I do not care for thy trifling and childish sorrows, when the deep sorrows of millions require my attention, when the welfare of my race is at stake. And yet I shall be good to thee, Viracocha. Thou needst not fear the old *Camasca;** she will not harm a hair on thy head. She will try to relieve thy troubles and protect thee from the results of thy follies. She will try to make a man of thee; but thou must BE a man, Julio de Carrera, and stand by what thy heart acknowledges to be right. Thy people say, I am in league with the Prince of Darkness. Believe it not, my son! It

---

* Witch or sorceress.

is not for evil, but for good that I strive. I want to dry the tears and gladden the hearts of millions. I know our race has succumbed to yours, and the Indian is not strong enough to drive the foreigner from the land of my fathers. But I see a way of securing the happiness of both races, of restoring my people to their rights as human beings, without injury to thee and thine. This is the great object which I seek to accomplish before I die. My sands of life are running fast. My days are numbered. I have not much time to lose. Art thou ready to behold what I shall show thee to-night? Two visions thou shalt see. Two roads are before thee. Wilt thou take to the right? I shall show thee what awaits thee at the end. Wilt thou take to the left? I shall show thee what there is to the left. If thou art a coward, if thou fearest like a child, if thou believest the stories with which monks and nurses or fools may have frightened thy ignorant mind, retrace thy steps. Go home to thy bed and forget what thou hast heard. If thou art a man who believes in God, no matter how thou callest Him, and in doing good to thy fellow creatures, come with me. The potion is ready, the veil will be lifted, thine eyes shall see! Art thou prepared?"

Carrera hesitated, doubted, feared. But he had gone so far that he would have considered it dishonorable or cowardly to recede, and this consideration prevailed over his scruples of religion and the terrors of superstition so powerful in those days.

"I am prepared, Mamita!"

"Then, come," she said, rising from her seat. "Thou art welcome to the house of Mama Rucu. There was a time when I should have received thee in a palace. It is a miserable hut to which I invite thee now. And yet I might live in splendor. I might buy more acres than thine eyes could survey, if I would take for myself what belongs to my race. But I shall share the fate of my kindred, and live as they live, sleep as they sleep, and die as my betters have died. Come in!"

CHAPTER VIII.

THE FIRST VISION.

Carrera turned to follow her, when she motioned him to stand back: "Wait! One word before I receive thee under my roof. I ask thy promise, as a cavalier, that what thou shalt hear or see to-night shall remain buried in thine own bosom. Whatever I do for thee to-night, is for thee alone, and must remain thy secret as well as mine."

"Your caution is unnecessary, Mother," said Carrera. "Nobody shall know that I have been here. I promise silence, on the honor of a gentleman."

"Good! And now, come in!"

They entered. The interior of the hut was divided into two compartments by a curtain, and, like all Indian cottages, was without flooring. The *cuyes* (a species of guinea pigs, which almost every Ecuadorian Indian owns), frightened by the appearance of a stranger, took to their holes. A dim candle burned on a primitive table. On an adobe bench, protruding from the wall, a bed had been improvised. Pots and crockery of Indian workmanship were piled up in a corner. The old woman lifted the curtain. A slow fire of aromatic woods was burning under a small kettle, and a couch of sheep-skins and shawls was placed near the fire.

"Make thyself comfortable, my son!" said Mama Rucu. "Take off thy sword, hat, and cloak. Nobody shall touch these things. There is a bed which I have made for thee. Thou wilt need it." She then hobbled to the fire, and took a calabash, which supplied the place of a drinking vessel, and, with a ladle, poured into it some of the liquid that was boiling in the kettle.

"What I have here is a great and powerful decoction. It is made from a vine growing far, far away from here, on the banks of the river Napo, on the other side of yon mountain range. The vine is called Samarucu, the consolation of old age. Prepared, with the addition of a few innocuous herbs, it confers upon those who drink of it the gift to see the future. It is harmless. I have been taking it for many years."

The author of this truthful narrative might here insert that the Samarucu is still in use among the uncivilized Indians of the Napo Province. The most wonderful virtues are ascribed to it by the natives. Its effects are similar to those produced by the *hashish* of the Orientals.

"Take a sip!" said Mama Rucu, "and we shall see how it affects thee."

Carrera obeyed.

"Now, listen. The person thou shalt see now is probably the one uppermost in thy mind at present. Whoever she may be, she will be the clue to what thou shalt see next."

Suddenly Carrera made a start, and, throwing out his arms, he made a few hasty steps toward the rear wall of the hut, and exclaimed: "Dolores!"

"I thought so!" said the old woman.

"She is gone!" said Carrera, passing his hands over his face and rubbing his eyes. "And how natural and life-like she stood before me there, near the wall. I could have sworn she was there in reality."

"It is well!" muttered the witch. "Thou art susceptible. Thou shalt see a great deal. Now, drink the rest. Take it all. Leave not a drop in the cup. It is a most precious draught."

Carrera obeyed, without hesitation.

"Stretch thyself upon that bed. Put thy cloak and

sword under thy head. Lie still, and wait for what will come. Close thine eyes. It is well! And now listen to my words. It was Dolores that appeared first. Well, then, the great Moon, under whose rays we are now reposing, and whose power is in the draught thou hast taken, will show to thee, in a long series of visions, what awaits thee, if thou linkest thy fortunes to those of the woman, Dolores. Lie still, my son, and confide in me. I shall assist thee, if the potion should prove too strong for thee." And, with these words, the old woman sat down on her couch before the fire. Perfect stillness reigned in the cottage, interrupted only by the chirping of the crickets, and, at rare intervals, by the detonations of Mount Cotopaxi.

A feeling of delicious languor came over Carrera, and lazily he stretched himself and closed his eyes. He soon felt as if he were at home again. There was his room, his bookcase, his bed, his windows. There was Mariano, too, beckoning him to come. He followed him into the reception room. A lady, deeply veiled, stood before him. Another veiled lady stood in the door. The first lady lifted her veil, and he beheld Dolores. She spoke to him. She spoke long, earnestly, appealingly; but he could not catch her words. She drew nearer to him. Her hands were in his. Her eyes met his, and, in the next moment, she was in his arms. But soon the scene changed. A mass of people filled the street before his house. They cheered him wildly as he showed himself in the door. Hats were flung up, and thundering *rivas* rent the air. But suddenly the faces and voices of the men changed from joy to madness, from acclamations to fury and imprecations. Knives and daggers were raised against him. He could discern the brutal face of Castro, the notorious chief of the ruffians of Quito, who looked at him with the fierceness of hatred and rage. Carrera was seized by the mob. His clothes were torn from him. He was hurled into the street and carried away by a surging mass of humanity. He felt a stinging pain in his back. He felt the hot blood trickling down his limbs. The maddened crowd surrounded him with wild shrieks. He felt like one oppressed by a terrible nightmare. He uttered a loud, piercing scream. Mama Rucu quietly arose from her couch, walked up to his bedside, and placed her hand on his burning forehead. It had a soothing effect. The anguish under which he had been laboring passed away; but he felt crushed and helpless. The painful vision had disappeared. His tormentors were gone; but his strength would not return. He lay in a pool of blood, his own blood, in an out-of-the-way part of the city, under a garden wall. He heard the voices of the fiends that had tormented him, but they were away in the distance. At last he saw two ladies hurry by, followed by two or three male servants. He recognized Dolores again. She looked at him. She must have seen him. Why did she not stop? He called her by her name. She must have heard him. Why did she not stop? Again a dreadful feeling of anguish came over him. He fainted away.

How long he thus lay in a swoon he could not realize. Suddenly it was clear to him that he was in Mama Rucu's cottage again. But the scene was changed. Several Indian men and women were in the room whom he did not know. They bent over him wistfully and shook their heads, exchanging low whispers. Where had they come from? What did they want? He tried to raise himself from his bed; but again he felt Mama Rucu's hand upon his forehead, gently pressing down his head, and he heard her whisper: "Be quiet!" A long pause followed, during which he saw nothing. Impenetrable darkness surrounded him and kept him inclosed until it became painful. At last lights broke through the darkness. What lights were they? Tapers? Yes, tapers burning upon an altar. He was in a church. He saw the pictures and the statues of the saints. He found himself kneeling before the altar, with Dolores by his side. The priest stood over them. The peals of the organ reverberated through the edifice. It was a wedding he witnessed—his own wedding, and Dolores was the bride; and the organ kept on pealing and pealing without end, until he saw nothing. Darkness surrounded him again, but the organ continued to play. At last he saw a new sight. A man was groping his way through the darkness. It was Paredes. How he hated him! And yet he followed him, his sword clutched in his right hand, ready to stab him to the heart. Inexplicable pangs lacerated his bosom, but he could not realize what made him suffer. And now Dolores appeared again, but there was no love in her eyes. The expression of her face was haughty and cold. He joined her, and they walked on together in silence and estrangement for many a weary mile, over mountains and rivers, and through forests and defiles, and every now and then he saw, peeping through the branches of the trees or through the bushes, as if lurking along the road, the hated face of Paredes.

At last a forest received him, such as he had never seen before. It was a forest of gigantic trees and impenetrable brushwood. The reports of arquebuses broke through the stillness. Indian arrows whirred through the air. It was war, with its terrors, that now came on him. He felt that a battle was raging around him. Sometimes he was in it; sometimes it was far away from him. At last an Indian woman stood before him. Her face and figure were familiar to him. Her appearance carried him back through a long vista of years. His heart went out to her. She spoke to him. He heard her voice. It was a voice of inexpressible kindness and sadness. She spoke but one word. She said: "Fly!" Sadly he pointed to a tattered banner which was stuck into the earth. She averted her face and wept. He took her hand, kissed it, and bathed it with his tears. Deep, unfathomable regret, and the abject sadness of despair now seized upon his soul, and his whole frame was shaken with sobs. The woman in the meantime had disappeared, and again the din of battle sounded through the forest. Again he was bleeding from many wounds. He dragged himself from tree to tree, passing through a rain of arrows. He heard the howls of savages. Naked Indians, such as he had never seen before, with war-paint on their faces, closed in upon him. His sword broke. He dropped upon his knee and uttered a last prayer. Then blow fell upon blow, until consciousness and life ebbed away. A leaden heaviness weighed him down; a deathly sickness seized him, and he broke into a loud and agonizing groan.

CHAPTER X.

THE SECOND VISION.

AT this moment Mama Rucu dashed a handful of cold water into his face, and he awoke. "Bathe thy hands and face in this basin of cold water. Thy first vision is over."

Carrera did as he was told, and the effects of the potion passed away, leaving only a certain faintness, which he soon overcame.

"By the Virgin, Mother, you have made me see strange things!"

"Not I," said the old woman; "it was not I. It was the wonderful power of the Samarucu. Art thou ready for the second draught?"

"How long have I been asleep?"

"Perhaps an hour." The old woman had filled her calabash from the fluid in the kettle again, and presented it to her visitor. "Take a mouthful at first."

"Must it be now?"

"It need not be now; but thou wilt require a good,

sound, long sleep after the two visions, and the sooner they are ended the better it will be for thee."

"Shall I have to suffer such agonies again?"

"Not this time. I do not know what thou hast seen; but as, during thy sleep, I pierced the veil which covers thy future, I am almost certain that thy second vision will be pleasanter than the first. Take a sip, my son!"

"Your will shall be done, Mamita! Here is to your health!" He swallowed a mouthful of the potion, and handed the calabash back to the woman. Again the effect was instantaneous. Again he gave a sudden start, and, stretching forward his arms, he exclaimed: "The mysterious Indian maiden! There she stands!"

"Glory to Pachacamac!" shouted the witch. "Hail to thee, Viracocha!"

"Who is this wonderful apparition? Her forehead is encircled with a diadem, holding a large emerald of exquisite beauty."

"The emblem of her royal race. May the great Sun bless the last of his living children!"

"She is gone!" said Carrera, with a sigh of disappointment. "Oh, that I could see her again!"

"Thou shalt see her again, my son! Thou shalt see her again!" repeated the old woman, chuckling with satisfaction and delight. "Just finish this wonderful draught; the potion of life; the key to the future; the unraveler of all mysteries; the godlike Samarucu. Do not spill a drop of the precious liquid."

Carrera obeyed silently, and drained the cup to the last drop.

"And now do as thou didst before. Lie down and keep quiet."

And again he imagined he was in his bed-room. Again Mariano beckoned him to step into his reception-room. Again he saw the two veiled or masked ladies. And again Dolores approached him and spoke to him, long, earnestly, appealingly. He could not understand her words, but they seemed to produce no impression upon him. At last she turned to depart, and politely he escorted her down stairs. With a formal bow he took leave of her. Shortly afterwards the scene changed. Again his house was surrounded by a tumultuous mass of men, whose cheers and acclamations greeted him as he showed himself in the doorway. But this time their welcome did not change to rage. He was carried away by them, but only smiling faces surrounded him, and only joyful sounds struck his ear. He was borne along, on the shoulders of men, until the procession halted in front of the government palace. At the same time another procession filed into the square. It was a long procession of Indians, headed by warriors carrying a palanquin, similar to those on which the ancient Incas were carried by their faithful subjects, and in it stood erect and majestic, yet full of indescribable grace and modesty, the mysterious Indian maiden with the emerald diadem.

On the steps of the palace she alighted, and was received by him. Hand in hand they ascended the staircase, under the enthusiastic acclamations of the multitude, while salutes were firing and the church-bells ringing. His heart swelled with pride and tenderness.

The scene changed, and the din of battle again fell upon his ear. Yet it was not a hopeless and agonizing struggle as before, but victory seemed to be with him wherever he went. Again he traversed the tropical forest; but this time the beautiful Indian maiden was at his side. The dark face of Paredes disturbed him no longer, but the bright and open countenance of young Sanchez smiled on him and his companion. Suddenly the ocean expanded before his view. Ships were in the harbor, men-of-war carrying many guns, But it was not the well-known flag of Spain; it was the cross of St. George and other strange emblems that floated in the breeze. A number of boats set out to receive him and his Indian bride, and the guns of all the ships belched forth their thunders as he stood on the deck of the main vessel, surrounded by smiling men in strange uniforms and speaking unknown tongues. The sounds of martial music rent the air, and the vivas would not end.

Other battles followed, crowned with new victories. Thousands of Indians followed him, wherever he went. The troops of Quito were pitted against the regular troops of Spain. But they were not unaided. Those strange soldiers, who spoke unknown tongues, were with him and made his army successful in every encounter. At last he found himself at Quito again, but not in his own house. It was a palace he inhabited, and men of first quality surrounded him and did him reverence.

He was not oppressed by darkness and anguish, as during his first vision, but brightness and happiness greeted him everywhere. The beautiful Indian was again at his side, and threw her arms around him. A feeling of delicious repose spread over him, and he fell into an enchanting swoon, which was followed by a loss of consciousness, and a long, unbroken, dreamless sleep.

CHAPTER XI.

TOA.

Whether he slept hours or days, he did not know. When he awoke the rays of the sun greeted him through the open door of the cottage, and the Fool stood smiling before his bed, awaiting his orders.

Carrera gazed at him lazily, but said nothing. He had not yet realized where he was. He tried to recall the scenes of the previous night, but a pleasant feeling of languor prevented all mental exertion.

"Good morning, your Grace!" said the Fool after a pause. "I hope your Grace has passed a good night."

Carrera again looked at the man, and tried to remember who he was. The Indian seemed to understand his inquiring gaze: "I am your Lordship's Fool," he said in an explanatory manner. "I brought your Lordship to Mama Rucu's cottage last night."

"What time is it?" asked Carrera at last, without attempting to rise.

"It must be seven or eight o'clock, your Lordship."

"Have I slept here all night?"

"Most certainly your Excellency slept here all night."

"Where is Mama Rucu?"

"She went out to collect medicine herbs with the dew drops on them. There is great power in the morning dew."

"Have I been here alone?"

"Not alone, my Lord. Your Lordship's Fool was in attendance, preparing your Lordship's breakfast."

"When will Mama Rucu be back?"

"I do not know, Master."

"But I want to see her before I go."

"I do not know, Master."

"Did she go far away?"

"I do not know, Master. But I know a cup of chocolate will revive your Lordship's spirits. Shall I bring it?"

The Fool set the table, and Carrera, who had not supped the evening before, partook of a most inviting breakfast. After he had finished, the Fool cleared away the dishes, and disappeared. The young man then tried to recall the events of the preceding night. He remembered that he had passed through two distinct concatenations of dreams or visions, but they had become somewhat obliterated and blended in his mind. He endeavored to separate them in his recollection, and to trace the order in which the sights he saw had succeeded each other. He owned that they were unintelligible to him. The occurrences in which he had played a part, seemed to be entirely inexplicable. How could such things happen, and why should they happen to him? His visions could not have been the foreshadowing of real events. They must have been the result of the beverage he had taken. They appeared unnatural and unreal to him as the hallucinations of a heavy nightmare. The object of his visit to Mama Rucu had not been accomplished. He had come to consult her about his own affairs, and she had given him a potion which, for the time being, must have disordered his brain, and filled it with the phantoms of a madman's fancy. And yet there was a continuity of evolution in what he had seen which was astonishing. But what could it all mean? How could he, a peaceable and inoffensive youth, become the hero of events of such magnitude and violence?

While he was thus pondering, a female voice of wonderful melodiousness struck his ear, the same voice that he had heard in his dreams.

"Is Mama Rucu at home?"

"She is not!" said the Fool.

"When will she be back?"

"I do not know." Suddenly the Fool gave a half-suppressed exclamation of surprise, and then whispered some words which Carrera could not hear. He determined to see the possessor of that voice, and stepped before the door of the cottage. But he saw nothing extraordinary. A female, dressed in the garb of a common Indian, stood before him. Her face was covered with a shawl in the fashion which the Indians had learned from the Spanish women, leaving but one eye exposed. And even that was shaded by the folds of her heavy shawl; and Carrera, blinded by the glaring rays of the sun as he emerged from the darkness of the hut, could not discern anything.

The Fool stood hat in hand, looking doubtfully from one to the other.

After a long scrutinizing look at Carrera, the woman said: "I shall wait!" and again, Carrera was satisfied that it was the voice he had heard in his dreams.

"Will you take a seat, Niña?" he said beckoning her to the bench in front of the house.

"Thank you, Señor," said the woman, and sat down; but she bowed her head so low that Carrera could not look into her uncovered eye. The Fool, by this time, had disappeared.

"You are not of Quito, Niña," continued Carrera.

"I have followed Doña Carmen Duchicela from Riobamba," replied the woman, without looking up.

"Do you belong to her suite?"

"I do not."

"To whom do you belong?"

"To myself first; to the Shyri Toa next."

"The Shyri Toa!" exclaimed Carrera. "Is there such a person as the Shyri Toa?"

"There is."

"Where is she?"

"Everywhere, and nowhere. She is a wanderer without a resting-place in the land of her fathers."

Carrera was strangely fascinated by the melodious intonation the Indian gave to her words. But still more the mystery of the Shyri Toa attracted him. Should he be the chosen one of all the men of Quito for whom it was to be solved? This woman knew her, and belonged to her suite. He would pursue his inquiries.

"Why does she hide herself?"

"Why does she hide herself?" repeated the woman musingly. "Why does she hide herself? Because she wants to live. Not for herself. Life has no charm for the homeless fugitive; but she wants to live for her race, whose rightful sovereign and last hope she is. If she were to show herself in public, she would be seized and imprisoned by the Spaniards. She would lose her liberty, and very probably her life.

But why, Niña?"

"Because, while she lives, the Indians recognize her as their rightful Queen. Her commands would be obeyed from the banks of the Guayas and Esmeraldas to the mountains of Pasto; from the Tumbez to the Napo. While she lives, her people have a head which thinks, a mind which plans for them, a will that directs them. Destroy her, and the Quito Indians are a herd without a shepherd, and their subjection will be complete. While she lives, the Indian heart still hopes. With her death, dies the last hope of our race."

"And do you really think the Spaniards would kill her?"

"Did they not kill Tupac Amaru in Peru? What had he done? Peaceably he had held his court in the inaccessible fastnesses of the Eastern Cordillera, whither no white man had ever penetrated, except as an applicant or a fugitive. They inveigled him by treacherous promises. They entrapped him into their power. He trusted the promises of the men who had betrayed Atahualpa. For such confiding credulity he paid with his life. They murdered him without cause, without trial, without excuse. The Viracochas thought their dominion was not secure while Tupac Amaru lived, and, therefore, they murdered him. Would they not do to Toa Duchicela, the Shyri Queen of Quito, what they did to Tupac Amaru, the Inca of Peru? No, Señor, Toa must hide from the Spaniards, if Toa wants to live."

Carrera was deeply moved, not only by the words of the Indian, but by his rapidly growing conviction that this woman, of such unusual intelligence and elegant grace, who hid her face from him so carefully, could not be a low-born Indian. If her appearance was not another vision, a mere continuation of his dreams of the previous night, he felt assured that she must be the Shyri Queen herself.

"And, moreover," continued the woman, "what are your countrymen seeking now? What have they been seeking since Benalcazar entered the burning ruins of ancient Quito? The Treasure, the great Treasure of Atahualpa and Rumiñagui! If they could seize Toa Duchicela, they would put her to the rack. They would break her limbs on the wheel to extort from her the secret of the Treasure. Of course they would fail. Toa would die with sealed lips, as so many of her race have died. But why should she needlessly expose herself to these tortures? She is safe as long as the secret of her abode remains the secret of her own race. No Indian will betray her."

"But was not Rumiñagui betrayed to the Spaniards by his own servants?"

"Yes, but he was a usurper, a tyrant, a rebel who had put to death all of the members of the royal house whom he could get into his power. The Indians owed no allegiance to Rumiñagui."

"It must be a sad and joyless existence," said Carrera, sympathetically, "to hide away in huts and hovels or in the wilderness."

"It is, Señor," said the woman, deeply affected. "It is! I know the Shyri Toa well. She is but human, and but a woman, with the instincts, desires, feelings, hopes, and the heart of a woman, yearning for love, for domestic happiness, and peace. She is not a savage, Señor. She appreciates the comforts, the luxuries, the refinements of civilization. It is natural that she should long for a home, that she should long to live in a pleasant and permanent abode, by the side of a husband, the mother of children, and surrounded by loving friends; that she should yearn for rest and security, instead of being driven forth into the snowy *paramos* of the mountain, or into the rainy lonliness of the tropical forest. Why should she not long for a sheltering roof over her head, for a homestead, however modest, which she might permanently call her own, instead of forever shifting from place to place; from the mountain to the valley; from the ravine to the jungle; fleeing at the approach of danger, like the wild beast of the forest, ever changing her abode for fear of discovery, ever hiding like a criminal, ever wandering like an outcast in the land which is her's by right divine?"

"Lady," said Carrera, with deep emotion, "you make me ashamed of my own race. Oh, that I could say that the fears of your Queen were unfounded."

"But you can not, Señor, you know you can not. The Shyri Toa might trust herself to you, perhaps to a few noble Viracochas, but she can not trust herself to your rulers, or to your people. The mystery of her existence is her only safety."

"But thus far she has not trusted any one of us. She has not shown herself to white men at all."

"Are you sure that she has not? You, Señor, may have seen her yourself. But if she keeps away even from the best of your race, even from those who have shown sympathy for the Indians, and a feeling heart for their sufferings—and there is no lack of such good men—she does it for their sake. She is safe enough herself. No power on earth could take her while she confines her secret to her own race. But she might compromise her white friends, if she had any. They might be questioned by the authorities, and exposed to vexatious inquiries and demands. They might even be required to assist in her arrest, and their refusal would involve them into difficulties. The Señora Toa is too proud to expose her friends to dangers on her own account. She would not exact sacrifices from those who owe her no allegiance. As to the Indians, she has a right to their sacrifices, and requites them by a continuous self-sacrifice. To watch over the welfare of her race; to neglect no means and no opportunity to ameliorate their condition, and to lessen their sufferings, or to direct the hurricane of their long pent-up indignation, if it should have to break forth, is the great and only object of her arduous, joyless, restless, and, perhaps, hopeless life."

"And I hope," said Carrera, "that noble, magnanimous, self-sacrificing lady will also be discreet and generous enough not to sacrifice the lives and fortunes of thousands of both races, in a fruitless endeavor to array an unarmed and undisciplined mass of untutored Indians, against the genius and organization of a superior civilization which, so far, has proved invincible, not only in the New World, but likewise in the Old."

"Don Julio de Carrera," said the girl solemnly, and for the first time turning her uncovered eye upon him, brilliant with the fire of enthusiasm, indignation, and unyielding courage, "you are a stranger to me; a stranger to the Shyri Toa. I know you only by report. I know your heart beats with sympathy for the outraged and the oppressed, and that more than once you have protected the children of my race, in spite of personal danger to yourself. The Shyri Toa knows it, and respects you for it; and if it should ever be in her power to show you her gratitude, she would do so. But what her plans may be for the unknown future; what she will do, or not do; from what sacrifices she will shrink, and what sacrifices of lives and happiness she will make, are questions she will debate with her own conscience, and with those who represent the royal house of Atahualpa and his nobility in her councils. Death, under circumstances, may be preferable to life, and the destruction or self-immolation of a race may be preferable to eternal oppression and degradation. But the Shyri Toa is not a wild visionary, Señor Carrera; she will weigh these matters well. The time may come, and, perhaps, has come, when the white natives of this country will be as impatient of Spanish oppression, with all its crushing extortions and humiliations, as the Indians are of their hard task-masters. Then, perhaps, both currents may be directed into the same channel; then, perhaps, a combination may be effected for the deliverance of both. But I shall not trouble you with these dreams, Señor; I see Mama Rucu slowly descending the slope of Rucu Pichincha, and our chat will soon be at an end."

"Señora," said Carrera, "I have listened with wonder, and what you said has taken root in my soul. I shall ponder over your words; but I want to see the noble lady who has spoken them. There is no use of further disguise, Lady Toa! No one but a Queen would have spoken as you have. I am a gentleman who, whatever his failings may be, has never been charged with a breach of faith. Your Ladyship's secret will be safe with me. I shall die rather than betray it.

"I know it, Don Julio! I know you must be loyal as as your heart is good, and to you, the first of all the Viracochas of Quito and Peru, I have shown, and shall again show, my face. Behold!" she said, throwing back her shawl, and then slowly dropping it down to her waist. "Behold, then, the unfortunate, the restless, the Shyri Queen, Toa Duchicela, the granddaughter of Atahualpa, the inhabitant of caves, forests, *páramos*, and ravines, the poorest, and yet the richest, the weakest, and yet the most powerful inhabitant of her kingdom."

There she stood before him. It was the same maiden that had appeared to, and disappeared from, him so mysteriously but two days before. It was she whom he had seen in his visions under the influence of Mama Rucu's potion. There she stood before him, a picture of beauty, with the expression of indescribable sadness and resignation in her smile, but the fire of indomitable courage and determination in her eye. There she stood before him, graceful, elegant, and refined, with the long and heavy hair of the women of her race streaming down her back and lending an additional charm to her agile and plastic figure.

Carrera drank in her features with an unfeigned expression of admiration, which could not have been offensive to any woman, however devoid of vanity she might have been. A long pause followed, during which his eyes rested on her, while she received and returned his searching and admiring look with modesty and dignity. At last she extended her hand to him.

"Shall we be friends, Don Julio de Carrera?"

"A more devoted friend," answered Carrera, kissing the proffered hand, "your Highness will and could not have among the men of my race."

"We shall see, Don Julio," she answered musingly, "we shall see. It is dangerous to be a friend to Toa Duchicela."

"It is danger by which true friendship is tried and proved."

"I shall hope to return your friendship. But there comes Mama Rucu and we must part. Mama Rucu, although not strictly a member of my royal cabinet," she added with a roguish laugh, "stands high in my confidence and I consult her on all occasions. I have important secrets of government to discuss with her to-day," she continued with another charming laugh, "and I regret that our interview must terminate."

"But shall I not see your Highness again?"

"Of course you shall, if you care to continue our acquaintance."

"Can I be of any service to your Highness?"

"Do not call me by that title. It sounds like a mockery from the lips of a white man. To me you can be of no service, Don Julio. I ask no service for myself. But you can be of great service to my unfortunate race," she said impulsively and enthusiastically, and then she added, hesitatingly, "if you wish to be. Listen! Before we enter into a compact, we must know and understand each other. I may have deceived you. Perhaps I am an imposter, and not the Shyri Queen. My plans, if I should disclose them to you now, might appear visionary. After you have seen what I intend to show you, you will judge them differently. To-morrow I shall show myself to my people. I shall do so publicly in the Church of San Francisco. And yet it will be done in such a manner as not to attract the slightest notice or attention, as far as your people are concerned. Doña Carmen Duchicela, of Riobamba, my grand-aunt, the only Indian princess whose title your government has recognized, has presented a necklace of wonderful emeralds to the Convent, for the image of the Virgin, and high mass will be celebrated for the souls of her deceased relatives and ancestors, at ten o'clock. The Church will be crowded with Indians, who will go there to see Doña Carmen Duchicela, as *your* people will believe. But these Indians will come to see ME; for I have had it given out that I shall show myself on that occasion. Come and judge for yourself. Bring your best, your most honorable, your most reliable friend. I have to depart from the policy of entire seclusion, which I have pursued until now. My future plans require that I should enter into certain relations and negotiations with some of your best men. Bring only one friend, for the present; but choose well. You shall know that I am what I claim to be. My people shall be my credentials. After you have seen the moral power I wield, I shall let you judge of the material resources that are at my command. Meet me on the day after to-morrow on the mountain-path where I appeared to you first; but come alone. Come shortly after night-fall. I have trusted myself to you; will you trust yourself to me?"

"I will, Lady."

"Then do as I have told you. And now go, and leave me with Mama Rucu. Good bye, Don Julio de Carrera. Do not forget that you have promised to be my friend."

When Carrera returned to his room, he beheld, to his great surprise, that a small tripod vase, or vessel of antique

Indian workmanship, stood on his table. He lifted the lid. The vase was filled with gold coins, of the reign of Charles the Fifth. Carrera drew back in amazement, while the blood rushed to his face, coloring it deeply. A letter lay under one of the legs of the vase. He drew it forth, and opened it. It was written in excellent Spanish, and in a large and round, although somewhat unpracticed and unsteady hand. I read thus:

" *Señor Don Julio de Carrera.*—The actions of princes must not be judged by the rules applicable to those of ordinary individuals. What would be boldness and immodesty in a lady of private station, may be but an act of dignity and self-respect on the part of a Queen.

" Don Julio de Carrera has proved himself on more than one occasion the kind friend and protector of my race. It is my duty, as the head of that race, to express to him our gratitude. Gratitude, however, as we understand it, consists in deeds, not in words. I have learned that our friend is the victim of embarrassments, from which he should be relieved. It is in my power to help him by an insignificant loan, and I consider it my duty to do so.

" Do not be offended, Don Julio. I mean no offense or disrespect. I can spare the small amount involved in this transaction until the time when it may suit your convenience to repay it. If upon the arrival of that time, Toa Duchicela should be no more, you will devote this fund to the alleviation of the sufferings of such of my subjects as may be most deserving of your sympathy or commiseration.

" Forgive this intrusion into your private affairs, and in order to show me that you have forgiven it, I beg you not to mention the matter, and not even to allude to it at our next interview.

" I am your sincere friend,

Toa II,

" *Queen of Quito and Purruhá.*"

BOOK II.
REALITIES.

Allí quedaba el mísero difunto
Y allí con el sus frívolos intentos,
Sus fábricas, sus vanos pensamientos,
Sus torres, sus chimeras, todo junto:
Allí de solo un golpe, en solo un punto
Mostraba la ruyndad de sus cimientos,
Que lo que en semejante vasa estriba
Su misma pesadumbre lo derriba.
    PEDRO DE OÑA, *El Arauco Domado*,
        Canto XVI., p. 265.

BOOK II.

REALITIES.

CHAPTER I.

JUAN CASTRO.

Before we proceed with our narrative, we must return to Paredes, and ascertain his doings during the night which Carrera spent at Mama Rucu's cottage. On Don Manuel's return home, after the barren discovery of the subterranean passage, described in a previous chapter, he ate a hasty supper, and sent for his Mayordomo, whose arrival he awaited, while nervously pacing the room.

"Don Tomas," he said, "you and I must follow this matter up. If there is anything in it, I should divide it with you, rather than with those strangers."

"Well said, Señor, and many thanks for your Lordship's kindness and confidence."

"To-morrow they will be with us again. Hence, if we want to get ahead of them, we must work to-night."

"I understand, Señor!"

"Well and good! But there is a matter that must be attended to first."

"What is it, Señor?"

"Our companions of the afternoon might be tempted to do the very same thing. I should like to know that they are comfortably stowed away in their beds. Suppose you get on your horse, Don Tomas, and try to see them both. Make any excuse you see fit. Tell their servants that you have a message from me, which you are instructed to deliver personally. If they are in bed and asleep, you need not wake them. If they are up, you might say that I ask them to breakfast with me to-morrow."

"I understand, Señor," said the Mayordomo, as he left the room."

He was not gone very long, when the valet of Paredes made his appearance, and announced that Juan Castro begged to be admitted to his Lordship's presence.

Juan Castro, the king of the rabble of Quito, who will play an important part in this story, a butcher by trade, was a ruffian, with all the fierceness and viciousness of a ruffian; but the general saying that bullies are cowards was not corroborated by his case. If he was reckless of the bones and lives of others, he was as reckless of his own. To break a horse fresh from the *potreros* of the coast, to bait an untamed steer fresh from the *paramos* of Mounts Cayambi or Antisana, to engage in a brawl with four or five men against him, were feats from which he shrank no more than from abusing a defenseless woman or beating an unresisting Indian. His brutality made him an object of fear, while his great physical strength and power of will made him a leader of the populace, whom he could sway at pleasure. While he was the terror of all those of his class who dared to oppose him, he was a protector and shield to those who did his bidding and followed his lead. In the French Revolution he would have been one of the noisiest partisans of Marat; at Quito he was the ally of all those who sought to disturb the public peace or to foment riots and insurrections.

To Paredes he presented himself with cringing submissiveness.

"Well, Castro, I see you have kept your word like a man. You have not betaken yourself to a sanctuary or left the city. How do your matters stand?"

"I thank your Excellency most gratefully for the kindness you have shown to me, and for which I shall consider myself eternally your Excellency's debtor."

"Enough of that, my good man! Give us an account of your troubles. Is Mama Catita dead?"

"No, your Excellency, thanks to the Virgin; for her death would have put an innocent man to a great deal of trouble."

"Had she been beaten very severely?"

"Well, your Grace, I do not know. I am ashamed to say that I had taken a little too much of her abominable rum yesterday afternoon; besides, it was dark, and there was so much confusion that I can not remember how it came. We were all to blame, but I did less than any of them."

"Does she charge it on you?"

"She did at first; but I went to see her very early this morning, before she could make her statement to the authorities. I told her—but you must not betray me Señor—that I would pay her, innocent as I was, rather than get into trouble. She then commenced to haggle about the amount, and I paid her half of it down, and promised to pay her the other half next week. Hence, when the notary came, she said that she preferred no charge against me, and that she was too weak to submit to an examination."

"Well, Castro," said Paredes, in his blandest manner, "I think you are still in a very bad predicament. If she should feel death upon her, she would tell, and it would go ill with you; for there is no doubt in my mind that you are the one who did it. But the *Alcalde del Crimen* is my particular friend, who will do anything to oblige me. He will, if it becomes necessary, at my request, leave a loop-hole for your escape. It may be a somewhat difficult matter, but having taken an interest in you once, I am determined to help you through"—

"May God and his Holy Mother bless your Grace through

eternity. Juan Castro will be your most devoted, your most faithful servant, whose eyes, and ears, and arm, and dagger, if necessary, will always be at your disposal."

"Take a glass of this fine liquor, man," said Paredes, whose friendly condescension increased as the interview progressed.

"A thousand thanks for your Excellency's kindness to one so humble as myself. May your Grace live many years, and death to your enemies!"

"How is your sister, Castro; the girl whom they call the 'Flower of Machángara?' You have every reason to be proud of her."

"Well, your Grace, she lives with my mother, and mother and I do not agree very well"—

"I understand. But still a brother naturally takes a jealous interest in the honor and reputation of a sister. You may not care for her much at present, but let her be made the subject of questionable remarks or insinuations, and your feelings of indifference would at once give way to intense concern. Would they not?"

"Of course they would. But why does your Excellency ask these questions?"

"Well," said Paredes, evasively, "I have no special object in doing so. I do not think there is much truth in the rumors I have heard."

"Rumors! Has your Grace heard any rumors about my sister?"

"Not exactly rumors, Castro; only surmises, you know; perhaps mistaken surmises at that."

"Your Grace would oblige me very much by acquainting me with the nature of these surmises," said Castro, getting uneasy and excited under the artistic treatment of Paredes.

"Does your sister still receive the visits of young Roberto Sanchez?"

"I have not been to my mother's house for many months, Señor. I never heard that my sister received his visits."

"Well, there may be no harm in them, Castro. They may be pure friendship, you know. But if a nobleman constantly visits a girl whom he could not possibly marry, the neighbors, you know, will draw their inferences"—

"I see! I see!"

"These inferences may be entirely mistaken; and in this case, I have no doubt, they are; but, nevertheless, such inferences will be drawn, and spoken about, and repeated until they become a matter of public notoriety. It can not be very pleasant for a brother to know that his sister has been made the object of such notoriety."

Castro ground his teeth, but said nothing.

"Under the circumstances, perhaps, you would do well to watch over the conduct of your sister, and to exercise a little brotherly authority over her. You might make her save appearances, at least. Your sister is too good to be the mistress of any nobleman, Roberto Sanchez not excepted."

"I kiss your Excellency's hands for having opened my eyes to this matter. I had not heard of it before, and had not thought of it in the way a brother should think of such matters."

"And now, Juan Castro, take another glass of this excellent *mistela*, and then leave me, for I have several important matters to attend to, this evening. Whenever you are in trouble, come to me, and I shall protect you to the best of my ability."

Castro left and a few minutes afterward the Mayordomo returned from his mission. He had gone to Carrera's house first, but Mariano would not let him see his master, claiming that he was in bed. The man then went to the barracks, and easily caught a glimpse of Count Valverde, who sat alone in his room, brooding in silence. "Something must have afflicted my master, to-day," said his servant to the Mayordomo. "He is not like himself at all. I neversaw him so before."

The Mayordomo felt satisfied that Mama Rucu's curse had made a deep impression on the mind of the Spaniard, and left him to his meditations without delivering his Master's message. Don Tomas then returned to Carrera's house, but his repeated attempts to penetrate to that gentleman's bedroom were frustrated by the astuteness and fierceness of Mariano.

Still Paredes, on hearing his servant's report, saw no cause for apprehension, and so the two returned to the mountain that night, with a relay of fresh Indians, who were threatened with death if they should dare to betray the secret of the expedition.

But their work of the night proved as fruitless and unsatisfactory as their labors in the afternoon. Nothing was discovered. No clue to the secret of the subterranean passage could be found; and, exhausted, angry, and disappointed, they returned to the villa shortly before daybreak.

Mama Rucu was right when she told Carrera that his friend Paredes was in the bowels of the earth, burrowing and digging for what he should never find.

Next morning when Paredes returned to the spot, he found the bronze plate gone and the passage closed. The ceiling of the passage seemed to have caved in and choked it up completely. How this destruction had been accomplished, and by whom it was done, Paredes could not discover. Baffled in his avaricious hopes, he hastened to inform his two companions of the check with which their explorations had met. And now we shall leave both him and Carrera, in order to secure a better acquaintance with other characters of our story.

CHAPTER II.

DOLORES.

TWENTY-FOUR hours have elapsed since Carrera's return from Mama Rucu's cottage. It is morning. Mass has just been said in the private chapel of the Marquis, because the condition of the Marchioness makes it extremely difficult and painful for her to leave the house. The old lady has retired for a long conference on spiritual and other matters with her confessor and friend, the curate of the parish. Dolores and her aunt, Doña Catita, are in their dressing-room, the latter combing the long and beautiful hair of her niece. The two ladies are dressing for a call they intend to make on Doña Carmen Duchicela, of Riobamba, an Indian princess, related to the royal house of Atahualpa, who has come to spend a few weeks at the Capital, to offer her devotions at the celebrated shrine of San Francisco.

Dolores is the ruling spirit of her father's house. Her mother, a confirmed invalid and a lady of indolent disposition, leaves everything to her daughter's care. Her father, a vain and weak-minded, but very ambitious man, worships her as the brightest ornament of his family circle, and the most accomplished lady of Quito. He recognizes her superior intellect, seeks her advice on almost all occasions, and invariably defers to her opinion. His sister, Doña Catita, a worn-out flirt, who can hardly bring herself to realize that her day is gone, clings to her niece because, through her and with her, she can still connect herself with all there is of social attractions and love-and-merry-making in Quito. Moreover, Doña Catita has little or no property of her own. She is dependent on her brother, and, as he is ruled by his daughter, Doña Catita is politic enough to propitiate the power behind the throne. Add to all this the adulation which Dolores receives at the hands of the young gentry of Quito, and we have an almost irresistible combination to make her, what thousands of others would have been in her place, a spoiled child.

But Dolores is a child of the Ecuadorian table-lands, quick-witted, clear-headed, self-reliant, with never-failing presence of mind, cool—cold almost—reflecting, reasoning, perhaps calculating, never carried away by passion or illusions, young in years, but old in her views of life and her opinions of human nature. When we say young in years, we leave room for allowance, Dolores is no longer in her teens. She has already tasted the cup of bitterness and disappointment. She is a widow. After a short year of married life, her husband fell a victim to the prevailing mania for dueling. Unprepared for the dreadful shock, Dolores saw his bloody corpse brought home to her father's house, and years could not efface the impression that fearful event produced. His death was a severe blow to her hopes, because he died before his father, and left her nothing. She had not loved him passionately, but the loss of a husband was to her the loss of that competency and independence which had been within her grasp. Now she looks to the future, not through the rosy haze of youthful hopefulness and confidence, but with a constant regard to her own position in life, and its difficulties and probable embarrassments. Her father loves her blindly, and dotes upon her and gratifies all her wishes; but her father will not live forever, and on his death her brother, now in Lima, will be the head of the family. On him she would then be an humble dependent; and if he should marry, which emergency must arise sooner or later, what would her position be?

"Is it not strange," said Doña Catita, "that Señor Carrera has not been here for two evenings in succession?"

"Why do you find it strange, Auntie?"

"Because he hardly ever misses a night."

"Well, the night after their gambling extravagance he probably needed rest, as we all did; and, by the way, he played not only unluckily, but also very foolishly. He is no match for Paredes or the Count."

"And why did he not come last night?"

"Do I know? And why should I care, Auntie?"

"Well, my child, you are certainly aware that he loves you."

"At all events, he wishes me to believe it."

"Surely you do not dislike him?"

"Oh, no, Auntie! I like him very well. I am not in love with him. I have often told you, Auntie, that I am not in love with anybody. Julio de Carrera is a gentletleman, but whether he would be eligible as a husband remains to be seen."

"I am curious to hear your objections to him, Doloritas; for I must confess that, of all your admirers, he impresses me most favorably."

"You love me, Auntie dear, do you not?"

"What a question, my darling!"

"Well, would you wish me, whom you love, to be the wife of a poor man?"

"Is it settled that Carrera will be a poor man?"

"Is it settled that he will be a rich man? His uncle is a rich man. He may leave everything to Don Julio. But his uncle, although old, is yet robust and full of vitality. He may marry again and have children of his own. He is a very pious man, and may leave most of his property to convents and churches. O, dearest Aunt! I can not, I will not be poor. I have been reared in affluence. I have been accustomed to have all my wishes gratified. It would break my heart to change to poverty, and to live, like so many of our noble families, that have nothing but their titles and what little they can grind out of a few wretched Indians."

"But, darling, Don Julio may be his uncle's heir after all, and you should consider this very great probability, and not throw him away entirely. There is a difference between not committing one's self and giving no encouragement at all. He may lose heart, and be weaned away from you entirely. Nearly every girl in town would be delighted with him for a husband, and if you starve his affection some one else will get him into her net, and by encouraging him, and meeting him more than half way, secure him."

"You are not altogether wrong, Auntie; perhaps I have been too reserved with him."

"I have noticed that you treat the Spanish Count with a perceptible preference."

"I must confess that I am interested in the Count. He is a real Count of old Castile. I often think how greatly I should prefer a life in Spain to this dull, slow, uninteresting, out-of-the-way city of ours."

"But, my child," said Doña Catita, "you want a rich husband, and the Count has nothing but his title."

"Does he not stand high in the favor of the Viceroy? And is it not probable that His Highness will soon help him to a profitable position? Do not most of these Spanish officers enrich themselves in the colonies?"

"That may be all true, Doloritas, but it may take a long time, and you should not wait until your youth and beauty fade. There is no danger of it just now; but you are no longer so very young, my child. Look at me, and take a warning example. If I have remained an old maid, in this country, where ladies are so scarce, it was my own fault. I frittered away opportunities until they ceased to present themselves."

A long pause followed, which was broken by Doña Catita: "What do you think of Paredes, child?"

"He is a man, Auntie. He has all the energy of a man. He lacks the graces of scholarly refinement, and, perhaps, is not as scrupulously honorable as Carrera; but he will make his way in life. He looks to success, and his own affairs are prospering, while those of almost all his young friends are sadly deranged."

Here the conversation of the two ladies was interrupted by the entrance of Santos, the nurse, whom our readers already know: "Niña, your father, the Marquis, wishes to see you for a few moments."

"I am coming, Mamita," said Dolores, arising hastily, and throwing a shawl over her head and shoulders, she repaired to her father's room, which was in another part of the spacious mansion.

The Marquis received her at the door. "One moment, Daughter, dear," he said, leading her to his room. "Your young head generally sees more clearly than mine, with all its gray hairs. I am puzzled, and I want your opinion and advice."

"What is it, dear Papa, you wicked flatterer? Do you want to turn the head of your own child?"

"Listen," he said. "You know I have seen the new member of the Royal Audience, but I have not told you what passed between us. The first time I waited on him, he told me that I stood high at Court; that the King had frequently heard of me, and had even condescended to order his Secretary of State to write me a confidential letter in his name concerning affairs of grave importance. This letter the new Auditor has brought with him from Spain, and he said he would give it to me as soon as he had opened his trunks and boxes. The next time I called upon him, he said nothing about the letter, but he seemed to be in raptures over my horse, 'Chimbo,' your favorite. He said that the possession of such a horse would make him perfectly happy "—

" Papa, you have not given ' Chimbo' away?"

" What could I do, Daughter dear? He is the new Auditor, and I have cases pending in the Royal Audience. It would have been highly impolitic not to conciliate him. And so I said the horse was his, and should be at his disposal the moment he sent for him."

"And so my poor Chimbo is gone," said Dolores, with a sigh. " It is too bad!"

" Before I left the Auditor, I ventured the question whether he had already unpacked his trunks and boxes; but he said that he had not yet had the time. He said that he would first of all open the box containing his dispatches and correspondence, and that I should have the King's letter the next time I called on him."

" Well?"

" When I called on him a day or two afterward, he regretted that he had not yet been able to find the letter. He said that he had searched for it, but had not found it in his dispatch-box. He promised, however, that he would go over his papers again in order to find it."

" Did you see him since?"

" Yes, my child, yesterday."

" Had he found the letter?"

" No, child, he seemed to be much alarmed about it, and said that the unaccountable disappearance of the letter had caused him extreme uneasiness, because he was satisfied that the letter contained matters of vital interest to me, and of great importance to the colony."

"And you did not understand him, Father?"

" Understand him! What do you mean?"

" That he has had this letter in his possession all this time; that he has not mislaid it at all; that it is ready for delivery to you; but that his Excellency, the Auditor, wants money for placing it in your hands. That's what I mean, Father, dear."

"Fool, fool that I was!" exclaimed the Marquis, beating his forehead with his fist. "You are right. The Spaniard wants money, and the thought that this was the cause of his procrastination had never entered my mind. But who could have thought of such meanness? Caramba! Don Alonzo Sanchez is right, after all, about these Spanish cormorants! And now, Doloritas, what shall I do? Perhaps the whole thing is an invention. Perhaps the letter he speaks of is some indifferent and unimportant circular or routine document of no moment, gotten up for the express purpose of extortion. Shall I pay him money to get it?"

"You gave him the horse, Father, because you said you had cases pending in his court, making it desirable to gain his good will. If you do not give him money for the King's letter, you will not gain his good will, and you have sacrificed my noble Chimbo to no purpose."

"You are right, Daughter; you are always right. What a wonderful head for business you have. But suppose we are both mistaken. Suppose I should offer him money, and he should refuse it"—

Dolores gave a ringing laugh: "Then send me to a convent, Father, for the rest of my days. Now, Father, if I had to do this piece of work, I should do it in this way: I should make up my mind first how much it will take to satisfy the Spaniard's rapacity. Then I would tell him that I wanted him to look upon me as his confidential friend; that the voyage to America must have cost him a great deal; that it must cost him a great deal to establish himself in a strange city; that he would require money, and that nothing would please me better than if his Excellency would condescend to accept a loan from me for his present needs. You must also tell him that you have no immediate use for the money, and that he might keep it as long as he pleased. You will then see, Father, how soon the King's letter will be in your hands. If the letter contains nothing, then consider that you have spent your money to win your cases. If the letter is important, you must have it, and you can not get it in any other way. We shall have to buy it from the Spaniard, Papa."

The Marquis paced the room uneasily, and finally, stopping before his daughter, said: "You are right, child; you are right. I shall do as you say. A small amount of money would not accomplish the purpose. I shall have to give him a great deal, and it inconveniences me very much to do so at present. Still, there is no help for it. I shall do it at once. Will you be here when I return?"

"I intended to call on Doña Carmen Duchicela, the Indian princess, with Aunt Catita."

"You will not find her at home now. She will attend high mass at San Francisco at ten o'clock, and it will nearly be twelve before she returns to her house. Wait till I come back, and then make your call. I may want to speak to you again after I have seen the Auditor."

"I shall wait for you, Papacito!" said Dolores, kissing her father as he turned to go.

CHAPTER III.

THE KING'S LETTER.

Dolores was right.

The Marquis poured his golden rain into the lap of the Spanish judge, and the result was that the latter immediately found the letter. "He had found it where he had least expected it to be. He had inadvertently misplaced it. How COULD he have been so absentminded? How COULD he have searched for it everywhere except where he had originally placed it? Sheer forgetfulness, Señor Marquis —most unaccountable forgetfulness."

And now to the letter. It was a most astounding document. The Marquis read it and re-read it, and could not make up his mind whether to rejoice over the confidence of his sovereign, or whether to be bewildered by the responsibility his Majesty compelled him to shoulder. The Marquis was still turning the sacred document in his loyal hands when Dolores opened the door:

"Well, Father."

"You were right as to the Auditor, my child. He is a greedy scoundrel, who, I fear, will continue to bleed me. But that letter, child! It contains the most difficult, the most responsible task ever forced upon me, and it is of such a nature that I can not, dare not consult about it with anybody. O, that I could at least have the support of your opinion!"

"And why can you not, Father? My opinion is the cheapest and the nearest commodity at your command."

"Yes! yes, my child! But I do not know whether I can let you read this letter. You are a woman, a young woman. You might unintentionally betray the important secret it contains."

"Father," said Dolores, sternly. "If I have ever been unworthy of your confidence, why have you continued, unsolicited, to honor me with it until this very day, when the result has proven that I was not mistaken?"

"It is true, child, you are a wonderful woman, and I can not do without you. But will you swear, Dolores, never to breathe these secrets of state to any living soul, either directly or by hints, allusions, or indirections?"

"I shall swear if you command it, Father."

"Swear by the Holy Trinity."

"I swear."

"Well, then, read the letter."

Dolores read:

"Madrid, *Oct.* 15th, 1591.

"To His Excellency, the Marquis Vicente Guitierrez de Solando:

"*Most Excellent Señor:*—His Most Gracious Majesty, the Catholic King, our Lord Don Felipe II, whom God may preserve, has instructed me to write to your Excellency from notes made by me under his Majesty's own dictation.

"His Majesty, who takes the greatest possible pains to keep himself informed as to the affairs of all his dominions, has been highly gratified by the zeal displayed by your Excellency in His Majesty's service, and by the judgment and loyalty for which your Excellency has been distinguished. Placing implicit confidence in your Excellency's devotion and ability to carry out a difficult and delicate task, His Majesty has instructed the undersigned to communicate to your Excellency the following orders, which will require the strictest secrecy and the utmost caution on the part of your Excellency, if His Majesty's object is to be successfully accomplished.*

"His Majesty has learned with great regret, that resistance will be attempted at Quito, and perhaps also in other cities of Peru, to the collection of the *Alcabala*, the introduction of which in the Viceroyalty of Peru, has been made imperative and inevitable by the pressing and overwhelming necessities of His Majesty's service. The turbulent disposition of most of the Peruvian colonists and their proneness to insurrection and rebellion are well known to His Majesty. His Majesty remembers the civil wars which disgraced the early history of his Peruvian possessions, and their frequent and dangerous resistance to the royal commands. His Majesty is fully determined to prevent a repetition of the horrors and devastations of internecine strife. But the necessities of His Majesty's service have sadly depleted his American possessions of available troops.

---

* See the introductory chapters of Gayarre's excellent essay on Philip II. of Spain.

Under these circumstances, it becomes not only a necessity, but also a duty of statesmanship and good government to resort to strategy. If the wild and dangerous beast of rebellion can not be overcome in open contest, it must be ensnared or entrapped. The dragon must be destroyed, no matter how it is done.

"If, therefore, His Majesty's strong and, to all appearances, but too well-founded apprehensions of armed resistance should unfortunately be verified at Quito, His Majesty commands your Excellency secretly and with all the caution such a difficult and dangerous task requires, *to induce some gentleman of influence, social standing, and popularity, to side with the insurgents, and, if necessary or possible, to place himself at their head, in order to break the dangerous force of their movements, to be informed of their intentions, and to guide them into such channels as to secure the final and easy victory of the lawfully constituted authorities.* To such a man, entire indulgence and a full pardon for all the treasonable acts or utterances of which he may have to be guilty, apparently, in order to serve His Majesty, are hereby fully guaranteed under His Majesty's own hand.

"The selection of such a man could not be intrusted to the Royal Audience, the members of which are Spaniards, and not so situated as to enjoy the advantages of such intimate acquaintance with the characters and dispositions of the leading natives of your city, as would be indispensable in making a prudent choice. Nor can this task be confided to the municipal authorities, for these have fomented and prepared the rebellion by protesting against His Majesty's orders, and sending remonstrance after remonstrance against the imposition of the *Alcabala*, to His Majesty's Council of the Indies and to His Majesty personally. The ringleaders of the present municipality will hereafter have to be proceeded against.

"For these reasons, His Majesty has concluded to confide the task of making this difficult selection to your Excellency, a native of the colony, a man of judgment and patriotism, and, above all, a loyal, trusty, and zealous servant of His Majesty. In this choice, your Excellency will be guided by the greatest care; for the consequences of a mistake would be irreparable. The man whom your Excellency will take into your confidence must not only be the right man, but must also be sure to accept. Any mistake in this regard would be fatal.

"His Majesty also desires your Excellency to send from time to time full and accurate reports of the condition of affairs in the Viceroyalty, and of all events that may transpire there, to the undersigned. His Majesty desires your Excellency fully and freely to criticise, in these reports the doings, acts, and measures of the Royal Audience and its individual members, and to give accurate information of the disposition, merits, and demerits of the leading men at Quito, whether natives or Spaniards, and whether in public or private station.

"In order to protect the privacy of these communications, secret orders are herewith inclosed, directed to the Superintendents of the Royal Mails at Quito and Lima, because His Majesty does not desire your Excellency to correspond with this office through the medium of the Royal Audience, but entirely unknown to the same.

"In case of an extraordinary emergency, His Majesty desires your Excellency immediately to address His Highness the Viceroy, who has already been notified that such communications from your Excellency are specially desired and authorized by His Majesty.

"The undersigned now hopes that your Excellency has fully comprehended the meaning and purport of this dispatch, and the full scope which His Majesty intends to give to the exercise of your Excellency's discretion; and with the sincerest wishes that your Excellency may live many

years in the enjoyment of all possible earthly happiness, the undersigned has the distinguished honor to remain,
"Your Excellency's most obedient servant,
"JUAN DE IDIAQUEZ."

And, on the outside of this remarkable document, there was the following indorsement, in the King's own handwriting, and with his own signature:

"All that is said in the within letter has been written by my command, and has my full sanction.
"Yo EL REY." (I, the King.)

This dispatch was accompanied by secret orders to the mail superintendents and postmasters to transmit all letters of the Marquis to the Secretary of State with the greatest possible dispatch and secrecy, and without submitting them to the inspection of any officer or tribunal, not even that of the Royal Audience or Viceroy, and threatening severe punishments in case of disobedience or of a violation of the secrecy which these orders enjoined. The dispatch itself contained frequent corrections of phraseology and punctuation, which were evidently made by the King himself, for Philip II loved to wade through volumes of dreary pages, and correct the grammar, syntax, and style of his subordinates, as well as to attend to the minutest details of the cumbersome, complicated, and destructive machinery of his government.

These documents had reduced the Marquis to a state of helpless despondency and bewilderment, from which he hoped to be extricated by the clear-headedness and intellectual resources of his daughter.

His eyes rested upon her while she read, and silently he awaited her opinion. Dolores calmly and attentively perused the document, and, when she had finished it, went over it for a second time, re-reading certain passages.

Then dropping the hand which held the papers into her lap, she rested her head on her other hand and looked out of the window.

"Well, child?"

"Well, Father!"

"What do you think of it?"

"The royal confidence, if you can justify it, Father, may be of great advantage to you and your house."

"But what shall I do?"

"That remains to be seen. In the first place, Papa, do you really believe that there will be a rebellion?"

"Yes, my child, the people, high and low, are unanimous. Even the clergy seem to be in favor of resistance. Our Curate here talks downright treason. The Dominicans and Franciscans loudly denounce the *Alcabala*. The Jesuits alone are loyal. With the encouragement of the clergy, the rebellion would seem to be irresistible. I understand, from the new Auditor, that the Alcabala is to be proclaimed to-day. The collection of the tax will be resisted at once. In fact, it will be impossible to collect it here in Quito, and from here the fire will spread to Latacunga, Ambato, Riobamba, Cuenca, and Loja. The Government will be powerless for years to come. Then a long struggle may follow, which will plunge us into a war like that of Fernando Jiron or Gonzalo Pizarro."

"If this is your opinion, Father, then select your man at once."

"But whom shall I select. I have thought of several, but there are weighty objections to each of them."

"Of whom have you thought?"

"Well, daughter," said the Marquis, tenderly, "I have thought of your own interests and your own prospects. The man who renders the King such a great service, will be entitled to His Majesty's grateful remembrance, and, as the estates of the ring-leaders will be confiscated, His Majesty will be enabled to show his gratitude without expense to his own treasury. It is natural that I, as a loving father, should have thought of those first who aspire to the hand of my Doloritas."

" Dear old Papa ! And of whom have you thought ? "

" I know that my naughty child will have her own way, and you shall have it, if your choice is a good one. But if you should want to know my preference "—

" I am dying to know it, Father ! "

" Then," continued the Marquis, " I should have to tell you that, considering everything, I am most favorably impressed with Julio de Carrera."

Dolores broke into a short, roguish laugh.

" Why do you laugh, child ; is he objectionable to you ? "

" Not at all, Father. I should be very willing to accept him for a husband, provided "—

" Well, what ? "

" Let us postpone this part of the question to some other occasion. Julio de Carrera, Father, would never fulfill the commission you wish to assign to him."

"And why not? Is he not one of the most popular men, if not the most popular young gentleman of Quito? He is worshiped by the rabble. They would at once follow his lead."

" Very true, Father; but Carrera would never participate in a movement merely for the purpose of betraying it. He is scrupulously honorable."

" But is it dishonorable to serve the King ? "

" No, Father, although opinions may differ as to the kind of service. It would not be considered honorable, for instance, to act as the King's executioner ; and yet it may be called serving the King, to execute those whom he has sentenced to death. All I can say, is this, Carrera will never put himself at the head of a rebellion or insurrection. But, if he were to do it, he would not do it for the purpose of betraying it.

The Marquis sat silent for many minutes. At last he playfully pinched his daughter's cheek, and, shaking her gently, he said, with great warmth: "You are right again—always right, my child. The role the King wishes me to assign to some one is not so very honorable or desirable, after all. But no matter; the King's commands must be obeyed. All I have to do is to find the man who possesses the necessary qualifications and who will accept. I thought of old Sanchez, who is one of the loudest resistants. Such storm-cloud men are easily changed by a ray of Royal sunshine. But Sanchez is too old"—

"And would not accept such a task," interrupted Dolores. "He is an enthusiast, like his son, and, I am afraid, has sealed his doom. But I thought, Father, you wanted to select one of my admirers?"

"But your admirers are too chivalrous and honorable."

"You are mistaken, Father. There is but one Carrera among them. But, if the almost unerring instincts of a woman should not fail me this time, if I am not more wofully mistaken than I have ever been, I believe I have your man."

"Well, daughter," asked the Marquis, greatly excited, "who is he?"

"Manuel Paredes!"

The Marquis stared at her in blank amazement for several moments, then he clapped his hands, wildly struck the table, and exclaimed: "By all the angels and saints of heaven, you are right! Of all the men in the kingdom he is the one who will answer our purpose!"

"And do you really think, Father, that there will be troubles here to-day or to-morrow?"

"I do."

"Then go and see him or send for him at once."

CHAPTER IV.

THE QUEEN AND HER PEOPLE.

WHILE the Marquis was in attendance upon the new member of the Royal Audience, an immense multitude of Indians had been pouring into the Convent Church of San Francisco, filling every available space of the massive edifice. Numbers that were unable to gain admittance were kneeling outside, blocking up the entrance. A great many white people and *mestizos*, who had come to catch a glimpse of Doña Carmen Duchicela had to turn back, unable even to reach the door of the crowded church. By common consent possession had been given up this day to the Indians, who had flocked to Quito from all the surrounding hamlets and villages. They had crowded in with such eagerness that they seemed to have forgotten their usual deference to their white masters, and would not give way for any caballero who should attempt to squeeze through the squalid multitude. Only once their ranks had opened voluntarily, like the waves of the Red Sea for Moses and the Israelites. It was when Carrera and Roberto Sanchez, preceded by Mariano and the Fool, had entered the building. But the human waves closed after them again, and the two young friends were probably the only representatives of the white race inside the sacred pile. A convenient place near one of the pillars had been yielded to them, from which they could enjoy a full view of the places of honor reserved for the Indian Princess and her suite.

Seats had been prepared for Doña Carmen and a few of her companions, which they occupied during the *requiem*, while during the whole of the mass they knelt, according to the custom of the country. Doña Carmen Duchicela was surrounded by a number of Indian *Caciques* and their wives. Among the former, the venerable form of Don Sebastian Collohuaso, the *Cacique* of Ibarra, occupied a prominent position. But the greatest deference was paid to a very old Indian, with snow-white hair, who stood nearest to the Princess, and who was eagerly pointed out by the few who knew him to the many who wished to see his face.

And had these thousands of Indians come to see Doña Carmen? Our readers know better. For Doña Carmen Duchicela not an Indian would have left his cottage in the country. Her father, Cachulima, was the first native Lord who welcomed the foreign invaders, the murderers of his kingly nephew and his noble brother, Chalcuchima. Cachulima was the first native Lord who had come to kiss the hand that had smitten his race and destroyed its freedom and independence. It might be said in his defense that he welcomed these strangers because he hoped that they would deliver him from the usurpation of the terrible Rumiñagui, who had murdered all the other Princes of the blood in order to secure the crown for himself. But was not the usurpation of Rumiñagui but the result of Pizarro's invasion and his treacherous faithlessness to confiding Atahualpa? No; in the eyes of the loyal Indians of Quito there was no excuse for Cachulima. The Spanish Government had rewarded his submissiveness. He was the only native Lord who was permitted to retain his lands and vassals, and to remain exempt from all the degrading restrictions and slavish regulations to which the conquered race was subjected. There was no sympathy in the Indian heart for his daughter, Carmen Duchicela. Not for her had they crowded the church this day; but by that wonderful and still unexplained system of telegraphy which, even at the present day, astonishes the uninitiated by the unaccountable celerity and mysteriousness with which its messages are transmitted from place to place, without regard to distance, it had been given out that Toa Duchicela, their rightful Queen, the legitimate sovereign of the country, the direct lineal descendant of Cacha and Atahualpa, would avail herself of the presence of her distinguished relative to show herself to her people at a most convenient public place, where thousands could see her, and satisfy their loving and anxious minds that their Queen still lived, and was still among them. Thousands of Indian men and women went to bend their knees, not before the Christian altars, which only their lips revered, but to prostrate themselves with all the blind devotion and loyalty of their race before Toa, their unfortunate, but ever rightful, Queen. Of these thousands not one had betrayed her secret; not one had breathed it to any of the enemies of their race. Not a white man knew it but the two who were there at the Queen's own invitation. Not a negro, not a mestizo knew it. Faithfully, loyally, scrupulously, the poor, down-trodden, outraged, starving Indians had kept the secret, which any one of them might have sold for enough money to buy his freedom, and to live in affluence and luxury for the rest of his days. Toa Duchicela was as safe among them in the crowded church, and in the heart of the city of Quito, as she could have been in the mountainous wilderness of Llanganati or in the impenetrable forests of the Napo.

Carrera's eyes sought her in vain. He could not discover her among the companions of Doña Carmen, who occupied the most conspicuous seat. He had already communicated this disappointing fact to his friend Roberto. The religious function was over. The procession of priests filed away, and disappeared; but the organ pealed on as usual after the celebration of high mass. And now a sudden commotion became noticeable among the multitude of kneeling Indians, who, thus far, had cowered on the cold stones, almost motionless. A surging sea of Indian heads inclosed the cavaliers; thousands of necks were eagerly stretched, and thousands of eyes strained, in the direction of the old lady who sat in the seat of honor. But still not a sound escaped the vast assembly, and nothing was heard but the peals of the great organ reverberating through the massive edifice. And now Doña Carmen Duchicela made a motion as if attempting to arise from her chair. This seemed to be the preconcerted signal, and the suspense and eagerness with which every eye hung on the group surrounding her, were almost painful to behold. The white-haired old Indian and the Cacique of Ibarra approached Doña Carmen's chair, and bent over her, as if to offer her their arms and assistance.

At this moment a figure, which until then must have been concealed by the high back of Doña Carmen's chair, arose behind it. She wore the garb of a common Indian, and her head and face were covered by a coarse and heavy woolen shawl. But with a majestic and graceful motion of her arms, she now opened this shawl, and dropped it down to her waist, uncovering the beautiful face and the indescribable eyes of Toa. Her head was encircled with a golden diadem, to which, on her forehead, an immense and magnificent emerald was fastened—the emblem of the old Shyri Kings. Her beauty was so radiant, and the apparition so surprising, that Roberto Sanchez, who had not seen her before, could not restrain an exclamation of astonishment. It passed unnoticed, however, for it was drowned in the general and ill-suppressed utterances of delight which now broke forth from the multitude. The sight which the two cavaliers beheld during the next few seconds defies all description. It was as if the hearts of thousands had gone forth to that one being that held them all. A sigh, changing into a low moan, ran through the multitude. Arms were stretched out to her; folded hands were raised to heaven, as if in prayer; tears stood in almost every eye; love, devotion, self-sacrifice beamed in every countenance; and when Toa slowly raised her shawl, and covered her.

head and face again, a loud, heart-rending wail arose, mingled with many a violent sob. Old Doña Carmen now had arisen and hobbled away, heavily leaning on the arms of her two aged companions, and the uninitiated would have supposed that the multitude had wept in compassion for her bodily infirmities. At the same time, however, the old Indian raised his arm, as if in deprecation, yet with the air of conscious authority, and the wailing ceased, and was followed, first by an instant of oppressive stillness, then by a general movement toward the door.

The royal reception was over. Queen Toa had shown herself to her people, and had received the homage of her subjects. The whole scene had passed off in a few seconds —an infinitely shorter time than its description required.

Roberto seized Carrera's arm with both his hands, and said, rapturously: "She is superb! Every inch a Queen. By the Virgin! I would serve her rather than our Philip."

CHAPTER V.

MOTHER, DAUGHTER, AND SON.

Near the southern approaches of the city, at a considerable distance from the center of population, not far from where the bridge over the Machángara now stands, there was a small house, inhabited by Mariquita Yeaza, the widow of a common soldier named Castro, and her daughter Mercedes, who eked out a scanty living by sewing and embroidering for the rich, and by selling refreshments to those travelers who chose to offer their prayers or thanksgivings upon leaving or returning to Quito, on or from a journey, in the chapel of the *Señor del buen viage,** on the hill south of the River Machángara.

---

* The Lord of the Happy Journey.

Late in the afternoon of the great day on which Toa Duchicela had shown herself to her faithful subjects in the Church of San Francisco, Mercedes was busily bending over her embroidery, while her mother attended to necessary house and kitchen-work, or ministered to the patrons of her shop. The latter department of their domestic economy was exclusively under the mother's charge; for Mercedes had abandoned the shop since Roberto Sanchez had become a regular visitor to the house. A little Mestizo girl had taken her place as Doña Mariquita's assistant.

Busily Mercedes bent over her frame, but her thoughts were not on the embroidery. Quite near her chair stood a harp, to which she frequently resorted, interrupting her work in order to try some tune which she was evidently composing; and when she returned to her needle, her lips moved audibly, as if endeavoring to accommodate words to her melody. At last she threw her needle away, and, sitting down to her harp, struck up a prelude, and then began to sing, not loudly, but softly, as if still rehearsing her own composition, and with all the sweetness and tenderness of love, resignation, and grief:

> "No me llames por mi nombre,
> Que mi nombre se acabó!
> Llámame la flor marchita
> Que del arbol se cayó!
>
> "Las lágrimas que derramo
> Amargas i saladas son;
> No te dan vida, florcita,
> Ni me alivian el corazon."*

---

* Call me not the name I bore,
  That name, alas! to me is lost.
Call me but a faded flower,
  Upon the earth by tempest tossed.

Remorseful are the bitter tears
  That to mine eye-lids start;
They bring not life to fading flower,
  Nor ease to aching heart.

Her voice grew fainter and weaker as she proceeded. Her fingers ceased to touch the chords, and as the last sounds of instrument and voice died away, the girl buried her head in her hands and broke into a flood of bitter tears.

Suddenly she gave a start. A hand had touched her lightly upon her shoulder. Her mother stood behind her and asked: "Why do you weep, Merceditas?"

Doña Mariquita was a tall and spare woman of about forty-five. She was dressed very plainly, and covered with the inevitable shawl from which the women of the Andean table-lands seem to be inseparable. The battle of life had furrowed her cheeks and sprinkled her hair with gray, but it had not bent her head or subdued her courage. Bitter experience had taught her the habit of self-reliance. Fate had dealt roughly with her, and, in her way, she had drawn lessons from it, which were not of a purifying or ennobling character. Doña Mariquita knew the value of a competence; and there was little that she would not have sacrificed in order to attain it. Still she was full of kindness to her daughter, whom she treated with great fondness, not only because she was her daughter, but also because she looked upon her youth and beauty as capital, from which, while it lasted, golden interest might be drawn. It was Doña Mariquita that had encouraged the visits and pretensions of Roberto Sanchez. Mariquita Yeaza de Castro knew that her daughter was too poor and too low down in the social scale to entertain any expectation of a rich and noble husband. But poverty and want pinch cruelly, and relief, even temporary relief, from the gnawing cares of indigence, was thought highly desirable by a woman of Doña Mariquita's character, and not too costly at any price. If her daughter, a child of the people, could not aspire to a wealthy and noble husband, why should she not strive to, and have a wealthy and noble lover, provided a generous, open-hearted, and open-handed youth could be attracted who would do the right thing by Mercedes, or, more properly, by her mother? There was danger in this respect. The young cavaliers of Quito were unscrupulous and licentious enough, but mostly too poor to be considered eligible by this worthy matron. But fortunately, or unfortunately, chance threw Roberto Sanchez into her way, who, to an unbounded generosity, and a sense of loyalty rare in those days, united a supply of ample means with which his rich and indulgent father provided him.

"Why do you weep, Merceditas?"

Mercedes had cause to weep, as her mother was soon to learn. The way of the transgressor is always hard. After the days of illicit bliss the days of trial were to follow, and Mercedes had discovered that those days were soon to come. To add gall to this bitter discovery, the visits of her lover had not been so frequent, of late, as in the earlier days of their love. Sighs and tears, such as the girl had been unable to repress in his presence, are not to the taste of a young cavalier, however loyal his intentions may be.

"The dazzling toy, so fiercely sought,
Has lost its charm by being caught."

The story is so well known that it does not bear repetition. Doña Mariquita had, therefore, every reason to ask: "Why do you weep, Merceditas?"

Ask a woman why she cries, and you will open the floodgate of her tears. Mercedes threw herself into her mother's arms and continued to weep.

"This is quite a touching sight," said a coarse and sneering voice, which filled both mother and daughter with sudden fear. It was the voice of Juan Castro who had entered the room unobserved, and stood in the door, his face flushed with rum and excitement.

"And to what are we indebted to the rare and extraordinary pleasure of seeing the Señor Don Juan?" asked the

Doña Mariquita, who, although greatly vexed and alarmed by his visit, had not lost her presence of mind.

"Ask your sniveling daughter, there! Ask the neighbors! Ask the whole town, and you will know, if you do not know already, why a visit of the son and brother has become necessary."

"I do not understand you," said his mother, without looking at him. "It is so uncommon for Juan Castro to remember that he has a mother and a sister."

"I can not say that I enjoy the remembrance. The conduct of that young lady has not been calculated to develop brotherly pride and affection. It would have been better for me not to have had a sister."

"And why, pray?"

"*Al demonio* with your questions!" he replied with an oath. "As if you did not know what I mean! I am not easily flattered by your high connections. Do you two women think that it is very pleasant for me to have our name and family disgraced by Roberto Sanchez?"

"If the honor of any name and family were intrusted to your keeping, Juan, I should pity the family," answered Doña Mariquita, while Mercedes continued to cling to her mother tremblingly, and in silence.

"For how much have you sold that girl?"

"If I had to sell her, Juan, in order to keep ourselves from starvation, you would be the last person in the world who has a right to complain. What have you done for your family? What have you ever contributed to the support of your mother and sister? How have you repaid me for bringing you up and establishing you in business?"

"Nonsense, Mother! Devilish little have I received from you of my father's estate."

"Your father had no property, and you know it. What I had was my own, and not your father's."

"I have not come to quarrel with you. I have come to

tell you that the disgraceful visits of Sanchez must stop. These visits must stop, do you understand me."

"But if they should not stop?"

"Then I must infer that it is very profitable for you to let them go on. And if I am to share the shame, Mother, I must share the profits, too. Have I expressed myself with sufficient clearness?"

"And if I tell you never to set your foot in this house again?"

"You will not tell me anything of the kind, Mother. You know I am not to be trifled with. You know I am to be feared."

"Will you murder us, as you attempted to murder the old *Chichera*, Doña Catita?"

"She has found to her expense that I am not to be contradicted or counteracted by anybody. You will either put a stop to the visits of Sanchez, or you will let me share in the proceeds. And, by the way, I am in difficulty just now. One or two ducats would help me out."

"I have no money in the house," said Doña Mariquita, turning pale.

"We shall see about that," rejoined Castro, swaggering up to the bureau.

"Stand back!" commanded his mother, throwing herself in his way.

"Give way!" he shouted, seizing her by the arm, "and do not provoke me. I know now that you have money in the house."

A scuffle began. The woman was determined, and so was her son. With a loud scream, Mercedes threw herself between them to protect her mother, but he flung her back with such force that she fell to the floor, upsetting her harp which fell with a moaning sound. In the next moment Castro would have overpowered his mother, if a new party had not appeared on the scene. Roberto Sanchez, with drawn sword, and the fire of indignation in his eye, now faced the ruffian.

"Stand back, you blackguard, and if you ever dare to come here again, I shall cut you to pieces"—

Castro was not afraid of any man. But Roberto Sanchez was armed, and Castro was unarmed. Roberto was a nobleman of high standing, and the strong arm of the law would have been on his side. Discretion, therefore, became the better part of valor.

"I see, it is your time now, Señor Don Roberto," he said, slowly retreating. "You claim rights by purchase here, which it may be too late for me to dispute. But we shall meet under more favorable circumstances."

"Your threats are ridiculous, Juan Castro," said Sanchez. "If it is money you want, you should act differently. And as for your courage, there are better opportunities to prove it than by abusing two defenseless women, whom you should consider it your duty to protect. Listen, man! I have something to tell you which you will like to hear. You claim to be a son of Quito. Well, then, Quito has good use for you now. The Procurator-General, Don Alonzo Bellido, has been arrested to-day by order of the Royal Audience, for advising the people to resist the collection of the Alcabala. He must be set free to-night. Do you understand? We shall all go to the Palace, and *force* the President, if necessary, to issue an order for Bellido's release. I know, your influence among the commoners is great, and the Cabildo relies on your zeal. Get your men in readiness for to-night, and as you will need money, here it is. You shall have money enough, but do not act the brute to your helpless mother and sister."

Juan Castro hated Roberto Sanchez, and did not intend to be deprived of his revenge. But money and the prospect of a riot tempted him beyond his power of resistance. Worse than all, he hated the native Spaniards, and a demonstration against the foreign authorities was one of his favorite pastimes. What course he should hereafter pursue as to Sanchez might be made a subject of future deliberation. All appearances indicated that for the rescue of his sister, he had come too late. But Sanchez had given him money, and more money might be drawn from the same source. To bleed him in his purse might, after all, be wiser policy than to run the great risk of attempting his life. At all events, Castro determined to consider. For the moment he was satisfied, and so he said cheerfully: "Many thanks to your Grace. I shall show myself worthy of the confidence of the Cabildo. In the meantime, I beg your Excellency's pardon for my rudeness. I see it was all a mistake on my part. Your Grace shall hear from me to-night. Death to the Audience and Viva el Señor Alonzo Bellido!"

With these words he hurried away without deigning to look at his mother or sister, who felt that although the danger had passed away for the time being, a dark cloud had arisen on the horizon, which might still be fraught with destruction.

That same night the first blow was struck by the Commune of Quito. The first overt act of rebellion was committed. An immense multitude appeared before the Government Palace, headed by gentlemen in masks, and by men of the Castro stamp, with open visor. The President of the Royal Audience, Don Manuel Barros de San Millan, was completely taken by surprise. No outbreak had been apprehended so soon, and consequently no precautions had been taken. The mob demanded the immediate release of Don Alonzo Bellido, and the terrified Auditors assented without hesitation. The cowardly President even went so far as to assure the people that a mistake had been made by some one; that his authority had been exceeded, and that it had not been his intention to arrest the Procurator-General. Bellido was borne home on the shoulders of men. From the balcony of his house he addressed the people.

He thanked them for their sympathy and kindness, and assured them of his unswerving devotion to their rights. He entreated them to go home peaceably, and to commit no excesses, so as not to disgrace their just cause. He vowed that while he was Procurator-General their rights should be protected. At the same time he expressed loyalty to the King, who must have been misinformed, and had evidently acted under the advice of evil counselors, with whom the responsibility rested. Still, while trusting to the justice of His Majesty, it behooved them, like prudent men, to be on their guard against the continued influence of His Majesty's evil advisers. The people of Quito had taken a lawful, but a bold step, and it would be necessary to prepare for the consequences. The rights of the Municipality must be maintained, but he doubted if it could be done without a struggle. He hoped to God that struggle might be averted; but, if it became inevitable, he, for one, was ready to go to the bitter end, and to sacrifice his life, if necessary, in the cause of law and justice, without which life itself would be unbearable.

His speech electrified the people, and was received with thunders of applause. The hour had come and had furnished the man. The Revolution had found a head to direct it. And a clear, cool, far-seeing, and determined head was that of the ill-fated Alonzo Bellido.

CHAPTER VI.

CARMEN DUCHICELA—THE OLD FAITH AND THE NEW.

We must go back to the evening preceding the scene at the church, described in another chapter. A large house in the Plaza of San Francisco, owned by the Convent, patronized by the liberality of Carmen Duchicela, had been placed at the disposal of the Indian Princess, for the time of her stay in Quito. All the nobility, ladies, and gentlemen, and nearly the whole clergy of the place, had called on her shortly after her arrival, and visitors were continually offering their services to her, in the usual Spanish style. She was overwhelmed with attentions and besieged with invitations, most of which she declined. The Spanish colonists looked with contempt on the common herd of Indians; but Doña Carmen was the representative of Royalty; and Royalty, even conquered Royalty, never loses its charm in the eyes of poor humanity.

In Peru intermarriages between the conquerors and the Indian Princesses had been frequent. The celebrated historian, Garcilazo de la Vega, was the issue of such a marriage. In Quito such unions could not take place, because Rumiñagui, the usurper, had killed off the Princesses that had been left behind when Atahualpa went south, and had even carried off or murdered the Virgins of the Sun, who always were of the best blood of the land. The visit of Doña Carmen, therefore, created great excitement at Quito, because she and her son were the last known representatives of the royal blood of the Shyris. Her son, however, had not come with her to Quito, as the management of the family estates, at this season of the year, required his presence at home.

The hour of the night-bell (*toque de la queda*) was fast approaching. All her white visitors had left. Doña Carmen felt somewhat fatigued with their attentions. Don Sebastian Collahuaso, the Cacique of Ibarra, had remained with her, and was now joined by the old Indian whom we noticed at the church. He entered the room after the last white face had disappeared. An Indian servant girl stood in the door awaiting the orders of her mistress.

"How I hate them," whispered the old man to Don Sebastian Collahuaso, as they both respectfully took up their positions near Doña Carmen's chair."

"Peace be with you, Prince Cundurazu; we must wait and bear. Our Lady seems to be fatigued."

"Yes, my dear Don Sebastian, I feel tired and exhausted. These people are all very kind to me, but it is very tiresome to receive so many. Such a constant stream of visitors interferes with my devotions. At my age, on the verge of eternity, the vanities of this world lose their charm, however highly I may have prized them once. I am very much beholden to you for your assistance, Don Sebastian. You must be fatigued likewise. I shall keep you no longer."

"I am sorry, Doña Carmen, that I must trouble you for a few minutes longer. But I must speak to you on a very important subject."

"Is it of such importance that it can not be postponed until tomorrow?"

"It is, Lady Carmen. Now we are alone in the house— I mean nobody is with or around us, but the children of our own race."

"Don Sebastian, if you had entered into the spirit of the new faith, you would know that there is in reality but one race, which is the human race, and that we are, all of us, children of our heavenly Father, and consequently Brothers and Sisters."

"A pretty way of treating their Brothers and Sisters they have, those foreign children of your heavenly Father," sneered Cundurazu.

"Hush, old friend. You and I shall never agree on this subject. Let us hear what communication Don Sebastian has to make."

"Knowing your views, I might have kept it from you, Lady Carmen. But good faith requires that you shall know what we intend to do. You will not be compromised by it in any way. And as you may, perhaps, desire to see your nearest female relative—"

"For God's sake, Don Sebastian, do you mean to tell me "—

"That the Señora Toa is in the city? Yes, Doña Carmen, I do."

The old lady turned pale, and looked very uneasy. After a pause, she said: "And why have you brought her here, into this hot-bed of danger?"

"She is perfectly safe here, Doña Carmen; safer, probably, than in the remotest hamlet of the country."

"And you, Prince Cundurazu, I have no doubt, are planning and plotting with her, dreaming of impossibilities and struggling against the inevitable."

"Coya,"* said the old man, "The Senora Toa is my Queen "—

"Whose life you have made wretched and miserable, making her a fugitive and a wanderer, while she might have lived in happiness and peace. For the sake of a worthless bubble—for a mere phantom—the perpetuation of Shyri Royalty, which must end, even in this form, as it has ended in substance, you have sacrificed that unfortunate girl. Why did you not leave her with me, where she was unknown and safe? The special privileges conferred

---

* Royal Princess.

upon my father by the King of Spain have descended to me, and will descend to my son. I might have protected her, even if her origin had been revealed, especially if you had let me carry out my wish of marrying her to my son. But, no; you have filled her mind with hallucinations and illusions, and have unfitted her for a quiet, useful, matronly life, and doomed her to hide in caves, in ravines, and in the wilderness, in order to keep up the spirit of discontent and false hope among the children of our race. The only consolation they might have—the consolation of true religion—you take from them, by secretly keeping up heathenism among them, and you have nothing to give them in return, nothing, nothing; for what can your plots ever lead to? What could our Indians ever accomplish against the power of Spain? If they could not crush the invaders when we were the millions and they the few hundreds, how can you expect to shake off the yoke when the hundreds have multiplied into the hundred thousands? You afflict me, my friends, by your vain struggles and visionary hopes. And where is that poor, dear girl now?"

"She is here, in the house, Doña Carmen, waiting to embrace her kinswoman."

"Here, in the house! God bless her. Why did you not tell me before? Where is she?"

"Here, Auntie dear," said Toa, who had listened to most of this conversation, in the adjoining room, and now, with outstretched arms, flew to the old lady. But the latter had already slipped from her chair. Stronger than the new faith, stronger than her religious convictions, stronger than her loyalty to the authority of the conquerors who had dealt so generously with her house, was the power of blood and ancient custom. Carmen Duchicela, the loyal subject of the King of Spain, and the favorite of his Church, instead of receiving the homage of her young relative, upon whom she had lavished her charities, instantly forgot the present, and at once flew back to the past, and throwing herself in the dust before the Lady Toa, clung to the feet of the granddaughter of Atahualpa, the legitimate representative of Indian sovereignty.

"Rise, Auntie, dear," said Toa; "nay, Mother, I should say—for you have proved a mother, a guardian angel, a benefactress to me, your wayward, disobedient child." With these words she lifted her up and silently held her in her arms. The two women were locked in each other's embrace, and a long pause followed, during which only sobs were audible. The two strong men, hardened in the school of adversity, had melted like children, and Prince Cundurazu especially could not stem the flood of his tears. But soon the silence was broken. The members of Doña Carmen's Indian suite and her numerous retinue of servants crowded into the room, and prostrating themselves before the Lady Toa, kissed the hem of her humble garment, or, true to the old Indian custom, seized her foot and put it on their necks or shoulders.

"I thank you, children," said Toa, vainly endeavoring to repress her tears, "with all my heart I thank you for your love, your loyalty, your devotion. But leave us now. I have not seen the Señora Carmen for years, and I have much to say to her. Leave us now, children. I shall see you again, and shall speak to each one of you. The Great Sun will protect you, and his sister, the Moon, will smile upon you, and Pachacamac will once more favor the cause of our race."

"You must not speak to them thus, Lady Toa," said Doña Carmen, regaining her composure, and with an expression of reproachful sadness. "The gods you name were false gods, and we are Christians. The Sun and the Moon are but the works of the true God. Where was the power of Pachacamac and the Sun and the Moon, when the true God came into this land? They were like chaff and withered leaves before the hurricane. Go, now, my children; I want to speak to the Shyri Toa."

Reluctantly the Indians obeyed this command, leaving the two ladies alone with Don Sebastian Collahuaso and Prince Cundurazu.

"And now, children," said Doña Carmen, "what do you intend to do?"

"The Shyri Toa," said Cundurazu, "must show herself to her people. Our people believe in her existence, but this belief would soon die out without the evidence of their own senses. They must see her, and they shall see her in the church to-morrow, in order to be confirmed in their loyalty."

"And what is your object, my friend, in preserving a loyalty, which, while it is useless to my darling Toa, can only help to make our race miserable by increasing its discontent with its present condition?"

"Doña Carmen," replied Cundurazu, "we have great plans"—

"The old, old story!"

"But listen! It is not the old story. No longer do we hope for deliverance through our own unaided exertions. I am ready to admit to you now that this would be in vain. But there will be an outbreak here against the authority of the King of Spain. The children of our conquerors have become as dissatisfied with their foreign tyrants as we are. If they will give us our rights, we shall aid their rebellion and make it successful. We have millions of men and our great treasure. All the resources of war are at our command. This country can shake off the yoke of Spain. It can be made an independent kingdom under a sovereign of its own, assisted perhaps by one or more of the powers that are now at war with Spain. I grant our new King must belong to the detested race of the conquerors. But he shall marry the Shyri Toa, and she shall confer upon him her rights as the successor of Cacha and Atahualpa. She shall be a real Queen, and will be able to protect her race."

"And who is the husband you have selected for her, you restless, indefatigable, incorrigible schemer?" inquired the Señora Carmen.

"We have not settled yet upon any particular individual; it is only the general outline of the plan on which we have agreed. We shall have to leave a great deal to the decisive power of the events before us."

"And you, my child," asked Doña Carmen, "do you approve of all these visionary schemes?"

"My dearest Aunt, I have devoted my life to the cause of my race. The plan of Prince Cundurazu may succeed, and it is my duty to try it, trusting to the guidance of our friends here and to the mercy of the Gods. If this plan fails I have another."

"My poor child," said Doña Carmen, "do not sacrifice yourself and the lives of others to such fruitless beginning. I see no hope but in submission and in the grace of God. These schemes can not succeed. How can this poor country shake off the yoke of the greatest power in the world? And what good would your success do to our race? The Crown of Spain has always been the friend of the Indian. Numberless laws were passed for our protection. Who has disregarded them? Who has prevented their execution, or perverted them into instruments of additional oppression? The Colonists—the very men with whom you propose to coöperate. Have you forgotten the rebellion of Gonzalo Pizarro? What was its cause? Why did Peru then arise against Spain? Because the Government wanted the Indians to be free, and to be protected like human beings. Against this intention the Colonists rebelled, and the Government yielded in order to crush the rebellion. What little protection we enjoy lies in the Government of Spain and in the Council of the Indies. Let these Colonies shake off the Spanish yoke, and the Indian will lose his last and only friend. It is true,

the Spanish officers who are sent here disregard the
benevolent laws and intentions of the Home Government. But it only shows how much worse we should
be off if that last restraint were removed. No, child,
you will never succeed, and if this country should gain
its independence, it would be the deadliest blow to our
people."

"Not under a King of our own making," said Cundurazu, " with Toa as his Queen."

"You are a visionary, Prince Cundurazu," continued
the old lady, "and you are leading this child to destruction. Toa! Dear Toa! Flesh of my own flesh—my
child, my darling child! Be warned by one who has been
a mother to you! Abandon this life of adventure, of restlessness, of danger, and of utter hopelessness. Come to
me again. You know my son. He is good, kind-hearted,
and true. He will be a loving husband to you and an affectionate father to your children. He will give you the
blessings of a home; he will cherish and protect you, and
your life will be passed in usefulness and happiness. Renounce your empty title; it is a heritage of defeat and
death. The glory of our royal house has passed away
forever, and will never be restored. I am old, and my
days on earth are numbered. I remember the past, and
can judge of what the future will be. By the sacred
memory of our fathers, by the living God, in whom I believe, and who has proved stronger than the Sun or the
Moon and Pachacamac, by everything that I hold dear on
earth and in heaven, I implore you to return to me, and
to exchange peace, comfort, and happiness for restlessness,
misery, suffering, and death. Our race is an inferior race,
which has had its days of power; but those days are gone,
and will never—can never—return. We are suffering for
the idolatry and the errors of our Fathers, and nothing remains for us but patience and hope, and a firm trust in

Him who died on the cross for the meek, the down-trodden, and the lowly, who will be with Him in Paradise."

Toa was deeply moved. She loved her Aunt and longed for the happiness her self-imposed martyrdom had thus far denied her. But visions of another love, and dreams of greatness and glory, and the noble ambition of liberating her race steeled her determination. She bent over Doña Carmen, kissed her fondly and tenderly, and then said, with a voice trembling with emotion: "Aunt, Mother, benefactress! How dear, how good, how noble you are! For all your love, I thank you! I can never repay it. It grieves me to the heart that I can not obey you. If I feel remorse for what I consider the performance of an imperative duty, this remorse lies in my love for you. The thought of grieving you is almost unbearable, and yet, Doña Carmen, I can not do otherwise. The heavenly powers made me the rightful Queen of our people. Shall I abandon them for my own comfort and happiness? Shall I settle down quietly and selfishly, and think of myself only, while my people are crushed by the most revolting and heartless tyranny? The foreigners are making them beasts of burden. They kill them by thousands in the factories and mines. They are grinding them into dust. They whip them like dogs. They hunt them down like wild beasts. They tear the wife from the husband. They snatch the child from the arms of the mother. They doom our people to disease and starvation. They kill them for pastime. And I, the rightful Queen of these unfortunates, should quietly turn my eyes away from their sufferings and abandon them to their fate? No, Doña Carmen! While there is hope, be it ever so remote and so faint, I shall work and plot and struggle, as long as the Gods give me strength. And if all hopes fade, and our enterprise fails on this side of the Cordillera, I shall have my revenge on the other. Yonder, along the headwaters of the mighty

Marañon, the dominion of the foreign invaders rests on an insecure and trembling foundation. I can not cope with them in the plains and on the table-lands, but there in the tropical forest, where wild Nature will come to my aid, I shall destroy them; I shall crush them as they have crushed my people here. Not a vestige shall be left of their towns. Not a white face shall be left to tell the tale of horror. I know a mighty chief, Quirruba, the King of the Jivaros. He loves me and wants me for his Queen. I can fire his heart to deeds of daring and revenge. I can unite, through him, the Jivaros, the Zaparos, the Napos, the Macas, the Hambayos, and other tribes, in a great confederation, and with one blow I shall wipe out the Spanish dominion in the country of the great rivers and the great forests"—

"May the Lord have mercy on thy soul!" interrupted Carmen. "I shall hear no more. Peace! Peace! Be silent, for the Virgin's sake. I can not, I must not listen to this any longer. Toa, my unfortunate child, I can only pray for you. May God enlighten you and show you the dreadful error of your ways. If my incessant prayers and burning tears can move Him, He will have mercy on you and turn you away from this horrid path. Toa, my child, I am sick in body and mind. I can not listen to this any longer." And with these words the old lady buried her face in her hands.

"Forgive me, dearest Mother," said Toa, tenderly. "Forgive your unfortunate child. My heart beats and bleeds for you; but I can not abandon my race. Our ways, Mother Carmen, have deviated, and we must part. If, after you leave Quito, we should never meet again, my tenderest thoughts will ever be with you. But, Doña Carmen, I can not, I must not act otherwise. You have been brought up in a different school. You have not seen the sufferings of our race. Your house and your vassals have enjoyed exceptional privileges. Your father was a friend to the foreigner, while my father and grandfather were his victims. You have adopted the faith of the invader, and judge things differently. I cling to the old traditions and to the old faith; and my people's sufferings point out to me the path of duty. Auntie, dear, however our views may differ, however your religion may condemn my doings, I know you will never betray me."

Doña Carmen roused herself from her stupor and said sternly:

"Toa! In my opinion you are violating the laws of God and man. My religion teaches me that those who rule over us, derive their powers from God, and that God's will must be done. You are a heathen and a traitor to the King of Spain. Your life is forfeited. My judgment condemns you, my heart deplores you. My duty to my Church and my King would compel me to abandon you, nay, to deliver you to your judges. But, Toa, though a Christian and a loyal subject to the King of Spain, my benefactor, I am a scion of the house of Shyri-Duchicela. That house may have had some weak and a few bad representatives, but no Shyri-Duchicela ever was a traitor to his house, race, or friendship. I can pity you, Toa; I can weep and pray for you, but rest assured I should forfeit all hope of salvation in the next world, and all happiness in this life, rather than to betray you. But now I am exhausted, my children. I am worn and weary, and you must let me retire. In the meantime, Toa, let this house be your home. While I have a roof over my head, Toa Duchicela shall never be without shelter. But do not tell me more of your plotting and scheming. I could not listen to it again."

With these words the old lady called her maid, embraced and kissed Toa once more, and then, supported by the servant, left the room.

The Queen was now alone with her Ministers, and a long and anxious discussion followed, during which Toa was informed as to the state of opinion and the disposition of the leading men of Quito. She learned that as to all present indications, old Alonzo Sanchez and Alonzo Bellido would be the natural leaders of the expected revolutionary movement, and that Bellido, especially, was a man of great power and daring, and would give vitality and shape to the rising of the populace. Don Sebastian Collahuaso thought it highly desirable to communicate with either, if not with both of these men at once.

The cock proclaimed the hours of approaching morn, when the three conspirators retired to the rooms which had been assigned to them by Doña Carmen.

CHAPTER VII.

THE STATECRAFT OF MURDER.

The day after the scene at the Church of San Francisco, Count Valverde was in attendance on Don Manuel Barros, the President of the Royal Audience, who had requested the pleasure of a visit from him, on business of the utmost importance to the service of the King. On presenting himself at the Palace, the Count found that the Royal Audience was in session with closed doors, and hours passed before he was ushered into the presence of the dull and bad man in whose weak hands the coming crisis should find the reins of government. His Excellency apologized for having kept the Count in waiting, but the delay was inevitable. It concerned the very business upon which his Excellency wished to confer with the military commander.

Did Count Valverde have in his company of arquebusiers, two men who might be relied upon for a secret service of the utmost delicacy and importance?

The Count thought that almost all his men could be relied upon. They all had seen service in one or the other of the many wars waged by Philip II. Yes, but it was not strictly a military service that would be demanded of them. The service to be performed was of such a nature as to require men who were not troubled with scruples or sympathetic weaknesses, but who were ready to do anything the King's interests demanded. They should be well paid for what they were to do, provided they could hold their tongues.

Would his Excellency condescend to acquaint Count Valverde with the nature of the service required? It would aid him in a proper selection of the men. His Excellency would not do so directly, but he hinted that it was of prime necessity that these two men should be unerring marksmen. Count Valverde now understood the worthy head of the Government. Not soldiers, but assassins, were wanted. Somebody had been doomed, and Valverde was called upon to furnish the executioners. The Count was startled, but not surprised by this intelligence. The dagger and the pistol of the assassin, as well as the secret midnight visit of the executioner in disguise, were integral parts of the system by which King Philip governed the great empire in which the sun never set. And the example of the terrible spider who sat lurking in the Escurial, in the center of his web, was faithfully imitated by his representatives and instruments abroad.

At any other time, Count Valverde would have furnished the men without asking a question. But the fearful prophecy of Mama Rucu, with the remembrance it had revived, was still fresh in his mind; and so he asked whether his Excellency would assume all the responsibility. His Excellency would. And would his Excellency give the necessary orders to the men, or would he, the Count, be required to do so? The President took a ring out of a drawer, broke it asunder with a hammer, and handing one of the halves to the Count, explained that the men might be sent to the Palace, with instructions faithfully to obey the orders to be given them by the party that would present the other half of the ring.

Count Valverde was a subaltern officer, and the man before him was the President of the Royal Audience, next in dignity to the Viceroy of Peru, and to the President of the Audience at Lima. And, hence, although Valverde greatly doubted the policy of the measure to which the Government seemed determined to resort, he considered it his duty to remain silent and to obey. He bowed and prepared to withdraw; but the President detained him. It would be necessary to be prepared for every emergency. The other night the populace had assailed him in his own Palace, and found him unprepared and unprotected. He was helpless in the hands of a lawless mob, and compelled to accede to their outrageous demands. This must not occur again. The royal authority must be maintained. Would Count Valverde be kind enough to transfer all his men to the Palace? A mere guard of honor, such as the President had had hitherto, was powerless in case of need. The President had given orders for the removal of the bureaus that now occupied the lower floor of the Palace, so as to furnish quarters for the soldiers.

"And when will these rooms be ready for the reception of my men?"

"To-morrow," answered the President. "Let your men be concentrated in the Palace to-morrow, as early as you can. The royal authority must not be defied again."

With these instructions, the interview terminated. The President seemed greatly alarmed. He was evidently troubled by fears for his personal safety much more than by his regard for the royal authority.

Count Valverde did not relish the orders he had received. He was vexed at the idea of having to exchange his comfortable quarters in the barracks, for some unfinished or unfurnished office-room in the Palace. Much less did he relish the command to detail two men for a secret service, the object of which evidently was murder. He did not know who the victim was to be, or whether more than one blow was to be struck; but would not he, as the military commander, be held responsible for a deed committed by soldiers? And if such a dark deed should lead to an outbreak of popular fury, would it not direct itself against him? He had but one company of arquebusiers against a mob of thousands; for he was confident that the native militia would either lend him no assistance or side with the mob. He took the ring out of his pocket and looked at it. Was this mean piece of metal to be the forerunner of death and destruction? He felt a sinister presentiment that his own death was in the command which the broken ring conveyed. The President evidently was blundering. Valverde had no confidence in his Excellency's capacity. Should he instruct his men to report to him, before carrying out the orders which they were to receive? He might exercise discretionary powers, and prevent some act of disastrous folly or imprudent cruelty. While he was thus pondering, he had unknowingly been made the object of sneers and insulting questions. A crowd of boys and loungers, belonging to the rabble of Quito, had collected and followed him. Their courage grew as their numbers increased.

"There goes the *Chapeton*,"* said one.

"He is the fellow who is to teach us obedience," said another.

"Down with the Spaniards!" exclaimed a third, and the cry was immediately taken up, "Down with the Spaniards! Down with the Alcabala!"

Count Valverde looked around indignantly. "Stand back, you hounds," he thundered, laying his hand on the hilt of his sword, "or I shall kill a dozen of you."

---

* A nickname given by the Creoles to native Spaniards.

The rabble fell back in terror, but immediately rallied again, hurling a volley of epithets, and even a few stones, at the officer.

"They do not deserve any pity," thought the Count, exasperated, as he put the broken ring in his pocket. "They are all rebels and traitors, and deserve to die, those low-born dogs, as well as their betters who lead them on."

Here a stone knocked off his hat, and broke his plume, while a shout of derision followed the assault. The Count might have fared badly, had he not been near the barracks. Three soldiers, who were lounging at the next corner, saw his danger, and hurried to his rescue, easily scattering the mob with their swords.

Grinding his teeth, and with compressed lips, the Count entered the barracks. "The President is right," he thought. "It is necessary to strike terror to their cowardly souls," and turning to an orderly, he said : "Tell Juan del Puente and Ildefonso Coronel to come to my room immediately. I want to see them."

Twice more that day the broken ring changed hands.

CHAPTER IX.

THE PROCURATOR-GENERAL.

Alonzo Bellido was a man of about forty-five years of age. He was a man of scholarly attainments, but his companions, unlike Carrera's, were not the Muses. History and the law were his favorites. He was a great jurist, who had carefully studied and pondered over the history of Spain. His mind dwelt on her ancient liberties; on the rights of representation in the Cortes, and their subsequent rise and decline; on the history of provincial *fueros*, the privileges and immunities of municipalities, and on the brutal violence and reckless disregard of law, justice, and custom with which Charles V and Philip II had crushed out nearly all that had survived of popular liberty and municipal or provincial rights in the mother country. Bellido was a philosophical thinker of great clearness, and a natural lover of justice, whose whole being revolted against measures which, like the imposition of the Alcabala, were palpably and flagrantly wrong.

That morning he had introduced a resolution, at the meeting of the Cabildo, pledging the municipality to resistance. The resolution was couched in terms of respectful loyalty, but it was outspoken and decided. It threw the blame of the measure on the King's evil advisers, who, unfortunately, had prevailed in His Majesty's councils; but it declared that until His Majesty had been fully advised in the premises, the Alcabala should not be collected in Quito, and that the Royal Audience should at once be petitioned to withdraw or suspend the proclamation made on the previous day. This resolution was adopted unanimously, when Bellido coolly turned to his colleagues, and said:

"Gentlemen! Do your Lordships know that they have signed their death-warrants?"

This question provoked a general incredulous smile, but Bellido proceeded:

"Yes, gentlemen; your death-warrants! Philip II never forgives and never relents. Think of Egmont, of Horne, of Montigny, of Orange, of Antonio Perez; think of his son, Don Carlos. Think of Don Juan of Austria! He who offends King Philip stakes his life, and loses it if he succumbs. You have now burned your ships. All future repentance and atonement, all subsequent proofs of loyalty, will be unavailing. Your death-warrants are signed. The only question now is, whether King Philip will have power to enforce them."

"What do you mean, Don Alonzo?" asked Señor Olmos, one of the Councilors.

"That we have entered upon a life and death-struggle. We are doomed if we remain under Spain. There are but two ways of escape for us—absolute independence, or a foreign protectorate, if not both."

And now Alonzo Bellido developed his plans into which it is not our purpose to enter minutely. Spain was at war with France, England, and the Netherlands. The two latter were maritime powers, whose cruisers infested every ocean. Communications should at once be opened with the governments of those countries. French aid would probably be the most acceptable to the people, because England and Holland were heretical powers, while Henry IV had made his peace with the Church. But, if French aid could not be procured, any other assistance would be welcome. The great smuggling trade that was carried on all along the colonial coast under the very nose of the authorities, would furnish means of communication, in addition to which deputies should at once be sent abroad to impress upon the enemies of Spain the great importance of a diversion in their favor in the very heart of Spanish power, in a colony from which so vast a portion of the Spanish revenues was derived. In the meantime, Bellido insisted the native militia should be reorganized and prepared for active service. The royal treasures should be seized everywhere. The members of the Audience should be arrested and detained as hostages. A provisional government should be formed that should assume control of all the inland cities, and secure the possession, for the Independents, of the seaports of Esmeraldas and Guayaquil. The success of the Revolution depended on the rapidity of its blows. We must not wait until the Viceroy sends an army to crush us; we must carry the war into Africa, and from Cuenca and Loja invade Peru, where the cities will receive us with open arms. If these views are carried out, Peru and Quito will be independent before the news of it reaches Spain. Then, by the time the King sends an armament against us, our negotiations with foreign powers will have ripened into some result. Foreign powers will be ready to help us whenever we show strength enough to help ourselves."

Altogether, Bellido's plan, bold and dangerous as it seemed to be, was that of a great statesman, but it startled and frightened the more conservative members of the Cabildo, who still thought and hoped that by petitions and remonstrances, backed, if necessary, by a show of forcible resistance, an accommodation might be effected with the Court of Spain, or with the Viceroy at Lima. Poor, deluded creatures! They did not know Philip II and the tools he selected for his service.

The discussion became excited, and at times angry and stormy, and had already lasted several hours, when one of the office-messengers approached Bellido and whispered to him, so as not to interfere with the speakers: "There is an old Indian in the ante-room whom I do not know, and whom I have never seen. He says he has a communication of the greatest importance to make, either to the Procurator-General, or to Don Alonzo Sanchez; but he insists on speaking to your Grace in person, and alone."

"An old Indian! Ridiculous! Didst thou not tell him I was engaged?"

"I did, Señor, but he said that what he had to say to your Grace referred to the very subject now under consideration."

"If that is the case, somebody must have sent him."

"Yes, he says he is the bearer of a message."

"Well, I think I will see him for a moment. Take him into my office."

. Bellido was struck with the appearance of the Indian. He looked as if he had lived over a century, and yet, having assured himself that he was alone with Bellido, he showed a quickness and intelligence which to the Procurator were surprising in one of the despised race.

"I thank your Grace for coming, and shall not detain you long. I do not come empty handed. To the support of the plan your Grace has conceived, I bring thousands of men and millions of treasure."

Bellido looked uneasy. "Why, man, are you crazy? What do you mean?"

"I shall at once give your Grace some proof of what I say. Your Grace has been maturing a plan for the separation of this country from Spain"—

"Man, you are a wizard. How could you have known that, if it were so?"

"Señor! Is there a house without Indian servants in this city? You think these Indians are mere beasts, and you speak before them without reserve. There is nothing of interest or importance that these apparently stolid and embruted creatures do not hear, see, remember, and when asked or instructed, report to—well, let me say to—us. Thus I know of your plan. I have known of it for weeks."

"But who are you?"

"Señor, I am a poor Indian, despised and trampled upon with impunity by those of our white conquerors who choose to do so. Why should you wish to know more? I come not of my own accord and without authority. I come as the messenger of my sovereign."

By this time Bellido was thoroughly aroused and interested. His quick mind saw at a glance that this visit had a deep meaning, and that it promised aid, unexpected aid, from an unexpected quarter. "Then, I am to understand that this legend of an Indian Queen, of whom we have heard so much and seen nothing, is not a myth but a reality."

"I am authorized to say so to your Grace."

"And your credentials?"

"Are in my hand. Your Grace will please to look at this paper, but I beg you to return it to me."

Bellido took it, and read:

"The bearer will speak for me and in my name.
"Toa Duchicela,
"*Of Quito and Purruhá.*"

"All this seems very strange," said Bellido, returning the paper to the Indian. "But I shall be glad to learn what you can do for us, and what we are required to do for you in return."

"Don Alonzo! I shall be brief. I trust in your honor. For the next few minutes my head, my limbs, my life, will be in your power, but not my secret. You may order me under arrest, and put me to the rack, as has been done to so many of my race, who were suspected of knowing what I have come to tell you voluntarily. I know I invite this danger by endeavoring to communicate on such matters with a *Viracocha*.* But because the task is dangerous, it has been confided to me. I am a very old man. My days are numbered, and it makes very little difference whether a few are added or taken away. I am unknown here. Nobody in this building ever saw me before. I can hide my tracks. You may break me on the wheel but you will discover nothing. I know this charnel-house, *la casa de la Municipalidad*, where hundreds of my unfortunate race were tortured to death before your Grace came to this city, nay, before your Grace was born. I am ready to suffer as they suffered; but you would gain nothing by it, Señor Procurator-General."

"I admit," answered Bellido, "that your experience justifies your distrust. But you are mistaken in me. You have come to me in confidence, and I shall not abuse it."

"I believe you, Viracocha. And now I shall answer

---
* White man.

your question. To the furtherance of your enterprise we can give thousands of strong arms and stout hearts, which although untaught and undisciplined, will be an avalanche as to numbers, and when led and supported by military science and skill, will be invaluable auxiliaries by their knowledge of the country, their powers of endurance, and their blind devotion to their Queen. But we can do more than that. We can give you treasures, gold, the sinews of war. We can give you what your race has sought for during three generations, but has not found and never will find, unless we give it to you—the treasure of Atahualpa and Rumiñagui."

Bellido's eyes dilated. He could hardly conceal his delight. This information, if true, placed the success of his great plans beyond doubt. Still he would hardly believe it. It was too good to be true. And so he said after a pause: " But does that treasure really exist?"

" It does, Señor Bellido. And to satisfy you that what I say is true, and what I promise shall be accomplished, I shall let you see the treasure. Mark me; you shall see it, only see it. Nothing can be taken from it except by order of my Queen, and she will use it only for the cause of our race. There must be giving and taking. For what we shall give you, we demand an equivalent more precious to us than gold or jewels."

"And what is it you demand of us, my unknown friend?"

" There are two things, Señor Procurator-General, which must be conceded to us before the co-operation I propose can be effected. In the first place, our Queen must be made *your* Queen; that is to say, she must marry the man upon whom you confer the royal dignity. Our Indians will not follow unless a Shyri-Inca leads. They obey their own sovereign, who is their head. Without this head, they could not be depended upon. Crown a King of your own race, and let him marry Toa Duchicela, and there is not an

Indian man, woman, or child in the kingdom that would not die in his defense. In the second place, we must have our rights, Señor. We have been ground to dust; we have been treated as beasts of burden. We must be treated as human beings. You have made slaves of us; we want our freedom. Give us our freedom, and your movement shall be successful. The two races can live together in harmony and peace. The Indian will till your soil and perform your labor, as a free man, more willingly than as a slave; and, if there are those among us who have it in them to rise to the higher places, do not plunge them back into the abyss of misery and degradation. Look at me! Do I not speak your language as well as any one of you; and yet I never knew of the existence of your race until Pizarro had landed in Peru. I do not demand an answer now. I ask you to reflect over what I have said. I ask you to see what I am willing to show you, in order to influence your decision. Meet me to-night, on the Chorrera road, on Mt. Pichincha, and, if you are willing to trust yourself to me, as I have trusted myself to you, you shall see what our race can do for your cause. I shall expect you shortly after dark. Come alone, and make no attempt to capture or betray me; it would be of no avail. Will you come?"

"Most certainly and gladly I shall."

And that same night, he met Cundurazu on Mt. Pichincha, where they found Carrera, and were soon joined by Queen Toa attended by a number of Indians.

CHAPTER X.

THE HIDDEN TREASURE.

"Are you ready to follow us?" asked the Indian Queen. The two gentlemen bowed and said, "We are."

"Then you will not object to a little formality, which, unfortunately, can not be dispensed with. You must allow yourselves to be blindfolded. Señór Carrera, whom I have known a few days longer than you, Señor Bellido, has expressly promised to trust me, as I have trusted him. And, as I could have no possible motive in doing harm to either of you gentlemen, I believe that you, Señor Bellido, will follow his example."

"I hate to be deprived of sight, even for the shortest time," said Bellido, "but I see no reason for refusing to obey your Highness. By the very fact of my coming here, I have placed myself under your Highness' orders."

"Well said, Señor. Let us lose no time, then. Take off your hats, gentlemen, and leave them to our attendants." With these words she threw a hood over Carrera's head, and fastened it with a bandage across his eyes. Cundurazu did the same to Bellido. "Give me your hand, Don Julio!" she added, seizing his hand, with a gentle pressure.

"I shall take the pleasure of leading you, Señor Procurator," said Cundurazu; and the party moved on at once, ascending acclivities and descending into ravines, now stumbling over rocks, now wading through sand or pumice-stone, or fording torrents, which came rushing down their mountainous beds. Physical exertion in such altitudes is very fatiguing, and our white gentlemen were frequently compelled to arrest the onward step of their

Indian leaders, in order to recover their breath and strength. The journey seemed to be endless and doubly trying, as not a word was spoken. At times it seemed to Bellido that they were purposely led in a round-about way, in order to deceive them as to the locality they were to visit. At last the procession came to a halt.

"Stoop down, gentlemen," said the silvery voice of Toa, "and walk on stooping until I tell you that it is no longer necessary." Again they walked on for a considerable distance, until Toa stopped them: "We are through and shall give you a little rest." For the last two or three minutes the distant sound of rushing waters had become audible, and now the travelers plainly heard a roaring torrent dashing and breaking itself against narrow and rocky defiles. "Uma! Is the water turned off?" asked Toa.

"Yes, Shyri!" answered an Indian voice. And really the noise of rushing waters suddenly began to lessen, until it had almost died away or changed into a mere ripple.

"We must march on further," said Toa, again taking Carrera's hand. "Be careful, we are descending. Take hold of my arm or you will fall. One more step and our descent is made. Now comes a last ascent; but you shall be carried the rest of the way."

Unseen arms seized the two *Viracochas* and carried them an additional distance. They were again ascending. At last a halt was made, and the bandage was taken from their eyes. Complete darkness surrounded them. They knew they were not in the open air, but they had no conception of where they were.

"I shall not blind your eyes with sudden light. You must recover your sight gradually," said Toa. And so it was done. A dimly burning torch appeared in the distance, and slowly came nearer, increasing in blaze as it approached. Another, and still another followed, enabling the gentlemen to examine the place where they found themselves. It was a subterranean vault or cave. Toa stood in the center, clad in a white alpaca robe, and wearing the emblem of Shyri royalty, a magnificent emerald fastened to a diadem. Next to her stood Cundurazu, arrayed in garments such as the nobles of the ancient kingdom wore. Two Indians, similarly dressed, stood behind him, while five or six torch-bearers posted themselves in different parts of the hall, so as to light it up completely.

But the eyes of the two gentlemen now fell upon another sight, which filled them with wonder and amazement. Piled up along the walls, and in the center of the cave, were monstrous gold and silver bars, heaps of golden vessels, ornamented with precious stones, and of exquisite workmanship, statues of precious metals, golden suns and moons, huge chains of gold, and a gigantic pile of gold coins, heaped up in the center, and bearing the stamp of Charles V., which showed that the possessors of the secret must have found means to secure the good will and services of the officers of the Royal Mint, at Lima. Next to this pile of coins a Spanish cloak was spread, and on it lay sprawling a complete skeleton, with a grinning skull. A large Spanish plumed hat lay on one side of it, and a Spanish sword on the other. Close to one of the walls of the cave rose a throne of gold, studded with emeralds, and on it sat a mummy, horrifying in its ugliness, its eyeless skull covered with a diadem, to which a large emerald was attached. A golden scepter rested in the lap of the corpse. The terror spread over the scene by the ghastly presence of grim death, seemed to mock the impression which the sight of such treasures had produced on the visitors.

A long pause followed. Carrera did not know whether he was awake, or whether he again lay dreaming in Mama Rucu's cottage. Even the strong mind and nerves of Alonzo Bellido were overwhelmed, and he waited breathlessly for what was to come.

"This," began Toa, solemnly, "is the treasure of my great-grandfather, Huaynacapac, and of my grandfather,

Atahualpa. The usurper Rumiñagui had seized it and hid it here, lest it should fall into the hands of the Spaniards. After his death the secret of its hiding-place was communicated to those who were the legitimate representatives of my house. Hundreds of my race perished on the rack, or in the flames, because they would not divulge its secret. Many knew it then. Many know it now. Most of them are poor and starving wretches, who, by taking but a handful, might secure comfort and plenty for the rest of their days. But the humblest of my subjects would perish of destitution, rather than take one grain of gold-dust of what is the property of our nation, subject to the disposal of its legitimate rulers. I am the rightful owner of what you see here; but I vow to Pachacamac the Great, and call the Sun and the Moon as my witnesses, that I should leave it here, buried and forgotten forever, rather than use it for any purpose, or with any view other than the liberation of my race."

A slow and deep murmur of approbation, uttered by her Indian listeners, followed this speech.

"This," she continued, pointing to the mummy on the golden throne, " is my father. Peace to his remains, and glory to his memory! This great and good man," pointing to Cundurazu, " rescued him when a suckling babe, from the murderous fangs of Rumiñagui, who had determined on the destruction of all that were of the royal blood of Atahualpa. The noble Cundurazu saved him, hid him, and educated him, and when death had claimed him, he brought him here to watch over these treasures, and enjoy the honors due under our laws and customs to departed royalty. This," pointing to the skeleton on the ground, " was a Spanish *Corregidor*, who had been most heartless and cruel to our race. His Indian victims could not be counted. Hundreds he sacrificed to his avarice and rapacity, until my father gave orders that he should be allured hither. One of our men offered to betray to him the secret of the great treasure. The tyrant greedily grasped at the offer, and imprudently allowed himself to be conducted to this place. He never left it. After he had seen everything the torches were extinguished, and night closed in upon him—a long, last, terrible night, without moon or stars, and never followed by a morning dawn, or the light of day. There you see his remains! He died a slow and agonizing death, in the midst of all the gold for which he had thirsted. Look around you, gentlemen; there is no visible egress here. You could not find your way out, even with the torches burning. You are our prisoners, and your lives depend on our mercy."

Bellido shuddered, but Carrera, though greatly awed, looked confidently at the speaker and smiled. He felt instinctively that his life was safer in her hands than in his own. She noticed and understood his smile, and returned it by a rapid, but unspeakable glance of tenderness.

"Yet, gentlemen," she resumed, "you have trusted us as we have trusted you, and you may consider yourselves as safe here as at your own homes. Our object to-night was to show you our power. Look at these treasures and judge for yourselves. But it is not money alone that we can give. If you say the word, thousands of hearts and arms will be at your disposal. All we ask in return is the freedom of our race, and the recognition of our rights as human beings. I have sent this trusted friend to you, Señor Bellido, with full powers to represent me and the interests of my people. I now reaffirm his authority. Whatever he may agree upon with you and the municipality of Quito, will have my full sanction. And whatever I undertake or promise will be carried out by my people. And now, Prince Cundurazu, take our friends back into the open air, where I shall soon join you. I desire to be alone for a few minutes with the remains of my father."

With these words Toa slowly walked over to the golden throne and prostrated herself before the ghastly mummy that sat in it, a mocking specter or royalty. Not another word was spoken. Cundurazu approached the two gentlemen and indicated to them by a sign that they must be blindfolded again. This time they both submitted as a matter of course. Again they were carried for a while by strong, unseen arms, and when their feet touched the ground once more, the same arduous and fatiguing march had to be made, up hill and down hill, over rocks and through ravines, now through deep sand, then, again, through mountainous streams that intersected their path.

Carrera's hand was in that of a powerful Indian, who led him along. Suddenly he felt that his hand had been released for a moment, and when it was seized again it was a smaller and gentler hand that held it with a slight pressure. He felt that Toa was at his side, and recognized it by returning the pressure.

"Do you believe me now?" she asked.

"I never doubted your word, Lady Toa."

"Do you still think that my hopes are visionary?"

"Your Highness has not confided your plans to me. Nevertheless, I recognize the great power which is at your Highness' command."

"Yes, Don Julio, a time of peace and rest may come after all, even for a fugitive and a wanderer like myself. What would life be to me without that hope?"

"And has your Highness never loved?" asked Carrera.

"Do you refer to the present or to the past? If to the past, I must answer, no. There are but few of my own race who are my equals, and those few are in Peru. Here in these parts the descendants of the few nobles who escaped the fury of Rumiñagui, and of the Spanish conquerors, are mostly without culture; and I am fastidious in this respect, for, strange as it may seem to you, Don Julio, considering my roaming mode of life, I am not without education. Doña Carmen Duchicela, on whose estate I was brought up secretly, has done more than a mother's part by me. I enjoyed all the advantages of her own children, or rather they enjoyed the advantages which her love and kindness had accorded to me. Learned men of both races had come from Lima, to teach her wayward, ungrateful grandniece whose present course and aspirations aggrieve her so sorely. Perhaps, if she had given me no education, I should not struggle and strive as I do now, and should be all the happier for it. The Jewish prophet is right when saying: 'In much wisdom there is much grief, and he that increaseth knowledge, increaseth sorrow.' Love? if you refer to the past, Don Julio, I had no time for it. The cares for my own safety, and the affairs of my wandering government would not have given love a chance to steal into my heart, even if there had been an object."

"And the present."

"Why should you care to know, Don Julio? What could Toa Duchicela be to you? Your heart is not free. Does it not belong to Dolores Solando, to whom but last night you made almost a declaration of love?"

"Señora! Your information is wonderful, although your informant is not quite correct. But how could you know that I was with Dolores Solando last night?"

"Ah, Don Julio, this is an additional evidence of my power, which verges on omniscience. There is not a house in Quito, whose secrets I could not learn, if I wished to know them. But do not be alarmed. This is not the power of witchcraft; but the clue to it is the devotion of my people, and their readiness to serve me. Do you preceive it now?"

"I do Señora! And as you know so much, you had better know it all. For years I had been in love with Dolores. I had never succeeded in securing an opportunity to declare myself. But when the opportunity presented itself at last unsought and unexpected, it was no longer welcome, but almost painful and embarrassing. A week before, I might have spoken, while I remained silent last night. A week before I should have made a proposal, while I had none to make last night."

"And what has caused this change?"

"Can you ask, Lady Toa? The eyes that I shall never forget, the silvery voice that is always in my ear, the majestic, and yet so graceful apparition, that is ever present to my mind—it is you, Shyri Toa, who have wrought this change."

"My poor friend! I told you once that it is dangerous to be a friend to Toa Duchicela. It would be tenfold more dangerous to love her."

"What would I not brave for you? Even if I did not love you, admiration and friendship would make me your faithful knight. But you have taken possession of my heart, Lady Toa, and I fear I shall not be able to recover it."

"Think twice before you commit yourself hastily, and perhaps very imprudently. The man who loves me, and whom I love, may become the foremost, the richest, the greatest man of the land, but he may also become a mere victim, sacrificed to the evil fortunes of my house. I have still sufficient control over myself to refuse such a sacrifice. Do not say more, Señor Carrera! Do not arouse the passions of an untutored and undisciplined nature; for then I might demand, exact, compel the sacrifice."

"Señora Toa, what you say of riches and greatness is nothing to me. I love you for your own sake; and the homeless wanderer, suffering for the misfortune of her royal birth, and denying herself all the comforts of existence and all the hope of present and perhaps future happiness, to serve—whether mistakenly or not—the cause of her race, is dearer to me than the powerful possessor of all the treasures you have shown to me to-night."

"Don Julio! I shall speak without reserve. Reserve may be an admirable quality for a young lady living under her father's roof, protection, and care. But I, the fugitive and the wanderer, have no time for reserve. I must speak truthfully, openly, plainly. You say you love me. Whether you say so under the influence of my presence, and will not say the same thing to Dolores Solando, when I am away, I do not know. Men are strange beings, and I do not know them enough. But whether you love me or not, whether you love me truly, or whether you mistake your present feelings of sympathy, pity, friendship, for love, I can make the confession that I love you. Why you should have stolen into my heart, I know not. It is enough to say that I love you, loved you before you knew of my existence. It may be a fatal and unfortunate love, and yet I love you. But, Don Julio de Carrera, love must play a secondary part in the great work of my life. I have a mission to perform, a goal to reach. If my love were an impediment to the task I have to fulfill, I would stamp out the last spark of it—no matter what the anguish of my heart would be. My people first, my own self last. I love you, Don Julio. With a woman's weakness, I confess it. But, with a Queen's firmness, I tell you that this love must be no hindrance to my plans, but it must be made subservient to their furtherance. If you can help me, if you possess the courage, the devotion, the generosity to carry out the plans which my friend and counselor has submitted, or is even now submitting to Don Alonzo Bellido, I accept your love, and shall return it with all the passion, the loyalty, the constancy of an Indian heart. But if you love only Toa, the mysterious and the weird, the woman Toa and not also Toa the Queen, whose mission it is to save her people; and if, instead of helping her, you will look coldly upon my great task as visionary, my heart would almost break; but I would refuse your love, and strive to forget my own weakness."

Long before she had finished this speech, she had snatched the bandage from his eyes, and now stood before him, holding both his hands in hers, and looking at him tenderly, earnestly, and sadly. "Yes, my friend," she continued, "among the loftiest cliffs of our giant mountains, in those lonely heights where almost all vegetation ceases— even there, you will now and then find, hidden under the snow, a beautiful flower, placed there as if to remind the daring traveler that there are other scenes brighter and happier than the dreary solitude of the wilderness. I shall look upon my love for you as the sad and lonely flower that grows under the snows of Chimborazo or Antisana, a forlorn hope, an outpost of a friendlier zone, inaccessible to me—a misplaced little unfortunate, that has no right to exist amidst the howling storms and under the chilling snows. I shall say: 'My life is the mountain wilderness, the loneliness of the Paramo, with its fogs and hurricanes, with its icy rocks and sands. The flower of love is there, hidden under the snow, but it blooms in vain. No human eye greets it, no friendly hand will pluck it, no loving bosom will receive it.'"

CHAPTER XII.

THE WARNING.

The party had nearly returned to the place from which they had set out on their mysterious journey, and the darkness of the night had begun to yield to the morning dawn, when a strange obstruction in their path suddenly arrested their progress. A crude portable chair had been placed across their way by its four Indian carriers, at a turning of the road, and seated in the chair was the shriveled form of an old Indian woman, with a mummy-like face, with white disheveled hair, and her eyes flashing and rolling like those of a maniac. It was Mama Rucu. Toa approached her, and affectionately bent over her, listening to what she had to say.

"It is you, Señor Bellido," said the Indian Queen, "to whom she wants to speak. Listen to her attentively. Treasure up her words in your memory; for they are the words of wisdom and truth."

The appearance of Mama Rucu, although Bellido had seen her before, filled him with superstitious awe. There was something weird and unearthly in her countenance and expression. Her appearance at this time and place was in keeping with the wonders of the night through which he had passed. He approached her with uncovered head, and waited to be spoken to.

"Yes, Yes!" the old woman said, with a hoarse laugh. "I know him. I have seen him before; but never so clearly as I did last night in my vision, after I had taken the draught of life—the Heavenly Samarucu. Come here, my son, come here! Let me feel thy hands! May Pachacamac protect thee in the hour of danger, which is approaching fast. Dost thou understand my language, my Son?"

"I do, Mother; speak on!"

"It is well! Ah, thou art the man! He is the man, Queen Toa; he is the hand that must strike the great blow; he is the head that must think the great thoughts; he is the bow that will send the arrow to the mark. Young man," she proceeded, turning to Carrera, "here is thy master. Follow his counsels, and thou wilt be safe. But now, Alonzo, my Son, let me tell thee that a great danger awaits thee. I have come to warn thee. Poor old Mama Rucu, who needs rest—it will soon be eternal rest—has left her couch long before the break of day to warn thee; to save thee! Behold! my limbs are weak with age. I could not have walked hither this morning. My strength is fast ebbing away. And so I had myself carried by these men, which is against the laws our conquerors have imposed. They will not allow us this comfort. But no matter! I had to come here to warn thee, my Son. Wilt thou heed my warning?"

"I will, Mother!"

"Thy life is in danger, and will be in danger for weeks to come. Do not ask me why or how. I could not tell. I have seen a dreadful vision. I saw thee weltering in thy blood—dying—dying—dead. Beware! Beware! Beware!"

"Of what shall I beware, Mother?"

"Of murder! The assassins are lying in wait for thee even now. Thy caution alone can save thee!"

"But how, Mother?"

"Do not leave thy house at night, or before the busy hum of day has begun to be heard on the streets. Do not go to thy house now. Wait a few hours, and then thou wilt escape this time. The danger is great. It will last for two moons. During two moons thou must beware. Live through two moons, and nothing shall harm thee. But if thou disregardest my words, thou wilt not re-enter thy house alive. And now I am done. I have said all that thou must know. Thy life is in thine own hands. Thou mayest keep it, or throw it away." And, with these words, she beckoned to her Indian carriers to move on; and, before Bellido had fully recovered from his astonishment, she was out of reach.

"Heed the warning, Señor Bellido, heed it!" added Toa. "I never knew Mama Rucu to err."

"I thank your Royal Highness for the advice. Mama Rucu's warning is evidently well meant, and I shall heed it as much as I can. But how could I, at this critical emergency, when my presence will be required everywhere, and at all times, confine myself to my house at night? I shall be cautious. I shall wear a coat-of-mail under my doublet; yet, if I am to be pursued by assassins, all precaution, I fear, will be in vain. My life, Lady Toa, is in the hands of God, and in Him I must confide."

"Your life, Señor Bellido, has become precious to us.

Our race looks to you and to my friend here," pointing to Carrera, "for that protection which our own weakness can not afford. I shall give orders to my subjects to watch over your safety, and to warn you in case of danger. Prince Cundurazu will confer with you this afternoon. And you, Señor Carrera," she whispered again, "will you be with Dolores Solando to-night?"

"Shyri Toa"—

"Enough! If the day passes without disturbances, I shall meet you at the Church of La Merced after dark. But, should we be unable to meet, you shall receive a message from me to-morrow. Take this, Julio," she said, giving him a small silver moon, with an emerald in the center, "and if you ever should want to send me a letter or a message, show this to any Indian, and say that your letter or message must reach the Shyri Toa. It will come to me as surely as the waters run to the sea."

CHAPTER XIII.

LYING IN WAIT.

STORES and shops occupied the ground-floor of houses at Quito then, as they do now. These shops are always without windows, and receive what little light and air they get through the door. Alonzo Bellido's house stood in the street leading from the southeast corner of the Great Square toward Mount Panecillo. Carrera lived on the same street, a short distance from Bellido. The day had hardly dawned. The streets were still quiet and deserted. Not even the tramp of the watch was heard. The door of one of the shops—it was a dram shop—in the house opposite to that of Bellido, was slightly ajar, and a man, who seemed to be lying on the floor on the inside, pushed his head through the opening and cautiously looked up and down the street. It was an ugly head, covered with bushy hair, turning gray. His face was disfigured with scars and adorned with a tremendous moustache and chin-beard. After the man had inspected the street in every direction, he drew his head back into the shop again, and rolled himself toward the wall, where a couch had been improvised of sheepskins and ponchos.

"I think we have waited in vain!" said the man. "He has not yet come home, and the Devil knows whether he will come at all. You are getting sleepy, Ildefonso."

The man to whom these remarks were addressed was lying on the other side of the shop, with an empty bottle before him, which he took up occasionally in search of a last drop. Both men were soldiers. They wore the uniforms of Royal Arquebusiers under the heavy black cloaks in which they had wrapped themselves; for the night had been very cool and the morning was very chilly. On the counter, in the rear of the dingy shop, stood an expiring tallow-candle, hissing and spurting in its socket and filling the room with nauseous smoke. Two arquebuses, ready mounted, and with matches burning, stood in the center of the room. The implements of death were prepared; but the victim was wanting.

"It strikes me, Juan," answered the other, "that those ink-worms, their High Mightinesses of the goose-quill, might have provided more generously for men to whom a task of such importance has been confided. May the Devil take their souls without delay!" And, with these words, the pious Ildefonso Coronel flung the empty bottle, the sight of which had worried him long enough, into one of the corners of the dark room, so as to send the pieces of the broken glass flying in every direction. At the same time, the dying candle on the counter gave its last spurt and went out, and a faint streak of daylight broke through the opening of the door.

"You should not complain, Ildefonso. You have had more than enough. Why, man, you are drunk now."
"I wish I were," growled the other. "So much the better for our job. I must have drink to be sure of my mark. If I have not fortified myself with rum, my hand is unsteady and my eye without clearness. By Santiago! man, I shall be completely sober in a few minutes, and then, so help me God, I could not hit a cow. Without a good dose of rum, man, I should miss an elephant."

"Stop! Listen! I think I hear something." With the same cautiousness Juan del Puente pushed his head out of the door again and reconnoitered the street. "It is nothing! not a soul is stirring."

"Who is to pay for this job?" continued Ildefonso Coronel, "and where shall we get the money? By the Holy Virgin, I do not trust these ink-fishes and quill-drivers. I hate lawyers. They can never be relied upon. They allure you into all sorts of things, and then slip away like eels. Why did not the Captain give us our orders and our money? Promises are good, but they do not buy olives. Thunder and lightning! Here we kill our fellow, and then perhaps they will prosecute us as murderers, instead of paying us our reward. Such things have happened before. Men were detailed to act as secret executioners and then their employers murdered the executioners."

"Ildefonso! You talk like a fool this morning. How many soldiers have they here? A very small band. Do they not want every man of us? Can't you see that the ink-worms and pettifoggers of the Palace are trembling for their lives? I never saw such cowardly fellows before. Do you think they could spare such marksmen as Juan del Puente and Ildefonso Coronel? They will get down on their trembling knees before us, ere these insurrectionary troubles are over. There, comrade, I was afraid you would drink too much, and so I kept back one bottle of what they gave us to warm ourselves with, if we should have to wait long. It comes in excellently now." And, with these words, he took a deep draught, and then handed the bottle to his comrade.

"So you kept this bottle back, you sly devil!" said the other. "And what else have you kept back? I do not like this habit of yours. It is altogether too wise for me. Who has appointed you my guardian? By all the devils of hell! I think you have kept other things back as well as the rum. Some money must have been paid on account. They always pay part of it down. Where is it? Why do you want to cheat me? Beware of me, Juan del Puente, I shall have my revenge if you dare to cheat me."

"Hand back that bottle, if you do not want to drink!" said the other, "and stop your slanderous tongue. Give me that bottle!"

"I am not in a hurry about it. If you hold on to what belongs to both of us, I shall do the same. Did not that scoundrel of an ink-worm call you back after both you and I had left the room? What did he whisper to you?"

"Man, you are drunk or crazy. Was not the door open? Could you not see both of us plainly? Do you want to insult me? Well, well, Ildefonso Coronel, if it should ever happen again that you lose your foothold in the mire, and lie sprawling on the ground, unable to get up under the weight of your armor, Juan del Puente will not again be a barrier between you and the Dutch cavalrymen."

This reminiscence mollified the distrustful Ildefonso, and after taking a long pull at the bottle, he said: "You are very cross this morning. I am sorry you can not take a joke. We have been comrades so long that you should know me better. Hark! What was that?"

"Indians coming to town with their fruit and vegetables. The streets will soon be filled with people. If our man does not make his appearance very soon, we shall have to postpone the job until the evening."

"If he must die, we might just as well kill him in the daytime."

"But it will not be so easy for us to get away, when the streets begin to fill with people."

"There is but a short distance between here and the Palace. We are not to go back to the barracks. We shall be quartered at the Palace. The ink-worms are afraid they might get hurt."

A pause followed, during which the bottle changed hands once or twice.

"What has befallen the Captain?" asked Ildefonso, at last. "He appears to be changed completely of late. I never saw him so serious and crestfallen before."

"I can tell you, but it is a long story. You were not with us at Neuss?"

"No!" said Ildefonso. "I had been sent to Brussels with prisoners."

"Well, you see—But stop! I hear voices!" and Juan pushed his head out of the door, as he had done several times before. He immediately drew it back again.

"Santa Maria! There is our man at last!"

In an instant Ildefonso was on his feet.

"But he is not alone. There is somebody with him. They are standing still at the corner, engaged in conversation."

"Well, what shall we do?"

"I hardly know!"

"Shall we shoot them both, so that the other can't tell?"

"Our orders are to shoot one."

"But if we shoot one, the other may turn upon us and then we shall have a row and an exposure; and the ink-fishes at the Palace will charge us with having bungled the job, and will refuse to pay us our money."

"There is something in what you say. Still, I hate to shoot a man without orders. He might be a loyal servant to the King."

"The Devil! Why should he, then, be prowling around with that arch-traitor and rebel, Bellido? Let us shoot them both and be done with it."

"Here they come. Let us decide quick!"

"But how?"

"Give me the dice-box. One throw; the highest commands."

"I am willing."

"Stop! It is not necessary. They shake hands and part. The other puts a key into a house-door, and our man comes this way. Ah! I see! His Indian porter is up already and has opened the door of his house. We can finish him as he passes through the entry. That'll be a neat way of doing it up. Get ready man!"

Noiselessly Juan del Puente now opened the door of the shop so as to uncover the range of the two arquebuses, and stealthily, like cats, the two men took their positions behind their pieces. The darkness of the shop enveloped them. It would have been impossible to see them or their arquebuses from the other side of the street. The sun had not yet arisen. Nothing could be heard but the steps of the approaching victim.

CHAPTER XIV.

THE DEED.

Bellido had spoken long and earnestly to his young companion. Carrera had never given much thought to political subjects. He had played with the Muses, as his college teachers had taught and encouraged him to do; but his mind had not been directed to the grave and serious problems which Bellido now unfolded to him. In a certain sense it was a new revelation. The Procurator's forcible statements and irresistible arguments produced a deep impression on his youthful listener.

Before they had reached the great Square, they met old Alonzo Sanchez wrapped up in his cloak and hurrying home. He stopped them as he recognized Bellido.

"By Santiago! Where do you come from, and where have you been?"

"Might I not ask the same question, Don Alonzo?"

"Of course you shall!" replied Sanchez. "The Cabildo was in session all night and applied itself to business thoroughly. Most of your excellent suggestions were acted upon; but we missed you very much indeed. We sent messengers in every direction and could not find you. For Heaven's sake, where have you kept yourself?"

"You shall know it all. It is a long and most exciting story. I shall give it to you as soon as I shall have snatched a few moments' rest. What I heard and saw last night, Don Alonzo, secures the success of our movement. I shall come to your house after breakfast and tell you all about it."

"Do not hurry away, Señor Bellido," said Sanchez detaining him. "I have important and highly gratifying news to impart to you. We have adopted your plan of organizing an armed force, and have appointed you Commander-in-chief."

"Thank God, Don Alonzo! not for my appointment, but for the good sense and energy of the Cabildo in preparing for war."

"Of course, you will accept the appointment?"

"How could I refuse? One condition, however, I must make. Your Grace must give me your son, Roberto, for my Chief-of-staff. He is a young God of war. Can I have him?"

"Take him, my good friend; the boy will be delighted with this distinction."

"And what else have you done?"

"We have written letters and dispatched messengers to all the cities of Peru. We sent them in hot haste. Most of them are gone!"

"Good! Good!" exclaimed Bellido clapping his hands, "you could not have done better. Oh, friend Sanchez, I never felt so happy and so hopeful in my life! But I must go home and get a little rest now I can hardly stand on my feet."

"But what, for the Virgin's sake, have you done?"

"Perhaps it would be cruel to leave your curiosity entirely unsatisfied; but do not ask me any questions now. We have the Inca Treasure and the Shyri Toa for us in this great struggle—millions of gold and thousands of men."

Old Sanchez raised his arms in amazement.

"And now, a fortune for an hour's rest. God be praised! Come, Don Julio!" and taking Carrera's arm, Bellido walked away, leaving his old friend stunned and speechless.

When they came to the corner formed by the Plaza and the street on which both Carrera and Bellido lived, a black cat darted across their path and disappeared under the stairs leading to the esplanade in front of the Cathedral.

"I do not like this," remarked Carrera.

"Were I a Roman," said Bellido, "I should turn back."

"You had better come with me, Don Alonzo. Here is my house. Stay with me until you are rested. Think of Mama Rucu's warning, which you promised to heed."

"What is the difference, my kind friend? Here is your house, and there is mine—a difference of perhaps forty or fifty paces. I fully intend to be cautious, and to beware of assassins hereafter. But there is nothing to be feared now. There is not a soul on the street. The door of my house, I see, has been opened already, so that I can enter it without the trouble of waking my porter. The day has dawned, and the sun will smile upon the city before I can reach my bed."

"And yet you had better come with me. Do not go to your own house now. Mama Rucu's warning has filled me with sinister presentiments."

"She told me not to return to my house before daybreak. Well, it is daylight now. Besides, I hope to get home before my wife awakes. The sky is bright and clear out-doors; but," he added with a melancholy smile, " I am afraid a storm has been gathering under my roof. Every minute now becomes valuable in order to get under shelter before it begins to pour. Good-night, or good-morning, rather, my young friend."

With these words Bellido went to meet his fate. How often great men are borne down with the pettiest cares. The brain that had conceived projects which, had they succeeded, would have crowned him with the unfading laurels of immortality, now cudgels itself with the uneasy question whether he would find his wife asleep or awake. The man who prepares to shake a whole continent to its foundations, and to conjure up a political earthquake of unheard-of magnitude, attempts to sneak, on tip-toe, into his bed-chamber, so as not to awake the termagant, at the mere thought of whom his courage fails and his wings droop.

Carrera looked after him, anxiously, while he took out his key to open a small door which had been cut into the main door of his house. As soon as Bellido had reached his own door, he turned back and waved his hand to Carrera. as if to show him that his fears were groundless, and that he was now safe at home. With this Bellido entered his doorway, and Carrera was about to follow his example, when he was startled and horrified by the detonations of arquebuses. Two shots were fired in rapid succession, and then two black figures, wrapped up in long cloaks, and their faces shaded completely with broad-brimmed, slouched hats, drawn down to their eyes, appeared on the street—as if the earth had vomited them forth—and rushed away from Bellido's house. One hurried on to the left, turning the next corner, around which he disappeared. The other came running toward the Plaza, so that he must pass Carrera. The assassin—for instinctively Carrera took him to be such—tried to pass him on the other side of the street. In an instant Carrera had drawn his sword, and made an excited plunge at the man. But Juan del Puente was a veteran who had not learned the art of war in vain. A Spanish foot-soldier, who had seen service under Alba and the Prince of Parma, was not to be trifled with by an inexperienced young Creole, who had never looked into the deadly eyes of Bellona. With one blow from his arquebus he shattered Carrera's sword into splinters, leaving him nothing but the hilt, and sped away to the Palace, before his antagonist could recover from his surprise. But Carrera had seen enough. He had seen the uniform and the weapon of the soldier under the man's cloak, when he reached out to deal the blow.

At this moment, Carrera heard loud cries and wailing in the direction of Bellido's house, from which he inferred that the assassins had done their work. Disarmed, as he was, his pursuit of the armed murderer would have been fruitless. But some assistance might still be rendered to his friend. He rushed down the street to Bellido's house. The double door was open, and in the spacious entry the ill-fated man lay on the stones, with his head in the arms of his Indian porter, who knelt over him. The porter's wife and children stood around them, wringing their hands and shrieking and wailing. Soon afterward Bellido's wife, followed by the inmates of the house, appeared upon the bloody scene, and beheld her husband in the speechless agonies of death. The neighbors, too, had been aroused by the noise, and in a few minutes the street and the house were alive with horrified spectators.

"A priest! A priest! Run for a priest!" shrieked the

women, and some of the servants immediately started off to procure the attendance of a clergyman.

"Send for a surgeon, for God's sake!" said Carrera. There may be help yet!" This order, too, was obeyed.

"Oh, my husband, my darling husband, beloved one of my soul! Thou canst not, thou wilt not die!" shrieked Bellido's wife, who would have received him with a torrent of abuse had he come home safe and healthy.

"Master! Dear Master! Our poor Master!" wailed the servants, while everybody wished to render assistance, and nobody knew how.

His wife knelt on one side of the dying man, while Carrera knelt on the other. Bellido looked at the young man intently, and tried to speak, but he could not. "Give room here!" exclaimed Carrera. "Do not crowd around so closely! Bring down a mattress, so that we can carry him up stairs!"

Bellido shook his head, as if to say that it was useless. Then with a trembling hand he motioned those nearest him to stand back, and dipping his finger into his own blood, attempted to write something on the stones with which the doorway was paved. But strength and consciousness soon forsook him; a stream of blood broke forth from his mouth, a convulsive gasp, a last despairing look, and all was over.

Mama Rucu's vision had been verified.

The Revolution had lost its head before it had fairly begun.

* * * * * * *

A priest arrived, but he found a corpse. A large number of people had congregated before the house, and began to crowd into the doorway, and even into the courtyard.

Carrera was beside himself. His whole being revolted against the cowardly crime, which had been committed here, evidently at the command of those in power. His inmost self was aroused. If he had ever hesitated to take sides in the impending struggle, he was determined now. The anarchy of the primeval forest was preferable to such a government.

Bellido's widow had to be torn away from the bloody remains of her husband by the women in attendance, and, while the neighbors and friends were preparing to place the body on a bier, Carrera stepped before the door, still holding the hilt of his broken sword. He had never spoken in public; but his indignation inspired him with eloquent words:

"Men of Quito!" he exclaimed, "a horrible crime has been committed. Our friend Bellido, whom we all loved and revered, a member of the Cabildo, the Procurator-General of our Municipality, has been murdered while entering his own house. I witnessed the crime from my own door. I saw the flight of the assassins after their dark deed had been committed. One of them passed my house. I attempted to stop him, but he broke my sword with an arquebus, and escaped to the Palace. He was wrapped in a black cloak, but when he raised his arm to parry my blow I saw that he wore the uniform of a Spanish soldier. Why should soldiers have killed Alonzo Bellido, who had harmed no one; who had committed no wrong, and whose only offense consisted in endeavoring to vindicate the rights guaranteed to the people of Peru by King Charles I? Soldiers would not have committed this dark deed without orders. It is evident that our friend's assassination had been commanded by those whose duty it should have been to protect the King's subjects from violence and crime. The hand that struck him dead is no more responsible for this deed than the arquebuses from which the two deadly shots were fired. The men who commanded the perpetration of this crime are the real murderers. But two days ago he was arrested by order of the Royal Audience, but liberated by the people. Now your friend, your counselor, your advocate, lies before you a bloody corpse. Who is to be held responsible for this deed?"

"The Audience! The Audience! The Spanish Commander! The Chapetones!" shouted the infuriated multitude.

"Let us have revenge!" exclaimed a dozen voices.

"To the Palace! To the Palace!" echoed others.

"Let the bells be rung, and the alarm be sounded."

"To arms! To arms!"

"Viva el Señor Carrera! Let him lead us to our revenge."

Like wild-fire the terrible news spread over the City of Quito. The sun had hardly risen when drums were beating, bells were ringing, and, the people flew to arms.

By eight o'clock the streets leading to the Plaza were filled with men armed with arquebuses, halberds, pikes, and clubs, preparing to storm the Palace. But the Palace was guarded. Valverde's company had barricaded the doors and windows, and their arquebuses and three or four light pieces of artillery, such as could be used along the mountain roads of the interior, frowned down ominously on the surging multitude in the Plaza.

The Rubicon was passed; the die was cast; the war had begun.

BOOK III.

THE REVOLUTION.

"Vor dem Sklaven, wenn er die Kette bricht,
Vor dem freien Menschen erzittert nicht."
SCHILLER.

BOOK III.
THE REVOLUTION.

CHAPTER I

PAREDES.

The ringing of the alarm-bells, and the tumult on the streets, awoke Paredes, who had passed the night at his villa. Rushing down the declivity of San Juan, he saw Juan Castro, accompanied by a dozen of his rabble followers. He was thundering at the door of a house to arouse its inmates.

"Up, ye sleepy devils! There is bloody work to be done. Come out as quick as you can, and bring your crowbars and pikes!"

"What is the matter, Don Juan?" inquired Paredes, beckoning to the ruffian to come to him. Castro at once acquainted his patron with the murder of Bellido and the determination of the populace to storm the Palace and kill the members of the Royal Audience.

A sinister smile glided over the dark features of Manuel Paredes. The Palace to be stormed? Count Valverde was his rival for the hand of Dolores. Count Valverde would have to defend the Palace; but he would hardly be able to hold it. Could Paredes wish for a better opportunity to rid himself of a rival?

"And do you think, Don Juan," he asked, taking Castro aside, "that the Audience has instigated this most wicked and outrageous murder?"

"Who else should have done it, your Grace?"

"I have my own views of the matter. Did you not tell me that the deed was committed by soldiers?"

(149)

"Yes, your Lordship; so it was."

"And who commands the soldiers?"

"Count Valverde."

"Well, do you suppose that these soldiers would have dared to commit such a deed without express orders from their commanding officer?"

"No, but the Count must have received his orders from the Audience."

"Yes, but would he have carried them out, if he did not approve of them? It is his duty to protect the subjects of the King, and not to murder them. I shall give you my reasons why I suspect Valverde. You remember the night when I saved you from the clutches of the guard?"

"Yes, your Lordship; and eternally grateful shall I be."

"The Count was with me on the balcony. He was pale with rage. He said, to fellows like you, no mercy should be shown, and that the day of reckoning was sure to come. He told me that the Viceroy had ordered troops to Quito, and as soon as they arrived, short work should be made of such rebels. He said that he had prepared a list of the most pestiferous traitors, and that your name headed the list of the commoners. Of the noblemen who should be put out of the way, he mentioned that very same Bellido, who was murdered this morning. Now you see, Juan Castro, how naturally it all follows. Count Valverde said that Bellido must die, and Bellido is dead. Count Valverde said that Juan Castro must die, and how long will Juan Castro live?"

"He will live longer than the Count Valverde, your Grace," said Castro, pale with rage and apprehension.

"You should have seen how anxious he was that night to bring out his Spanish soldiers and to fire into your party. He was greatly excited and censured me severely for vouching for you until next morning. I almost fear he added my name to his list for having taken your part."

Castro listened silently, but his looks expressed grim determination.

"If he has not put my name down already," continued the wily Creole, "he will do so to-day or to-morrow, for I do not intend to refrain from denouncing this infamous assassination, nor from laying the blame on those to whom it most assuredly attaches. Nay, more, Juan Castro, if my sword can contribute to revenge this deed, it shall not remain in its scabbard."

"Glory to your Grace!" exclaimed Juan Castro. "The Virgin be praised that you are on the side of the people in this cause. As to the Count Valverde," he added in a significant undertone, "leave him to me. His list will not be presented to the commander of the troops from Lima."

CHAPTER II.

SEIZING THE OPPORTUNITY.

The multitude was ready to rush on the Palace, and dash itself in an unorganized attack against it doors and windows, guarded as they were by a few, but resolute men, most of whom had seen service on many a bloody field. Suddenly the wave of human heads turned in another direction. The cry: "The Militia! The Militia!" was echoed from thousands of lips. Those nearest the Palace asked: "Where?" Those farthest from it answered: "In the Plaza of San Francisco!" And consequently toward San Francisco rolled the surging mass of humanity.

The Militia regiment, "Pichincha," was drawn up in the Plaza of San Francisco, almost in front of the elegant residence of the Marquis de Solando, who, at this crisis, was prudent enough not to show himself on the balcony, or at the windows. Dolores, proud like a Queen, and with a coolness and resolution rare in her sex, stood on one of the balconies, leaning against the house. Aunt Catita stood tremblingly behind her in the balcony door. Their female attendants pressed toward the window, and implored their young mistress not to expose herself so daringly. Dolores waved them back contemptuously, without averting her looks from the scene below. The young officers, Carrera among them, saluted her with their swords as they passed the house in order to take their places at the head of their companies.

The regiment Pichincha consisted of the very best native militia material. It was composed of municipal and government appointees of lower rank, tradesmen, shop keepers, and master mechanics, and officered by the nobility of the city. Manuel Paredes was its commander. He had just arrived, and seemed to be engaged in conversation with one of his aids.

About twenty paces from him, there was a group of officers who conversed in an undertone, darting now and then looks of distrust and hatred at their Colonel. One of them was Roberto Sanchez.

"Let us lose no time, then," he said. "The moment he gives the order to disperse the populace, or to march to the relief of the Audience, we demand his immediate resignation; and if he refuses, we cut him down."

"And let there be no weakness or indecision!" added another. "A coward and a traitor he, who falters or hesitates."

"Shall I tell Carrera?" asked a third. "His company is in the center, and he stands right in front of Paredes."

"No," answered Roberto. "Do not tell him. I love him dearly, and I feel sure he will be with us. But, brave as he is, he is not a man of decision. He would shrink from such bloody work."

"Attention!" commanded Paredes, who had now taken

his position; and everybody fell into his place, except the five conspirators, who slowly drew nearer to their Colonel.

Paredes looked at them and smiled. He had understood them, and divined that they were preparing for a blow; and he secretly rejoiced over the disappointment he had in store for them. In the meantime the populace had filled up every foot of ground in the Plaza, and listened breathlessly for what was to come.

"Comrades!" began Paredes, after a glance at the balcony where Dolores stood. "I have, this very moment, received an order from the Royal Audience, countersigned by Count Valverde, to lead you to the Palace for the purpose of protecting the Government, and dispersing the people who have assembled there."

Roberto Sanchez, followed by young Olmos, and young Garcia, drew uncomfortably near.

"Comrades!" continued Paredes, without seeming to notice them. "I shall not obey this order!"

A wild shriek of applause and rejoicing at once rent the air, and thousands of hats and handkerchiefs were waved, while the young enthusiasts who were ready to dispatch their Colonel, drew back in blank astonishment and surprise.

"If you demand," continued the Colonel, casting a stern look at the young conspirators, who were not with their companies, "that the order of the Royal Audience be obeyed, I shall have to resign my place as your Colonel, and surrender the command of the regiment to the officer next in rank."

"No! No! No!" shouted officers and men. "Viva el Colonel Paredes!" And again the shout was taken up and carried over the sea of human heads, from square to square, until it reached the little garrison of the Palace, who comprehended what it meant, for they had all foreseen and predicted the defection of the native militia.

"But I consider it my duty," resumed Paredes, as soon

as the tumult had subsided, "to explain to you the reasons of my apparent disloyalty and insubordination."

"Hear! Hear! Listen! Silence!" were the exclamations that welcomed this remark.

"It is well known to you all that the Royal Audience has ordered the exaction of a tax from which, by a *cedula* of King Charles I, of glorious memory, the Kingdom of Peru has been exempted for one hundred years. This time not having expired, the imposition of such a tax is plainly and palpably wrong and unlawful. It has been said that our Lord the King, His Majesty Philip II, yielding to the selfish advice of evil counselors, has disregarded the humble petitions and remonstrances of the Peruvian Municipalities, and commanded His Highness the Viceroy, and the Audiences, to proceed with the collection of the Alcabala. Of such a decision by His Majesty, however, we are not yet definitely and properly advised. It may be so, and it may not be so. Thus far we have had no proof of it except the word of men who murder the King's subjects whom they have been sent here to protect."

These words had hardly passed from his lips when another shout of applause and approbation rent the air. The common people, especially, cheered wildly, while Roberto who had quietly resumed his place at the head of his company, whispered to the officer nearest him: "The hypocrite! He is a traitor at heart to the cause his lips espouse. He wishes to gain our confidence now, in order to betray us afterward!"

"Yes, Comrades," continued Paredes, "it was a murder. I can not call it by any other name. Don Alonzo Bellido was a member of the Cabildo, which had elected him Procurator-General. He was a man of great parts and unimpeachable righteousness. He was not a native of our city, and yet the city had adopted him as a favorite child. He was beloved by the old and the young, by the rich and by the poor. He was a good man and loved justice.

He had done no wrong. When he was arrested the other day, no charge of any kind had been preferred against him. He was released at the intercession of his fellow-citizens, and the Royal Audience disclaimed all complicity in his arrest. He defended the rights of the city which had so lovingly adopted him. And for this devotion to your rights and interests he now lies, a bloody corpse, in his house. His wife has been deprived of her husband, his children of their father, the city of its best and truest friend."

Many of the men now melted in tears, while others vowed vengeance on his assassins.

"Is it possible that His Majesty can approve of such a crime? It would be downright treason to answer this question in the affirmative. Are the men who command the perpetration of such deeds worthy of being entrusted with the powers of government, the administration of justice, and the preservation of the public welfare?"

"No! No! Down with them! Kill them!" shouted the populace.

"Am I—are we—to receive orders from, and to obey the orders of, these men, before they have convinced us that they are innocent of this dark deed?"

"No! No! Never!"

"For this reason, Comrades, I shall not act under the orders of the Royal Audience or of the Count Valverde, until every atom of suspicion is removed. At the same time, I do not intend to draw my sword against the King, as long as there is hope that he will disapprove of these horrors and grant the prayer contained in our petitions and remonstrances. Under the circumstances, the only proper conclusion I can come to, as the Colonel of your regiment, is to do nothing. I shall not order you to shoot down your friends and brothers"—

A fresh outburst of applause now interrupted the speaker.

"And I can not and will not command you to attack the Palace, and to take the law into your own hands. I, therefore, command you to return to your quarters and disperse to your homes." And, as if to suit the action to the word, he returned his sword to its scabbard, and turned to go.

But he had now touched the popular heart, and the enthusiasm he had aroused knew no bounds. While the drums were beating, and the companies were marching off to their quarters, Paredes was seized by brawny arms, placed on strong shoulders, and carried in triumph around the Plaza. There was no end to the "Viva el Coronel Paredes!" That speech had made him the favorite of the hour. He had completely won the confidence of the populace. He felt that, with the masses, he had made his point. Whether he would also succeed with the leaders remained to be seen. With them, he apprehended, his task would not be so easy. Still he would try, and try at once.

There was one pair of eyes which followed him with an expression of especial delight and admiration, as he was borne along on the shoulders of the multitude; they were the eyes of Dolores.

CHAPTER III.

THE BESIEGED.

THE human wave now rolled back to the Plaza Mayor, where the arrival of Juan Castro and his followers soon imparted the necessary decision and aggressiveness to the multitude.

Many of the Militiamen reappeared, but most of them without their uniforms. Some of the nobility, in the disguise of commoners, joined the besiegers. Others, like young Sanchez and Carrera, and their friends, young Olmos and Garcia, were too proud and too bold to assume a disguise, and freely mixing with the people, gave encouragement and direction to the surging crowds.

The Government Palace was built on a platform, which formed what the Spaniards call a *Pretil* or esplanade in front of it, rising about twelve feet above the level of the Plaza, and occupying its entire western side. On the south side of the square stood the Cathedral, and on the east line stood the house of the Municipality. The west side was occupied by private residences, with porticos under them. The esplanade before the Palace was reached by a flight of stairs in the center, and one at each end.

Nearly the whole Plaza was swept by two pieces of artillery posted behind a barricade in the main door of the Palace, which had been left open to enable the guns to play on the assailants. Count Valverde, who could easily be recognized by the large waving plumes in his hat, leaned over the barricade and looked contemptuously on the mob below. Suddenly an orderly appeared and announced that the President wished to see him.

Don Manuel Barros de San Millan awaited him in the Audience Chamber. The four Auditors were with him. They all looked ashy pale, and fluttered about tremblingly. One shout below would draw them to the windows, while the next yell would frighten them away again.

President Barros affected some composure which he did not possess.

"My dear Count," he began, "what shall we do?"

"It is my business to obey your Excellency's orders," said Valverde, "whatever they may be. I have no suggestions to make."

"Do you think they will dare to attack the Palace?"

"I think they will," answered Valverde, with freezing politeness.

"Then we are lost!" shouted Auditor Meneses, the one who had recently arrived from Spain.

"Can you hold the building?" continued the President.

"If they are foolish enough to attack us only from the Plaza, I can repel the assault easily. If, however, they should scale the courtyard wall in the rear, they would hem us in on both sides, and make our position untenable."

"We must take refuge in the Church of La Merced," suggested Meneses.

"But how would your Excellencies get there? The streets are filled with people who will watch the rear entrances. No one can leave the Palace unobserved, at least not in the daytime."

"But, for God's sake, what shall we do?" urged the President.

"If your Excellencies had asked me that question yesterday, I should have advised to defer the blow against Bellido until after the arrival of troops from Lima. As the case now stands, I have but one suggestion to make."

"Let us hear it! Let us hear it!" exclaimed the Auditors in a chorus.

"I should negotiate to gain time. I should even advise to issue a proclamation disclaiming all complicity in the death of Bellido, and promising that the crime shall be investigated and the guilty parties brought to justice. I would suspend the collection of the Alcabala until another appeal can be made to the Viceroy and to the Court at Madrid."

"Good! Good!" shouted Meneses. "Let us do it at once!"

"And if they refuse to be pacified?"

"Then, we must try to hold the Palace until night sets in and then attempt to escape to a sanctuary, either in some disguise, or by cutting our way through."

"And if it should not be possible?"

"Then, we shall have to put our trust in the Lord. I shall order my men to confession and prepare for the worst."

"But there must be no worst!" said the President.

"Let us negotiate! Let us send out a flag of truce. We can annul all our concessions afterward. They are null and void *ab initio*, because granted under duress. Let us promise — "

He could not finish the sentence. Two, three, four shots were fired in rapid succession, and were followed by a volley accompanied by unearthly yells on all sides of the building. The President and the Auditors threw themselves on their knees and began to pray, while Valverde hurried out of the room to meet the emergency. He was just in time. The populace in the great square had made a sudden rush for the esplanade in front of the Palace with the intention of forcing the main entrance; but they were quickly repulsed by the fire of the garrison and fled panic-stricken in every direction, leaving the square covered with their dead and wounded. The rapidity of this success enabled the Count to turn his attention to the wall of the court in the rear of the Palace, where Juan Castro and his men had nearly effected an entrance. Here, too, the Count was in time, and drove back the assailants with great slaughter. The struggle was over in a few minutes, and the Count returned to the presence-chamber of the Audience to report that, for the time being, they were safe.

But the relief of the Auditors was of short duration. The Rebels soon returned and fortified themselves in the adjoining houses, turning the seige into a much more effective blockade. A flag of truce sent out by the frightened ministers was fired upon by the populace and driven back to the Palace. The people were still too infuriated to allow negotiations. The death of Bellido and of those who had perished during the assault had not yet been avenged. The multitude thirsted for a victim; and a victim it would have.

CHAPTER IV.

A SUDDEN DEPARTURE.

And where was Carrera during the hours of suspense and anxiety, and the scenes of tumult and disorder that followed the unsuccessful attack on the Palace?

Feeling the necessity of a short rest after his sleepless and fatiguing night and the overpowering excitements of the morning, he had returned to his house, and without undressing, thrown himself on his bed. His rest was but of short duration. The tramp of horses was heard in his courtyard, and immediately afterward Lorenzo Viteri, the Mayordomo of his uncle's *hacienda* at Puembo, rushed into the young man's bed-room looking pale and excited.

"I beg your pardon, Master, for interrupting your repose. But I am the bearer of sad news. Your poor uncle lies on his death-bed. He was suddenly taken ill this morning, and I am afraid there is no help."

"For Heaven's sake, Don Lorenzo, how you have alarmed me. How is it possible! He was the picture of health when I saw him last."

"And yet you would hardly recognize him now. Your Grace must come with me at once. His Lordship wants to see you before he dies. He urged me to hurry, and commanded me to bring you without delay. I have everything in readiness. I brought five or six horses.. Before I came here I dispatched a physician to Puembo. It was difficult to get one, as all the leeches are busy with the wounded. And now we must follow. We must put the spurs to our steeds, if we want to find him alive."

At this moment Roberto burst into the room: "Julio!"

he exclaimed, "the Cabildo has sent for you. You must come with me at once."

Carrera informed him of the sad message he had just received. "I can not go with you now. I must be off this very minute."

"But, by all the Saints of Heaven, you can not disregard the order of the Cabildo. Your uncle is a most excellent man, but he has only one life to lose, while here the lives of hundreds are at stake."

"Roberto! He is my benefactor—my second father—to whom I owe everything."

"But suppose you find him dead. What good would your coming do him then, while not a minute must be lost here? We have staked our lives in this contest, and we must either succeed or die on the scaffold. Will you sacrifice all your living friends for the sake of a dying uncle? And, after all, he may not be so very ill; the Cabildo will not detain you, and perhaps in an hour, or even less than an hour, you may be ready to go."

"Young Master," said Lorenzo, "it is the dying man's last and only wish to see his nephew. Do not deprive him of this consolation."

"I must go, Roberto, I must."

"And Toa?" asked Sanchez, taking his friend aside.

"You must tell her what has called me away."

"How could I? Where should I find her, whom nobody can see?"

"Write her a letter in my name, giving her all the particulars, and take this," he said, kissing the silver moon she had given him, and then handing it to Roberto. "This piece," he whispered to him, "will put you in communication with her. Show it to Mariano, or any other reliable Indian, and he will take your letter, and return with her answer. And now, farewell. May the Virgin protect you!"

"O, Julio!" said Roberto, pressing him to his heart. "You go, and perhaps we shall never meet again."

"Do not be childish, Roberto. In a day or two I shall return to you;" and before Roberto could sit down to write the letter to Toa, he heard the tramp of the horses that bore away his friend. It was their last meeting on this side of the grave.

The pen was not Roberto's forte. He wrote with difficulty, and had spoiled several sheets of paper, before he succeeded in inditing the following epistle, full of sins against the then recognized method of spelling the language of Castile:

"I regret to inform your Royal Highness that my friend, Don Julio de Carrera, has been called away to Puembo, by the sudden and probably fatal illness of his uncle and benefactor. He left with a heavy heart, but he hopes to return soon, and to throw himself at the feet of your Royal Highness. His departure was so sudden as not to allow him the time to write. He, therefore, requested me to communicate these facts to your Highness, and to tell your Highness how it grieves him to be taken away from Quito. In fulfilling the commission of my friend, I avail myself of the opportunity to place my own services at the disposal of your Highness. Whenever your Highness should be in need of a stout heart, a strong arm, and a good sword, your Highness has but to remember your humble servant, who kisses your hands *   ROBERTO SANCHEZ."

After finishing and re-reading this document, and congratulating himself on his unexpected clerical success, he called Mariano.

"Dost thou know the Shyri Toa, my boy?"

"No, Señor!"

"Well, couldst thou find the Shyri Toa?"

"Nobody can find the Shyri Toa, Señor," said Mariano.

---

* The usual Spanish mode of concluding a letter.

"But I have a letter of great importance here, which must be delivered to the Shyri Toa."

"If your Grace will tell me where to find her, I shall deliver the letter."

"If I knew where to find her, I should deliver it myself, man. You must find her for me."

"It is impossible, Master. She is far, far away from Quito."

"These Indians are not without strong points," thought Roberto. Then he said aloud: "Mariano!"

"Señor!"

"Look at this!"

The effect was magical. In an instant Mariano was on his knees, and, with tears streaming down his cheeks, he kissed and petted the little silver ornament which Roberto had handed to him.

"What is the matter now, my boy?" asked Roberto, good naturedly.

"The letter! the letter!" exclaimed the boy. "Give me the letter, Master, and the Shyri Toa shall have it this very hour. And Mariano is your Lordship's slave. Command me, send me wherever your Grace desires. Mariano will go to the death for your Grace." And again he kissed the silver moon, and then reverentially returned it to Roberto.

"Now, listen!" said the young gentleman. "If I am not here when thou returnest, thou wilt find me in the House of the Municipality."

CHAPTER V.

VALVERDE.

It was a long, long day, but at last it drew to a close. The soldiers in the Palace were served with eatables and wine. And as the Revolutionists persisted in their inactivity, the vice of Spain demanded its rights. Dice rattled under the field-pieces; cards were shuffled under the arquebuses, and many a time the amount was won and lost that had been paid for the life of Bellido.

Tears and despair in the house of mourning; endless discussions in the session-chamber of the Cabildo; thirst for revenge, coupled with indecision and timidity among the surging crowds in the streets; abject cowardice and helplessness in the upper story of the Palace, and recklessness of life or death among the soldiers below, who gambled on, never pausing to consider whether they would live to-morrow to enjoy the money for which they played with such intensity: such were the scenes during which the hours wore on, until the sun had disappeared behind Mount Pichincha, and the day gave way to twilight, and the twilight to the shades of night.

" Juan del Puente, are you a Christian ?"

" Why, by Santiago!" replied the man who had just returned from a tour of inspection, " your Excellency has put this question to a man whose whole life has been devoted to the war for our holy religion."

" I have no doubt of that. But do you feel a craving for its consolations? You have reddened your hands in Christian blood to-day. It is true you have only obeyed orders; yet it must weigh on your mind. We are in a very desperate strait. The probabilities are against us, at least against some, and perhaps all of us. Do you not feel a necessity to unburden your conscience by confessing your sins?"

"But, even if I did, Señor Commander, what could I do? Our Chaplain has not come to the Palace with us. He was in bed when we left the barracks, and said he would follow soon. But this insurrection came upon us like a thunderbolt, and it seems the old gentleman was afraid to trust himself to the maddened crowds."

"This is a sad state of affairs, Juan del Puente. We must open a communication with the Convent of La Merced, or with La Compañia. They might send us priests, and I do not think the mob below would prevent their entrance."

"Yes, but how will our messenger get there? They would tear any man to pieces who should venture out of this inclosure."

"The only difficulty will be to get out. Once at the Convent, our messenger might come back in the disguise of a monk with the other friars."

"But, perhaps he would not come back. He might conclude to remain in the Convent. That would not be fair, your Excellency. We are all together now, and no man should have a better chance for his life than his comrades."

"But we might decide by lot who shall go. Then the chances would be even."

"That's true," answered Del Puente, who could not have resisted an appeal to his gambling propensities.

"There are two ways of doing it. Either let our messenger try to reach the Convent in disguise, or we might make a sortie with all the men we can spare, push on to the Convent, throw our man into the Church, and then fall back to the Palace. At the Convent our man might learn how matters stand outside, and whether we can hope for a favorable reaction. We might, through one of the friars, open communication with our friends in the city, and send messages to other garrisons."

"In this case, however, I must warn your Excellency against trusting the Friars of Mercy. Most of them are natives, and I am told they all sympathize with the Rebels. It would be better to appeal to the Jesuits, who stand by the King."

"I have considered what you say; but it will be tenfold more difficult for us to reach the Church of the Jesuits, than to get to La Merced. Moreover, the Superior of the Mercedarios is a Spaniard, whom I know, and whom I can trust. From the very fact of their sympathy with the Rebels, I infer that they will be allowed to come here to administer the sacraments of religion to our men. You are now fully informed as to my views, Juan del Puente. Go, then, call the sergeants and some of your best men together, and ascertain their preferences. Report to me as soon as you are ready. In the meantime, I shall notify the Royal Audience to prepare their communications to our friends outside."

In about half an hour Juan del Puente returned to his commander.

"Our men are ready, as I knew they would be, to carry out the plan of your Excellency; and they humbly present a few details which they beg your Excellency to consider. We are all of the opinion that it is impossible for any man to escape from the Palace unobserved. For this reason we all favor the idea of a sortie, which will lead to a stampede outside. We might drop our messenger in the disguise of one of the rabble, as we emerge from the palace. He would run along with the fugitives and be looked upon as one of the mob, or remain entirely unnoticed. We might pursue the mob as near La Merced as we can, without cutting off our retreat."

"Very well, Juan del Puente. Shall the messenger be selected by lot?"

"As a matter of course, your Excellency."

"Every name to be put in the urn?

"Comrades in life, comrades in death; every name to be put in; your Excellency alone to have the option whether or not to withhold your name."

"Can you read or write, Juan del Puente?"

"No, Señor Commander."

"Who can?"

"Idelfonso Coronel can read a little, but he can not write. Diego Narvaez can write."

"Then let him and my adjutant do the writing; and, as mine would be the greatest danger if I should be selected, let my name be put in the urn along with the others."

"Your Excellency's commands shall be obeyed."

A little table was placed in the lower corridor, and by the flickering light of a torch, the soldier, Diego Narvaez, and Valverde's aid, Guzman de Tapia, wrote down each name on a slip of paper, rolled up the slips, and put them in the hat of Ildefonso Coronel. Every man who was not on guard stood around the table. The writing had not proceeded very far, when the betting commenced.

"Five to one that my name will not be drawn!"

"Ten to one that my name will not come out!"

"If anyone will give me the odds of twenty, I bet that my name will be drawn."

"Taken!" shouted half a dozen voices.

"Who shall draw?"

"Juan del Puente! He is the ugliest of all!"

A shout of laughter, a yell of acclamation, and Juan del Puente bent forward to draw. The lurid flame of the torch threw an unsteady and fantastic light on the powder-begrimed countenances of those rough and reckless men, as they pressed around the table to hear the decision.

"Shake up that hat once more!" shouted Ildefonso Coronel, distrustful to the last.

"Silence!" commanded Guzman de Tapia, Valverde's Adjutant.

Juan del Puente had drawn a name, and, as he was unable to read, he handed it over to the Adjutant who opened the paper, read it and turned pale. Silently he handed it to Diego Narvaez, who had assisted him as scribe. He, likewise, was so struck with consternation that he neglected to make the announcement, but continued to gaze upon the paper with a blank stare.

"Well, why do n't you read?"

"What is the matter?"

"The name! The name!" shouted the men.

Diego Narvaez motioned them to be silent, and then read with a faltering voice:

"*His Excellency, the Count Valverde!*"

A long silence followed, during which not even a loud breath was drawn. The men looked at each other in amazement. They were not prepared for this result. At last, the Count emerged from the darkness of the courtyard, where he had witnessed the scene unobserved.

"Comrades," he said, "there is no danger which, for your sake, I would not brave. The verdict of fate is a righteous one. This great task, upon the success of which our present safety and, perhaps, our eternal salvation may depend, belongs to me. I swear to you, by the most holy Trinity, that if I do reach the church, I shall not stay there. I shall either return to the Palace, or you may pray for my soul. Do you believe me?"

"Yes! Yes! Long live our noble commander!"

"And now to our work. Señor Guzman de Tapia will remain in command of the Palace. He will be my successor, if I should be killed outside. Juan del Puente will command the sortie. He will succeed the Señor de Tapia if he should fall. And should Juan del Puente, too, meet with a soldier's death, let Diego Narvaez be his successor. For the present, let no man despair. Each one of us is a match for twenty of the rabble outside, and help will come, must come, if we can hold out for a few days. And now I shall withdraw to prepare my disguise. Señor de Tapia and Juan del Puente, assume your commands."

"Thirty volunteers for Juan del Puente!" commanded Tapia. Nearly twice that number rushed forward; the necessary selections were made in an instant, and the chosen ones drawn up in line.

"Let three men carry axes, and bring baskets for five!" commanded Juan del Puente.

"What for?" asked Guzman de Tapia.

"There is a bakery on our way to La Merced. We may not find it open. Therefore, the axes; and the baskets are for what we shall find. We have enough to eat for a day or two, but this thing may last longer, and it may be well to lay up a crust for the future."

"Viva Juan del Puente!" shouted the soldiers.

"Diego Narvaez," commanded Tapia, "take twenty men and follow Juan del Puente outside to protect his rear. Keep up a fire in the opposite direction, and rush to his aid if he should be pressed too hard. And now God and the Virgin be with you all."

"Santiago! Santiago!" shouted the men.

CHAPTER VI.

THE SALLY.

JUAN DEL PUENTE was right. Not a man could have escaped from the Palace unobserved. Fires had been kindled all around the building, so as to light up its walls and windows. The Revolutionists had posted themselves in the adjoining houses, and guarded every street leading to the Great Square. Almost the entire male population of the city was out, and, although the turbulent crowds of armed and unarmed men did not venture into the immediate vicinity of the Palace, they completely blockaded all the avenues by which it could be reached. A large quantity of pitch had been collected in the Square of La Merced, from which men were busily preparing torches.

Suddenly one of the doors in the wall inclosing the Palace court was thrown wide open, and Juan del Puente issued forth at the head of his thirty dare-devils, opening a destructive fire into the dense ranks of the citizens in the street leading to La Merced, which was but two or three squares from the Palace. His party was followed immediately by the men of Narvaez, who advanced in an opposite direction, and opened fire on the men who had collected under the shelter of the arcades and porticos lining the Great Square. By these, and by the men stationed in the windows of houses, the fire of the soldiers was returned, and not without effect; but in the street the old story of regulars against an armed mob repeated itself. Completely taken by surprise, the crowds nearest the Palace broke and fled, sweeping along with them even those who would have stood their ground and offered resistance.

Count Valverde, in the ragged disguise of a man of the populace, soon caught up with the fugitives, and ran forward, as if in deadly fear, toward the Church of La Merced. His own men came charging along, shouting wildly for the King. Their shouts were replied to by the garrison inside, who supported them with acclamations, with the blowing of trumpets, and the incessant beating of drums. For a moment it seemed as if the whole force of defenders had sallied forth from the Palace. The panic-stricken citizens shrieked and yelled, the women screamed in the balconies, and the reports of the arquebuses spread terror in every direction.

The bakery was still open, and had been doing a brisk business. When the rush came, the baker attempted to close his door, but a blow from the ax of one of the soldiers threw it wide open, and felled the baker to the floor.

Four or five soldiers rushed in and filled their baskets with what the shop contained.

The panic of the besiegers, however, was not of long duration. The smallness of the attacking party soon became evident. Before the House of the Municipality the more disciplined forces of the insurgents, consiting mainly of the Militiamen and old soldiers, had been massed, in order to defend it against a possible attack of the Royalists. A strong detachment of these men was soon in motion, and advanced, sheltered by the porticos under the private residences, and opened fire on the twenty of Narvaez, driving them back to the sally-port. With a bold dash, the insurgents might have captured the men of Narvaez and cut off the retreat of Del Puente, or forced themselves along with the latter's men through the open gate. But, unfortunately, they hesitated at the end of the sheltering portico, and confined themselves to an exchange of shots. But even thus the position of Narvaez became critical, and Guzman de Tapia, leaning over the walls, ordered him back into the Palace court, while the bugle-horn blew the signal of retreat to Juan del Puente. It was high time. Juan Castro had rallied his men, after the first rush of the fugitives had swept by, and, gliding along the houses, endeavored to take Juan del Puente in the flank, and drive him into an intersecting street, where he would have been overpowered. But the veterans were too quick to be caught. Snatching up their wounded, and dragging them along, they succeeded in passing the dangerous crossing, before Castro's men had fairly come up. These latter could not follow Del Puente too closely, as they would have exposed themselves to the fire of their own friends under the porticos.

Two of the soldiers were left dead outside, and three were brought back wounded, while the loss of the citizens was much heavier. The royal messenger had been set adrift, and five baskets full of bread formed a welcome addition to the scanty stores of the garrison.

The engagement had not lasted over ten minutes. Valverde would have reached the church in safety, could he have hurried on. But the fire of his own men who had lost sight of him, compelled him for a moment to turn into an intersecting street. When he again ventured into the street leading to the convent, he found himself in the midst of Castro's men. Only a short distance now separated him from the sanctuary, the door of which stood open.

Fortunately, the men of Castro were engaged in a council of war.

"If those fools under the porticos had not kept up their fire," said one, "we might have captured the Spanish dogs."

"I can not understand, why they came out," said another.

"It was bread they wanted," said Castro. "They have plundered the bakery. Thunder and lightning! They have nothing to eat. They can not hold out much longer."

"Who is that fellow?" asked another, pointing to Valverde, who had glided by, apparently unconcerned.

"It is a strange face. I have never seen it before."

Castro turned around, and looked at the Count, who now walked boldly towards the church door. "I do not know the fellow," said the ruffian, "and yet I think I must have seen that face before." With these words, he started to follow the Count, who doubled his steps as he drew near to the church. He saw that he had been observed, yet he would not arouse suspicion by running, as long as it was not absolutely necessary for his safety. Castro, accompanied by some of his gang, soon overtook him, and passed him just as he entered the sheltering edifice. The pursuers entered the church with him. The building was but dimly lit, but, by the glare of the fires on the streets, Castro looked him straight in the face. The Count had trimmed his long moustache, the pride of the Spanish nobleman, and cut his hair. He had used white powder and the actors brush to give himself the appearance of an old man. Yet such a disguise would not bear close inspection by the watchful eye of hate. As the Count doffed his hat on entering the sacred edifice, Castro became assured that he had recognized his man.

"The coward!" he muttered, but loud enough to let Valverde hear it. "He has deserted his men to save his own miserable life."

Valverde winced under this taunt, but he would not betray himself. He had an important mission to perform. He carried letters to persons outside, who must not be compromised. He had to despatch messengers to Lima and Pasto. Everything depended on his cautiousness and discretion. Affecting therefore the utmost unconcern, he repaired to the darkest corner of the church, and prostrating himself before an image of the Virgin, buried his face in his hands, and seemed lost in meditation and prayer.

"Could I be mistaken?" muttered Castro. "Impossible! Rodriguez! Watch that man. And you fellows, guard every outlet of the church and convent. That man must be the Spanish commander. If he has not come to take refuge, he is here for mischief. We must watch him closely."

CHAPTER VII.

THE HORRORS OF NEUSZ.

THE Count had gained the church. But how to communicate with the Superior, whom alone he could trust? What if the Superior should be absent from the Convent? Some men were kneeling in the church and praying; but in vain did Valverde strain his eyes to penetrate the darkness, in order to discover a friar. People came and went, but he saw no friar. The precious minutes glided away, and brought no means of communication. Should Valverde venture into the Convent? He did not doubt that he was watched. Of course he was safe in the sanctuary; but should he endanger his purpose by attracting attention? At last he saw the white robes of the Friars of Mercy. Now was the time. He arose and approached them. The unsteady light of a taper burning upon an altar trembled upon their faces. Thank the Lord of Hosts! Valverde recognized the venerable form of his countryman, the Superior.

"Reverend Father!" he said, "I beg to speak to you."

"I can not listen to you now, my Son. My duty calls me hence."

"But I must say three words to your Reverence. It is a matter of the utmost importance."

"Speak to Father Alphonso, my Son. He will attend to you."

"What I have to say is for the ear of your Reverence alone," persisted Valverde, and then he added in a low whisper: "For the sake of the King listen to me!"

The Superior now looked closely at the Count, and turned pale as he recognized his features.

"Father Alphonso!" he said, "proceed without me! I must speak to this man." And, turning to Valverde, he added: "Follow me."

Through the darkness of the church, the Superior led him to a door, which communicated with the corridors of the Convent. Less than seventy years before, a great temple of the Sun had stood on the spot now occupied by the church and monastery of La Merced. The Christian edifice had arisen upon the ruins of the Pagan temple. The Sun of the heathen had paled before the Cross. The luster of the emerald and *borla* had vanished before the splendor of the Castilian crown. The bronze of the Peruvian had given way to iron, out of which the fetters for the conquered race were forged.

Silently the twain walked through the lonely halls of the

Convent, the stillness of which formed a striking contrast with the tumult outside. Their steps resounded on the cold stone pavement of the massive corridors. At last the Superior opened a door, which led to his cell. It was scantily furnished in the rude style of native workmanship, and contained only a large wooden crucifix fastened to the wall; a table, a few chairs, a bookcase, and several pictures of Saints and the Virgin. A side door communicated with a smaller cell, in which the bed of the Superior stood. The Superior himself was an old man, whose originally dark complexion had been darkened still more by exposure to many climates. He was not very learned, but zealous and enthusiastic, a forerunner of the ecclesiastical age which was soon to follow the military age, in which our story is laid.

Not a word had been spoken until now. The Superior closed and bolted the door, then turned around and embraced the Count, who devoutly kissed his hand.

"And now, my dear countryman, how did you come here?"

"Father," answered Valverde, "you are a priest, a friend, and a Spaniard. I come to you as to my confessor, my countryman, and a loyal subject of the King of Spain. To come to you, I ordered that sally to be made. There are other souls that need your spiritual assistance, and the King's cause demands your aid." And now Valverde briefly narrated the occurrences in the Palace, and acquainted the Superior with the hopes entertained by the besieged to communicate, through his instrumentality, with their friends outside.

Uneasily and with painful suspense the monk listened to his young friend. "My dear Son!" he began, after Valverde had finished, "what you ask of me is a matter of extreme difficulty, not because I shrink from personal danger, but because I am destitute of all means to help you. The brethren of our convent are all natives, and, I am sorry to say, strongly sympathize with the cause of their countrymen outside. I am their Superior, and they must obey me; but they dislike me, perhaps hate me, for being a Spaniard. They could not be intrusted with messages to our friends. They would surely betray us. Moreover, it is questionable whether we could communicate with anybody. The houses of those who are known to be in sympathy with the cause of the King were to be sacked this morning. The mob began with the house of the Marquis de Solando. The timely intercession of Manuel Paredes alone prevented its destruction. At his request, Municipal Guards were detailed to protect the houses of the suspected; but, while protecting them, they hold their inmates as prisoners, allowing access to no one excepting those who are well known to be on the side of the insurrection."

"And where is the Marquis?"

" He is said to have left the city."

" Could you not dispatch couriers to the Viceroy and to the commander of our garrison at Pasto?"

" Where is the native whom I could trust, and if I were to send Spaniards, they would be seized, searched, and perhaps murdered."

" It is not necessary that our messengers should carry letters. Verbal commissions would be sufficient. The insurrection has not yet passed beyond the limits of the city. Once away from Quito, our messengers might travel ahead of the news they carry."

" I shall try, my Son, I shall try. But destroy these letters. No papers must be found. We know what they contain." And, with Valverde's acquiescence, he burned the hastily written notes which the latter had brought.

" And is there no hope, Father, that our friends outside will rise and come to the rescue of the King's Ministers in the Palace?"

" None—at least not now! We must put our faith in the

Lord, and trust that ⸱ me will bring a reaction. Our friends here are few, and these are cowed, frightened, terrified. Help must come from abroad."

"Then what is to become of us in the Palace?"

"I have heard that it is not the intention of the Cabildo to murder the Ministers. They are to be made prisoners and kept as hostages."

"And what is to be done with the soldiers and myself?"

"I do not know, my Son; but you are here now. You are within the walls of the sanctuary. The Church will protect you. Powerless outside, I am still the Superior here. And even our native Friars would not allow you to be harmed within this sacred inclosure."

"No, Father, I can not stay here. I must go back to the Palace."

"You are raving, my Son."

"No, Father, there is no alternative. My duty is plain. Do you think I should desert my comrades in the hour of need? I promised to return, and return I shall or die. Why should I live a disgraced man, a deserter, who ran away from his post and abandoned the most important and critical command a military officer ever held at Quito? To stay here would be the destruction of all my hopes in life, and a disgraceful end of an honorable career. I can not, must not stay."

"But how will you return?"

"You will send some of your brethren to confess my men. The Eucharist will be carried in procession to the Palace, and even those rebel fiends will not undertake to stop it. Why should not I join the procession in the disguise of a Friar? But, first of all, you must hear what I have longed to tell you. I want your opinion, your advice, Father. I am sadly troubled in mind. I am not a coward. God, whose holy battles I have fought, knows I am not; and yet, Father, I fear. It is not death at the cannon's mouth I fear; but it is a prediction which haunts me. A horrible prediction twice made to me and by different persons at different times, but almost in the same words."

"Explain yourself, my Son!" said the Monk. "I am listening. The Virgin knows how anxious I am to help you."

"It was about six years ago, in summer, that I lay, under the Prince of Parma, before Neusz, a fortified town in the Low Countries. It was defended by a Dutch commander, named Kloet. He was a most godless heretic and infidel, but I must do him the justice to say a man of almost superhuman bravery. Even the Prince regarded him with unbounded admiration. But, Father, in order to be brief—for time presses, and I can not stay long—I shall not refer to the particulars of that memorable siege. One of the churches of Neusz was dedicated to St. Quirinus. His bones were kept there in a holy shrine, and had been left untouched even by the pestiferous Calvinists, who held the town against us. But on Santiago's Day, when our whole camp celebrated the festival of the patron saint of Spain, the wretches, to mock us as it were, entered the church, took out the remains of the Saint, and, after reviling and defiling the blessed relics, burned them in the open square."

"O, horrible! How can human beings so far forget themselves," exclaimed the Monk.

"But that was not all. They had captured two of our brave boys, and, infuriated by their master, the devil, they roasted them on the same fire which had consumed the sacred relics."

"The fiends!"

"This latter deed they denied subsequently, but the burning of the relics they admitted when we questioned them. Well, we took the town by storm, and scenes of carnage followed, which may appear horrible to many, but which were no novelty to men who had been engaged in so long and fierce a war. Our men thirsted for revenge for the cruel murder of our comrades and the fiendish indignity inflicted upon the relics of the saint. The Prince of Parma wished to spare the commander, and was about to give orders to that effect; but Archbishop Ernest, to whose dominions the town belonged, was with the Prince, and protested against such leniency as blasphemous. To gratify him, the orders to save Kloet were not given. He was to be left to his fate, whatever it should be."

Valverde paused for awhile, as if to collect his thoughts, wiped the cold perspiration from his forehead, and then continued:

"It was my company that first reached the Captain's house, and I was swept along by the current. Officers, you know, are powerless on such occasions. During the sack of a city the common soldier will listen to no command. Nor did I wish to give any commands. I was burning with indignation myself; I was six years younger than now, and hated the Calvinists as heartily as they hated us. They had murdered our men; now it was our turn to get even with them. Such is the fate of war! My men found the Dutch commander in his bed. He was wounded. His wife and daughter attended him. When I entered the room, the soldiers had thrown a rope around his body by which they dragged him from his couch. 'Don't hang him!' said one. 'It is too easy a death for the damnable heretic.' 'Burn him! Burn him!' shouted others, 'as he burned the remains of the saint and our poor comrades.' Kloet denied all complicity in these occurrences, and begged for a soldier's death; but our men were inexorable. They concluded to make an example of him; and stripping him completely, they covered him with a thick coat of pitch, and, by a chain drawn around his chest, hung him out of his own window, and, lighting the pitch, consigned him to the flames."

Yells in the street below interrupted the speaker. He

started from his seat and listened intently; but, as the noise soon subsided, he resumed his narrative:

"While the soldiers were engaged in their preparations for the execution of the doomed heretic, his wife and daughter clung to my knees and implored me to interfere. They appealed to me as a soldier, as a gentleman, as a Christian, to save him, or at least to let him die a soldier's death. Both of them were beautiful women, and the pallor which overspread their countenances, together with their long, disheveled hair gave them, almost an unearthly appearance. They offered any ransom, their own lives or honor, to save the man. My heart had been steeled to such scenes; yet I was strangely moved. Their appeals were most piteous; but I had heard such appeals before. One thing, however, troubles me to this day, although I did not heed it much at the time; both of them offered to become Catholics if I would save their husband and father."

"This was, indeed, a critical case," interrupted the monk.

"But what could I do? The Archbishop, his Sovereign, demanded the death of the man. The Prince had given his consent. The soldiers clamored for it. The great crime that had been committed, and for which he, as the commander of the place, was responsible, had to be avenged. Perhaps, even if I had tried, I should have been powerless to save him. I might have saved Kloet for the moment, but he would have been executed all the same afterward. Hence, I should only have compromised myself, without averting his doom."

"I really do not see what you could have done, my Son—under these circumstances."

"When fire was set to the coat of pitch with which they had covered him; when the first shrieks of the victim were heard in the room, the scene changed. The wife released my knees which, until then, she had held. At the same time, she tore her daughter away from my feet, and, holding the fainting girl with one arm, she pointed to me with the other. I shall never forget the expression of her face. I still see her terrible eyes, starting from their sockets, and rolling like those of a maniac. In her white nightdress, with her long hair streaming down over her back and shoulders, she looked like a ghost; and her voice, which had turned hollow and shrieking, sounded as if it came from the grave. 'Not another word of imploration, Daughter,' she said. 'No more! No more! No appeal for mercy, for honor, for humanity, to that stone! God is just! God will avenge! Yes, the veil that covers the future is rent asunder before my eyes. My gaze pierces through a long vista of years. I can see your end, Spaniard, *yours*—and it will be that of my husband. Do you hear? He is a prisoner of war, whom you should protect from the murderers under your command. But there is justice; there will be retribution. Yes, terrible retribution. Do you hear his shrieks? Such will be *your* shrieks, Spaniard! Do you see his agony? Mark it well, for such will be *your* agony. Like him, you shall die in the hands of infuriated enemies. Biting fire shall lick the skin from your flesh and the flesh from your bones; and howling and rejoicing fiends shall dance around you and mock you, while death creeps upon you slowly, and preceded by what shall seem to you eternities of most excruciating pain. Look at him! Hear him! Remember him! His place will be yours! It is you! It is you! It is you!' With these words she broke into a hoarse and terrible laugh, and suddenly fell swooning upon the floor, while the horrifying cries of her burning husband gradually changed into hollow and unearthly moans."

"How pale and agitated you look, my Son." said the Friar. "Let me give you a glass of Xerez; you seem faint and weak."

"No, Father, let me finish." Several of my men, who

had listened to the fearful imprecation, now attempted to seize her and bury their swords in her bosom. 'She shall never wag that wicked tongue again,' said one of them, as he lifted up his arm to strike. But I stopped him. 'No, men,' I said, 'let us return good for evil. They are but women. Let our war be against the men.' I ordered the ladies to be conveyed to the Prince of Parma, and told one of my men, whose influence over the others was known to me, that I should hold him personally responsible for the two women, until the Prince had decided what should be done with them. The Prince, as I told you, Father, was enthusiastic in his admiration of Kloet, and he protected his widow and daughter. Weeks afterward, I saw her again. She was completely broken in spirit, and meek as a child. I told her that I had saved her life and her daughter's, and that I regretted my inability to save her husband; and, you may call it wrong or superstitious, Father, I begged her to take back her curse. It was difficult to make her comprehend what I meant. She did not seem to remember what she had said; and, when I repeated her prediction, she shook her head and answered: 'Spaniard, what I said to you after my husband was hung out of the window, I do not know. The burning match is the last I remember. Then consciousness deserted me. If I said anything after that, it was not I that spoke; it was the Spirit of the Lord that spoke through me. How can I take back what I did not say? I have forgotten it all, but the Lord will remember it. He will be as merciful to you, as you were to my husband.'"

A long pause followed, during which the Friar seemed to meditate over the narrative, and to prepare his opinion.

"But this is not all, Father. Her prediction haunted me. I have never been able to forget the scenes of that night; and when my friends at Court procured me the opportunity of trying my fortunes in America, I gladly welcomed, and promptly accepted it. The voyage across two oceans, the change of scenes and associations, the peaceful repose of a residence in the Andes, had gradually succeeded in effacing the dreaded reminiscence, when the prediction was again and most forcibly brought back to my mind by an almost literal repetition."

"Is it possible?" exclaimed the Friar. "A repetition here in America!"

"Here in Quito."

"In Quito—you amaze me! By whom, and where?"

"By Mama Rucu, the Indian witch."

"Mama Rucu! And why did you go to see Mama Rucu? Why should you have resorted to witches and sorcerers for that comfort and light which true religion alone can give?"

"It was altogether unsought, Father. I had never heard of her—I had never seen her before. I never dreamt of going to her or consulting her. I had gone in search of the Inca Treasure with a Creole friend. We went to a spot where we had good reasons to presume the existence of a subterranean passage. We discovered the passage, and just as we were in the act of entering it, Mama Rucu appeared on the mountain side above us, and wildly and menacingly said something in the Quichua language which I did not understand. After she was gone, my friend ordered one of his Indians to enter the passage, but the Indian refused, and would suffer the severest punishment rather than obey. My friend explained that Mama Rucu had filled the minds of her Indian listeners with superstitious fears. To show the groundlessness of such superstitions, I entered the passage and explored it. I learned afterward that Mama Rucu's imprecations had been hurled against the first man who should enter the passage. As I entered first, the curse attaches to me. It is the same, identically the same, as the imprecation of the Dutch commander's wife; only with this difference—Mama Rucu fixed the time when it should come to pass."

The monk clapped his hands in astonishment.

"Before the rains of winter shall again descend upon the plain of Aña Quito, I shall die in the hands of infuriated enemies; and biting fire shall lick the skin from my flesh, and the flesh from my bones. We are now in the beginning of the dry season. If, therefore, these prophecies are to be verified, it will be during this summer. Still, I should have risen above what you will denounce as a groundless superstition. But here comes this revolution. I am the commander of the garrison. I am expected to hold the Palace with a handful of men against thousands. I have repulsed the first attack with great slaughter. Other attacks will follow. The traitors are vowing vengeance for the death of Bellido, and those of their number who perished during the assault and our sally. What will, what must my fate be when they have overpowered our little garrison? They look upon me as the author of those deaths, and I shall be the victim. It all follows so naturally, Father. The problem has worked itself out with the irresistible logic of fate. The toils are closing around me, and there is no escape. For this reason I have come to you, Father, come to you because you are a Spaniard, a countryman, and because you are a priest. The time is flying fast. I must hasten back to the Palace. The moments are precious. Hear my confession, grant me your absolution, and enlighten me, advise me, guide me as to the great burden that weighs upon my soul."

CHAPTER VIII.

NEGOTIATIONS.

Doña Carmen Duchicela sat in an easy-chair. The Cacique of Ibarra and Prince Cundurazu stood at her side. Toa was in an adjoining room reading a letter which Mariano, Carrera's Indian servant, had just handed to her.

"Yes, Don Sebastian," said the old lady. "I shall return to Cacha as soon as my preparations are completed. This is a sinful place, inhabited by a godless and murderous people. I long for the quietness of my country retreat, where I can worship God in peace, and without being frightened by the din of battle in the streets, and by the howling of licentious mobs."

"My dear Lady," said the Cacique of Ibarra. "Do not leave us yet. God knows whether we shall ever meet again."

"We *shall* meet again, Don Sebastian, if you are a Christian. We shall meet where there will be no separation, and no earthly troubles, my friend."

"I am so sorry that you should shorten your visit. If you go, I must go likewise; for my remaining after your departure might arouse suspicion, and expose me to dangers. And, yet I had wished to remain longer."

"Go, Don Sebastian! Go! The sooner the better. Go home to your wife and your children. Not if you go, but if you stay, will you be in danger. Believe me, Don Sebastian, your projects are visionary, and can only lead to destruction."

In the meantime Toa had read the letter, with all the expressions of angry impatience. After she had read it, she began to pace the room endeavoring to compose herself. As last she stopped before Mariano, who awaited her orders in reverential submissiveness. "Wait outside, my good man, until I send for thee!" She then went to the door leading to the other room, and said: "Auntie, will you excuse Prince Cundurazu for a moment?"

The old man at once hurried into her presence: "What is the pleasure of my Queen?"

"Read this!"

He read, and then silently handed back, the letter. "He leaves me," said Toa, "when I want him most. But yesterday I declared my love for him, and to-day he is gone."

"He is a *Viracocha*, Shyri!"

"What dost thou advise now, my fatherly friend?"

"Thy question comes late, Shyri."

"Was it not thy advice, man, that I should marry a *Viracocha*, to make him King of our land?"

"Yes, Shyri, but the selection was thine own."

"And thou hadst approved it!"

"It was not my province, unasked to gainsay the choice of my Queen."

"Was he not the only *Viracocha* who had ever drawn a sword in defense of one of our race?"

"Yes, Shyri, his impulses were right, but didst thou test his metal? The mica may glitter, but is it gold? The vulture may soar over the highest cliff, but is he a condor? Thou shouldst have chosen a man of iron. Dost thou know that this youth is not a toy of wax? The writer of this letter is a man of iron. Take him! The great *Viracocha* whom they murdered this morning, had vouched for him."

"O Cundurazu! Wise old man! With all thy wisdom and experience, thou dost not know the heart of a woman. Dost thou think it is like a gold chain that I can take away from one man's neck, to hang it around another's?"

"The heart of common women, I may not know, Shyri. I loved but one woman, and thy grandfather Atahualpa took her for himself. But thou art a Queen, and a Queen's love by right, belongs to her people. If the cause of thy people demands a transfer, or a sacrifice of thy affections, thou must and wilt make the sacrifice."

Toa was silent. Were not the words of Cundurazu but the echo of what she had told Carrera on their return from the mountain? "And yet," she said after a pause, "he may love me. His uncle is his benefactor."

"If his filial duty and gratitude proved stronger than his love, why should not thy Queenly duty prove stronger than thy affections?"

"We shall discuss this hereafter. What is thy advice now?"

"Send for his young friend. He offers his services, and we need them. The death of the great *Viracocha* has disturbed our plans. We must have some one to communicate with the Cabildo. Let young Sanchez be sent for."

"But where shall I receive him? We must not compromise Doña Carmen, nor abuse her confiding kindness. I shall meet him on the mountain."

"No, Shyri, the mountain is too far distant. We must meet him somewhere near the Cabildo. Meet him in the Church of San Francisco, where we can escape, in case of treachery, through the vaults and the ravines under them."

Mariano found young Sanchez in the Municipality Building, with the defense of which, against a possible attack from the Palace, he had been intrusted. His heart beat faster when he learned that Queen Toa desired to see him.

"Where is the Shyri Toa?" he asked.

"I shall take your Grace to her," replied the wily Indian.

"And whither must we go?"

"This I am not to tell, Master. Have the kindness to follow me."

"Wait for me. I shall be back presently." Thus saying, he rushed to his father, who was in conversation with Francisco de Olmos, Diego Nuñez del Arco, Juan de Londoño, and other members of the Cabildo, with whom he had already discussed the problem of an alliance with the mysterious Indian Queen.

"Father, I am to see the Shyri Toa. What shall I tell her on behalf of the Municipality?"

"Oho!" exclaimed Londoño. "So you are to see her! Well, gentlemen, would it not be a capital stroke of policy, to seize that mythical personage, and make her divulge the secret of the treasure? We could do better with her money than with her Indians."

"Señor Londoño!" thundered the young man, "this would be infamous!"

"Señor Roberto," replied the other, laying his hand on the hilt of his sword, "such language requires castigation."

"Peace! Peace!" interposed the bystanders.

"Son!" said old Sanchez. "Curb thy heedless tongue, and learn how to speak to thy betters. Excuse the boy, friend Londoño. He is too hasty and impulsive. I beg your Grace's pardon, in his name. Still, it strikes me that we should gain nothing by such an attempt, while we should throw away all the advantages that might be secured by coming to an understanding with that Queen of Mystery."

"I defer to your wiser counsels, Señor Sanchez," said Londoño. "What I said, was merely a hasty suggestion, thrown out for the sake of discussion. Yet, allow me to advise caution with reference to the Indians. We might unchain an element of fierceness, that we could not curb again. These Indians will demand concessions; and such concessions will conflict with the interests of some of our best men. Such concessions might prove ruinous to the *Encomenderos*,* and we might thereby raise up enemies, where we are now surest of friends."

---

* Landed proprietors to whom Indians had been assigned, or, to use the term from which the system derived its name, "*recommended for*

"I admit," answered Sanchez, "that the problem is one of great difficulty. As I understood from Bellido, the Indian Queen offers us her treasures and the services of her people. What does she demand in return, and how much are we prepared to grant?"

"And how do we know that she will really put us in possession of treasures?" continued Londoño. "And what can her Indians do? To speak frankly, I do not think they would be of much service to us in case of war."

" Gentlemen;" said young Sanchez, " Queen Toa waits to receive me. If you have nothing to propose, I shall candidly inform her that it is useless to negotiate with the Cabildo. Is it your pleasure that I shall carry this message to her?"

And again an excited discussion arose, which led to nothing, and which was several times interrupted by Roberto Sanchez, who insisted that he must go. It became painfully evident that the master-spirit of the Revolution was gone, and that there was no one to replace him. At last it was agreed that Roberto should confer with the Shyri, and obtain from her an authorized statement of her demands.

In the darkest recesses of the Church of San Francisco, Roberto Sanchez bent his knee to the Indian Queen, and

the purpose of being instructed in the Christian religion." In return for this great benefit, which implied nothing less than the salvation of their souls, the Indians had to till the lands of their proprietors, or to requite the religious and spiritual benefits which they were supposed to receive, by work in the factories or mines. The *Encomenderos* did not trouble themselves much (hardly at all, if we are to believe the noble monk, Las Casas, supported as he is by the intrinsic probability of the charge) for the souls of their Indians, and as to whether or not they received the necessary Christian instruction; but were very anxious to enforce the fullest performance of the price with which the Indians had to purchase their eternal "salvation."
" Being recommended," therefore, for the purpose of Christian instruction, was but another name for being consigned to slavery.

swore upon the cross of his sword that whatever cause of distrust she might have against others, HE would be her loyal and faithful cavalier, her trusty messenger to the Cabildo, and the defender of the rights of her race. How different his blunt and emphatic declaration sounded from the vague and uncertain language of Carrera. Roberto's words were music to the ears of old Cundurazu; and the enthusiastic nature of Toa responded sympathetically to the stormy impulsiveness of the youth who, regardless of consequences and the prejudices of the age, threw himself into the breach for a cause of which, until then, he had never thought. But it was not the wrongs of her race, it was the silvery voice and captivating grace of Toa, and the romantic mystery which surrounded her, which carried him away. And as he listened to her pathetic and burning eloquence, and felt the charm of her magnetic presence, the image of Mercedes, longing and weeping for him, in her lonely house in the suburbs, faded from his memory and paled in his heart.

"I beg Your Highness' pardon for this plain statement of objections raised, not by me, but by certain members of the Cabildo. It was urged that the Indians were indifferent to our cause or unable to comprehend it. No Indian, it was claimed, participated in the attack on the Palace."

"And why should they sacrifice themselves for a cause which does not concern them?" answered Toa. "Make *your* cause *their* cause, and you shall see what they can do."

"It was the Señor Londoño who asserted that they would not be able to render us any valuable assistance."

"I can prove their ability this very night. Do you want me to take the Palace? I can do it. Let the Cabildo but say the word and the Palace shall be in your hands. But not a drop of Indian blood shall be spilled, if I can prevent it, until we have secured a guaranty of our rights. What ability have the Viracochas shown in this assault on the Palace? They allowed themselves to be driven like llamas on the mountain heaths. If the Viracochas are in earnest, why do they not take the Palace at once?"

"They do not intend to storm it for fear of sacrificing the lives of the Auditors, whom they wish to retain as hostages."

"Fear! The Viracochas fear! The men of iron are afraid. They want hostages to protect their lives. When the men of our race embrace a cause they do not ask what becomes of their lives. Still, if you wish to save those miserable extortioners in the Palace, it shall be done. I can take the Palace, and deliver the Ministers into your hands, without hurting a hair on their sinful heads. Give us but a trial, and you shall see what my children are made of. But, Don Roberto, they will not move without my commands; and these commands I shall not give until our rights are secured."

"For this very reason, the Cabildo has instructed me to obtain from Your Royal Highness a statement of your demands."

"Prince Cundurazu will acquaint you with what we ask. I shall leave you with him. And now, Don Roberto, whatever the result of our negotiations may be, whether they succeed or fail, I accept the offer of your friendship, and shall treasure it up in my heart. You have given it as a cavalier to a lady, Don Roberto, and the lady will hold you to it. Mark me, if we should never meet again: what you promised to Toa Duchicela for her sake, was pleasant music to her ears, but shall be no duty imposed upon you. But from the promise you made in favor of my race, I shall never, never release you. And now farewell, my friend. Call on me if adversity should befall you. I am a homeless wanderer, and yet a powerful Queen. Toa Duchicela will never forget or forsake the friends of her race."

With these words she extended her hand to him, which he

covered with burning kisses. She then withdrew to a side chapel, and threw herself on her knees before a Christian altar, and sent up fervent prayers, not to Christ or the Virgin or to the Supreme Being of the Christians, in whose existence she partly believed, and whose greatness she acknowledged; but to that unknown God who, to her mind, was greater and higher than the Trinity of the foreigners, greater than the sun and the moon, the gods of her own race, to Pachacamac, who had ruled the heavens and the earth long before the Sun-God had revealed himself to the first Inca; long before the powerful Carans dethroned the feeble chiefs of the Quitus, long before the Christian God was heard of in the land of her fathers.

With a few words, Cundurazu disclosed to Sanchez the great plan for which he had gained the approbation of Bellido. Peru was to be made independent of Spain, and to be governed by a native *Viracocha*, who was to be the husband of Toa. This plan, however, was not to be communicated to the full Cabildo at present, but young Sanchez was to submit it to his father, who should carefully prepare for, and win to, it the leaders of the Revolution. In the meantime, the provincial office of defender of the Indians, whom the Spanish law classed as "*personas miserables*," with minors, women, lunatics, idiots, and paupers, and which office was now held by a corrupt tool of the *Encomenderos*, should be conferred on Carrera or some other trustworthy friend of the conquered race. The ordinances forbidding Indians to be transported in chains should be strictly enforced. The laws forbidding them the ownership and use of arms and horses, and all laws discriminating against them as to dress, property, and the comforts of life should be revoked. Forced labor in the factories and mines, or on public buildings, should be prohibited. All services rendered by the Indians should be voluntary, and should be paid for. Upon the acceptance of these conditions, by a solemn act of the Cabildo, Queen

Toa would co-operate with the Cabildo in the storming of the Palace. As the Indians were still unacquainted with the use of firearms, and in order to spare lives, she asked for the assistance of a few arquebusiers. The attack should be made this very night. With the aid of a few arquebusiers, Queen Toa would deliver the Palace and the Ministers into the hands of the Cabildo before the break of day. Upon the marriage of Toa to the future King of Quito, the Inca Treasure should be delivered to the new government for three purposes—1. To maintain the royal state; 2. To carry the war against Spain to a successful termination; and, 3. To indemnify the *Encomenderos* and the owners of Indian slaves for their losses by emancipation, and to reward the men of the Revolution for the services rendered to the cause of independence.

With this information, Sanchez returned to the Cabildo. He was to meet Cundurazu within the next two hours at the same place to acquaint him with the determination of the Municipality. But he was to come alone, and in case treachery should be attempted, he pledged himself, on the honor of a cavalier, to warn the counselors of Toa through Mariano or any other intelligent Indian.

The report of Robert Sanchez threw the Cabildo into a maze of doubts and perplexities, and again the discussion threatened to become endless. By this time, two parties had distinctly developed themselves. The one was the party of action, and favored bold and energetic measures. It adopted the full programme of Bellido, and soon became known by the name of *Bellidistas*. The other party had no programme of its own, but objected to all decisive and radical measures. It proposed nothing, but doubted everything. It claimed to be in favor of action, and yet it could not resolve to act. Its policy was to temporize and to await developments in a guarded attitude of defense. It became the party of hesitation, which was soon joined by all the secret friends of the King, and by all those who feared that the new dispensation would endanger their pecuniary interests. The nominal chief of this party was Londoño, while Paredes soon became, of course secretly and unknown to almost all its members, its real head. Openly, Paredes embraced the cause of the Bellidistas, and seemed to be one of its loudest and most determined advocates. The leaders of the party of action were Sanchez and Olmos. As these differences of opinion soon grew into bitter dissensions,.they divided the people of Quito against itself, and speedily weakened, and finally undermined and overthrew, the cause of the Revolution.

But let us return to our narrative. Where men will disagree in debate, events will turn the scale. The helpless discussions of the Cabildo, were interrupted by the arrival of a party of Municipal scouts, who had intercepted the Royal mail-carrier, a short distance from the city, on his way from the coast to the capital. His mail-bag was taken from him, and delivered to the Cabildo. That body at once determined to open it, and to examine its contents, among which were two documents of startling importance. The one was a dispatch from the Viceroy to the Audience of Quito, which contained the alarming information that a military expedition was in process of organization, under the command of old Pedro de Arana, to proceed by sea to Guayaquil, and thence by land to Quito. The preparations were nearly completed, and the vessel should sail in a few days. If upon his arrival at Guayaquil, Arana should learn that the city of Quito had submitted to the collection of the Alcabala, he was to return to Callao; if not, his orders were to proceed to Quito, and to increase his forces among the friends of law and order, in the towns on the road. He should have full power to arrest, try, and punish those who had rebelled against the King, as well as those who had given encouragement to the rebels, or had refused to assist in the suppression of the rebellion. His instructions were such that no man's life or property was secure at Quito. There was not a man in the assembly which, with breathless attention, listened to the reading of this ominous dispatch, who would not be at the mercy of the royal commissioner. And worst of all was the fact that Arana was a rich man, whom it would not be easy to bribe. Executions and confiscations, would be the order of the day, should the dreaded Spaniard who had graduated in the school of Alba, enter the capital of the ancient Shyris. Even submission and obedience would then be too late; and who would have dared to speak of submission now?

The other document was a letter from the son of the Marquis de Solando at Lima, to his father at Quito. It contained the announcement that the young gentleman would return to Quito on the staff of Arana. It also stated that the Viceroy had treated the writer with great kindness and condescension, and had informed him that in dispatches from the Court of Madrid, the Marquis had been spoken of in high terms, and mentioned as one who should be consulted as to the measures to be taken for the pacification of the colony, and the rewards or punishments of the leading men of Quito.

These documents at once secured the ascendancy of the party of action. They silenced, at least for the present, the voices of those who favored procrastination. The danger had become imminent, and not a day was to be lost. The attack on the Palace should be made, and the persons of the President, and the Auditors be secured, at once. Help must be accepted from whatever quarter it could be obtained. The Cabildo decided with a rush to accede to the demands of the Indians, for the time, which meant that many, if not most of those who voted to do so, did it with a mental reservation that all such concessions might be revoked, whenever it should become expedient or desirable hereafter. A series of ordinances were enacted, embodying the demands of Queen Toa into Municipal

Laws. The attack on the Palace, however, should not be left to the Indians alone. The majority of the Cabildo, entertained a very low opinion of Indian usefulness for military operations. Pedro de Guzman Ponce de Leon should be put in command of the Arquebusiers of the City, who were to keep up a fire from the porticos, and the neighboring houses, to drive the soldiers from the doors and windows of the Palace, while the Indians should make the attack in front, and on the south side. In the rear, Juan Castro's men were to renew their operations, which had nearly proved successful during the first attack. Roberto was dispatched to Queen Toa, to signify to her the acceptance of the Cabildo, and to act as her military adviser. At the expiration of two hours the attack should begin. The ringing of the Cathedral bell should be the signal.

In the meantime orders were given for the arrest and imprisonment of the Marquis de Solando. His house should be searched, and should he not be found there, detachments of mounted men were to proceed to his *haciendas* at Chillo and Tambillo, to seek for him there and bring him before the Cabildo. The estates of the Marquis were an inviting prize to his political enemies. Not only the Marquis, but all the other open adherents of Spain should suffer for their disloyalty to the popular cause.

CHAPTER IX.

A DOMICILIARY VISIT.

Paredes not being a member of the Cabildo, was not in the session chamber, but he was in the building, and soon learned that letters compromising the Marquis had been intercepted. He concluded at once that the arrest of the Marquis would be ordered by the Cabildo. It was of the utmost importance to warn him, if at his house, or to send a messenger ahead of the mounted men of the Cabildo, in case the old gentleman should be at one of his *haciendas* in the country. The house of the Marquis was guarded by Municipal Guards. These men would admit Paredes, he knew, but they would also inform the searching party of his visit, and this might cost him the confidence of the rebels, which he had won so skillfully and in the face of such difficulties. What should he do? There was but one way, and it was a desperate one. He would forestall the men of the Cabildo, and search the house on his own responsibility, with volunteers whom he would gather on the street. One line to Dolōres, which he would slip into her hand, one word which he might whisper to her, would answer his purpose. Fortunately, as he left the Municipality Building, he discovered his Mayordomo in the crowds around the main entrance. "Don Tomas," he said, taking him aside, "send for one of my fastest horses and let it be brought to the Plaza of Santa Clara. Have it in readiness there for yourself, and then follow me to the house of the Marquis de Solando. Be quick about it, Don Tomas! You have befriended me a thousand times, and I want your help now more than ever. You know I love Dolores Solando, and to win her I must save her father, no matter what he thinks of the Alcabala. Do you understand me, Don Tomas?"

"I do, master, and you may rely on me. I shall hasten to give the necessary orders."

"But be sure to be back in a few minutes. I must have you with me to warn the Señorita, and learn from her where her father is."

Don Tomas succeeded in giving his orders without a moment's delay, and rejoined his master before the latter had left the Great Square. The first group of armed men they met, Paredes addressed thus: "Señores! Letters implicating the Marquis de Solando have been intercepted by the men of the Cabildo. He is plotting the downfall of our cause, and must be made a prisoner. I have information, which I consider trustworthy, that he has returned to his house in disguise, in order to be near the scene of action. Will you come with me to search for him and to take him?"

"We will! We will!" clamored the men. "Down with the Marquis! Viva el Señor Paredes!" and to San Francisco marched the party, increasing in numbers and violence on the way.

Paredes felt sure that the Marquis was not at his house; but if he should be there, Paredes would manage not to find him. The old gentleman had several *haciendas* in the country, and it was necessary to know at which one he had taken refuge, so as not to lose time. If he could be given an hour's start of his pursuers he would be safe.

"Let a strong party go to the rear of the house to prevent his escape through the garden." commanded Paredes, thus considerably diminishing his followers. "Search all the out-houses, ranchos, and stables in the rear, and I shall take charge of the main building."

The Municipal Guards at the door at first denied them entrance, but when they were confronted by Paredes in the name of the city of Quito, they gave way and admitted as many as Paredes chose to let in. "Enough, my friends!" said the cunning Creole, "we must not terrify the ladies—it is the man we want;" and with a commanding gesture he ordered the Municipal Guards to stop further incursions.

"Now, my friends, search the lower part of the house. Quite likely he may be hidden in the quarters of the servants. A dozen of us will suffice to search the rooms above."

Nevertheless, a much larger number followed him upstairs, and it would have aroused suspicion to keep them back.

Dolores, pale as death, but composed and courageous, awaited them at the head of the main staircase. When she recognized Paredes, who had assumed the sternest possible look, she felt relieved.

"I regret, Señora," he began in a courteous, but hard and determined tone; "I regret that it has become my painful duty to arrest your father."

"My father has left the city," replied Dolores, likewise assuming an air of haughty determination.

"As in such cases it would be the duty of a daughter to conceal the truth, your Ladyship will pardon us for doubting your word. We must search the house!"

"Search it, then! I shall show you the way."

"As you please, Señora," said Paredes, with a deep bow and significant look, which she eagerly scanned, but was unable to interpret. But when he, as if by accident, touched his Mayordomo, who had pushed himself forward, she concluded that his look had an object, and that she must be on the *qui vive*. The party now entered the room next to the staircase, the lady leading the way. It was a sitting-room leading into the main *salon*. Aunt Catita was there, and gave a wild scream at the entrance of the armed men. This led some of the men to believe that the Marquis was really in the house, and they rushed forward, passing Dolores. By this time Don Tomas was at her side, and, unnoticed in the tumult and confusion which followed, whispered to her: "Where is your father, Señorita?" She looked at him, distrustfully, and then looked at Paredes, who had opened a large wardrobe, and stood back for some of his followers to search it. As he turned around and took in the situation, he gave a nod imperceptible to all but her. "I am his Mayordomo," whispered Don Tomas," and must warn your Ladyship's father!" Dolores moved away from him, but as she passed him, she whispered the word: "Tambillo!"

Three hours afterward the Marquis was on his way to

the coast. An hour later the mounted men of the Cabildo arrived at his *hacienda* at Tambillo, but the nest was empty—the bird had flown.

CHAPTER X.

HATUNTAQUI, THE GREAT DRUM OF WAR.

ARMED men were hurrying to and fro. The news that another attack should be made on the Palace had spread like wild-fire. The streets of Quito, usually so quiet and dark at night, were lurid with the blaze of torches. Torches were fastened to the balconies of the friends of the popular cause—and who would now have dared not to be its friend? And torch-bearers hurried to and fro, or stood around the groups of armed men stationed in the streets, and discussing, in eager suspense and anticipation, the event that was to come. Anxiously the multitudes awaited the ringing of the great Cathedral bell, which was to be the signal for the final attack. Wild rumors concerning the contemplated co-operation of the Indians were carried from group to group. The mysterious Indian Queen, hitherto a myth, was to become a reality to-night. Some even pretended to have seen her, dressed in a robe resplendent with gold and precious stones. Still, but few Indians were to be seen, and the wiseacres shook their heads incredulously. All at once, a deep, hollow, but penetrating sound, like the noise of a volcanic explosion, was heard, and startled everybody. No one had heard such an unearthly sound before. Another soon followed, and still another, and each could be heard all over the city. At the same time the streets filled with Indians. Every house vomited them forth. From every rancho they emerged. Out of the lanes and ravines which ran through the town and were not then arched over and hidden from public view, as now, the Indians issued forth, uttering deep, gutteral, and unintelligible exclamations. They were armed with clubs, knives, pikes; with anything they could lay hands on, and those who had no weapons carried stones in their ponchos, ready to sling them at their enemies. It seemed unaccountable where they had all come from in so short a time. The Plaza of San Francisco and the street leading from it to the Great Square were soon filled with them. The mysterious and terrific detonations, which so puzzled the Creoles, became louder and more unearthly as they approached the Great Square. Some of the whites at last interrogated the Indians as to those unearthly sounds. "Hatuntaqui! Hatuntaqui!" was the reply.

"Hatuntaqui," in the Quichua language, means "the great drum of war." And it was one of the great drums of war that, carefully hidden away, had survived the Spanish conquest, and was now brought forth once more to rally the children of the sun to deadly combat. They did not know whom they were to be led against, and whose cause they were to espouse, and they did not care. They knew that their Shyri Queen was among them, and that she had commanded the great drum of war to be brought forth from its hiding-place, and that was enough. But very few of those Indians had heard the sound of the great drum, because nearly two generations had passed away since it was beaten last under the banners of the terrible Rumiñagui, the face of stone; but they knew it by tradidition. They had had heard their fathers and their mothers and their grandfathers and grandmothers tell of the miraculous power of those great drums, the sound of which could be heard at the distance of many miles. And they knew that when that drum was sounded every male Indian must come forth and follow it to battle. It was the sound of resurrection to their ears. What they heard as a tradition in the misery of their lowly cottages had become a reality. The *Hatuntaqui* was beaten again, and the Indians followed it as in the days of Atahualpa; followed it, as if sixty years of slavery and suffering had not intervened; followed it, as if there had been no Spanish conquest; followed it, as if it were an old familiar sound which they had heard but yesterday. And as the large and unwieldy contrivance came in sight at last, borne on the shoulders of two powerful Indians, and beaten by a third, they wildly brandished their worthless weapons, and shouted: "Hatuntaqui! Hatuntaqui!"

As yet the sea of Indian heads had no direction, but waved to and fro in apparent aimlessness. Their generals had not yet appeared upon the scene. But the suspense was of short duration. A very old man, dressed in a white alpaca robe, in which we have seen him already, and with a weapon of bronze in his hand, appeared among them. Few knew him, although many had seen him in the Church of San Francisco, when Queen Toa showed herself to her people. But whether they knew him or not, they knew that he was a man of authority, and unhesitatingly they intended to follow him. They knew by the traditions of their race that he wore the garb of a great Indian Prince, who would, by rights, be their general. It soon became known that he was the mighty Curaca Cundurazu, who, in the days of Atahualpa, had defeated the treacherous Cañares in many a bloody conflict. He must be ninety or a hundred years old; but he appeared to them as the impersonation of all the glories of the past, and they received him with joyful acclamations. He commanded silence by a wave of his hand, and swinging himself on the shoulders of two men, who proudly supported him, he said:

"Children, the Kingdom of the Shyri Incas will come again. Did you think that the *Hatuntaqui* was broken, and that its sounds should be heard no more? There it is again! Do you see the great drum of war? Do you hear its mighty sounds? Do you know what it means?"

"*Hatuntaqui! Hatuntaqui!*" shouted thousands of voices.

"I am Cundurazu, the Curaca of Purruhá, a descendant of its ancient rulers, the great kings, through whom the house of Duchicela, by marriage, united with Toa Caran, the only daughter of the Shyri of Quito. I have led your grandfathers to battle, and I shall lead their grandchildren to-night. I saved the life of Autachi, the son of Atahualpa, the father of Queen Toa, and brought him up to reign over you in secret. I watched over his child Toa, and with the aid of our father, the Sun, and your strong arms, and with the assistance of friendly Viracochas, I shall restore her to the throne of the Shyris. Behold her—there she comes!"

A palanquin, borne on the shoulders of four Indians, now appeared in the Plaza of San Francisco, and turned into the street leading to the Great Square. Toa, dressed in the robes of the Incas, sat in it on an elevated seat, and by her side, on a powerful steed, rode Roberto Sanchez, hat in hand. Her forehead was encircled with the great diadem of the Shyris, distinguished by the immensity of its brilliant emerald. A girdle in the shape of a serpent, studded with precious stones, encircled her waist, and in her right hand she held a staff, to which the golden image of the Sun was fastened. The Indians threw themselves on their knees, and stretched out their arms to the one being who was dearer to them than life. Toa rose from her seat, and commanded them to rise likewise, which they did with enthusiastic acclamations.

"Children of Quito, Purruhá, and Caranqui!" she said. "You all know Toa Duchicela, the daughter of Autachi, the son of Atabualpa. She has come to restore the empire of her fathers. The good Viracochas will help her. The bad Viracochas must be overthrown. The men of the Palace are our oppressors, as they are the oppressors of our Viracocha friends. When the Cathedral bell shall ring, the Palace must be taken by you, my children. The friendly

Viracochas will help you. The false rulers in the Palace must be made prisoners, and delivered to our Viracocha friends. The venerable Curaca of Purruhá, the greatest of the surviving heroes of our race, will lead you; and Toa Duchicela, the Shyri Inca, will behold, with her own eyes, the valor of her people. Our Viracocha friends have doubted your heroism, because they never heard the sound of the Hatuntaqui, which rallies the children of the Sun to victory. The great Coya-Priestess, whom the people call Mama Rucu, has prophesied that our empire will rise again, and that a union will be made between our people and the friendly Viracochas, as the Kingdom of Purruhá was once united to the Empire of Quito."

With these words she turned to Roberto Sanchez: "And now, my friend, take my place for an instant, and let me have your horse. My people are not trained to understand the art of words; it is a symbol which they must see."

Roberto was wild with excitement, and thrilled with enthusiasm. He helped Toa from her palanquin, and lifted her on his horse. For a moment he hesitated to take her place, but a look from her reassured him, and he ascended her throne. Immediately she held out her hand to him, and hand in hand they remained for a few seconds, during which the air rang with acclamations: "Hail to the great Viracocha! Hail to the Viracocha Shyri! Hail to the Inca Viracocha!"

Toa then rode through square and street up to the very front of the Palace, so as to let all her followers see that she was there. After this she slowly returned through the dense multitude and, dismounting, resumed her seat on the throne, while Roberto Sanchez remounted his horse.

And now the great bell of the Cathedral rang loudly and rapidly through the lurid night. The signal was given. The struggle was to commence. True to the agreement, the Arquebusiers of the Municipality opened fire on the soldiers in the doors and windows of the Palace, and one of the first victims was young Guzman de Tapia, the aid of Valverde, who stood leaning over the barricade at the main entrance, gazing with blank astonishment at the proceedings of the Indians, which, to him, were unintelligible.

Cundurazu brandished his weapon, and vainly endeavoring to press forward through the living wall of his followers, shouted: "Beat the Hatuntaqui! Forward to the Palace! Let the cry be Toa Duchicela!" And with the swiftness of the mountain-current, the living wave rolled into the Great Square, and up to the entrances of the Palace. The garrison opened a heavy fire on the assailants. The field-pieces belched forth destructive thunder and mowed down the foremost ranks of the Indians. But the places of those who fell were immediately filled up by the masses behind them, who pushed forward with irresistible impetuosity, seeming to court death under the eyes of their Queen. There was no panic, no stampede, no wavering, no turning back. Before the guns could be reloaded, the Indians had overrun the Esplanade, broken through the barricade, poured through the main entrance, bore down the soldiers by the mere weight of numbers, ever increasing, and ever pushing on, and soon filled the Palace court, its lower halls and corridors. The assault was successful before it had fairly begun. And during all this time, the bell of the Cathedral was kept ringing, and the terrific Hatuntaqui, like the thunders of Mt. Cotopaxi, boomed through the night.

CHAPTER XI.

THE CURSE OF MAMA RUCU.

Of the preparations and events described in the foregoing chapters, nothing was known in the Convent of La Merced. About five or ten minutes before the great bell of the Cathedral gave the preconcerted signal for the attack, a solemn procession issued from the Church of the Mercedarios, and slowly moved toward the Palace. Friars bearing torches or censers preceded it, and were followed by four *mestizos*, carrying a Baldachin, under which the Superior walked, holding in his hands the holy Eucharist, or, as the Creoles called it, "La Magestad." The ringing of a small bell announced the progress of the procession.

Wherever it appeared, the people fell on their knees, uncovering their heads, and reverentially allowing it to pass. It had already advanced one square from the church, when it met with an unexpected obstacle. Juan Castro and some of his men were kneeling in the center of the street, obstructing the passage of the procession. About half a square behind them, in the direction of the Palace, was a multitude of armed and unarmed men. The procession itself was completely surrounded by men on their knees.

"Most reverend Father," began Juan Castro, with his head bowed low, "whither do you intend to go?"

"Clear the way, children!" commanded the Superior. "Do you dare obstruct the passage of the Lord's Majesty?"

"Most reverend Father," continued Juan Castro, "your life will be in danger if you proceed an inch farther. Firing will commence in a few minutes, and I do not wish a hair on your holy head to be harmed."

"Out of the way, man!" resumed the Superior. "We carry the most holy sacrament to the dying Christians of the Palace, as we have administered it to the Christians outside. Cursed be he who stops the progress of this sacred procession!"

"Father!" replied Castro most reverentially and bowing his head still lower, "far be it from me to stop the progress of your Reverence. With my own body I shall protect you. But it is your own safety, Most Reverend Father, and the safety of the holy men who are with you, for which I am alarmed. Let me warn you, Most Reverend Father, not to proceed any further—at least, not now. The signal for the attack may be given at any moment and it will provoke the fire of the garrison."

"Your solicitude, my son," said the Superior, "is commendable; but your zeal exceeds your discretion. There is no fighting now, and there will be none in the presence of the *Magestad*. Give room, children; the Lord is with us and will protect us."

"I have warned you, Father," answered Castro, reluctantly preparing to obey, "and having done my duty, I shall submit to your commands. Room for the Lord's Majesty! Give way for the most holy sacrament!"

But at this moment, the great bell of the Cathedral gave the expected signal, and the firing instantly commenced and was vigorously replied to by the garrison. The multitude behind Castro, nearer to the Palace than the procession, broke and fled to escape from the deadly missiles of the besieged. Great as the reverence of the people was for a procession with the Eucharist, the instinct of self-preservation overcame all other considerations. A panic knows no laws, human or divine, and onward came the rush of fugitives bearing down everything in its way. Juan Castro and his men, who had been kneeling, were on their feet in an instant, and in the next minute the rabble and the sacred procession were one inextricable mass of confusion, pressing back toward the Church and away from the Palace. Not until they were out of the range of the arquebuses of friends and foes, could the current be stemmed. The monks and their ministrants had been lifted off their feet by the pressure of terror-stricken human beings around them, and were swept along by the irresistible wave of men, running for their lives. Several of the monks were thrown down and trampled upon. The Baldachin under which the Superior had marched was overthrown and fell, and was soon torn to pieces by the throng. The friars were separated from each other in an instant. Some were pressed against the walls of houses. Others were swept onward, and those who had been overrun vainly endeavored to rise to their feet, new fugitives stumbling over them and keeping them down.

At last the stentorian voice of Juan Castro rose above the din, while his herculean arms endeavored to restore order, and to check the panic.

"Stand, ye cowards!" he shouted. "Stand! Let the hares run, but let the men rally! We must press on to our charge!" And as if to rally the men, he took a position at the entrance of the Square before the Church, casting fierce glances at every white robe he could discern. "Help the Reverend Fathers! Draw them out of the crowd. Do not trample upon them, ye brutes. Have you no respect for the ministers of religion, in your abject cowardice? There!" he screamed, rushing to the relief of one of the friars, whose robe was tearing under the feet of those tumbling about him, while he anxiously attempted to raise himself on his knees.

As Castro lifted him up, the monk tried to draw his hood, which had fallen on his neck, back over his head and face, in order to conceal his features. But it was too late. The eye of hate had recognized him. It was Count Valverde.

"A most holy man!" yelled Castro, tearing the hood

from his captive's gown, and holding his arms in an iron grip. "Come to me, men of Quito! Quick!"

Powerful as the ruffian was, Count Valverde shook him off with the strength of despair, and made a rush in the direction of the church. But Castro immediately caught him again, and a fierce struggle followed, which terrified and amazed the beholders. Juan Castro had dared to lay hands on a holy man. A few seconds more, and the wrath of the populace would have turned against the perpetrator of such a sacrilege. But the face and beard of the man with whom he struggled were not those of a monk. The crown of his head was without the shaven mark of priesthood. "It is the Spanish commander!" yelled Castro. "Do you not see his face, ye brutes? It is the assassin of Bellido, the murderer of our brothers!"

That was enough; and a dozen strong men seized the unfortunate Count, mocking all further resistance.

"Off with the robe which he has shamelessly desecrated!" commanded the leader of the populace. And in an instant the priestly robe was torn from the shoulders of the Count.

"Give him a coat of pitch!" yelled Castro. "Black will become his crimes better than the color of holiness and innocence."

During all this time, the firing was kept up around the Palace, the detonations of the Hatuntaqui rose above the reports of musketry, and the Cathedral bell rang the death-knell of the ill-fated captive.

The tumult, the noise, and the confusion were so great, that it was impossible to notice, in one part of the square and streets, what happened in another. The Friars of Mercy rushed back to their Church, as soon as they had extricated themselves from the crowds. Some were carried back by the men who had lifted them up from the stone pavements. The Superior, clinging to the Eucharist, was one of the last to re-enter the holy edifice; but even he had not seen the event which we have just described; and not until all his brethren had returned and gathered around him, he found that the Count was missing. Again he left the church, to find and save his countryman; but the shouts of hatred and revenge were suddenly drowned by the louder shouts of victory, which arose around the Palace. The tide of humanity now turned back to the Palace, and the anxious priest was seized by a wild vortex which would have swept him along helplessly, had he not, with an effort, broken away from the current, and slowly and despondingly returned to his church.

"Let us pray, my brethren!" he said, overcome with agitation and solicitude. "Let us pray! Let us pray for the Christian cavalier, whose soul will, at this moment, be summoned to appear before the Lord of Hosts!"

Count Valverde, in the meantime, had been dragged away toward the place where the torches were making. What was the attack on the Palace to Juan Castro now? He had other work to do. The man who, as he thought, had doomed him to death, was in his power, and Juan Castro never forgave. Joaquin Valverde's last hour had arrrived, and he knew it. The curse of the Dutch commander's wife, and the predictions of Mama Rucu were to be fulfilled. His only prayer now was, that the fearful agony might be short.

The cry, "They have taken the Spanish commander," was carried on wings of lightning from group to group, and was answered with the fiercest shouts of triumph and revenge. "Death to the assassin of Bellido! Death to the author of the great slaughter! Kill him! Tear him to pieces! Burn him! Burn him!"

Count Valverde commended his soul to God. He knew that no human power could save him, and, brave as he was, he trembled at the approaching doom. Deathly pale, his garments torn from his body, his face and bare breast covered with blood, he was exposed to the indignities of the exulting fiends around him. They tore handfuls of hair out of his beard; they pulled him by his moustache; they spat in his face, and kicked him in the back; they struck him over the head with their torches; they beat him and pulled him until he was no longer able to maintain himself on his feet. At last the mob and its victim had reached the place where a large quantity of pitch had been collected, from which that night's great demand for torches had been supplied. The fiends now stripped the Count of the tattered remnants of his clothes, and covered him with a thick coat of pitch, as the Romans under Nero are said to have done to the early Christians.

"A chain! A chain!" clamored some of the ringleaders. And a chain was brought and drawn around the body of Valverde, under his arms. The other end of the chain was then fastened to a strong hook in a blind wall inclosing an orchard or garden.

And now the Christian knight, who for many a year had fought for the extermination of heretics, under the Prince of Parma, was doomed himself to die the death of a heretic. Another instant of intense suspense and futile hope, a last look up and down the street, vainly endeavoring to descry the approach of rescuers from somewhere, a last silent and fervent appeal to the Mother of Christ, and the coat of pitch, in which they had enwrapped him, was ablaze, and wild shrieks, which even this strong and determined man could not repress, announced the fulfillment of the terrible prophecy, that "biting fire should lick the skin from his flesh, and the flesh from his bones." He could not throw himself on the ground, as the shortness of the chain prevented it; but by pressing and rubbing his body against the wall, he instinctively endeavored to put out the flames. But these convulsive attempts only protracted his sufferings.

And the fiends danced around him, shouting, sneering, howling, rejoicing. Their numbers increased as the agony of the victim progressed. Indians, too, fresh from their victory at the Palace, infuriated by the struggle, and by the sacrifices it had entailed, now joined the mocking crowds. To the subjects of Queen Toa, the dying man was not the accidental representative of continuous authority, but the impersonation of the Spanish conquest, the embodiment of the foreign power, by which their fathers had been enslaved. And in the mistaken idea that his death, together with the victory of to-night, would terminate their subjugation, they danced around the dying Spaniard, shouting the monotonous and half-forgotten war-songs of their race. Valverde's death was to them the confirmation of all their hopes. Had not the great Coya-Priestess, whom the Viracochas called Mama Rucu, predicted it? And had she not also predicted the restoration of the Shyri-Inca Empire? And was not the literal fulfillment of the one prediction, proof and guaranty of the speedy verification of the other?

There was not a friendly eye to look upon the unspeakable sufferings of Valverde. None but infuriated enemies witnessed the murderous sacrifice. He saw them but for an instant, after the pitch had been set on fire; for the flames at once deprived him of his eye-sight; but he heard their yells and imprecations, as long as there was a remnant of life in his quivering, hissing, roasting body. His shrieks gradually changed into moans, his moans into sighs; then there was an end to all sounds, and only the convulsive motions of his limbs betokened that life had not been quite expelled. But even these convulsions ceased, and nothing but an unsightly mass of charred and steaming remains, was left of what, but a few hours ago, was the noble person of the commander, who had held the Palace for his master, the King of Spain. And not a voice was heard to say: "May the Lord have mercy on his soul."

The rest is easily told. It was with some difficulty that the wretched Auditors were prevailed upon to come forth from their hiding places, and to surrender to the representatives of the Cabildo. Their joy upon learning that their lives were to be spared, was equaled only by their fears before. They laughed and wept, and chattered promiscuously, and promised acquiescence in anything the Cabildo might see fit to ordain. They would suspend the collection of the Alcabala, and order back the troops that were coming from Lima. They would co-operate with the Cabildo for the purpose of inducing the Home Government to yield. They were as obsequious now as they had been harsh and tyrannical a few days before.

BOOK IV.
THE REACTION.

"Y quando estaua ya, segun barrunto,
Un falso Rey no léjos de elejirse.
La fuerza del tronido fue de modo,
Que presto se dexó deshecho todo."

PEDRO DE OÑA, *El Arauco Domado,*
Canto XVI, p. 280.

BOOK IV.

THE REACTION.

CHAPTER I.

MORNING.

The first rays of the rising sun were gilding the tops of Mt. Pichincha, when a weary traveler, mounted on a sorry jade, slowly passed the chapel of *Señor del Buen Viage*, at the southern entrance of the city. He seemed to be asleep, or at least struggling with sleep, for he nodded and reeled in the saddle, and came very near falling off, when his horse suddenly stopped in front of a dram-shop well known to travelers and their beasts—the *tienda* of Doña Mariquita, the mother of Juan Castro.

Without taking the trouble of tying his horse, which showed no disposition to go farther than compelled to go, the traveler, who was covered with ponchos, and had his face and neck still wrapped up against the cold air of the night, entered the shop, the door of which stood open. He looked around, but there was nobody inside. Female voices, however, were heard in the court outside, one of which—a most melodious voice—seemed to be struggling with sobs. The stranger began to divest himself of such of his garments as had become superfluous since sunrise, then stretched his weary limbs, and, drawing near the back door, endeavored to catch the conversation outside.

"Yes, Mother," said the voice of Mercedes, "hand in hand they stood before all the people, he occupying her throne, and she mounted on his horse. He is lost to me forever. They say she is beautiful, that Indian Queen, and possesses the treasure of the Incas. Her love will make him the richest and greatest man in the country, and he will never return to me."

"Well, child," answered Doña Mariquita, "if she blesses him with her treasures, he will be enabled to provide for you and your child as becomes the richest man in the country. You ought to congratulate yourself on his good luck."

"How can you talk so, Mother? Did you ever know what love is? What would wealth be to me if I had to lose him?"

"I know what love is, Mercedes, and for this reason I know that it can not last. There is an end to all things, and nothing ends so suddenly as a man's love. Lose him you must, sooner or later, and it is better to lose him when he can shower wealth into your lap, than to be discharged by him with a miserable pittance or a scanty allowance, which he will cut off on his marriage to some Señora. Do not be a fool, child! You are still young and beautiful, and many a caballero would give a small fortune to possess the Flower of Machángara. As to your Don Roberto, leave him to me. You shall not suffer from his neglect or desertion, if these reports are true. But I do not believe half of them. Who ever heard the like before? I have seen more wars and revolutions in my day than you will ever live to see, but I never heard such things before. But hold! There is a customer in the shop. Go to your room, Merceditas, and let us think of breakfast. Where is that little huzzy, Panchita! To run away and leave the shop without telling me!"

The tears of Mercedes flowed on as she sat on the stone bench in the court of the house and pondered over the news she had heard. What was this Revolution to her? What did she care for the *Alcabala*, or the rights of the colonists? Even the death of Valverde and the many victims of last night's bloody work failed to touch her sympathetic heart. There was a sight more terrible to her mind's eye than all the scenes of slaughter. It was Roberto Sanchez, her own Roberto, the father of the child which she carried under her heart, seated upon the throne of that Indian witch and heathenish imposter, while she was mounted on Roberto's horse, holding him by the hand and leading him on to perdition. This whole Revolution was now a tissue of wickedness in the eyes of Mercedes. It was begotten in crime, and could only lead to destruction. Why should these men rise against their master, the King of Spain, the Lord's anointed, and against the Ministers to whom he had intrusted the government of the colony? Such treason was a crime and a sin, and men engaged in these nefarious doings would not shrink from breaking vows and breaking hearts. Their patron-saints would abandon them to the wiles of Indian witchcraft. Their cause was doomed, and they were doomed in this world and the next. Oh, if she could but save her Roberto, and draw him back from the fearful abyss into which he was about to plunge!

* * * * * * *

"Is it you, Don Tomas, so early in the morning?" said Doña Mariquita. "Good morning to you, *Compadre*. Where do you come from?"

"From my master's *hacienda* at Chillogallo. Give me an *agua gloriada*,* my dear *Commadre*. This must have been a horrible night here in Quito."

"Horrible, *Compadre*! Most horrible! Have you heard of it already?"

"Reports came to us at three o'clock in the morning, but they were greatly mixed, and wonderfully incredible."

And while he was sipping his *agua gloriada*, Doña Mariquita entertained him with a most inaccurate, distorted, and exaggerated account of the events of last night.

---
* Hot water with sugar boiled in it, and a strong addition of rum.

"I can hardly trust my ears, *Commadre!* If there was such bloody work, I must hurry to see whether any harm has befallen my master. *Adios, Commadre!* And with these words Don Tomas paid for his dram, and after giving Doña Mariquita the customary Spanish embrace, he remounted his horse, and repaired, as fast as it was possible with such a jade, to the city residence of Don Manuel Paredes.

Paredes had just returned home. Great as his powers of endurance were, he required rest after the terrible tension and excitement of last night. His schemes thus far had met with unexpected success. He had not failed in anything, and even blind luck or chance seemed to have declared in his favor. If he had planned and shaped the events of yesterday, he could not have shaped them more advantageous to his purposes. In less than twenty-four hours, he had made himself the most popular man of Quito; one of his most dangerous rivals was out of the way; he had saved the Marquis, and thus secured an indisputable claim on the daughter's gratitude; the lives of the Ministers had been spared, and now he had but to play his cards properly, and he might be appointed commander of the armed forces in place of the unfortunate Bellido, or at least name his successor. The latter seemed to be the safer course to the discerning mind of Paredes, because it would not expose him to the revenge of those, whom, as commander, he would have to betray. It would be better to assign this part of his task to other hands, and if he was not very much mistaken, Don Pedro Guzman Ponce de Leon, was the man for it. His military experience entitled him to be first named in this connection. Moreover, he was an *Encomendero*, who had great pecuniary interests at stake. He was in debt, and would want money. He belonged to the party of procrastination, which would soon develope into the party of reaction; and he was a man without strong opinions, and not burdened with scruples or convictions. Don Manuel would sound this man, and prepare the way for his appointment, if he proved practicable. Such were the thoughts of Paredes, as he returned home, long after the taking of the Palace, for a few hours of rest. He had not yet reached his couch, when his Mayordomo burst into the room.

"The Virgin be praised, Don Tomas. I see success in your eyes."

"Yes, your Grace, the Marquis is on his way to the coast. He would surely have been caught, if we had not warned him."

"Let me embrace you, Don Tomas, and rest assured of my eternal gratitude."

"He sends his best love to your Grace. He swore that he would never forget how much he owed to your Lordship. He wanted to write a note to his daughter, but I would not let him. I insisted that every minute was precious, and so he just dashed these lines on a piece of paper, before he mounted, and told me to give it to Señorita."

Paredes took the paper which the Mayordomo had handed to him. It contained these words: "Take my place under the Royal Commission and confer with Don Manuel Paredes, as to whom I absolve you from all obligations of secrecy. Your loving father."

CHAPTER II.

THE SECRET OF DOLORES SOLANDO.

THE guards had been withdrawn from the house of the Marquis. With the dawn of day they had been ordered off. A litter, carried by four men and followed by servants, both male and female, moved out of the door in the direction of the neighboring Plaza of Santa Clara, as Don Tomas drew near the house. The Marchioness, partly of her own volition, and partly following the advice of her daughter, had determined to take refuge in the Nunnery of Santa Clara. Her health, would probably not have resisted another shock such as the intrusion into her house of an armed mob, searching for her husband. She would stay at the convent until the storm had blown over. Doña Catita accompanied her on foot to see her properly installed, and then to return to the mansion-house, which Dolores refused to leave. Doña Catita would have preferred the security of the Convent, but, as her niece insisted on remaining at the house, come what may, Aunt Catita considered it her duty not to leave her entirely alone. But she had exacted a promise from Dolores, that at the first symptoms of a new outbreak, they should join the Marchioness at the Convent.

It had been a trying night to Dolores; a night that had made her older in mind, and colder at heart. The news of the death of Valverde had struck her dumb. Speechless she had listened to the tale of horror, which she learned shortly after the occurrence, from one of the Cabildo-men detailed to guard her house. At first, she seemed incapable of comprehending him, and not until he had repeated his story, she realized what it meant. She beckoned him to depart, and then sat motionless and brooding for a long while. But she shed no tears. Aunt Catita, who was with her, respected her silence, and waited to be spoken to. Dolores had buried a hope, and she keenly felt the disappointment. A few days before his death, he had asked for her hand, and she had promised to consider his offer. Supported by the favor of the Viceroy, he would make a fortune in the Colonies, would make her a real countess, and take her with him to Spain, where she might have dazzled the Court with her wit and brilliancy. And now that hope was destroyed; and the horizon of her existence would probably remain forever bounded by the impassable mountains of Quito. But this was not all. It had become a dreadful certainty to her that a fatality hung over her, which she could not avert, and that the course of her life was influenced by a dark and mysterious power, the decrees of which could not be resisted. "Aunt Catita," she said, after a long pause, folding herself closely in her shawl, for the coldness of the night began to be felt in the room, which, like all the houses of Quito, was without a stove or fireplace, " will you not go to bed?"

" Who can go to bed amidst such horrors, my child?"

" Your health will suffer, Auntie. You have suffered such a fright during the evening, and now this new horror; you must be cold as ice. Go to bed, Auntie, and warm yourself."

" The poor Count!" said Doña Catita. " What a brave gentleman he was. And to think of it; but two days ago, he was here full of hope and promise, and full of love for you. Now he is dead. And such a horrible death!"

"My love is death, Aunt Catita," said Dolores, coldly, "Do you remember how my husband was brought into this house; nay, into this very room?"

" Remember? How in the name of the Virgin could I ever forget it?"

"Well, he *was* my husband. The Count *might* have been my husband. I confess to you that I frequently thought of him as my husband—and behold his end! There is a dark power over me, Aunt Catita, which I must not provoke. If I do marry, I must not marry the man I love, and I must not love the man I marry."

" I do not understand you, Doloritas. You talk wildly."

" Do I, Auntie? This is news to me. No, Auntie, I am clearly aware of what I say, and I mean it. If you knew what I know, you would not say that I talk wildly."

" You alarm me, child. What do you mean?"

" I mean what I have never told a living soul before,"

she said solemnly, "except my confessor, who said I should not fear as long as I remained worthy of invoking the aid of the Virgin and the Saints against the powers of darkness."

"For Heaven's sake, Doloritas, explain youself. You make me tremble from head to foot." And pale, and shivering, Doña Catita approached her niece, and took both her hands in hers. "O what a frightful night this is! There! Do you hear?"

"I hear nothing, Auntie. Compose yourself. They have taken the Palace, and the bloody work seems to be over."

"Yes, but there are things to fear, other than murder and bloodshed, and you have made me fear for you."

"Not for me, Auntie. It is not I for whom there is cause to fear, but for the man I should marry, or wish to marry."

"O tell me what you mean!" And kneeling by her niece's side, she threw her arms around her, and nestling to her, expectantly hung upon her lips.

"I do not know whether I do right in telling you; and surely I should not have told you, had it not been for the horrors of this night. Listen! Many, many years ago—I was a very young girl, almost a child, then—I took a walk or rather a romp with a whole bevy of girls, followed by their Indian maids up the mountain. Panchita Olmos, Carmen Aguirre, Mariquita Remos, Conchita Valdez, and others were of the party. We had bathed in the Cantera, and to get warm again, we dashed up the hill, ran races on the plateau, and acted so wildly and improperly, that we should have been dreadfully ashamed of ourselves, if anybody had seen us. But you know the mountain is always lonely, and so nothing happened to disturb our merrymaking, until we found ourselves unexpectedly, almost in front of Mama Rucu's cottage."

Aunt Catita gave a start, and nestled more closely to her

niece. The elder lady at this moment was the picture of trepidation, which strangely contrasted with the quiet repose and imperturbable self-possession of Dolores.

"A bantering discussion soon arose, as to which of us would have the courage, to have her fortune told. I believe if we had all gone together, there would have been no talk of fear. But Carmen Aguirre said she would not enter that cottage alone for the world. To this Panchita Olmos replied (I remember the conversation as if it had been yesterday), that that was quite natural, as no white woman would dare to enter that cottage alone. I then told them not to be too sure of that; for I knew one who would. At this there was a general laugh, and Panchita called me a braggadocio, and dared me to verify my words. Now, you know, Auntie, dear, if I have a weakness, it consists in a perhaps unfeminine desire to show that I am not afraid."

"Yes; and it will be the death of you some day, if you persist in it. You might have been killed this morning, when you insisted on keeping the shutter open and looking out, while they were throwing stones at our windows. But proceed, my darling!"

"I accepted the challenge at once, and said I would go. The girls did not believe it: and so I told them that not I, but probably they would be the cowards, and run away while I was inside. If they had any sense of honor, they would wait for me. And with these words I started to go. Had the girls really thought that I intended to go in, they would have stopped me; but as they expected I would turn back at the door, they allowed me to proceed. I must confess, Auntie, that I felt very faint, when I came close to the old witch's hut; but I should have died rather than retrace my steps. As soon as the girls saw that I was in earnest, they became frightened, and called me back, nay begged me to come back; but I merely courtesied to them, and entered the hut."

"Holy Virgin protect us!" exclaimed Aunt Catita, crossing herself. "How could you, my child?"

"At first I saw little or nothing, but when my eyes had become reconciled to the smoke and darkness inside, I saw Mama Rucu. She stood before a kettle boiling over a fire of aromatic woods. In one hand she held a calabash which she filled from the kettle. Her other hand rested on her stick or crutch. Her back was turned to me. She could not have seen or heard me, for I had entered noiselessly. Yet she knew I was there."

"Santa Maria!" interposed Doña Catita, shivering by her niece's side.

"At first she did not turn around, but said in Quichua: 'Young blood! Young blood! But cold blood! cold blood! Will draw blood, will draw blood!' Not knowing that these words were intended for me, I stood irresolute, whether to make my presence known, or whether to turn back. But my courage soon wilted, and I decided to leave unobserved, when to my amazement, the old woman, still without turning her face to me, said: 'Stay! Thou hast come to have thy fortune told. Wait till I give thee the clue to thy future, as I see it now.' And then she turned around. Auntie, it was horrible to have those burning, piercing, rolling eyes on me. I felt as if I should faint, but she pointed her crutch at me, and it seemed to uphold me, as if by some magic power. 'Young woman!' she said, 'Death is in thy hand; not to thee, but to him to whom thou givest it in marriage. Even thy thought of marriage is death to him whom—'"

At this juncture Aunt Catita fell into an hysteric fit, and with a wild scream, followed by sobs and tears and laughter, dropped on the floor. The excitement and horrors of the last twenty-four hours had momentarily overpowered her. Dolores called in her attendants, and with their aid soon restored her aunt to consciousness, but the thread of the narrative was not resumed that night.

And now the night has worn away at last; the sun has arisen; Doña Catita has accompanied the Marchioness to the Convent, and the Mayordomo of Manuel Paredes presents himself to Dolores, and receives the generous thanks of the daughter, whose father he has saved.

CHAPTER III.

HOW THE NEWS WAS RECEIVED.

On the very day when the Cabildo of Guayaquil on the coast, was about to make official proclamation of its adherence to the policy of resistance inagurated at Quito, the movement was nipped in the bud, by the arrival of Don Pedro de Arana, whom the Viceroy had sent to enforce obedience to the royal decrees in the ancient Kingdom of Quito. Arana came with an armed force, small in numbers, but well equipped, and sufficient to overawe the malcontents at Guayaquil. He had arrived in the nick of time. He was informed at once of what had been projected. There was an abundance of informers. The loudest rebels of yesterday endeavored to exculpate themselves by informing on their accomplices. But Arana was too prudent to alarm the whole kingdom by punishing mere intentions. He accorded to every one a most gracious reception. He seemed to be perfectly deaf to all evil reports. He acted as if nothing at all had happened. He took it for granted that the people among whom he had arrived, were indisputably loyal. He judged everyone by his own professions, and thus he saved Guayaquil, and with it his base of operations. His force was so small, that he could not afford to turn men into enemies, whom he expected to enlist as his friends. His policy succeeeded admirably. The men who would have drawn their swords against him two or three days ago, proclaimed their anxious readiness to serve under his command.

A few days after the arrival of Arana, the Marquis de Solando arrived at Guayaquil, and by his high title and the fame of his great wealth, gave tone and encouragement to the Royalist cause. Yet it was no child's play to crush the rebellion. With the whole interior of the country in arms, protected by the wretchedness of its roads and by almost inaccessible mountain-passes, which a few men might defend against a whole army, policy, negotiations, intrigue, bribery, promises, and diplomacy would be more effective than a military campaign.

*   *   *   *   *   *   *   *

Still worse than at Guayaquil, the popular cause fared in the towns of Peru proper, south of the river Tumbez, and outside of the Kingdom of Quito. The Viceroy's hands fell heavily on those who meditated resistance. At Callao, the port of Lima, the spirit of disaffection had spread to the fleet. But the Viceroy seized some of the officers and leading citizens and ordered their immediate execution. Men were executed at Cuzco, Arequipa, La Paz, and other towns, without trial or any of the formalities of civil or military law. The spirit of disobedience was crushed before it had time to grow. Terror stricken, the Peruvian colonists banished all thoughts of resisting the collection of the Alcabala. The rebellion, thus far, was confined to the city of Quito; yet, if it should spread to the towns between Quito and Guayaquil, and if it should prove successful there, an outbreak in Peru would become inevitable. On the defeat of the rebels at Quito, therefore, depended the maintenance of arbitrary government in the Viceroyalty. Thus every eye turned to the Capital of the ancient Shyris, where the fate of those rights and privileges was to be decided which had been stamped out in Spain, under King Philip's father, on the bloody field of Villalar.

*   *   *   *   *   *   *   *

And how was the news received at Puembo, where Carrera watched at the bedside of his dying uncle? It is high time that we should return to our young friend.

Carrera found the old gentleman in a stupor, from which his attendants thought he would never awake. To every body's surprise, however, he rallied toward evening, and gladly recognized and welcomed his nephew. The patient's condition even seemed to improve. For hours at a time he would feel relieved, and was able to converse with Carrera; to give directions to his Mayordomo concerning the management of the estate; to listen to the news from Quito, for which messengers were sent to and fro regularly, and to comment upon it; to listen to the consolations of his spiritual adviser, and to say a kind word or to administer reprimands to his servants and Indians. Then, again, he would relapse into a stupor, which lasted for hours. And so the days wore on and swelled into weeks, and still Carrera was chained to the bedside of the dying man, who would not allow him to leave the room longer than necessary for a little exercise in the open air.

At the end of the first week Carrera sent a letter to his friend Roberto Sanchez, requesting him for the return of Toa's silver moon, as he wished to write to her. It was not without a pang of jealousy that he had heard of the manner in which Toa and Roberto had appeared before the people. And he had received no explanation of this strange demonstration. Had Toa abandoned him already? Had she transferred her affections to Roberto? Had she taken umbrage at Carrera's departure from Quito? Her own solemn declaration that she would subordinate her love to what she considered her duty to her people seemed to confirm this supposition. Nervously he waited for an answer from Sanchez, but no answer came. The Cabildo had sent Roberto's father to Latacunga, Ambato, and Riobamba to organize the forces of the Revolution there. He had taken his son along as his trusty lieutenant, and the latter had left no word as to when he would return. After another week a letter came from Roberto, full of affectionate reproaches and insisting that Carrera should return to Quito, if he had not done so already. It also stated that the writer was organizing a company at Latacunga, and would have to remain there for some time. Carrera sent a messenger to that city with another letter, but both messenger and letter returned. The man brought the news that Roberto had departed for the neighborhood of Ambato, in order to collect horses for a cavalry corps which was then in process of forming. Having no specific instructions the man did not feel authorized to follow him, uncertain whether or where he should find him. Thus another week was lost, and, in the meantime, great changes were preparing at Quito, and a change was developing in the mind, feelings, and opinions of Carrera.

To the former we shall refer briefly. Paredes had carried his point. Pedro Guzman Ponce de Leon had been appointed commander-in-chief of the armed forces of the Municipality, and enlisted a great many men, whom he was preparing for active service. But these men were kept at Quito, where many of them grew tired of idleness, or demoralized by inactivity and by the fierce contest of conflicting opinions which raged around them. The party of action advocated a forward movement. The Quito forces should march to Riobamba and Guaranda and defend the mountain-passes by which Arana was to approach. There they would defeat him surely, and then might follow him into the low-lands, covered with tropical forests, where it would be easy to annihilate a beaten foe. Guayaquil should be taken from him, and communication with the sea being once established, the success of the movement would be secured. Pedro Guzman approved of all this in theory, but he did not act upon it in practice. He always prepared, but never was ready. He vowed great things, but never performed them. And the Indians, too, were backward. The resolutions which the Municipality had adopted during the night of the bloody conflict, had never been publicly proclaimed. Endless negotiations followed. The men of the Cabildo wanted gold, nominally to carry on the war, in reality, however, to enrich themselves. The Indians refused to furnish it until their rights should be secured,- and the first steps taken to carry out the programme of Cundurazu and Bellido. In the meantime the doubters, who disputed the existence of the treasure, had it all their own way. The best men of the Revolutionary party had been skillfully removed from Quito. Sanchez had been sent to the south, and Olmos to the northern provinces, nominally to organize the Revolution, in reality, however, to be out of the way. In the meantime the days wore on, the precious moments were wasted and the party of reaction slowly but irresistibly continued to recover the ground it had lost, and to confound and demoralize its antagonists. Still, all was not lost. A bloody event of startling magnitude soon rallied the earnest and the honest men and gave fresh impulse to the popular cause. The nature of this event will be disclosed in the following chapters.

Equally fatal to the aspirations of our heroine, however, was the change in the opinions and feelings of Carrera. Had his uncle died shortly after the nephew's arrival at Puembo, what a different course would the events of this story have taken. But the patient lived and lingered on, and impressed upon the unformed mind and character of Carrera the stamp of an old man's well-matured opinions, deep-rooted prejudices, and vast experience.

The murder of Bellido, he granted, was a crime, a great crime. But who had ordered it? Had it been proved that it was the work of the Audience? Might not a private grudge, an adverse party to a law-suit, or a love intrigue have been the moving cause? Those reckless soldiers would assassinate any man for a sum of money. And even if the murder was committed at the instigation of the Audience, should it follow that we must rise against the King, because some of his ministers had abused the power confided to them? And what right had the popular party to complain of murders? Was not the murder of Valverde an act infinitely more cruel, wanton, and fiendish than the assassination of Bellido?

From this point Carrera's uncle passed on to the utter hopelessness of the rebellion, and he supported his arguments with heavy artillery from the arsenal of Peruvian history. In the times of Gonzalo Pizarro the colonists had rebelled against the home government. They would not submit to the royal ordinances declaring that the Indians should be treated as freemen. Gonzalo Pizarro was made Protector of Peru, the colonists flocked to his standards and defeated the Viceroy, who was slain on the field of Aña Quito; and yet, when the Royal Commissioner La Gasca came, alone and empty handed, he soon had an army under him, Gonzalo Pizarro was ignominiously routed, his whole army deserting him at the critical moment, and the leaders expiated their treason on the scaffold.

And what was the fate of the rebellion of Hernandez Jiron, who had swept everything before him, and appeared almost under the very gates of Lima? The whole country was disaffected. Hernandez Jiron made himself the representative of the popular grievances. He had an army under his command consisting of men who had grown old in the art of war. He had defeated the forces of the government in several engagements. And yet he failed and died a traitor's death at the hands of the executioner. Spain was the greatest military power of the globe. Her armies had swept over Europe. Her resources were inexhaustible. Would the Creoles of Quito, inexperienced in the art of war, and divided in their own councils, be able to cope with the colossal strength of the mother country? It was a childish dream, a ridiculous vision, an *ignis fatuus* which could only lead to destruction. Even temporary successes could not avert the final doom.

The imposition of the Alcabala may have been a nominal breach of a royal grant; but that grant had been given in ignorance of the future wealth and greatness of Peru. Every age has its own necessities, and one King can not legislate for unborn generations, because he can not foresee the necessities of his successors. He may have been a wise man in his day; but that day has passed, and his successor, although bound to revere the memory of the Kings before him, must be the judge of his own exigencies, and of his own times.

An alliance with the Indians! Ridiculous! The Alcabala might be burdensome, the loss of their Indian slaves would be ruinous, to the colonists. Surely, they would submit to the Alcabala a thousand times, rather than release the Indians, who tilled their lands, worked their mines, herded their cattle, and served in their factories. And what assistance could those miserable beings render in case of war? Unacquainted with the use of firearms, abject and cowardly, broken by an iron rule into blind submission, they might murder prisoners, slay the wounded, and rob the dead, but how should they withstand the shock of infantry, or the charge of cavalry? Their treasure, you say? It is a myth, Julio, a nursery-tale with which we were amused in the days of our childhood, a legend resting on mere suppositions that have never been verified.

At this juncture, Carrera interposed a remonstrance. He had not been pledged to secrecy as to the existence of the treasure, and he gave his uncle a detailed account of all he had seen in the cave. The old man listened to him in amazement, which soon gave way to an air of incredulity. Without pursuing the subject of the treasure, he asked him how he had become acquainted with Toa. Carrera said that he had met her at Mama Rucu's cottage. His uncle then inquired what had taken him there. This question was very embarrassing, but he concluded to make a clean breast of his past delinquencies, and to throw himself on the charitable forbearance of his uncle. Nevertheless, he kept the promise of secrecy which he had made to Mama Rucu, and said nothing of his visions during the memorable night he had spent at her cottage. But he showed him the letter with which Queen Toa had accompanied her present or loan. The old man read it, and reread it, and then fell into a long silence, which was at last broken by Carrera, who asked his forgiveness for having allowed himself to be led astray by the temptations of the card-table.

"That you have played recklessly and perhaps foolishly, Julio," said the old man after another pause, "is but too natural for a young *Caballero* of your station. It was an experience that every gentleman must go through, and I hope you have profited by it. If I blame you for anything, it is for not having confided in me, your best and only friend, as you should have done. But I preceive with amazement that you have allowed yourself to be drawn into a most dangerous complication, from which you must be extricated. Now listen to the advice of an old man, who looks upon you as his own child. You are my heir, Julio de Carrera. I have kept the knowledge of this fact from you till now, for reasons which you will understand; but as you would know it soon after I am gone, I might as well tell you now, that your future is secured, and that you will be one of the richest men in the Kingdom of Quito!"

"Uncle!"

"No thanks! No protestations! If you want to prove your gratitude, follow my advice. This is all the return I ask. Your path through life will be easy and pleasant. All you have to do is to be what I have been. Apply yourself to the management of the estates, which will be yours, and, as you are a lover of books, you will not lack occupation for your leisure hours. Flee from the dangers that your improvidence has conjured up. The treasures of that Indian witch would prove your inevitable destruction. You do not need them. Where is the nobleman of Quito that would not envy your position? With the exception of the Marquis of Solando, there will not be a wealthier man in the land. What more do you want? What wishes can you entertain that my wealth will not gratify? The possession and enjoyment of what I shall leave you nobody will dispute. What SHE may give you would involve you in endless troubles. It would be taken from you and prove your destruction in the end. You can not marry a woman who, by the very claim she sets up, has placed herself in an attitude of rebellion against our Lord, the King of Spain, and the security and welfare of this colony. Her life is forfeited to the executioner, and her treasures to the Crown; and even if she would wish to subside into obscurity, it would be too dangerous for the public peace to let her live. For the Virgin's sake, Julio, I shudder when I think of the danger with which you have played. And yet there must be more than you tell me. You have made love to her, have you not? She pretends to reciprocate your affection in order to inveigle you into certain ruin. Tell me all, my son. Keep nothing from me. The lips of a dying man are sealed, Julio. Your secret, if it is a secret, will die with me."

What resistance could Carrera offer to such an appeal? He confessed how Toa had won his heart, and how she reciprocated his affection.

"Poor, deluded youth!" continued his uncle, "how childish and unsophisticated you are! Do you not see that she has played the same game with others—that she has allured others with false hopes of her love and treasures, in order to use them for her ambitious purposes? Did she not appear in public with your intimate friend, Roberto Sanchez? Would Sanchez, who is a shrewd fellow, have consented to lend himself to such demonstrations, if she had not played with his affections and fired his susceptible heart? Her wiles may deceive young men, but they are as plain as daylight to me. She wants a party among the nobility, and she endeavors to build it up by turning the heads of our young *caballeros*, while stimulating their greed with promises of her gold. They will secure neither the one nor the other. She will ruin and betray them."

Here the old man fell into a stupor, and Carrera had time to ponder over what he had heard. His uncle's words had sunk deep into the young man's heart. They had instilled the poison, which did its work.

On the next day the conversation was resumed. "I am afraid, Julio," said the patient, "that you will be involved in great trouble. As soon as this revolution shall be crushed—and, believe me, it will be crushed—searching inquiries will be made into its causes and into the conduct of all that were directly or indirectly implicated. You are one of these men. The seditious speech you made after the murder of Bellido will not be forgotten. Your enemies—and everybody has enemies—will make the worst of it. They will say that you gave the word for the attack on the Palace. You have communicated with the rebel and pretender Toa. You have seen her treasure and received money from her. It is as certain as fate that you will be proceeded against. You are in danger, my poor boy, and that danger should be judiciously averted.

"But how can it be averted, Uncle?" asked Carrera who, brave as he was, could not resist a feeling of great alarm at the thought of a prosecution for high treason.

"In the first place you should make a timely submission. You should side with the friends of the King. You should, if possible, manifest your loyalty by some signal act"—

"Uncle!" remonstrated the young man.

"Let me proceed! In the second place you should fortify your position by a wise marriage. I have long had a match in view for you, and until you told me of that foolish affair with your Indian Princess, I had believed that your own inclination coincided with my wishes. The woman to whom you should engage yourself, without delay, is Dolores Solando "—

Carrera gave a start, which encouraged the old man, whose eyes, as he pronounced the name of Dolores, carefully scanned the countenance of his nephew. "Yes!" he proceeded, " Dolores Solando! Her father is the head and front of the loyalists; not, perhaps, intellectually, but his great name and wealth will be of vital importance to the royal cause. He has almost become a martyr to that cause. His person was in danger. His house had been invaded; his wife's life might have been sacrificed. He has joined Arana, and will be in a position of almost unlimited influence with the Royal Commissioner. Who would dare to assail his future son-in-law? Engage yourself to Dolores and you will be safe. But aside from this consideration, the match would be a splendid one in every other respect. It would add to your wealth, to your name, position, and influence. You would become the founder of the first and proudest family in the kingdom, and be to this country what a grandee would be in Spain."

And thus the old man continued to argue and to preach, and every word he said was weighty, plausible, convincing. His reasoning was irresistible and overcame all objections. And when doubts arose in the mind of Carrera, while he promenaded in the orchard in the rear of the house, how quickly were they dissolved when he submitted them to the scrutiny of that wise old man.

And at last the closing hour arrived, and the dying man exacted promises which his grateful nephew could not refuse. He promised to renounce the heathen Toa and her delusive treasures, and be a suitor to the hand of Dolores. He promised to be as loyal to his King as he would be obedient to his God. And with the crucifix in his hand, and another appeal to Julio by look, word, and gesture, the old man breathed his last in the arms of his nephew. And the Jesuit father who had attended him during his sickness, appeared upon the veranda fronting the court, where the servants and *peons*, and their women were assembled, and raising his arms brought the multitude to their knees:

"Let us pray, children!" he exclaimed. "Let us pray for your good Master, Don Ramiro de Carrera y Pareja, whose soul has just been summoned before the throne of God."

CHAPTER IV.

LAYING THE MINE.

LATE in the afternoon of the day following the burial of Carrera's uncle, Dolores sat writing a long letter to her father, which was to be sent by a secret messenger, while Aunt Catita was deeply engrossed with the wonderful adventures and heroic feats of Amadis de Gaul, when Paredes was announced.

"Auntie!" said the young lady. "I am afraid you will have to betake yourself to one end of the room, while I shall take my visitor to the other. I have to confer with him on matters of the utmost importance to father."

"I might stay in the adjoining room, Doloritas."

"No, Auntie, it would not be proper. And, besides, I want you near enough so as not to leave me alone with him, and yet far enough not to hear our conversation. Forgive me, Auntie, but it is for father's sake. There will be no love making, I assure you."

Manuel Paredes now entered, and after some preliminary conversation touching the absorbing topics of the day, followed Dolores into a remote corner of the *sala*, where she seated herself on a sofa, while he took a chair beside her.

Aunt Catita took a seat on an ottoman in the opposite corner, and wrapping herself up in her shawl, soon seemed to be asleep.

"I have startling news of the utmost importance!" he said in a whisper.

"Proceed!" she said in a quiet, and yet commanding and business-like tone, as if she had been born and brought up to the direction of affairs of state.

"Old Sanchez, after organizing the Revolution at Latacunga and Ambato, had proceeded to Riobamba, with but a few armed followers, and was about to submit his plans to the Cabildo there, when he was seized by the *Corregidor*, and thrown into prison. His followers, on hearing of his arrest, and being too few to liberate him, dashed back to Ambato, where his son was, who with a hundred mounted men, immediately hurried to his father's rescue. In the meantime, however, the *Corregidor* ordered the old man to be tried for high treason, and had him convicted and executed."

Paredes stopped to see what effect this news would have on his beautiful listener. But not a muscle of her face moved; she sat there as cold and motionless as a marble statute, and merely whispered: "Proceed!"

"Young Sanchez arrived two hours afterward, and at once took possession of the town. He wanted to hang the *Corregidor*, but that official had escaped in the nick of time. Sanchez then hung two of the men who had served on the court-martial which had sentenced his father. He then left forty men to guard the town, and to arm and organize the rebel element, and with the others he started in pursuit of the *Corregidor*. They rode day and night, but finally met with the advance guard of Arana, who had divided his forces, which in my opinion was a great mistake. Roberto's horses were worn out when the two parties met, and to this circumstance alone, we owe the salvation of Arana's detachment. The meeting seems to have been a surprise to both parties. But that young Sanchez is a fiend! He fell on the King's men with such impetuosity that they broke and fled after the first fire, without discovering that the attack on them had been made by a mere handful of men. The officer in command of the Royalists vainly attempted to rally them. He was slightly wounded, only very slightly, Señorita; you need not be alarmed"—

"Why should I be at all?" interposed Dolores, coldly.

"Because—well—because," said Paredes hesitatingly, "because it was"—

"My brother, perhaps."

"Yes, but it was a mere scratch, I assure you. The freshness and fleetness of his horse saved him." Here Paredes paused again, and again Dolores, without changing her attitude, quietly said: "Proceed!"

"Reinforcements were soon brought up, but Roberto, having ascertained the enemy's superiority, returned to Riobamba. On his way back, he captured the *Corregidor's* private secretary, who was making his way to the royal camp, and hung him to a tree."

"He is a man of decision!" said Dolores calmly.

"I received this news by a special messenger, two hours ago, and took it to the Cabildo, where it at once and completely re-established the ascendency of the Bellidistas. Everybody is distrusted now, who has counseled delay and moderation. The party of action is supreme again, and as soon as this news becomes public, we shall have to apprehend a fresh outbreak, which may, and probably will, threaten the lives of the President and of the Auditors. The majority of the Cabildo is now opposed to all further procrastination. Unfortunately, old Olmos has returned with troops from Ibarra, and the Extremists have a leader again. He demands an immediate proclamation of independence, the election of a King, and his marriage to Toa Duchicela, the Shyri Queen."

"And who is to be selected for this sacrilegious mockery of royalty?"

"On behalf of the Shyri Toa, her representatives have presented the name of our young friend, Don Julio de Carrera."

Dolores slightly compressed her lips, and the color rose to her face for a moment, but only to give way to sudden paleness. It was the first involuntary betrayal of her emotion, and did not escape the scrutinizing eye of Paredes. But she immediately recovered her self-possession, and remarked, with an ironical smile: "You see I am a prophet, Señor Don Manuel. I had predicted royal honors for your amiable friend."

"His name has met with some favor among the men of action, because from his youth, inexperience, and softness of character, they suppose that he will be wax in their hands, and that they will be able to govern through him and in his name."

"And will he accept this crown of insanity?"

"He is to be sounded first. If he refuses, somebody else will be selected. But," said Paredes, with peculiar zest, "it is believed that he will accept, because he has been carrying on a love-intrigue with the Indian Princess for some time. He is said to be madly in love with her, and has been the recipient of her bounty. The gold with which he has paid his enormous gambling debts has come from her."

This time Dolores did not betray her emotion, but asked, sarcastically: "And where is His Majesty now?"

"He is still at Puembo; but I have been informed that he will return to Quito this very night."

"And do you apprehend any danger that such a hair-brained scheme will be carried out?"

"Most certainly I do. And if so, our influence will be destroyed. The leadership of the Revolution will pass into the hands of those who mean that it shall be successful.

The command of the forces will be taken from Guzman and be transferred to old Olmos, with young Sanchez at his side. The Indians will rise in every province. The Inca Treasure will be at the disposal of the rebellion, and the men of action, having burnt their ships and cut off their retreat, will fight for dear life, with the scaffold before them in case of defeat, and untold wealth, honors, and power in case of victory. The situation is exceedingly serious, Señorita."

"But if Carrera refuses, as he certainly will?"

"Worse for us! Then the probabilities are that Sanchez will be selected in his place, who is a lion, while Carrera is a llama."

"How do you intend to meet this emergency?"

"I have a plan which I think will prove successful, if we can be sure of Carrera's refusal to lend himself to the scheme of the rebels."

"Proceed!"

"Allow me to close that door first!" said Paredes, rising. "I am afraid of Indian listeners. Their sense of hearing is very sharp, and they are all spies of their Shyri Queen." Paredes went to the door and stepped out into the hall, where, to his great annoyance, he met Mama Santos, the nurse whom our readers already know. He entertained no doubt that she had attempted to listen; but he felt assured that she could not have heard the conversation, which had been carried on almost in a whisper. Mama Santos bowed to him and then entered the room.

"Señor Ortiz," she said in her calm and dignified way, "wishes to pay his respects to their Ladyships."

"Tell him," said Dolores, "I regret exceedingly that I am unable to see him. Tell him that I am ill to-night, but that to-morrow, or at any other time, I shall be delighted to receive him."

Mama Santos left as quietly as she had come, and Paredes closed the door behind her.

"Now we are safe!" he said. Your good old nurse is a spy, Señorita. I do not doubt it in the least; but she could not possibly have heard us."

"Proceed with your plan!"

"The dangerous scheme which we have every reason to fear, can, in my opinion, be frustrated only by springing it prematurely and exposing it to ridicule by some signal failure in its inception.

"Explain yourself, Don Manuel."

"I have great influence with the rabble, not so much owing to the position which I took as the Colonel of our Regiment on the day of the outbreak, but principally owing to my power over that worthless fellow, Juan Castro, the King of the Ragamuffins. I have sent word to him to come to my house this evening; and, if my plan meets with your approval, Señorita, I shall have all the necessary preparations made for a demonstration to-morrow, provided Carrera has returned or will return to Quito to-night. We must not give him time to consult with the men of action, or to be influenced by them. His return will not be known. The probabilities are that he will not see any body to-night. I shall visit him myself and stay with him, so as to keep him from falling into other company. I shall influence his flexible mind against the scheme; and, if I succeed, the premature demonstration to-morrow which Castro will organize, will finish the business."

"What shall be the object of that demonstration?"

"To proclaim Carrera, King.* The rabble shall offer

---

* As to this event, I have followed the account given by Padre Velasco in his History of Quito, and adopted by Lorente in his History of Peru. My learned friend, Dr. Pablo Herrera, formerly Equatorian Minister of Foreign affairs, doubts the reality of this episode, as in his researches among the old archives he has not been able to discover any confirmation of it. But Pedro de Oña, who wrote his poem "El Arauco Domado," a few years after the event is said to have taken place, distinctly speaks of an attempt to set up

him the crown, and it shall be done in such a violent and indecent manner as not to tempt him very greatly. The whole thing will appear ridiculous, and his refusal to accept will kill the movement, and make it appear in the light of a farce. It will arouse the public mind as to the folly of all such schemes, and thus form a powerful lever to bring on the reaction which we all desire. Do you approve of my plan, Señorita?"

"Thoroughly. It does honor to your genius. There is only one modification which I shall propose."

"I am waiting for your orders, Señorita."

"I shall lend you my personal help in the matter. You, Señor Paredes, may prepare Juan Castro and his rabble. As to Señor Carrera, leave him to me. I shall vouch for his refusal."

"Never! Never!" exclaimed Paredes, springing to his feet.

"And why not?" asked Dolores, rising likewise and fastening one of her sternest and most piercing looks on him.

"Señorita!" urged Paredes. "Have you forgotten that I love you, and that he is my most dangerous and now probably my only rival. No, I could not and would not consent to this. I would have the Revolution succeed rather than let you speak to him on this matter. How could you influence him otherwise than by holding out the inducement of your love and your hand?"

Dolores had listened to him with quiet determination, and without averting her eyes from his.

"Have you ended, Señor?"

"false kings." Under the circumstances, I have done no violence to historical truth by incorporating the episode referred to in my story. On the whole, I have endeavored to follow the course of historical events as accurately and closely as possible, considering the almost pitiable scarcity of the materials on which I had to rely.

"I have!"

"Have you nothing further to say, nothing to take back?"

"Nothing!"

"Do I understand you to threaten disobedience to the King's orders and disloyalty to the King's cause?"

Paredes felt nettled by the commanding tone with which she spoke to him, and for a moment his eyes flashed, and he met her severe gaze with a look of defiance; but it was only for a moment. He winced under the fierceness of those cold eyes, and said in a deprecating tone: "I have no orders from the King's Majesty. My powers are discretionary."

"Under whose commission do you act, Señor? To whom was the King's letter directed?"

"To your father, the Marquis."

"Exactly. And all the powers which you claim you derive from my father who has conferred them, and may recall them if the necessities of the King's service should demand it. Do I understand you to deny this, Señor Don Manuel Paredes?"

"I do not."

"And who represents my father since he is gone? Who stands in his stead by virtue of the power which I have placed in your hands?"

"It is you, Señorita!"

"And you, Señor, have recognized this fact by coming to me as to all matters concerning your task and authority. Do you admit that?"

"I do!" said Paredes, who had already weakened under the searching scrutiny of her cross-examination.

"Then you also admit that I now represent the King's Majesty, and that I am clothed with his commission; and you may further understand that I am not to be trifled with."

"But, Doloritas"—

"Not another word until we have come to a proper understanding. Your plan has my sanction, and I command you in the King's name to carry out that part of it which I have assigned to you. Do I understand you to refuse?"

"Allow me to say but one word."

"Do I understand you to refuse? Do you threaten to counteract me in what I deem absolutely necessary for the safety of our cause?"

"Well, and if I do?"

"Then I shall revoke your commission at once, and shall so inform my father."

"And if I do not choose," said Paredes, firing up again, "to submit to the well meant but mistaken ideas of your Ladyship; if I do not choose to complicate the King's cause with a love intrigue; if, with all due deference to the great intellect and wonderful genius of your Ladyship, I must decline to be guided as to a certain part of my plan, by your Ladyship's opinion, but insist that this great task must be performed by men"—

"Then I shall denounce you to the Cabildo, and Don Manuel Paredes will have shared the fate of Count Valverde before sundown to-morrow."

Paredes turned pale, yet he struggled to maintain his self-possession. "You are joking, Señorita. The daughter of the Marquis of Solando will not betray the King's cause and the man who has saved her father's life."

This appeal staggered Dolores, but it was now a trial of will. She had to conquer or be conquered; and her decision was made. Drawing her shawl closer around her shoulders, she said: "This interview has terminated, Señor Paredes. I expect your apology, or your immediate departure."

"Doloritas!" began Paredes, appealingly.

"Leave me at once!"

Paredes stood hesitating. "No, Señorita, we can not and must not part in anger."

"Leave me, Señor, or I must make you go."

The struggle drew to a close; the stronger will was in the ascendancy. Dolores turned away.

"Forgive me," he began, "if I spoke hastily."

No answer.

"If it is a crime to love you madly, I am a criminal."

"Confine yourself to matters concerning the King's service," she resumed, without turning to him. "We are not discussing love. Do you acquiesce in my view of what shall be done?"

A pause.

"Have the kindness to answer my question. It is the last I shall ask."

"I am your slave, Dolores, even if you sacrifice and reject me."

"Your answer is in the affirmative?" she inquired, turning around.

"It is!"

"Your hand, Don Manuel! Let us forgive and forget."

"Forget?" he said, bitterly; "forget that the services by which I hoped to secure your possession should be but the cause of my losing you forever?"

"Don Manuel, as you have spoken like a reasonable being again, I shall be frank with you. I do not love Julio de Carrera."

"The Virgin be praised! God bless you for those words!"

"I do not love him, and never shall."

"And will not give him cause to believe that you love him?"

"I have told you that I do not love him. The rest you must leave to me."

"But you will never belong to him?"

"Can you not be satisfied with what I have told you?"

"Oh, it is but a straw to a drowning man."

"And will you never learn patience, Señor Paredes? Let us first attend to the King's interests and to my father's business. There will be a time for everything. Let us not waste the precious moments now, when the fate of the Colony is trembling in the balance. Go, and perform your part of the task, and I shall perform mine. Go, now, Don Manuel, and if I do not send a messenger to you before ten o'clock to-night, telling you to stop, let the mine be sprung to-morrow. And now, go. Good night, my friend."

Paredes kissed her hand, and slowly turned to go. Dolores had followed him a step or two. Before he had reached the door he turned back again. Their eyes met. They both glanced at Doña Catita, who, by this time, was really asleep; and again their eyes met, and a moment afterward they were locked in each other's embrace, and hung upon each other's lips.

"Go, now," whispered Dolores, pushing him away. "Go! You know enough, and now you must go."

Paredes went; but before he had left the room she called him back.

"Don Manuel," she asked, "tell me the truth, is my brother severely wounded?"

Paredes hesitated.

"Answer me!"

"Yes, Señorita, he is severely wounded."

"Is my brother dead?"

He made no reply.

"Tell me truth. My brother is dead?"

"He is dead."

"Leave me!"

CHAPTER V.

THE TURNING POINT.

For several minutes Dolores stood motionless in the middle of the room. A world of thoughts flashed through her brain; but her eyes remained without a tear. The bullet that had laid her brother low had changed her position in life completely. She was now the only child of the great and wealthy Marquis of Solando. No longer a dependent on a brother's bounty, she had become an heiress whose hand would be a prize coveted by the noblest houses of Peru. She could give it to the man of her choice, be he never so poor, or she might exchange it for a rank and station higher than her own. That insignificant life which stood between her and greatness had been taken away. The boldest dreams of her ambition might now be realized. Did she think of the sufferings of a grief-stricken father? Did she calculate the terrible effect this dreadful news would produce on the waning health of her mother? Who can look into a woman's heart and fathom its hidden depths? Had she loved her brother? Was there room for anything but self in that cold heart which, a few minutes ago, had beaten against the breast of Paredes? Did she love even Paredes, or was her affection for him but an appetite, a wild passion which, to please herself, she yearned to gratify? Did she picture to herself the wild charge of young Sanchez, and the reeling form of her brother as he fell bleeding from his steed, and perished with a bullet in his breast, under the hoofs of maddened horses? Or was it her own future which engrossed her thoughts, as she stood silent and motionless in the center of that large and elegant room, the scene of so many of her social triumphs?

At last she turned around and moved toward the door. Cautiously she opened it, and looked out. There was nobody in the hall. "Guambra!" she exclaimed. "Guambra!" No answer. She passed along the corridor, and found her little Indian maid cowering on the floor, with her head on her knees, and her shawl over her head, fast asleep. It was now nearly dark. Dolores woke the drowsy child, and commanded her to bring lights, and to send up Raimundo, the white steward of the mansion.

"Raimundo!" she whispered to him. "Go to the house of Don Julio de Carrera, and see whether he has returned from Puembo. If not, wait until he comes, and tell him he would confer a great favor on me, by coming here at once. Tell him that I wish to see him, on a matter of the utmost importance. But be quick, and do not let any of our Indians know what you are about."

Slowly and with apparent calmness, but full of inward impatience and agitation, she paced the room while she awaited the return of her messenger. He did not stay long. The Señor de Carrera had just returned, but he regretted that he was not in a fit state to present himself to her Ladyship. Overwhelmed with grief and fatigue, and laboring under a serious indisposition, owing to a fall with his horse, he was unable to leave the house this evening, but he would hasten to pay his respects to her Ladyship early after breakfast to-morrow morning.

Dolores bit her lips, and returned to the *sala*. She would see that man at her feet yet, and then her revenge would come. Her resolution was taken at once. There must be no to-morrow at a crisis like this. If he would not or could not come to her, she must go to him.

"Aunt Catita!" she said, laying her hand on that lady, who awoke with a start.

"How you have frightened me, child! What is the matter? Is your visitor gone?"

"Yes, Auntie, he is gone, and we must go, too."

"Go to bed, you mean. It is very early, and I want to finish this book to-night."

"Put it away, Auntie. I must ask you to help me do a very improper thing; but there is no help for it."

"I do not understand you, child. What is it?"

"You must dress yourself, and go out with me."

"Go where?"

"To a young gentleman's house."

"I hope you are in your right mind, Dolores."

"Perfectly! And if I could tell you all my reasons, you would agree with me that we must go. It is on father's business. Come, Auntie, and while we dress, I shall tell you as much of it as I can, without betraying father's secrets."

* * * * * * *

Carrera was in his bedroom. His horse had fallen with him while crossing a deep ravine on his return from Puembo, and he felt shattered physically, morally, and mentally. And this was the reason why he had, although very reluctantly, postponed his visit to Dolores, although his heart had leaped with secret joy when he received her message.

Carrera felt that it was probably a great mistake, not to have dragged himself to the Solando mansion, in spite of his physical ailments; but the words were out of his mouth before he had reflected. Dolores would be offended. He would have to make a desperate apology in the morning. Perhaps he should, after all, rise from his couch and go there at once? But would she expect, and would she receive him, after his thoughtless refusal?

He was still weighing this matter, when Mariano entered the room in great agitation, and announced that two masked ladies had come to the house, and demanded to see the *Caballero*. They were waiting in the reception-room. Two masked ladies? Who could they be? He never dreamed that Dolores could be one of them. It must be Toa! There could be no doubt of it. But how should he meet her? What should he say to her? If it was Toa, he felt he was lost. He had pledged his love to her, and she had come to hold him to his word. Once again under the charm of her presence, he would not be able to break with her at once. He would have to temporize. And yet he had vowed to his dying uncle that he would renounce her. What an embarrassing situation! Why had she come? Was it not the height of boldness and impropriety thus to intrude upon his privacy? And yet, after what had passed between them, how could he tell her that he loved her no longer?

Racked by these perplexing doubts he made hasty toilette, and betook himself to his reception-room. The two masked ladies stood at the table in the center of the room. Carrera felt reassured and yet puzzled as he beheld them. Neither of the two resembled Toa in figure; yet who could they be? Where was his memory? Had he forgotten his visions in Mama Rucu's cottage?

The taller of the two ladies pointed to his servant, Mariano, who stood in the door awaiting orders. "Leave us, Mariano!" said his master. Mariano obeyed and closed the door behind him.

The lady then removed her mask and to Carrera's infinite surprise and astonishment, uncovered the beautiful face of Dolores Solando.

"Señorita Dolores!" he exclaimed.

"Yes, Don Julio. As you would not or could not leave the house to-night, I had to be guilty of this great impropriety and indelicate intrusion for which I ask your pardon. But what I have to say to your Grace admits of no delay. To-morrow it would be too late, and so I have come to-night to warn you, perhaps to save you."

Carrera had not yet recovered from his surprise, and did not know what to answer. Dolores led the way to one of the window-embrasures, while Aunt Catita placed a chair against the hall-door, and sat down, turning her back on her niece and Julio. The latter handed Dolores a chair which she declined.

"Thank you," she began, "I shall stand. I shall not occupy your time any longer than absolutely necessary. Do you know what the morrow will have in store for you?"

"No, Señorita. I arrived but a little while ago, and nobody has been here to see me."

"It is well! And as you are still in ignorance of what will happen, I shall inform you. You are to be proclaimed King to-morrow, and are expected to marry Toa Duchicela, the Indian Princess, as your Queen."

"By the Holy Virgin, Señorita, it is impossible."

"I know what I say. My information is reliable, as you will find for yourself before twenty-four hours have elapsed. Now, Señor Don Julio, I do not know which side you have taken in this contest, although from your intimacy with Roberto Sanchez, and from the fact that the crown is to be offered to you, I presume that you have sympathized and perhaps co-operated with the men of the Cabildo. I am equally ignorant of the exact nature of your relations to Toa Duchicela. There was a time when I thought I knew the object of your affections, but that time has passed, and I shall not refer to it."

"And why should it be past, Doloritas?" interposed Carrera, endeavoring to seize her hand, which she withdrew.

"Do not interrupt me. I have not come to speak of love or to humble myself to one who has taken pains to show me his indifference. I am not an Indian princess, and have no treasures and no kingdoms to bestow. I know you have made love to Toa Duchicela. You are a man, and men are changeable, and claim the right to transfer their affections from one woman to another. Yet I desire to prove to you that the change of your heart has not affected the friendship which I have always entertained for you, and which I entertain for you even now. For this reason I have come to warn you. There was no time to be lost. To-morrow it would have been too late. Give her your love. Marry her if you choose. But do not sacrifice yourself, your career, your life, by espousing the lost cause of the rebellion."

"Listen, Señorita!"

"No, listen to me! I shall divulge secrets to you which you must not breathe. I put my own life into your hands, but I trust to your honor as a cavalier. You will not betray one that has risked her reputation, and perhaps her life, to save you."

"How could you believe"—

"I do not fear it. I should not be here if I did. But listen! This rebellion must fail. It is doomed to defeat, and those who participate in it sincerely will die on the scaffold. Its leaders will betray it. The King's friends now control it. The commander of its armed forces, Don Pedro Guzman, is secretly on the King's side. He will never move unless it be in the interest of the King. The loudest advocates of resistance are secretly with us. There are members of the Cabildo, who, while co-operating with the insurgents, are in communication with Arana. I could name them to you if it were necessary. But no matter! There are, no doubt, many who are sincere in the position they have taken. I pity them, for they are betrayed and ruined. The very words they utter to their most confidential friends will be brought up in evidence against them. And now, Señor Don Julio, could you but for a moment harbor the belief that, under these circumstances, the cause of the insurrection can succeed?"

"I do not, Señorita!"

"And you will not sacrifice yourself by espousing it?"

"Am I not already sacrificed? Have I not compromised myself by the speech I made on the day of Bellido's assassination? They say that I gave the word for the attack on the Palace, and they say that King Philip never forgives."

"Leave that to me, Don Julio. My father stands high in the confidence of Arana, and is in communication with the Viceroy at Lima and the Court at Madrid. He will have ample power to protect you, and I, Dolores Solando, tell you that no hair on your head shall be harmed. And even without my aid you will have a splendid opportunity to redeem yourself. To-morrow they will offer you a crown."

"It is impossible, Señorita. Who would be so insane as to do that? And why should I be singled out as the victim?"

"You will not accept, then?"

"Accept! Do you think I am out of my right mind?"

"Do you give your word of honor that you will refuse?"

"I do!"

"And that you will take no part in this hair-brained rebellion?"

"Oh, Dolores! Do I dream or am I waking? I can hardly trust my senses. Is it reality that you care so much for me?"

"Do not ask me, Don Julio. Let my presence answer your questions. I have your word," she added, extending her hand, which he seized and covered with kisses.

"You love me, Dolores?"

She said nothing, but looked at him affectionately.

"Oh, speak the word! You love me, Doloritas."

"Enough! I must be hence. Aunt Catita will grow impatient."

"No! No! I will not let you go," he said, seizing both

her hands, "until you have spoken the word which will give me life or death."

"Think of your Indian Princess," she answered with a roguish smile, "you fickle, faithless man."

"Be generous, be magnanimous, be yourself, Dolores. I may have been bewitched by her wiles and by her strange power; but I never loved her. You are my first and only love. I knew not how intensely I loved you, until you came to me to-night."

"Let me go, Don Julio! I must not add another impropriety to those which I have already committed. Please let me go, Julio. There is a time for every thing. We shall talk of love hereafter. I must go now."

"But you shall not go, life of my soul. Not now! Tarry but a minute, and tell me that I may hope and live for you."

"How silly you are," she replied, with a faint show of resistance. "Let my conduct answer your questions. And now I have said enough."

"The angels of heaven will bless you, Dolores. And will you be mine?"

"Will you never cease asking?"

"Only this one question. I shall not ask another. Will you be mine, Dolores?"

"I must go!" And she started to go; but it was to be intercepted by his arms and pressed to his heart and covered with burning kisses which she did not return.

"You will be mine, love?"

"I may be yours," she whispered, tearing herself away, "but on condition that you let me go at once." Then turning back, she said, with a look which drove him wild with joy: "Good night, Julio!"

And down stairs he accompanied the ladies, who had resumed their masks, and would have escorted them home had they not positively declined it. Raimundo waited for them with an escort of servants, and the next moment they had disappeared in the darkness. And the vision in Mama Rucu's cottage had not yet returned to Carrera's memory.

CHAPTER VI.

THE BLAST.

Carrera was now fully satisfied of the hopelessness of the rebellion, and the thought struck him that it was his duty to warn his friend, Roberto Sanchez, and to save him if it was not too late. He concluded to leave Quito in search of the hot-headed enthusiast, and to travel on until he had found him. With this determination he arose early on the morning following the visit of Dolores, and ordered Mariano to make the necessary preparations, and to accompany him on the journey. But Spanish America in those days did not differ from the Spanish America of to-day. It takes so long to make preparations for traveling, as to bear out the Spanish proverb, "To get away from the inn is half the journey." In spite of all the impatience of Carrera, the day was far advanced before everything was in readiness. And now he would go out to learn the latest news, and to ascertain the probable whereabouts of his young friend. He would also take leave of Dolores, to whom he desired to prove, by his expedition, that he intended to be zealous in the King's cause. As to the contemplated hair-brained offer of a crown to himself, if such an offer was to be made, he would forestall it by a few words with old Olmos, or Sanchez, the father, whose death he had not yet learned. And Toa! should he see her? No; how could he meet her? In what light would he now appear before her? It must be confessed that his dread of such a meeting had contributed somewhat to his resolution to leave the city. He would return the sum she had advanced to him, as soon as he came into full possession of his inheritance. He endeavored to persuade himself that she had bewitched him, and that the potion which Mama Rucu had given him was an elixir of love, the effects of which, as he felt confident, had fully worn away. It seemed impossible to him, as he now felt, that Toa's wiles could have ensnared him, had he remained in undisturbed possession of his sober senses. But now the spell was broken, and he realized the full danger of the delusion under which he had labored. He stood in the doorway down stairs, giving his last orders to Mariano, when his attention was arrested by a wild tumult in the street. A disorderly multitude, entirely composed of men of the lower and lowest orders, came marching down from the Plaza, rending the air with wild acclamations. As they caught sight of him, they broke into enthusiastic *vivas!* and hurried toward his house, filling the street completely, and crowding into his doorway and *pateo*.

" *Viva el gran Senor de Carrera!* Long live our King! Long live our Shyris, Carrera and Duchicela!"

Dolores was right, then. He had doubted it until this moment.

" What are your wishes, my friends?" he inquired with a smiling face and a palpitating heart. He had not expected that the offer of a crown would be made to him by a mob. He had prepared himself for an argument with the revolutionary leaders, but this demonstration was a terrible surprise.

" Long live the first gentleman of Quito, who shall rule over this Kingdom and save us from our enemies," shouted one; and repeated *vivas* followed this announcement.

" I do not understand you, my friends," said Carrera, retreating toward the staircase, as the mob crowded around him. " Have the goodness to stand back, and let some one explain your wishes."

" Castro will speak for us!" exclaimed several voices.

"That I will, with your Highness' permission!" said Castro, as he elbowed himself through the crowd, and, hat in hand, presented himself to Carrera.

"I wish you would, Don Juan," rejoined Carrera meekly, "for I do not understand the meaning of these acclamations."

"The people, most excellent Señor!" began Castro, "want a King. We want a leader to protect us, to save us from our enemies. The Alcabala-men are murdering our friends. They have murdered the good Sanchez, as they assassinated Bellido. The troops of Arana are moving on the Capital. They will murder us all. Our leaders are divided in their councils. There are too many of them to agree. We must have one head to direct and command. King Philip has forfeited his rights by destroying our *fueros* and taking away our privileges. We are Americans and not *chapetones*. We want an American to rule over us and be a nation by ourselves. In this crisis the people look to your Excellency, the most magnanimous and the most beloved *caballero* of Quito. Your Excellency shall be our King and the husband of Toa Duchicela, the Shyri Queen, and we will defend your Majesties with the last drop of our blood. Will we not?"

"Yes! Yes!" shouted the multitude. "Long live their Majesties!"

"But listen, friends!" said Carrera, "I am greatly beholden to you for your kindness and good opinion and feel highly flattered by your confidence, but I regret the mode and cause of its expression."

"No! No! No!"

"Let me speak, my friends! I am a young man, untried and inexperienced in affairs of state, to which I never paid much attention. You should not come to me with your wishes or grievances; but you should present them to the Cabildo, where they will be properly considered and judiciously acted upon. You should know, my friends, that I am powerless to do anything for you. It is the Cabildo that has the disposal of your armed forces and the general direction of your affairs."

"The Cabildo will approve of our selection," rejoined Castro, "if your Excellency will but consent."

"Yes! Yes!" shouted those near by, while those that were in the rear crowded forward more and more, until Carrera's position became exceedingly uncomfortable and embarrassing. Some of the men had even taken positions on the staircase, thus cutting off his retreat.

"Were you sent here by the Cabildo, my friends?" inquired Carrera.

"It is all the same, most excellent Señor!" replied Castro. "The Cabildo but awaits your Excellency's decision."

"But do you bring me any message from the Cabildo?"

"I vouch for its concurrence and approbation," answered Castro, pompously.

"I do not ask for any concurrence or approbation," resumed Carrera, hesitating to utter the word which, in all probability, would turn this fierce mob against him, "all I ask is this, that in so grave a matter as your future welfare, you should consult with those who have the power to be of service to you."

"We shall defer to your Highness' opinion," replied Castro. "We shall escort your Excellency to the Cabildo and have the proclamation made from the balcony of the building."

"On to the Cabildo!" shouted several voices. "Let us carry our King on our shoulders!" And before Carrera could say a word, he was seized by strong hands and placed on the shoulders of two stalwart men.

And now the critical moment had arrived.

"Not one step further, my friends!" exclaimed the young man, who had turned deathly pale. "It must not, it can not be!"

"What can not be?" demanded Castro, changing his manner and tone.

"I can not be your King. If I have your confidence and your affection, I beg you to desist from this visionary scheme and let me go." And with these words he attempted to break from the men who held him; but it was in vain.

"But your Excellency must accept," whispered Castro. "We have risked our lives for your Excellency; and you can not, you shall not abandon us."

"But, my dear friend," remonstrated Carrera, "do you not realize that such a wild undertaking could never succeed?"

"Let him down," said Castro to the men who carried Carrera, while the mob were pressing around, vociferating and gesticulating, and then, placing his hands on his victim's shoulders, he whispered to him: "It is death to you to refuse. You must accept or die." And as he stared at him ferociously, the dream in Mama Rucu's cottage suddenly came back to Carrera's mind. Yes, those were the dreadful eyes that had stared at him in his dream. His heart sank. Now he understood the meaning of that dream. He knew that a dreadful ordeal was before him, and he prayed to God and the Virgin to protect him.

"Juan Castro," he said, "are you a Christian?"

"That is not the question now," replied the ruffian, still in a whisper. "You have to decide on the spot whether you will sacrifice us or yourself. Consent, and you shall be safe. Refuse, and your life will not be worth a *maravedi*. Be quick about it."

"Santa Maria, Mother of God! I commend myself to thy care."

"You are a traitor, then, to the cause of the people?" resumed Castro, in a loud and angry voice.

"I am no traitor, Juan Castro. I am your friend and

the friend of the people, a devout Christian, and a loyal subject to the King of Spain!"

"Hear it, men of Quito! Hear it!" shouted Castro, with a stentorian voice, "this man, for whom we were about to lay down our lives, rejects the honors which we have proffered him. He declares that he is a loyal subject to King Alcabala, the murderer of Bellido and Sanchez. He will not aid the cause of his native city and country. What shall we do with him?"

"Accept, Señor de Carrera! Accept! Accept!" exclaimed some of the men. "Do not abandon us in the hour of need. A King alone can save us, and you shall be our King."

"But will you not give me time to consider?" entreated Carrera. "This proposition has been a perfect surprise to me. I can not accept it without previous reflection. Give me a short time, at least, to consider." And his eyes glided over the sea of heads that surged around him, in the vain expection of relief or rescue from somewhere. But he saw nothing but the turbulent mob of his assailants. There was a number of armed soldiers among them, but they seemed to be in sympathy with the rabble.

"You can not escape from us that way, Señor Don Julio de Carrera," rejoined Castro. "Your decision must be made now."

"I do not intend to escape. Let me return to my house" —they had him out on the street by this time—"and you can go in with me and guard all its doors and windows. I pledge you my word of honor that I shall not attempt to escape."

"Time is too precious, Señor," said Castro. "Arana is marching upon Quito, and not a moment must be lost."

"Take off your hands, man," replied Carrera, vainly seeking to release himself. "Is this the manner in which you would treat your King?"

"But you refuse to be our King."

"I must!" exclaimed the young man, who had now resigned himself to the inevitable, and determined to try the effect of sternness. "Your proceeding is treasonable and sacrilegious. Unhand me, I say, and stand back!"

With these words he freed himself from the hold of Castro, and attempted to draw his sword. But it was in vain. He was at once seized and disarmed by half a dozen powerful men, and again found himself in the iron grip of Castro.

"Men of Quito " yelled the latter, "this traitor would draw his sword against us. He would strike down the people who came to offer him a crown."

"Kill him! Kill him!" clamored those near by, and the dreadful cry was taken up by those in the rear.

"I have not harmed any one of you—I have always wished you well," remonstrated Carrera, but his voice was drowned by the tumult.

At this moment an *arriero*, with a drove of donkeys and mules, endeavored to pass the next intersection of the street, but found himself stopped by the multitude.

"Let us put him on an ass, and make a Carnival-King of him, if he will not be a real King."

"Yes! Yes! And he shall run the gauntlet, too."

"Up with him! Tie him to the ass. That's the steed for him."

In an instant his doublet was torn from him. His vest and shirt were next pulled off his back and torn into shreds, and he was hustled forward to the corner. The Arriero attempted to turn back his animals, but the mob seized one of the donkeys, cut the ropes by which its load was fastened, and then pulled the animal through the crowd toward Carrera. Some of the men disentangled the ropes from the load of boxes on the ground, and shouted: "Now, let us tie him on the ass;" which was no sooner said than done.

"There is a crown for him!" said another, snatching a

hat from a poor Indian's head, and slamming it on Carrera's.

"And now for switches! Let us pay him his royalty."

The procession moved on, mocking its unfortunate victim, yelling, sneering, and cursing. Some threw mud, others threw stones at him; others belabored his bare back with canes and switches. A garden was reached, inclosed with an aloe hedge. The mob at once broke into the inclosure, and cut down the tough, long-bladed leaves, which, as the reader knows, end in spines. With these blades they struck him unmercifully. The skin of his back broke in a few seconds, and the blood spurted forth and covered those around him. In a few minutes Carrera's back was an unsightly mass of raw flesh and blood, with pieces of lacerated skin hanging down from it. And still the procession moved on, and the hooting, yelling, and cursing continued. No rescue came. No help from anywhere. The shopkeepers had closed their *tiendas* at the approach of the tumultuous mob. The citizens had shut and barred their doors and windows, for fear of violence to themselves or their families.

At last the procession had reached the suburbs, and approached the steep banks of the Machangara, in the rear of the Nunnery of Santa Clara. Carrera had lost his consciousness, and, apparently lifeless, hung from the ass. The mob had exhausted its fury, and some of the men had become ashamed of their work, and were anxious to get away from it. Others had dropped off, and the crowd had considerably diminished when it came to a halt. Castro, too, who was sure of his victim's death, had disappeared. As soon as the mob found itself without its leader it evinced an anxiety to stop.

"He is dead!" said one of them.

"Let us drop him in the river!"

"No; drop him right here, by the garden wall," said

another. "It is over with him. Let us go back to the city, and see what has happened."

"Come along!" shouted another, who, breathless from running, had just joined the crowd. "The people are clamoring for the surrender of the President of the Audience. He is to be dispatched next. There is work to be done! Come along."

"Cut down this dead traitor! Cut him down!"

It was done. The ropes with which Carrera was tied were cut, and heavily, without a sign of life, he fell to the ground, and lay there, bleeding and motionless.

When consciousness returned to him, he found himself lying in a pool of blood. He attempted to raise himself but this effort gave him a terrible pain in the back, and brought him down again. A second attempt was followed by the same result. The pain was so intense that it threw him into a swoon. When he came to again, he tried, without moving, to ascertain where he was. His head rested on the base of a garden wall. As far as he could see without turning, it was the place he had beheld in his first vision in Mama Rucu's cottage. That vision now came back to him with terrible distinctness. He could not descry any human being as far as his eye could reach. All was lonely and lifeless around him. Was his situation a reality, or another vision? If it had not been for the pain that racked him he would have believed that he was dreaming. By attentively scanning the features of the locality before him, he came to the conclusion that he must be near the *Quebrada* of San Diego, and that the garden wall above him must belong to the Nunnery of Santa Clara.

At last he heard voices, female voices. Two ladies, followed by four or five male servants, were coming toward him, apparently in great trepidation. They moved cautiously, yet hurriedly, constantly looking backward. A man now passed him, but took little or no notice of him.

The man rushed forward to meet the two ladies. "Your Ladyships can now enter safely," he said. "The Mother Superior has ordered the door to be kept open so that your Ladyships can slip in. But be quick, for the love of the Virgin! The demons of hell are let loose. They have sacked our house, and they are now before the Cabildo-building, clamoring for the lives of the President and the Auditors."

"Is there nobody in the street below, or in the Plaza of Santa Clara?" asked one of the ladies, reluctant to venture forward.

"The Plaza of Santa Clara is deserted; not a soul is to be seen there now. But God knows how it will be five minutes hence. Your Ladyships have no time to lose."

"Let us make haste, then," said the other lady, and Carrera recognized the voice of Dolores. "But what is that, there on the ground across our way?" she asked pointing to Carrera.

"Some man who has been murdered or badly wounded during the day; he will not trouble your Ladyships. Your Ladyships must pass him without looking at him. The sight might sicken your Ladyships."

And now the group had come up to the helpless man. Both the women averted their faces as they passed him. Aunt Catita even covered her eyes with her handkerchief, and, clasping the arm of Dolores, shrank away as far from the bloody sight, as the narrowness of the pathway allowed. Carrera now realized that this was his chance of salvation. If she would but look at him! But no! she passed him with averted eyes. Unmindful of the excruciating pain produced by the effort which, to his present condition, was almost superhuman, he raised himself on his elbow, and summoning the last remnants of his vital strength, he broke into the agonizing and despairing shriek: "Dolores!" and then fell back heavily, and fainted away.

"The man must know me," said Dolores, as they hurried

on to reach the door of the Convent in safety. "He has called me by name. His voice, too, is not unfamiliar. I wonder who it may be?"

"Hurry on, Doloritas, for Heaven's sake," said Aunt Catita; "let us get under shelter as fast as we can." And on they rushed until, almost out of breath, they had reached the Convent door, where they were waited for by the Mother Superior and some of her nuns, and overwhelmed with sympathetic caresses.

"Your mother is awaiting you with feverish anxiety," said the Superior. "You must see her at once. Your servants will stay with our own. We may need them all."

The ladies now rushed to the apartments fitted up for the Marchioness, whom the news of her son's sad death had not yet reached. Nobody in the Convent seemed to know of it, and Dolores deemed it most prudent to keep it to herself for the present. She would also ask the Superior to keep it from the Marchioness as long as possible. It was difficult enough to allay the present excitement of the old lady, who was lamenting the destruction of her property, and the absense of her son and husband.

It was not until about fifteen minutes had elapsed from the time Dolores and Catita had entered the sheltering walls of Santa Clara, that Aunt Catita remembered the wounded or dying man outside. A consultation followed, whether anything could be done for him, and whether it would be safe and prudent to attempt it. At last the Superior concluded that if no crowds were visible in the Plaza or in the adjoining streets, she would send out two men with a stretcher to bring him in. The Plaza and neighboring streets were still deserted, and so the men were sent out. They returned without the wounded man. They had easily found the place where he had lain. It was still marked by a large pool of blood; but the man was gone. There was no trace of him far or near.

CHAPTER VII.

AN UNDERSTANDING.

The riotous day had given way to a noisy and tumultous night. At about nine o'clock three men on horseback, fully armed and equipped for a journey, halted before the Convent of Santa Clara, and one of them dismounted and rang the bell. It was Manuel Paredes. The servant at the door opened the wicket and demanded to know his business.

"I wish to see the Señorita Dolores Solando."

"It is too late," answered the servant; "it is against the rules of the Convent to admit visitors at this hour."

"But I must see the Señorita on business of the utmost importance to herself and her father. If you will let me see the Mother Superior, I can satisfy her that my business admits of no delay."

"My orders are peremptory."

"But these are extraordinary times. Human lives are at stake. The Señorita Dolores is not a member of your order, and I know the Mother Superior will allow an exception to be made in a case of such urgency."

After long delays and protracted consultations inside, the door was finally opened and Paredes invited to enter. Telling his companions to ride ahead slowly, as he would soon overtake them, he led his horse into the convent court, and after tying him to a post, followed the janitress into the reception-room, where Dolores and her aunt awaited him, behind a double lattice-work of wooden bars, which separated that part of the room to which visitors were admitted from the part reserved for the inmates. A dim candle burned on a table near the door, leaving the ladies behind the bars in utter darkness. Paredes could not see their faces, but he heard the voice of Dolores asking him to be seated.

"I come to take leave, Señorita," he said, "and to receive your orders. I must be off this very minute."

"You alarm me, Don Manuel," said Dolores. "I hope nothing has happened to render your stay unsafe."

"Not at all. I leave on a mission which will soon be accomplished. I expect to be back within a week to place myself at the feet of your Ladyship."

"And where are you going to?"

"To the camp of Arana, with messages from the Royal Audience and the Cabildo. I shall see your Father, the Marquis, and shall take to him any letters or messages your Ladyships may wish to send."

"You are just in time, Don Manuel. I have written a long letter to him. Aunt Catita! Will you have the kindness to bring it to me. It is on my table, and," she added, in an undertone, "stay away, or stay outside as long as you can, without attracting attention."

"And now what has happened, my dear friend?" asked Dolores, as soon as they were alone. "What a fearful tragedy your plan has led to!"

"But it has succeeded. The scheme of the conspirators is dead. There will be no more plotting for a false king, unless unforeseen occurrences should change the situation. The reaction has set in. The party of action are still fierce and vow great things, but they have been foiled most skillfully in every respect, and the King's servants will soon be restored to power."

"But what of Carrera? I shudder when I think of his fate."

"Ah, then you love him still! Even dead he will be in my way."

"Is he dead? For heaven's sake say no, Señor Paredes!

His death would be our work, and the Holy Virgin knows I did not intend it."

"I do not know whether he is dead or alive. His body has not been found. The city has been searched in every direction. The most diligent inquiries have been made during the day, but with no result. Nobody has seen the body. Nobody knows what has become of it."

"It is dreadful, my friend.. It is dreadful, doubly dreadful because I suspect that your insane love for me has directed the blows that laid him low."

"I swear to you, Señorita, that I am innocent, and that I did not foresee, did not even dream of such a result. But the rabble of Quito is blood-thirsty and cruel, and when once aroused it seems impossible to control it. Yet, if in the King's service sacrifices become necessary or unavoidable, such sacrifices must be made. If I had to do this thing over again, I should not stop or hesitate even if I knew the lives of a thousand Carreras had to be sacrificed. But time presses, Señorita. Let us not waste it in vain regrets. What is past is past, and what is done can not be undone. I have news to tell you. Are you ready to hear it?"

"Proceed!"

"Your house has been taken possession of by the officers and men whom Olmos has brought from Ibarra and Cotocachi. They will do a great deal of damage, but that can not be helped now, and your father will have to be indemnified out of the estates of the guilty. Do you think they will find papers or documents which might compromise any of the King's friends?"

"Indeed, not, Señor Paredes. Proceed!"

"The mob, after having left Carrera for dead, reassembled in the Great Square, and demanded the lives of the President and the Auditors. But in this they were thwarted. The Audience was allowed to issue an order to Arana, commanding him to return to Guayaquil, and to remain there until the whole question can be referred back to the Viceroy and the Court at Madrid, in order to effect a compromise, if possible. The President and the Auditors are to be held as hostages for the fulfillment of this order, and I, being considered one of the most trustworthy partisans of the Cabildo, am to deliver the order in person to the Royal Commander."

"Very good! He will, of course, disregard it."

"If his forces are strong enough, he will. If not, prudence would dictate that he should comply with it, apparently. Once with Arana and your father, I think I shall be able to suggest a plan of action which will accomplish our objects with the least possible loss of time."

"And did this arrangement satisfy the populace?"

"With the distinct assurance that the Auditors shall die, if Arana refuses to withdraw to Guayaquil, it was easy to pacify the mob. If Arana disregards the order, means of escape to a sanctuary will be furnished to the Ministers. I have put everything in splendid working order. You will never have cause to be ashamed of your protegé, Señorita. There is but one difficulty in the way. Roberto Sanchez has asked for reinforcements. He has sent message after message, asking, demanding, begging, storming for troops. He declares that if the Quito troops had been moved four weeks ago, Arana would now be in the hands of the Cabildo, and old Sanchez's life would have been spared. The young man's courage and success thus far have won him the hearts of the people, and the Cabildo, seconding the popular demand, have ordered troops to be sent to him for active operations, in case Arana should refuse to withdraw."

"These troops will not be sent, really?"

"Yes, Señorita, it must be done. We must make a show of sending troops to the seat of war, if we do not want to betray ourselves. But these troops will be under the command of Juan de Londoño, who is with us. He will leave

Quito to-morrow with a small force; but it will take him a long time to get to Ambato, and he will never reach the place where young Sanchez wants him. If Arana disregards the orders of the Audience, Guzman de Leon is to follow Londoño with our whole force. But there is no danger of that. Guzman has played his part admirably and he will play it on as long as necessary."

"And Toa with her Indians?"

"The failure of the scheme to set up a pseudo King, with the ambitious Toa as his Queen, will disgust the Indians with the cause of the Cabildo. Our friends have wearied them with endless negotiations and arguments, with promises which we never intended to keep, and with demands for gold, which they are not inclined or able to gratify. No, Señorita, no danger threatens us now. We are on the high road to an easy victory. The only remaining difficulty is that unmanageable young man, Roberto Sanchez, and he is far away, where he can do no harm. I leave everything in a most satisfactory condition, and regret nothing but the necessity of having to be away from you."

"My thoughts and best wishes will be with you, Don Manuel."

"And your love, too, Dolores?"

"And my love, too."

"Then I am to hope, at last, that when all our difficulties are over, you will follow me to the altar."

"No, Don Manuel, for your own sake, I must not marry you."

"Dolores, what do you mean?"

"Let me speak frankly, Manuel Paredes, and you will see how much I love you. Yes, Manuel, I love you, more than I even loved my husband, because I respect and admire you as I admired no man before. You are a *man*, Manuel Paredes. There is none like you in this Kingdom. You have saved my father, you have saved and protected me, and you will save the King's cause. Both love and gratitude draw me to you."

"And yet you refuse to marry me '

"Listen! You have no rivals. The Count is dead. Carrera is dead. But you, Manuel Paredes, shall live. Know, then, that I am under a fearful spell, which, it seems, can not be broken. Do you believe in the predictions of Mama Rucu? Did she not predict the death of Count Valverde in your presence? You heard her curse, and you know how dreadfully it was fulfilled?"

"I do not understand you, Dolores."

"You shall, presently. I am cursed with one of her predictions. There is death in my hand when given in marriage. There is death even in my thought of marriage. That was her prophecy. Now consider how it was fulfilled. I disbelieved and defied her prediction, and was married. In less than a year the ghastly, bleeding corpse of my husband was carried into my father's house. I thought of marrying Count Valverde. I can confess it to you now. I did not love him, but the thought of exchanging the dullness of our provincial life for the gayeties and splendors of the court of Spain, had tempted me strongly. You know the result. Count Valverde is dead. There is death, then, even in my thought of marriage. And not a natural death. No! That Indian fiend has predicted a a bloody, violent, cruel death to those whom I should marry or even wish or intend to marry. And now Carrera! Before I learned to love and admire you, Manuel Paredes, I had thought of Carrera as a possible husband, and behold his terrible end. Can you reproach me, then, for not wishing to sacrifice you by giving you my hand in marriage, or even thinking of you as a husband? No, Manuel Paredes, I love you; and because I love you I want you to live and prosper. Your heart I accept. I love you too much to refuse it. Your hand I must refuse."

At this moment, Aunt Catita returned with the letter

Dolores had prepared for her father. " Quick For heaven's sake to your mother?" she exclaimed. . " Through the stupidity of one of the maids, who had become unmindful of our injunctions, she has heard of the death of her son and fainted away."

Before Paredes had left the Convent, the Marchioness of Solando had breathed her last, and Don Manuel had become the bearer of sad news for his great friend and patron in the camp of the Royalists.

CHAPTER VIII.

IN THE MOUNTAINS.

SEVERAL weeks had elapsed since the events narrated in the preceding chapters.

Arana had thought himself too weak to undertake the march on Quito at once, which would also have involved an immediate engagement with Roberto Sanchez, who had recruited his band with men drawn from Ambato, Mocha, and Riobamba, where he had seized the royal treasuries and levied heavy contributions on the estates and families of the colonists, who had joined the Royal Commissioner. Under these circumstances, the latter deemed it prudent to affect compliance with the mock-order of the Audience, and to withdraw his forces to the other side of the Cordillera, there to await the reinforcements which were coming to him from Cuenca, Loja, and the coast. Sanchez followed him with the little army of his own creation, under orders from the Cabildo, carefully to watch the movements of the Royal Commissioner, and to hold himself ready to strike at the first hostile demonstrations; but, if no such demonstrations were made, to respect the armistice concluded through the intercession of the Quito Audience until the final determination of the Viceroy should be known. The fiery Sanchez chafed under the restraints imposed by these orders, which he considered fatal to the Revolutionary cause; but in view of his own youth and inexperience, he did not dare to counteract commands upon which older and wiser heads had agreed.

The wily Arana, however, did not tax the impatience of his youthful antagonist too long. Reinforced by fresh levies, and relieved from his most pressing embarrassments by the opportune arrival of a vessel with supplies from Peru, the old fox suddenly broke away from Sanchez, and unmindful of the armistice, pressed on toward the Cordillera, which he prepared to repass by a side road, whereas Sanchez had expected his advance along the main road (*camino real*), on which he had fortified some of the most difficult mountain passes against the approach of the enemy.

Under these circumstances, left by himself in the heart of the mountains, and in danger of being cut off from his communication with Quito, if Arana succeeded in reaching Riobamba, Sanchez concluded to dash back into the tablelands, and thence, by a forced march, to reascend the Cordillera and to intercept the Royal Commissioner in the mountain passes before he had fully completed his arduous and difficult descent into the plains. If Sanchez could strike Arana in the wilderness, he would be at the mercy of the rebel mountaineers, who, availing themselves of the roughness of the wretched roads, the narrowness of the defiles, and the steepness of the precipices, might, by a lucky or skillful use of opportunities, decide the fate of the campaign without the aid of the sluggards at Quito. The plan was brilliant and promising, but its success entirely depended on the celerity of its execution. Unfortunately, however, the elements conspired against the youthful hero. Local rains, uncommon at this season of the year, made the roads so slippery that his men and horses could move along only with great difficulty and slowness. Thus two days were lost, while every moment was precious. The passage of the last ridge, which ordinarily might have been accomplished in a few hours, took him nearly a day, and compelled him to take a short rest in one of those romantic villages, hidden in the folds of the Andean mountains, while he sent scouts on fresh horses, seized for the occasion, to Riobamba and its neighborhood, to ascertain the whereabouts of Arana.

It was a cold, cloudless, and beautiful night—one of those weird summer nights under the equator, when the snowy dome of Mt. Chimborazo stands forth in bold relief against the deep dark-blue, starlit sky. Roberto Sanchez, covered with a heavy woolen *poncho*, stood on the veranda of the only habitable dwelling in the village, the house of the local *Alcalde*, whispering words of gallantry into the not unwilling ear of the *Alcalde's* daughter, who stood leaning against one of the pillars of the veranda with her eyes turned to the bright stars above them, while one of her hands heedlessly rested in Roberto's.

"Do not say to-morrow or next day, Señorita," said he, rather sadly. "To-morrow I am off. To-morrow I hope to fight, and there may be no to-morrow for me after that."

"The holy Virgin will protect you, Señor! You are too young and too handsome to die. I shall give you an amulet which I have worn ever since I was a child. I have it from my grandfather, who received it from a Moor in Granada, whom he had befriended by great kindness. It will protect you from balls and steel and from witchcraft, but not from water. You must never take it to sea, where its good qualities are perverted into evil and danger." And thus saying, she took the amulet from her neck and hung it around his.

"*Quien vive?*" shouted one of the sentinels, and the hoofs

of horses were heard resounding through the stillness of the night.

"*La Patria!*" answered a voice familiar to Sanchez. "Who commands here?"

"Roberto Sanchez!"

"Thank Heaven! It is he whom I must see."

"Do you bring reinforcements?" inquired the sentinel.

"No; but news and dispatches. Where is the commander?"

"There, at the house of the Alcalde."

Two horsemen, a caballero and his servant, presently appeared in front of the house and dismounted. In the next moment Roberto Sanchez was locked in the embrace of his young friend, Carlos de Olmos, the son of Señor Olmos, of the Cabildo, one of the few trustworthy leaders of the party of action. Señor Olmos had sent his son with important messages to Sanchez. A minute afterward the whole camp was astir, burning with anxiety to hear the news from Quito. The newcomer followed the young chief into the house, where they were joined by two of Roberto's officers. The one was his lieutenant, the veteran Pedro Perez, and the other was Roberto's adjutant, Garcia.

"Will you refresh yourself, *amigo?*" inquired Sanchez. "We have but little left, but it is at your disposal."

"Not until I have given you the news," said young Olmos, taking off his shawl, poncho, sword, and spurs. "I have traveled night and day to find you, and came very near being captured by the scouts of Arana."

"By the scouts of Arana?" repeated Sanchez, petrified. "Where do you come from last?"

"From Riobamba."

"From Riobamba?" continued Sanchez. "Man, what do you mean? Is Arana on his way to Riobamba?"

"He arrived there yesterday, and will continue his march to Quito to-morrow morning."

"Great Heavens! Then he has escaped from me, and all my hopes are blasted. I expected to head him off as he descended from the mountains. I should have crushed him among the cañons. Now it is over! With my handful of men I can not attack him in the plains. How strong is his force supposed to be?"

"From what I could learn, it is estimated at from fifteen hundred to two thousand; but this must be an exaggeration."

"Undoubtedly!" said Sanchez. "He could not have passed the Cordillera so swiftly with so large a force. And what has become of our army? Does it still exist, and will it ever move?"

"You strike the very object of my mission, Roberto," said Olmos. "I have not been sent by the Cabildo. They know nothing of my journey to your camp. My father has sent me. He wants me to tell you that he fears we are betrayed."

"By all the demons of hell!" shouted old Pedro Perez, while Sanchez listened eagerly, and turning pale. "That accounts for our inability to obtain reinforcements, and for the shameful inactivity of the authorities at Quito."

"My father fears," continued the young man, "that those to whom the most important commands have been confided are secretly in league with the King's Ministers."

"And whom does he suspect?"

"First of all, he suspects the commander-in-chief, Pedro Guzman; and what father merely suspects is clear as daylight to me. Guzman is a traitor, gentlemen, a vile and infamous traitor. He has frittered away our time and resources without making a move or striking a blow. He has paralyzed our energies, and demoralized our men. He has been playing into the hands of the enemy ever since he assumed the command."

"Just what I always thought," interrupted Sanchez;

"but why is he left in command? The scoundrel! I know him, and have always despised him."

"Because it seems that the party of the Bellidistas, to which your father and mine belonged, has lost its power. Our best men have been sent to the north, to resist an imaginary force from Bogota. The troops whom Londoño took south with him to reinforce you, also consisted of good and reliable men. But the men left at Quito are doubtful. A great many, perhaps half of them, may be trustworthy; but the others would side with Guzman and the traitors, rather than with the Cabildo. It is evident that the soldiers have been tampered with."

Sanchez buried his face in his hands, and exclaimed: "O my father! My poor father! Was he sacrificed in vain?"

"Under these circumstances my father can see but one remedy. He wants you to come to Quito with your whole force, if possible; if not, with at least fifty resolute men, and to come unannounced and unexpected, and with the aid of the loyal leaders and soldiers, to change matters by a bold *coup d' etat*, to remove and imprison Guzman and his traitors, to purge the Cabildo of its vicious elements, and then to push the war vigorously and boldly, and in accordance with the original programme of Bellido and your noble father. In the success of this *coup* lies our only hope. If it fails, we are lost and will be delivered to the hangman like sheep at the shambles. Your boldness, your dash, and the great reputation and popularity you have acquired, eminently qualify you for the task. Will you undertake it? Will you take the responsibility of acting without orders, and in spite of them?"

Sanchez had raised his head from the table while listening to this proposition. The words of young Olmos had given him new life, his eyes sparkled, and every nerve and fiber in his body quivered with excitement, and springing from his seat with outstretched arms, he pressed his friend to his bosom. "God bless your noble father!" he exclaimed. "Of course I shall do it, or perish in the attempt."

"Santiago! Santiago!" shouted Perez and Garcia. "On to Quito, and death to the traitors!"

"I shall make my preparations immediately. Our horses are too tired to start to-night; but we must march before daybreak."

"There is one thing to be considered," said Olmos. "Arana is now between you and Quito, and you will have to pass him on the way."

"He advances along the main road," said Sanchez. "We shall take to the mountains above or to the valleys below him. Arana will have to lose a day or two at Ambato; but we shall lose no time anywhere. By all the Saints of Heaven, I swear that we shall reach Quito before him!"

A tumult outside arrested the conversation. Some of Roberto's scouts had returned. They had met friends of the Cabildo, fresh from Riobamba with important news. Arana had detached two hundred horse under the command of a Spanish veteran, by the name of Juan del Puente, to set out in search of Sanchez' force, and to intercept and to capture him.

"We shall present our compliments to Señor del Puente!" said Sanchez after the scouts had been discharged. "If we can, we must give him the slip, because we must save our men for more important work. But if we can not, we shall try American bravery against Spanish brutality."

CHAPTER IX.

THE DESCENT.

"Do not forget," said the Alcalde's daughter, early next morning, as Roberto had snatched a farewell kiss from her not unwilling lips, "beware of water while you wear this amulet. From every other danger it will protect you."

And now the march began, and onward they toiled, up hill and down hill, over mountains and through ravines, over slippery and narrow paths with yawning precipices on one side, and perpendicular rocks on the other; now through defiles hardly wide enough for one man to pass, then again over the dreary *paramo* with its monotonous and oppressive desolation. At last they saw the plain of Riobamba at their feet, with its towns and villages almost hidden among the willow trees, and surrounded by fields of green clover.

But the troop of Sanchez had no time and inclination to scan the scenery which expanded before them for objects of natural beauty and grandeur. If they strained their eyes and anxiously looked down into the plain, it was to discover the men of Del Puente, who had been sent out against them.

Before making the final descent which would, for the present, take them away from the sheltering roughness of the mountains, Sanchez ordered a halt, to refresh his men and horses, and to await the return of the scouts whom he had sent ahead. The men had now spread themselves over what the Spaniards call a *meseta*, a small plateau formed by the protrusion of the mountain, from which they commanded the steep and narrow winding path which led into the plain below. There they disposed of the last of their provisions: they were now out of the wilderness, and the fertile country into which they were descending could supply their wants. Here the merry bottle passed from hand to hand. The weary limbs were rested after the long ride. Some that were soon to sleep the eternal sleep were stretched out on the ground and slept as quietly and securely as in the days of happy childhood. Others forgot, over the dice-box, or a soiled and sticky pack of cards, the danger that was before them. Still others discussed the political outlook, and shrugged their shoulders at the waning prospects of the popular cause. There was no lack of doubt and despondency. Blindly they had trusted and followed their leader, as long as success perched on his banners; but, since they knew that Arana had slipped away from him, and that the enemy was now between them and their friends at Quito, their confidence had been shaken, and dark forebodings began to fill their minds. Sanchez felt this as he passed from group to group, and noticed the half-concealed change in the tone, the smile, the laughter, the countenances of the men. The wilderness of the mountain bound them to him now; but would he be able to hold them together after having descended into the plain? Not unless the prestige of success could be restored, of which Arana's escape had deprived him. On the restoration of this prestige his own future usefulness seemed to depend. Hence, the conviction grew upon him that he must fight Del Puente instead of giving him the slip, as he had intended.

"*Quien vive!*" shouted one of the outposts.

"A poor Indian and a friend," was the answer given by a man in the Indian garb, with a bundle on his back, who came slowly climbing up the mountain road.

"Pass on," said the sentinel, who knew that Indians were always welcome and well treated at the camp of Sanchez; because, contrary to their usual disposition, they volunteered information and furnished provisions. To the

Indians all over the country Sanchez had become a superior being, by the favor bestowed upon him by Queen Toa, during the bloody night at Quito.

"I have to speak to the Viracocha who commands these soldiers," said the newcomer.

"I am the man, my friend. What good news do you bring?"

"May I speak to your Grace alone?"

"Yes, my good man," said Sanchez, taking him aside.

"Is your Grace the possessor of Queen Toa's silver moon?"

"I am, my friend!" answered Sanchez, showing him the trinket which he wore around his neck, "and I am a servant of Toa Duchicela, and a friend to your race."

"The great sun will protect your Grace!" said the Indian, kissing the silver moon. "I have a letter to deliver to your Grace from the Shyri Toa. Here it is!"

"God bless the Shyri Toa," said Sanchez hastily opening the letter. It read as follows:

"Señor Don Roberto Sanchez.—You are the only true friend I have found among the men of your race—the only one who has not deceived and betrayed me. The men of the Cabildo have not kept faith with me, and their cause is no longer my cause. The blood of my people shall not be spilled in vain. You will know by this time that you and your cause have been betrayed by the same men that betrayed me and my children. You have been asked to return to Quito, and I know you will come. I pray to Pachacamac that for your own sake and for the sake of my cause, you may not come too late. To prevent such a calamity, I have sent my servant, Uma, to you. He knows the country better than any of my subjects. He knows every mountain-pass, and he is familiar with byways that are known only to the Indians. He will show you in case of danger the shortest and the safest routes. His services will prove invaluable. You can trust him as implicity as you would trust me. Come as fast as you can and strike without a moment's delay. You shall want nothing during your march that my people can provide.

"I have but one word more to say, although I need hardly to say it to you. Distrust Manuel Paredes. He pretends great zeal in your cause, but he is as false as the serpent of the forest. I should have killed him long ago, had I not wished him to live in order to avenge my wrongs on one who has betrayed me worse than all, by making him experience the same sufferings that he has inflicted upon me.

"Your true and faithful friend,
"TOA DUCHICELA."

"In the plain below," resumed Uma with that dignified and unassuming calmness which characterized the old nobility of his race, "about half a league from where this mountain loses itself in the plain, is the great *hacienda* of San José, to which over three hundred Indians belong. The main building is large, and it is surrounded by a number of outhouses. The headquarters of the Spanish commander, Juan del Puente, are now at that *hacienda*. There he awaits your Grace to attack you as soon as you descend into the plain. He has sent out detachments to observe the two other outlets of this range, and has thus weakened himself to the extent of nearly one-half of his force. Your Grace will have to leave this road. There is a subterranean ravine about a hundred rods from here which descends from the mountain, and runs through the plain, passing the farm-buildings of San José. It is overgrown with shrubs and trees; but it is so deep and wide that two men abreast can walk through it. Your whole force can pass it, if you will leave the horses behind under guard. I have hidden *chasquis* (couriers) in the ravine who will inform the Indians at the *hacienda* of our coming. They will secure the horses of the unsuspecting Spaniards, while your Grace will fall upon the men. Your Grace can surprise them, and kill them. If your Grace will follow my advice, my head shall vouch for its success."

"I understand you, Uma. An angel has sent you to me. Is the ravine dry?"

"It was full of water yesterday, but it is nearly dry now."

Half an hour afterward the main force of Sanchez was in the ravine. Swiftly they descended into the plain, and cautiously they advanced toward the *hacienda*. Not a word was spoken as they pressed on. They were completely hidden from view. A dense growth of underwood and shrubbery covered the opening of the chasm. At some places the sides of it nearly closed on top, darkening the subterranean passage completely. Such ravines are not unfrequent in the Andes. They are formed and widened by the heavy volumes of water which, in consequence of the rains or the melting snows, rush down from the mountains.

The water had not entirely run out of the ravine. The men had to wade through it, and to stumble over the rocks which filled the bed of the stream. Their advance was necessarily slow. Suddenly it was arrested by the tramp of horses which they heard overhead. It terrified some of the insurgents, and filled them with apprehensions of a betrayal.

"What is this?" asked Sanchez of Uma.

"Let me climb on the shoulders of one of your men, and I shall see," answered the Indian. This was done, and Uma, carefully parting the shrubbery, pushed his head through the opening, and surveyed the plain.

A minute afterward he descended. "One of the detachments sent out to watch the other two roads, is returning to the *hacienda*. You must get them away before you strike."

"How can I do it?"

"Very easily."

At the suggestion of Uma, Sanchez now sent a command to the men left behind with the horses, slowly to recommence the ascent of the mountain, but to join Sanchez in the plain as soon as they should see two columns of fire arise, one on each side of the farm buildings of San José.

"For heaven's sake," said Pedro Perez, as he heard this order, "do not do this. You send away our means of safety and escape. Suppose we are betrayed by this man."

"No Indian will betray the friend of Toa Duchicela," replied Sanchez. "Those horses are of no use to us, nearer or farther. We could not reach them if we fail."

Sanchez then, at the dictation of Uma, wrote a letter, with the contents of which we shall become acquainted presently.

CHAPTER X.

THE SURPRISE.

"THE devil take you!" exclaimed Ildefonso Coronel, violently slamming down the dice-box with which he had been playing with his superior officer and patron, Juan del Puente, on the veranda of the farm building of San José. "You have taken all my money, as you have stolen the honors from me to which I was entitled."

"What do you mean, you ungrateful brute?" shouted Juan del Puente," "you are relapsing into one of your crazy spells."

"All my earnings went into your pocket. You have robbed me of money as well as preferment. Have I not done as much as you? Have I not fought as bravely as you? And now you are put in command of a detachment—and what am I?"

"Ildefonso Coronel, you are a fool! Have you forgotten

how often you won of me? And even if you lost to-day, whose money have you lost? Who has kept you in money ever since we are in America? Who has given you the chances which you were too stupid to discover for yourself? How often have I saved your worthless life? And are you not the first officer on my staff? Go to, Ildefonso, I have lost all patience with you. This very night you shall go back to Arana's camp. You had better try your luck among strangers, as you are dissatisfied with your truest comrade and your best friend. Get yourself ready. I shall appoint Rodriguez in your place."

"Well! Well!" said Ildefonso, who always broke down in the midst of his fits of anger, "how beastly you talk. When a fellow has lost as much money as I have, he can not show the temper of a lamb."

"But you are always abusive to the man to whom you owe your life and what you are now."

"Do not fall to preaching again. You know I did not mean it. Come! Give me another chance," and thus saying, he picked up the dice-box and shook it for a fresh throw.

"Enough! Here is the money you lost to-day. I do not want it now. You will owe it to me until next pay day, or until we play again. Now, it is time to prepare. In about an hour these rebels will have descended into the plain and we must make our preparations. Rodriguez! Have the horses been fed?"

"No, Señor Captain! Those devilish Indians are so very slow in bringing in the *alfalfa*."

"Take two or three of them and lash the life out of them as a warning to the others, and threaten to kill them all unless they have fodder enough for all the horses in five minutes from now."

The wild curses of the soldiers, and the piteous shrieks of the Indians, soon announced to Del Puento that his command had been fulfilled.

A few minutes afterward the detachment noticed in the previous chapter rode into the court-yard. Two of the foremost riders had an Indian between them whom they were dragging along. It was Uma.

"What news do you bring, Antonio?" inquired Del Puente.

"The rebels are not coming on the road of San Pedro. I soon satisfied myself of that, and, hence, concluded to return. On our way back, we saw them encamped on the mountain, right before us, and so we hurried to join you."

"And what is the matter with this Indian?"

"We saw him skulk in the bushes along the road. He first tried to hide himself, and, when he saw that we had noticed him, he sought to run away. His conduct was so suspicious that I ordered him to be seized. While my men were taking him, he put a piece of paper into his mouth, and endeavored to swallow it, but we choked it out of him. Here it is, Señor Captain. As I am not a scholar, I could not read it."

"Call the Mayordomo," said Del Puente. "He is right there. He can read."

The Mayordomo of the *hacienda*, a Spaniard by birth, took the paper and read it aloud. It contained the following lines:

"The Spaniards are right in front of me at San José. I can not risk an engagement now. I shall reascend the mountain and descend on the La Palma road on the other side. Meet me at the *hacienda* of Marcos Echerri, which I expect to reach to-night, under cover of darkness, and bring all the provisions you can get. We are entirely destitute and worn out by fatigue.

"Your friend,
"ROBERTO SANCHEZ."

"Good for him!" shouted Juan del Puente. "We shall get him to-night."

"There they go!" exclaimed Ildefonso Coronel, pointing to the mountain. And really a long line of horses, some with and some without riders, were now seen in the distance, slowly ascending the narrow serpentine path leading to the summit of the lower range.

"They will be completely exhausted by the time they get down on the other side," said Del Puente. "Have your horses been fed, Antonio?"

"Yes; we drove them into a clover-field while awaiting the arrival of my scouts."

"Do you know the country?"

"As well as my own pocket, Señor Captain. I have been stationed at Riobamba ever since I am in this miserable province."

"Well, then, push on with your men at once. I shall join you long before the rebels have descended on the other side. I shall stay here a few hours yet. This thing might be a ruse after all. They might want to get us away from here to get down. We must provide for every contingency. If you meet Ascásubi's detachment, take them along with you. And now be off. Leave this Indian to me."

Antonio and his troop departed, crossing over a wooden bridge covered with cross-staves and gravel, the very ravine in which the men of Sanchez were hidden. Their hearts leaped with joy when they beheld the success of their stratagem.

"And now," said Del Puente to one of his subalterns, "send a few scouts up that mountain, and let them be wide awake. In the meantime we shall attend to this Indian. Lift him up here."

Poor Uma was lifted on the veranda, and, surrounded by soldiers, he stood in well-affected trepidation before the Spanish Commander.

"What is thy name, man?"

"Mariano!" replied the Indian.

"What place dost thou belong to?"

"To the village on the other side of the range."

"Who gave thee this paper?"

"The Señor Roberto Sanchez."

"Dost thou know him?"

"I had never seen him before, but the men called him so."

"To whom wert thou to give the letter?"

"To a gentleman at Riobamba, who was to pay me for it."

"What is his name?"

"Aurelio Perez!"

"Dost thou know him?"

"No, Señor."

"Where wert thou to find him?"

"At the hacienda of La Palma, near Riobamba."

"Dost thou know that it is treason against the King's Majesty to carry such messages?"

"I swear by all the Saints of Heaven I did not know what the letter contained!"

"But thou knowest that Sanchez is a rebel?"

"I had never heard of him before. I have not been out of my native village for five years. I should not have left it now, but he made me go."

"How?"

"He said he would have me whipped to death if I refused; and he promised that the Señor Perez would pay me well."

"It is the greed for money, then, that has made thee a traitor to the King?"

"Misericordia, Señor; I knew nothing of the contents of the paper."

"How many men are there with Sanchez?"

"From seventy-five to a hundred."

"Didst thou count them?"

"No, Señor. I merely judged so from the quantity of clover which we had to cut for their horses."

"Are they in good condition?"

"Quite a number of them complained of sickness, Señor."

"Well, that's about all I care to know. And now to thee, man! Thou art a traitor to thy King."

"Mercy, Señor! Mercy!"

"Who is thy master?"

"The Señor Alvarez."

"Alvarez of Riobamba?"

"Yes, Señor."

"Well, he is a loyal subject to His Majesty, and for his sake I shall spare thy miserable life. But, as a warning example to the others, and to keep them from carrying treasonable correspondence, thou shalt receive three hundred lashes, well laid on."

"Mercy, Señor!" cried Uma, throwing himself on his knees. "I did not want to go. I did not want to leave my wife and my little ones. I was compelled to go."

"No matter! As soon as the Indians have brought in the fodder, Rodriguez, you will assemble them all in this court-yard, and in presence of the whole gang, have this man tied to a post, and see that he gets his three hundred lashes."

"For the Virgin's sake, mercy, mercy, Señor!"

"Take him away!"

Uma was taken away; his back was bared and he was tied to a post. Switches were then cut from the rose-bushes in the garden, and made ready for their bloody work. Some of the Indian farm-hands were compelled to assist at these preparations. To one of them Uma said, in a language which not even those who were familiar with the Quichua could understand: "Get on the roof of the house, and as soon as the *chasquis* announce that the foreigners have passed the *quebrada* (ravine) of San Marcos, give the signal."

The *quebrada* of San Marcos was one of those deep and broad ravines which frequently intersect the Andean plains in the neighborhood of the mountains. Its sides were very steep and it would take considerable time for men, on horseback, to descend on one side and reascend to the plain on the other. Uma's object in postponing the attack by the men of Sanchez, was to prevent Antonio's troop from galloping back to the hacienda as soon as they should hear the firing. He judged rightly that the reports of musketry would bring them back at once. The distance between the farm and the *quebrada* of San Marcos was not considerable. Antonio's troop might return before Sanchez had overpowered Del Puente. But once on the other side of the *quebrada* of San Marcos, it would take them at least half an hour to repass it. They could not gallop through it; they would have to descend into the precipice cautiously and slowly on the farther side, and to climb up with difficulty on the one nearest the *hacienda*. And in order to gain this time for his Viracocha friends, the noble Indian submitted his bare back to the cruel torture, and delayed the signal which he was authorized to give.

The horses were feeding and the Indians were driven into the court-yard. Two negroes, servants to the Spaniards—negroes always had to act as executioners in those days—took their places with Uma, one on each side. A Spanish soldier stood by to count the lashes. Uma's eyes were fixed steadily on the man on the roof of the building. And now the word of command was given and the negroes began to strike. They struck alternately. The thorns had been left on the switches and the very first blows lacerated the skin of the victim. "One—two—three—four"—went the count. Not a groan or a sigh escaped the lips of the Indian. "Twenty-one—twenty-two"—counted the soldier. Uma's eyes were on the roof. Some of the switches broke and had to be changed. The fresh ones always did fresh execution. "Forty!" The blood now flowed freely, and still Uma hung to the ring in the post without swerving. His eyes were on the roof. "Eighty!" The man on the roof sat motionless, but his eyes were not on the scene in the courtyard. Intently they scanned the distance far away. "A hundred!"

"Take a rest!" commanded the superintending officer. But now the man on the roof began to stir. "Proceed!" One—two." At this moment the man on the roof threw up his arms, and, in a loud, ringing voice, which brought the echo back from the mountains, shouted, "Duchicela!"

"Duchicela!" shouted Uma, dodging the last blow.

"Duchicela!" shouted every Indian; and in an instant, the Spanish soldier who commanded the execution, lay sprawling in the dust.

"Duchicela!" repeated the Indians, and in the next second the negroes were torn away from the sufferer and trampled down, and Uma was released, echoing the battle-cry: "Duchicela! Duchicela!"

The Spaniards were dumbfounded by this unexpected piece of Indian audacity, and would have fallen upon those unarmed creatures with terrible severity, had not another enemy monopolized their attention. One of the Spanish sentinels came running toward the gate of the court-yard, but the report of an arquebus was heard, and he dropped down dead. And now there was another and another, and some of the men of Sanchez rushed through the open gate.

"To your guns, men!" shrieked Del Puente. "Secure your horses!"

"The horses are secured, Señor Del Puente, and you, too," said a voice right behind him. It was Roberto Sanchez, who, with another party of men, after killing or driving away the sentinels, had entered the building through the windows. "You are my prisoner!"

Resistance was useless. Both Del Puente and Coronel

were overpowered and disarmed before they had recovered from their surprise.

The struggle inside and outside the building was of short duration. The Spaniards scattered in every direction, and were pursued by the men of Sanchez, who had captured and mounted the Spanish horses. And now the Indian carnival of revenge began. The heart-blood of the Spanish prisoners was exacted as the penalty for the blood of Uma. They were dispatched with clubs, hatchets, rakes, shovels, knives, or any other weapons that were in reach. They were literally torn in pieces by the infuriated Indians, whose savage nature, embittered by years of oppression, had been unchained. Before the Revolutionary commander could stop or even notice this carnage, most of the bloody work had been done. At the same time, two columns of fire arose on each side of the main building, the signal to the men on the mountain, who, soon afterward, were seen redescending the narrow path from which they had disappeared a short while ago.

"For heaven's sake!" exclaimed Sanchez, as he embraced the bleeding Uma, "what have they done to you?"

"I am safe, your Grace!" answered the Indian, returning the affectionate greeting of the young commander. "Do not waste the precious moments on me. Rally your men, for the enemy whom our stratagem has sent away, will soon be upon us."

"I know, my friend. Let the bugles be sounded, Garcia. We must get ready at once. But, first of all, your wounds shall be attended to."

"Leave this to the medicine-men of my race," said Uma. "I shall be with your Grace as soon as I can be of service again." And, with these words, he withdrew, calm and dignified, not a muscle of his face betraying the painfulness of his wounds.

"And now let us put a guard over these prisoners," said Sanchez to his lieutenant, Perez.

"Would it not be better to kill them?" suggested the old man. "A dead enemy can not fight again."

"Do not think of it, friend Perez. These two men are officers, and will be valuable hostages. Moreover, an exchange of prisoners may soon become desirable to our side. Let them bring in all the prisoners and have them well secured and guarded in this building until after the battle."

The horses of Del Puente's troop were in excellent condition, but not enough for all the men of Sanchez, and as his own horses could not be on hand in time for the engagement, the best marksmen were selected for infantry service. It is remarkable by what small numbers in those early Peruvian civil wars battles were fought which decided the most important contests.

The men of Sanchez had rallied in front of the farm buildings, when their commander joined them. A wild shout of welcome rent the air the moment they descried him. The gloomy despondency of the forenoon had given way to fresh courage and enthusiasm. The leader whom they had followed had retrieved himself. Again he had grasped success. Again he had won, confirmed, and strengthened their shaken confidence. The Spanish veteran, who had been sent out to capture them, had become their prisoner. It was almost too good to be true.

"Comrades and countrymen!" said Sanchez, as he rode up to the front. "This is no time for words. This time we took them by surprise. Now we must show them that we can fight. We are superior to them in numbers. Let us show that we are their superiors in courage. Thus far we have not met with a defeat; and another victory is within our grasp. Consider that our lives depend upon our success. To-night we shall sup in Riobamba! And now forward! 'Duchicela!' shall be the battle-cry. Let us take them as they emerge from the ravine."

This speech was received with loud acclamations, after which the final dispositions were made. A vanguard was sent forward under young Garcia. Sanchez himself led the main force, and Pedro Perez was assigned to the command of the reserve.

The Revolutionary force had not advanced very far, when the first of Antonio's riders emerged from the great ravine of San Marcos. This gave Sanchez a tremendous advantage. He had the enemy at his mercy. One part of the Royalists was ascending the ravine on the *hacienda* side, while the others were still descending into the precipice on the other side. The few that were out of the defile had no time to form, before the insurgents were on them. The Royalists could not withstand the shock. Their rout was complete.

Before the shades of night had allen, Sanchez with his prisoners was at Riobamba, and held it once more for the cause of the Revolution. But that cause was on the wane. It would have been better for the young commander not to allow his soldiers the luxury of a night's rest under the sheltering roofs of a large town. At Riobamba they learned what until now they had but partly known, or, at least, but vaguely apprehended. They were told of the helplessness of the Quito authorities, of their irreparable losses of time, spirit, and substance, of the apparent hopelessness of the popular cause, and of the large numbers and splendid equipments of Arana's forces. It demoralized and disheartened them, in spite of the brilliant success they had just achieved. When the trumpets called them to the rally of the morning, hardly one-half of the victors of yesterday responded to the call. The others had deserted during the night or at early daybreak, or were hiding away in or around Riobamba. Some had even spurred their horses to overtake Arana, in order to make their submission acceptable by its timeliness, and by the information they could give. Roberto's heart sank, when he saw how his band had dwindled down. Would he be safe with those who had remained? Would they not attempt to earn a full pardon with golden rewards, by delivering their leader, the arch-traitor, into the hands of the Royal Commander? Such treachery had not been uncommon in the civil wars of Peru. Yet, ho must run this risk. He had no alternative. His timely arrival at Quito, and if it were with a dozen resolute men, was the last hope on which his cause and his life depended.

And Arana? Should he turn back on the enemy in his rear and finish him before continuing his march to Quito? This was the course which the Marquis de Solando and other loyalists advised. But the old fox would not listen to it. Quito was the head and the soul of the rebellion. That head he would strike. Sanchez was but a distant limb which could not move or live after the head had fallen. With Quito in Arana's power, the troop of Sanchez would dissolve of itself. Hence, onward the old man pressed unmindful of the young enthusiast in his rear. But Sanchez did not long remain in the rear. While Arana advanced through the table-lands and the valleys, Sanchez climbed over the mountains, endeavoring to pass the Royalists, so as to reach Quito before them. The latter had the advantage of better roads and populated districts rich in provisions; but the rebels were guided by Uma and his men, who knew all the byways and recesses of the Cordillera; and while Guzman Ponce, Paredes, Londoño, and other traitors lulled themselves into a comfortable belief that the army of Arana formed a safe barrier between them and the guerrillas of Sanchez, the latter, worn-out and foot-sore, half-starved and half-frozen on the cold mountain-passes and paramos, but undaunted and clinging to their two principal prisoners, Del Puente and Coronel, appeared at the southern gate of Quito. And Arana was still a day's march from the Capital.

CHAPTER XI.

MARIQUITA.

"What does this noise mean, Mother?" asked Mercedes, while bending lovingly over the cradle of her babe. "Men on horseback were dashing by here, to and fro, shouting and cheering, while you were at church. Some one was hammering at our door, but the girl was out, and I was afraid to open. Besides, I could not have left the child."

Doña Mariquita who had just entered the room, placed her hands on her daughter's shoulders, gently turned her around and kissed her on the forehead: "He has come back, my child."

"Oh, Mother!" exclaimed Mercedes; and without another word, threw herself in Doña Mariquita's arms, and wept.

And again the tramp of horses was heard outside, and the riders shouted: "Viva el Señor Roberto Sanchez! Death to the Audience! Death to the traitors!"

"Have you seen him, Mother?" asked the girl with anxious expectation.

"No, child, I have not."

"When did he arrive?"

"Early this morning, and Santa Maria! what a commotion his arrival has caused. The city is wild with excitement. They say he has come to kill the Auditors, the commanders, and more than one-half of the members of the Cabildo."

"Oh, Mother, Mother! It is false."

"Still they all believe it. Guzman Ponce de Leon, the commander-in-chief, has fled to the Royal camp. He has taken with him one of the Auditors, the Señor Cabeza de

Meneses. The President and the other Auditors have taken sanctuary in the Church of San Francisco, which is now surrounded by a mob of fierce and excited men, who vow that nobody shall be allowed to carry food or drink to the unfortunate Ministers. Detachments of soldiers are searching the houses for the suspected. They are seeking Juan de Londoño and Manuel Paredes, whom Roberto wants to hang."

"Holy Virgin! Have mercy!"

"The Revolutionists are crazy with enthusiasm over your lover. He is the master of the town now, and does as he pleases He has disarmed one battalion, and imprisoned over fifty officers and men. They say he will shoot twenty to-morrow, in the Plaza of Santa Clara."

"O Mother, it can not be!"

"He is hurrying troops in every direction, They are fortifying Mt. Panecillo and the bridge near our house. They say that Roberto has dismounted but once since his return. He is in the saddle continually, and sees to everything himself. The King's friends are terrified, and the Bellidistas have everything their own way again, and swear that the world never saw a man like young Sanchez."

"And what will be the end of these dreadful doings?"

"Let us pray to God to have mercy on us all. Be composed Merceditas, and put your trust in the Virgin. You must be prepared for the worst."

"Oh my child! My poor little child!"

"This Revolution can not succeed. Who can prevail against the King of Spain, before whom the monarchs of the world are trembling? Arana is said to be at Machachi with a large army. He will soon be here, and all resistance will be in vain. He will take the city."

"He will take the city, and then?"

"And then, my poor Merceditas, that babe of yours will be without a father. It is dreadful, but it can not be otherwise—and the Virgin will give you strength to bear it.

You must not forget, Mercedes, that your child will want a mother, when his father is gone."

Mercedes had slipped from her mother's arms, and lay prostrate and sobbing, at the foot of the cradle.

"How glad I would be, daughter, if I could give you better consolation; but I know that the blow must come, and it is my duty to prepare you for it. Be brave, Mercedes, and think of your child. Roberto Sanchez has wrought his own destruction, and there is no help for him."

A knock was heard at the door of the shop below, and still another. "I must go down and see who it is," said Doña Mariquita, lighting a candle. "Be sensible, Merceditas. Perhaps things may turn out better than you fear; but you must prepare for the worst."

With these words, Doña Mariquita left the room, and descended to the shop. The street door was bolted and barred, and before she opened it, she asked: "Who knocks?"

"It is I, *commadre!*" said a male voice.

"Who is this I? Let me hear your name."

"Do n't you know me, Doña Mariquita, your *compadre*, Tomas Jaramillo? Open the door as quick as you can, for the love of God!"

"I do not dare to open the door to-night."

"But you must let me in, *commadre*. I am in danger."

"Then come around to the rear entrance. I shall open the corral door for you."

This was done. Mariquita led her visitor through the corral and court into the shop, and there they seated themselves by the dim and flickering light of a tallow candle.

"You must let me stay here for a day or two, *commadre*," said the Mayordomo of Paredes. "I should not know where to go, if you were to refuse me this shelter."

"But why should you want to hide yourself, Don Tomas? You have not done anything."

"But they are after my master; and, if they should take me, they would question me about him. They might put me to the rack to make me tell what I do not know. Upon my soul, *commadre*, I do not know where my master is. He was warned in the very nick of time. Five minutes later, and he would have been taken. Roberto Sanchez hates him. There is an old grudge between them. I know it, *commadre*. I have witnessed several of their quarrels. My master would be a dead man now, if Roberto Sanchez had caught him."

"*Por Dios!* What terrible times!" said Doña Mariquita, pouring out a glass of liquor for her visitor. "And who warned him?"

"That is the strangest of all the wonderful incidents of this rebellion. The warning came from a quarter where we should have expected the bitterest hostility, rather than an act of kindness. It came from the Indian Queen."

"You astonish me more and more, Don Tomas. Oh, tell me how it was!"

"A few moments before the men of Sanchez came dashing toward our house, an Indian, whom I had never seen, presented himself to my master. It is wonderfully strange!" said Don Tomas, as he paused to sip his liquor. "The Indian talked as if he had been a white man and a nobleman. 'Señor Paredes!' he said, as familiarly as if he had been my master's equal. 'Senor Paredes! I have come to return good for evil. I have come to save your life. I am the messenger of Queen Toa. She has just learned—you need not know how—that Roberto Sanchez, who at this very moment has entered the city, has determined to hang you within thirty minutes after his arrival, and she has sent me to warn you. You must flee at once. There is no time to be lost. Change your apparel. Don the garb of a Mestizo, and leave your house this very instant. The riders of Sanchez will be here in a few minutes.' And, with these words, the strange Indian left us thunderstruck. My master at first refused to believe him. But I hurried him into my room, made him change his clothes, and then we both left the house. Before we had reached the next corner, the men of Sanchez were at our door. By all the Saints of Heaven, it was a narrow escape!"

"And where is your master now?"

"I do not know. He may still be in the city. He may have taken sanctuary, or he may have gone to Arana's camp."

"And what did *you* do?"

"Through corrals and gardens and side streets, I made my way to the Recoleta of San Domingo, and there I hid until nightfall. Then I gathered courage and came here. And now, *commadre*, we must have a talk. There is a gold piece for you. Take it now for the trouble I may give you. And here," he added, as he displayed the bright pieces to the glittering and greedy eyes of Doña Mariquita, "are two more, which you shall have if you can keep me here in safety until the Royal troops have taken possession of the town. I came here because, of all the houses in Quito, I consider this the safest for me. The rebels will not trouble the house where their chief's sweetheart lives."

"My dearest *compadre*," said Doña Mariquita, with a sudden change of tone, "you have no idea how glad I am to be of some service to you. You will be perfectly safe here. Nobody shall know that you are here."

"You will not tell your daughter, of course?"

"Why, Don Tomasito, you do not think I am a lunatic? The girl shall know nothing about you. She would tell Sanchez. She is still madly in love with him, and could not keep any secrets."

"That is just what I expected, *commadre*," said Tomas; "and to show you how much I confide in you, I shall give you the rest of the money now. There! take it! There is no spark of distrust in me, and I hope you, too, will trust me. It will be to your interest."

"God bless you, *compadre*," answered the woman as she clutched the money. "You are the dearest man, and I should die rather than betray you. You will be as safe here as in the Bishop's Palace. But, tell me, *compadrecito,* how do you come by so much money? You seem to be possessed of a royal fortune."

"Ah, Doña Mariquita," said Tomas with a significant wink, "there is money to be made in these troublous times. There is more to be gotten where this came from," he added, jingling other pieces of gold and silver in his pockets.

"Of course, you came by it honestly," said the woman.

"I hope you do not take me for a rogue," exclaimed the Mayordomo with an air of virtuous indignation. "What I have here I made by serving the cause of our master, the King, whom it is my bounden duty to obey. It is God's command that the subject should serve, honor, and obey the King.".

"Of course he should," assented the woman. "It is a sin and a shame if he does not. Ah, if I were a man!"

"Why, *commadre?*"

"Well, you are a man, and I hear the gold jingle in your pockets. Would you have gotten it without opportunities, and would you have had these opportunities had you been born a woman?"

"Why, *commadre,* I would give all I have here for the grand opportunity which is within the reach of a woman whom I know. I should have enough to live in affluence for the rest of my days."

"What do you mean?" added Mariquita with eager intensity.

"What do I mean, *commadre?* I mean that some people have eyes and can not see; that they have ears and can not hear; that they have hands and can not grasp what is within their reach."

"Explain yourself, *compadre,* for the love of God!"

"Do you really require additional explanation, *commadre?* Where is your usual keenness? I never found you dull before. Can it be possible that you are blind to the glorious opportunity right under your nose?"

"Wait a moment, *compadre*," said Doña Mariquita. "I want to see whether our hand-maiden has come back. She might be listening."

Doña Mariquita left the shop, looked around in the courtyard, listened at the top of the staircase, and then returned to her visitor, closing the door behind her.

"Nobody can hear us, *compadre*. Now tell me what you mean!"

CHAPTER XII.

BETWEEN THE CUP AND THE LIP.

On the day after the scenes described in the preceding chapter, the vanguard of Arana appeared in the plain to the south of Quito. The Royal scouts dashed up to the very gates of the capital. Sanchez had labored with superhuman exertion, but he had not quite completed his preparations. On the next day, however, he hoped to be ready for an offensive movement, by taking possession of the villages and other commanding positions between Quito and Tambillo, at which latter place the Royal commissioner had temporarily established his headquarters.

But now nature demanded her rights. Instead of resting after the exhaustive fatigues and hardships of his march over inhospitable mountains, and through shelterless solitudes, Roberto had accomplished herculean tasks in seizing the reins of government, reorganizing the forces of the Cabildo, weeding out those who were suspected of treasonable intents, and hastily preparing his reconstructed battalions for the decisive conflict. He labored from the morning of his arrival until the early dawn of the following day. But then his strength gave way. His Lieutenant, Pedro Perez, had already succumbed to excessive fatigue, and was confined to his bed by a fit of utter prostration, of which Sanchez took warning. Leaving old Señor Olmos in command, the young hero, accompanied by his aid, Garcia, and a few of his most trusted men, whom he had constituted his body-guard, re-entered his paternal mansion, for the first time since he had left it with his poor father on their way to Ambato and Riobamba. The tears of the iron boy flowed freely as he lay in the trembling arms of his mother, who had watched and waited for him a long, weary night, anxiously expecting him every minute, and starting at every footstep in the street, in the hope that it would be that of her darling.

"But now, Mother, I must sleep. I could give ten years of life for an hour of sleep. Have the kindness, Mother, to see to the comfort of these gentlemen, and let me retire."

There he lay, locked in the healthy sleep of youth, with an anxious and haggard mother bending over him. He lay undisturbed by her burning tears which trickled down on his sunburnt face, bronzed by the winds and rains of the Paramo. There he lay, undisturbed by the dangers that had gathered around; undisturbed by the uncertainty of what the next moment would bring. His mother's eye watched over him. The unfortunate lady had lost her husband; would her son be spared? Was it possible that this rebellion could succeed? And what must be the fate of her darling if it failed?

Roberto's rest should not be of long duration. Two or three important messages came, which brooked no delay, and thus his sleep was broken repeatedly. Not until after sunrise, he fell into a sleep which might have been refreshing, had it not been for a terrible dream. He felt himself seized by unseen hands, from which he vainly endeavored to escape. He was pressed to the ground by a tremenduous weight, which soon rendered him incapable of moving his arms or legs. He tried to utter a cry, but his voice failed him. He could not give forth a sound. When, at last, with an almost superhuman effort, he broke into a groan, he awoke, with the cold perspiration on his forehead, and a heavy, inexplicable sensation of dark forebodings in his heart.

"Garcia! Garcia! Are you awake?"

No; the young man still lay stretched out on the sofa on which he had thrown himself the moment he had entered the room. There he lay, in the same position into which he had dropped the night before. Sanchez thought it would be cruel to wake him.

"Sentinel!"

The door opened, and the sentinel saluted.

"What time is it?"

"Nine o'clock."

"That's very late. Is there anybody waiting for me?"

"Yes, Señor. There is a woman below who wishes to see your Grace. There is also an old Indian, who says that he came by appointment."

"Yes! Yes!" said the young man, springing from his bed and beginning to dress himself. "Let him come in."

It was Cundurazu. He seemed sadly changed. Disappointed hopes had done what age alone would not have accomplished. They had bowed his head and bent his noble form. His step had lost its elasticity, and his eye its wonted luster. He was deeply moved as he returned the cordial embrace with which Roberto welcomed him.

"At last you come, my worthy friend. How is the Shyri Toa, and when shall I see her?"

"Your Grace shall see her after the victory, if we are still to hope for victory. She has gone to Tambillo to deliver the Royal Commander into the hands of your Grace."

"Oh, Prince Cundurazu! could she really do that?"

"She can! But hold! No human ear must hear what I shall say to you now. This has been a time of base betrayals, and I trust no one but you. The lion's strength is powerless against the serpent's sting. That young man might hear us."

"He is my aid, and fast asleep."

"No matter! Let us step on the balcony, and close the door behind us. Now we are safe. The ear that hears not keeps the mouth closed. Now mark! Arana is at Tambillo. His quarters are at an *hacienda*, at the foot of a wild mountain. His men are scattered through and around the village. He has guarded the roads in every direction, but he has not dreamed that the mountain wilderness above him might be fraught with danger. He is lying in wait for the ounces and panthers; but he has not thought of the condors overhead. There is a large cave in the recesses of the mountain at a short distance from the *hacienda*, accessible by paths and passes known only to us. The Shyri Toa will hide in that cave to-night two hundred of the most resolute Indians of Chillogallo and Tambillo. You must join her there with fifty picked men after midnight, when the foreigners will have surrendered themselves to sleep and security. We shall steal into the *hacienda*, kill the sentinels, seize Arana, and carry him away with us. In the meantime, your Grace will dash down from the mountain with your fifty men, who will seem a host to the panic-stricken, and scatter them in every direction. Then, returning to the mountain, your Grace will prevent the foreigners from pursuing us, and from rescuing their commander. They can not follow us into the mountains. We shall bring Arana as a prisoner to Quito. He shall remain in our custody—in yours'and mine—and the day afterward your Grace will be able to strike a decisive blow at his demoralized and headless army."

"May heaven reward you for this glorious plan!" said Sanchez, seizing the old man by both hands. "It will, it must succeed."

"If your Grace will keep it secret—secret as the grave.

Do not breathe it to your most trusted friend. Pick your men and take them with you, but let them know nothing."

"And when would I have to march?"

"It will be dark at seven. Send one-half of your men ahead. Let them leave the city quietly and unobserved. Uma will guide them. An hour later you may follow with the other half. I shall show you the way. It will be a rough and difficult road for your men, but it will lead to victory and salvation. We shall reach the rallying place at one o'clock. If we succeed, you will be King of Quito, and the Shyri Toa will be your Queen."

"Could she love me; could she really be mine, Prince Cundurazu?"

"She will belong to the liberator and protector of our race; and you, Señor Roberto, shall be the man."

This was a bright and dazzling vision. The young man's heart filled with all the happiness of glorious hope. His bosom swelled, his eyes dilated, his pulse beat faster. Glory, power, a throne, love, riches, momentarily arose before him in the distance, where, until lately, his mind's eye had beheld but the dreadful outlines of a scaffold. It was the last and brightest vision of his life's short dream, and the cruel awakening was near.

"There is but one difficulty," he said, after a pause. "I fear to leave the city. Treason lurks in every corner, and the traitors are kept down by the dread only with which I have filled them. If I go, there is danger of a reaction. The Royalists are incessantly tampering with my men. If, owing to my absence, I must relax my present unceasing watchfulness, they might rise against us and overthrow the Cabildo."

"Your absence can be kept a secret for one night. To-morrow morning our Indian *chasquis* will bring the glorious news to Quito that your Grace has captured the Royal Commander. The news of such a success will forever baffle the wiles of the traitors, and a few hours later your Grace will return in triumph with your prisoner."

"You are right, Prince Cundurazu. It is my last, my best, and perhaps my only chance. I am in the hands of God, and His will be done. I have much to do during the day; but, thank God, Arana gives us breathing time. He might have crushed me if he had moved on me yesterday. To-morrow I shall be in good condition, if he lets me alone to-day."

"He will, your Grace. From what our spies have learned, there is no danger of a forward movement for several days."

"Then we may hope for the best. I shall send the men whom Uma is to guide to San Diego at seven o'clock. Between half-past eight and nine o'clock I shall meet you with my men at San Roque. Will that do?"

"It will."

"Then God be with you, my dearest friend."

"May the Great Sun protect your Grace. But hold! This ring the Shyri Toa sends to the great Virococha, as a token of her friendship and alliance. She hopes to greet the wearer to-night."

"To-night I shall throw myself at the feet of Her Majesty."

Thus the interview terminated. In the meantime, the house was astir with detachment-commanders, members of the Cabildo, and others, who had come to receive orders, or consult with the young chief. The court-yard below resounded with the tramp of horses, and the stairs and corridors with the clanking of spurs, swords, and arquebuses. Sanchez dispatched his visitors with the most obliging politeness, and yet cutting them short and going to the very core of each man's business with the utmost rapidity. His breakfast had been brought, superintended by his mother, and he partook of it while listening to reports or giving orders.

"The two companies from Otabalo are reported doubtful," said old Señor Olmos. "Thus far, they seemed to be well disposed, but during the last few hours they have given cause for suspicion."

"That must be looked into," answered Roberto. "Keep them at the barracks. Do not put them in charge of an important position, until we are sure of their loyalty. Dissolve them, if necessary. Where are they now?"

"I believe that they were to be sent to the bridge of Machángara to-day."

"That must not be done. You must have this order countermanded, Señor Olmos. Let one company of the Pichinchas and one of the Ambatos be sent to the bridge to-night. You will not neglect this, my fatherly friend?"

"Most surely not!"

"And the Ministers?"

"Are still in the sanctuary, while the populace are guarding all the entrances to the church."

And now the business of his visitors having been dispatched, Sanchez descended into the court-yard to mount his horse, in order to make a tour of inspection. His foot was in the stirrup when a hand touched his arm. Turning around he beheld Doña Mariquita, the mother of Mercedes.

"God be with you, Doña Mariquita," he said, giving her the customary embrace. "I hope you are well. And how is Merceditas?"

"How can you ask, Señor Don Roberto? The poor child is dying to see your Grace, and in despair at your indifference."

"Let her take heart, Doña Mariquita," answered Roberto, turning to mount; "in a few days we shall see her, if we live. Give her my love in the meantime."

"But, Señor, will you not let me speak to you an instant?"

"Every moment is precious, Doña Mariquita. You can not imagine in what hurry I am."

"But only one second, for the love of God, and not before all these Caballeros."

"Well, well, we must be obliging to ladies!" he said, leading her to one of the servants' room in the court. "I suppose you are in need of money, Doña Mariquita. I should have been more thoughtful of your needs yesterday."

"Money, Don Roberto, money!" exclaimed the old woman, with well-feigned indignation. "As poor and helpless as I am, I should say, keep your money, if you were to send me back without a crumb of comfort to that poor and forlorn creature, who has been sitting up and waiting for you ever since your arrival in the city. Not a wink did she sleep during the last long night, not an instant did her wasting form press her bed. There she was, ever restless, ever moving about, now listening at the window, now rushing down to the door, imagining that she had heard your step. 'Surely he will come, Mother,' she said. 'I know he will come to see his child, at least, if he does not care for its mother.'"

"The Virgin bless my poor Merceditas, but I can not spare a moment now. This is a struggle for life. I fight with the noose around my neck, Doña Mariquita, and I must strain every nerve to save those that are intrusted to my charge. On the day after to-morrow I shall come to your house."

"But can you not come just for a minute this evening, when your most pressing business is dispatched. They say you are always in the saddle, riding from place to place, and inspecting every post and position. They have been fortifying the bridge near our house. Will you not come to inspect it, and then just alight for a moment to save the life of that grief-worn woman, the mother of your child?"

"The bridge of Machángara! You are right. Yes, Doña Mariquita, 1 shall inspect the bridge during the course of the day. And now let me go!"

"But do not kill the poor child by keeping her in this dreadful uncertainty. She will be restless and trembling all day. Every horse will startle, every noise will frighten her. Fix an hour when you can come, and if possible let it be in the evening, for the poor girl suffers most during the night."

"Let us see," said Sanchez, musing, "seven, eight, nine. Well, tell her I shall be with her shortly before eight o'clock, but only for a few minutes. And now I must be gone."

The next moment he was on his horse, and dashed out of the doorway, followed by his aids and guards. And Doña Mariquita looked after him. It was a long, stony look, and even after he was out of her sight, she still stood gazing at the doorway through which he had disappeared.

CHAPTER XI.

THE BRIDGE OF MACHANGARA.

It was nearly eight o'clock in the evening, when Sanchez, followed by about thirty mounted men, rode to the bridge of Machángara.

"*Quien vive?*" shouted the first picket he met, at a distance of about two squares from the bridge.

"*El Cabildo!*"

"Who comes?"

"The Commander-in-Chief!"

The sentinel saluted.

"What company dost thou belong to, comrade?" asked Sanchez, checking his horse.

"First Otabalo, my General!"

"And when were you sent here?"

"This afternoon!"

"Strange!" said Roberto to young Olmos, riding on at a slow pace, and halting again as soon as he was out of the sentinel's hearing. "Very strange! could your father have forgotten to countermand the order to send this company to the bridge? It was at his own suggestion that I decided not to send them here. There are doubts as to their loyalty, and this post is too important to be intrusted to any but our most reliable men."

"My father did not forget it, General. He spoke of it several times to-day, and told me that he had stationed the Third Pichincha and the First Ambato at the bridge. I do not understand how the Otabalos happened to come here."

"This is a riddle which stands in need of immediate solution. Gallop back to the Cabildo, Olmos, and inform your worthy father of this misunderstanding. Let him sift the matter, and ascertain who is responsible; and let the guilty parties be arrested, whoever they may be. Success, I assure you, lies within our grasp, Olmos, and we must not let treachery snatch it from us. Hurry on, now, and bring back a most accurate report. In the meantime, you, Señor Rodriguez, hasten to the barracks and bring the two companies that were intended to be here. Bring any available company; but let not a minute be lost. I do not like this mistake, and shall stay here myself until it is rectified. Hurry!"

These words had been spoken in an undertone, so as not to be overheard by Sanchez' own guard. Olmos and Rodriguez dashed back to the city, and Sanchez rode on to the bridge, where he was received with demonstrations of affection and enthusiasm which somewhat reassured him. He exchanged a few friendly words with the men, and then, followed by his own troop, rode back toward the city, halting at the house of Doña Mariquita. Here he dismounted, and turning to his men, he said: "Have the kindness to hold my horse, Señor Dávila. I shall be with you again in a few minutes. Good evening, Doña Mariquita"—the woman had appeared in the door of her *tienda*—"will you be good enough to send out some refreshments to these gentlemen, while I go in to see Merceditas." With these words he entered the house, and walked up stairs to the familiar room of Mercedes.

He had hardly dismounted, when three or four men on horseback, coming from the bridge, rode up to the men of Sanchez, who were forming different groups, and engaged them in a whispered conversation. At the same time a movement became discernible at the bridge among the Otabalo soldiers, some of whom rapidly mounted their horses, while others moved toward the front and rear of Mariquita's house. In a few minutes the post at the bridge was broken up and abandoned. Not the bridge, but the house, seemed to be guarded. At the same time an altercation had arisen between the men of Sanchez and the strangers that had come to them from the bridge. Swords were drawn, the cry "traitor" resounded, and a scuffle began, while a loud, piercing shriek was heard from the interior of the house. It was the voice of a female. An instant afterward, the voice of Sanchez was heard, but only for a moment. He shouted: "Dávila! Help! Help!" Then all was silence within, while the tumult increased outside. The men of Sanchez were now surrounded by the Otabalos, some of whom attempted to pull the Cabildo men from their horses, while others sought to hold the horses, and to reason with the riders. The Sanchez men seemed undecided; taken by surprise, and without a leader they were helpless against their well-prepared assailants, who outnumbered them, four to one. A few stray shots were fired increasing the confusion. One or two of the Sanchez men succeeded in cutting their way out and breaking away, yelling: "Treason! Treason! To arms! To arms!" Others were unhorsed and dispatched by their assailants, while still others seemed to yield to the combined arguments of persuasion and force, and allowed themselves to be swept along by the current which now had set in toward the bridge. About this time, a dozen horsemen emerged from the rear part of the house, dragging along a prisoner with whom they dashed over the bridge, followed by their accomplices, the Otabalo company, and by some of the men of Sanchez, who had changed sides in less than three minutes, to save their lives and to share the fruits of this act of treachery.

And now drums were beating in the direction of the city, and shortly afterward the alarm-bells were ringing, and two companies, headed by Olmos and Rodriguez came rushing breathlessly to the fatal spot. It was too late to save their commander, who was whirling away at this very moment, tied to a horse, toward the camp of Arana.

But might they not have saved him if they had dashed after his captors without delay? Perhaps! But the master-spirit was gone, and the tottering edifice which he alone had supported, tumbled down with a sudden, annihilating crash. The news of the kidnaping of Sanchez, struck terror into the ranks of the Cabildo-men. The blow was so sudden that it deprived them of all presence of mind; and demoralization, amazement, uncertainty, culminating in a panic, were its immediate effects. In vain the two Olmos and others attempted to stem the tide of discouragement and defeat. A blank feeling of utter hopelessness had seized the Revolutionary party. The cry "Viva el Rey," silenced for so long, was heard again ;·first timidly, but soon carried from mouth to mouth, until it startled the terrified Councilors of the Cabildo in their hall, and sent tidings of gladness and deliverance to the hearts of the Ministers in their sanctuary.

And now the downfall of the Revolutionary cause was

precipitated like the rout of Gonzalo Pizarro at Xapixaguano, by a mad rush of desertions to the Royalist side. Hundreds of leading rebels vied with each other to manifest their sudden conversion to loyalty by some signal act of meanness in the service of the King against whom they had rebelled. Each one wanted to be the first to make atonement for his past conduct. The fiercest rebels of yesterday, had suddenly become the loudest in advocating submission, and endeavoring to prove the utter hopelessness of further resistance, or in preparing to deliver their comrades to the hangman, in order to extricate their own necks. The Royalists, who had been lurking in places of concealment, or prowling around in disguises, now came forward in order to swell the tide of reaction. Manuel Paredes, the engineer of the plot by which poor Sanchez had been ensnared, and Juan de Londoño entered the Cabildo at the head of an armed force of Royalists, and spoke in a voice half reasoning and half threatening: "Gentlemen! We are betrayed! There is no use of further resistance. Our only salvation lies in making our peace with the Auditors, and throwing ourselves on their mercy. Let us, at once, proceed to the Church of San Francisco, and lead them hence to the Palace." The trembling Councilors had no alternative but to follow this advice. The same men that, a few months ago, had seized the reins of government, now headed the procession which, followed by a contrite multitude, repaired to the sanctuary, humbly to beseech the deposed Ministers to resume their power, and to deal gently with those who had offended against them. In triumph, the President of the Audience, with his three colleagues—the fourth had fled to Arana's camp with Guzman Ponce de Leon—were escorted back to the Palace that very night, through streets illuminated and festooned, as if the city were rejoicing over a great victory. The new government smiled kindly on its newly-won friends that night. No arrests were made. The President did not feel himself secure with Arana's forces eight leagues away from the Capital. But one ominous order he gave in secret, while smilingly shaking hands with his late enemies —it was an order to guard all the outlets of the city, and to allow no one to depart from it without a permit signed by the Audience or the President. At the same time, a messenger was dispatched to the Royal Commander at Tambillo, to announce to him that Quito was a loyal city once more, and that the King's Government had been restored. The Commander was notified that a festive reception awaited him, whenever it should be his pleasure to celebrate his triumphal entrance.

Such a complete and fatal change was wrought by one man's dismounting from his horse to enter an humble dwelling along the roadside. Had Sanchez kept away from that fatal door, had he dashed back to his headquarters with Olmos and Rodriguez to bring the faithful companies with which to garrison the bridge, or had he only awaited their arrival without dismounting, the Royal Commissioner would have been his prisoner before the dawn of another day. The traitors at the bridge would not have dared to assail the dreaded captain at the head of his body-guard, with re-enforcements in easy call. But such is the lottery of life. Your fingers had touched the great prize as they dived into the urn, but it slipped away as you closed them on the next number, which brought the deadly failure.

Pinioned and gagged, Roberto Sanchez had been carried out of the room of his child's mother. The blow was so sudden and so terrible that it stunned, but did not fell, Mercedes. She was like one awaking from a dream, unable at once to comprehend the situation. She heard nothing but one terrible sentence, which incessantly rang in her ears: "Ah, thou miserable viper, that I have warmed in my bosom, it is thou who hast sold me!" And the look he had given her! Oh, the terrible look! She covered her eyes with her hands, but still she saw that look. She buried her head in her shawl, but still that look was before her. It was like the dying look of Abel, that sank forever into the despairing soul of Cain. Oh, that look! It would drive her mad.

And now her mother entered the room.

"No, Mother!" screamed the girl. "I am not the viper that betrayed him. Mother! If he *was* betrayed, if this was a snare and a trap, may the curse of God crush those who laid it. May the guilty be forever doomed to the torments of perdition, no matter who it was, no matter who— and if it was you. If you did this, Mother, or knew of it, I cease to be your child, and curse you, yes, curse you, forevermore. May every *maravedi* of the blood-money for which you sold him, turn into burning fire or poisonous toads, as you hold it in your accursed hand. May you die without shrift and sacrament, surrounded and scoffed by heretics and Moors. For every Saint that you invoke, a Devil shall come to your side. May the planets strike you, may witchcraft blast you. If you did it, Mother, I wish you leprosy and plague so that you may live an outcast, begging at church-doors, and be driven, like a Jewess or a Lutheran, from the charities of the Bishop's Palace. You shall have no rest or sleep, and demons shall bar your entrance into church or chapel. I renounce you. I leave your house this very hour, this very minute."

And snatching up her child, with disheveled hair and flying garments, the unfortunate girl rushed out into night and darkness.

"For the Virgin's sake!" exclaimed her mother. "Run after her, Don Tomas, and help me to bring her back."

The girl rushed away in the direction of the bridge; but her paroxysm was of short duration. She had advanced hardly twenty paces when she sank on her knees, and bending over her child, broke into convulsive sobs and a flood of tears. In this attitude she was overtaken by her mother and Don Tomas, the Mayordomo of Manuel Paredes. The storm had spent its force, and the terrible strain was followed by a prostrating reaction. Meek, like a lamb, she allowed herself to be led back to the house. Meek like a lamb she listened to Mariquita's burning protestations of innocence and entire ignorance of the plot against Sanchez. And the poor girl finally believed her, and begged her pardon for the dreadful things she had uttered in the frenzy of despair. What should she do? The oak will stand or break; but the ivy must cling to something, and if it be a rotten beam of the wall that has just fallen. Poor Merceditas! Cling to somebody she must. She can not stand alone in the world. And thus dissolved in tears, she hangs around the neck of that mercenary mother, who has just stolen from her daughter what she loved best in the world. And this time Doña Mariquita does not ask her as she did a few months ago: "Why do you weep, Merceditas?"

BOOK V.
THE VALUE OF LIFE.

Que horcas eran dellos ocupados,
Que jaulas de cabezas bastecidas,
Que de soberbias casas abatidas
Y por su corupcion de sal sembradas,
Que prosperas haciendas confiscadas,
Que plaga de las honras, y las vidas,
Castigo merecido y justa pena
Del que contra su Rey se desenfrena.
     PEDRO DE OÑA, *Arauco Domado*,
          Canto XVI, p. 280.

BOOK V.
THE VALUE OF LIFE.

CHAPTER I.

ARANA.

ORDER reigned at Quito. Arana had effected his triumphal entrance. He had been welcomed with the ringing of bells and firing of cannon. The Audience and the Cabildo had gone forth to receive him, and to escort him to the city. A solemn *Te Deum* had been sung at the Cathedral, and those lately in rebellion had crouched before, and fawned upon, their new master. The Royal Commissioner had established his head-quarters at the house of the Marquis of Solando, whose guest he was. The Marquis and Dolores, being in deep mourning, could give no public entertainments, as they would have done under more auspicious circumstances; but they had yielded the largest and best part of the house to their honored guest, and overwhelmed him with attentions. Dolores, as we can easily understand, had entirely captivated the old gentleman, who had not seen her equal in America.

What Arana's policy would be, had not yet been developed. As at Guayaquil, he had smiled upon everybody. Two weeks had elapsed since his arrival, and but one sentence of death had been pronounced, and that was on Roberto Sanchez, the arch-rebel and traitor, the murderer of so many of the King's most loyal servants. Roberto had been sentenced to be dragged to the place of execution —the Plaza of Santa Clara—in a hurdle, to have his hands cut off and his eyes put out by the hangman, and then to suffer the extreme penalty by garroting. The estates of the Sanchez family were to be confiscated, their family-mansion was to be leveled to the ground, salt and ashes were to be strewn on the spot where it had stood, and a tablet was to be put up on the premises, with the inscription, that this was the place where the traitors, Sanchez, once lived, who had met with the doom which all traitors deserved. Young Sanchez had been brought back to Quito from Tambillo, at which place he had been delivered into the Commissioner's hands. He was now at the barracks, and—such is the fate of war—placed in charge of his own former prisoners, Juan del Puente and Ildefonso Coronel.

Nobody was surprised at his sentence. Nobody had expected it otherwise. The real cause of surprise was the apparent leniency of the Royal Commander. Few arrests had been made. The President of the Royal Audience had been deposed, and the senior Auditor Don Estevan Marañon, had been charged with taking the *residencia* of his late superior, a process well-known to Spanish law, and consisting in an account of his administration, which the deposed officer was required to give to the officer appointed to make the investigation. This measure against the worthless President had filled the popular party with a vague hope that the Royal Commissioner might, after all, be disposed to look upon their past offenses with a forgiving eye. Only two changes had thus far been made in the *personale* of the Municipal Government. Juan de Londoño and Guzman Ponce de Leon had been appointed Alcaldes in the places of Olmos and Garcia. This change, it must be admitted, was a violent one, as the Alcaldes had always been elected by the Cabildo, and not appointed by the King's representatives; but as these appointments had been designated as provisional, they had not given alarm or caused suspicion. Not to give alarm was the very object and purpose of Arana's present policy. Those of his intended victims who were at Quito, were within his grasp. They could not escape from him. They were his prisoners, even if he allowed them to go about. The ehtrances of the city were well guarded, and nobody was permitted to leave it under penalty of death, without a pass from the Commander. But there were rebels outside of the city, landed proprietors and gentlemen of note, who had compromised themselves during the Revolution. It would not be so easy to capture these, if they betook themselves to the mountains. Yet Arana wanted them in his net. He wanted them all. Not one should slip away from him. It was necessary, therefore, to allay their apprehensions and to induce them to come to the Capital. The way in which Alba had captured Egmont and Horne was the model after which Arana fashioned his policy. No second Orange should escape him, if he could help it. The moment he had his victims safe in his net, it would be easy to abandon the pretense of leniency, and resort to a policy of retributive severity.

It was forenoon. A large crowd of people had assembled around the house of the Marquis of Solando, forming groups on the sidewalks or on the Plaza in front of the building. In an age when newspapers were unknown, those who thirsted for news had no means of gratifying their curiosity other than personal exertion, to ascertain what they desired to know. The populace of Quito always lazy, gossipy and excitable, now hung around the headquarters of the Royal Commissioner, as during the Revolution, they had hovered around the building of the Municipality, to pick up, and greedily to swallow, the news and rumors of the day.

"Have they caught Juan Castro?" asked a wiry half-breed, who stood in a group of butchers and shopmen from the *Carniceria*, one of the most unruly districts of ancient and modern Quito.

"Indeed they have not!" answered one of the group.

"If he has succeeded in taking himself out of the city, they will never catch him. He will be shrewd enough to stay in the mountains, until the storm has blown over."

"Ah, but if he is still hidden in the city, that reward will fetch him. It is a big amount of money. His best friend would sell him for that."

"Hush! Who comes there?"

It was an elderly lady, all in black, followed by two women and a man servant.

"Oh, I know!" said another. "Do you see how she cries? It is the mother of Sanchez. She will beg for the life of her son."

The men now suddenly became quiet, and intently stared at the unfortunate lady as she walked or rather staggered through the doorway of the Marquis, so that her women had to hasten to her support. Most of those rough men had instinctively uncovered their heads in silent sympathy as they opened a passage for the Señora.

"There comes another woman in black, a young one."

"It is the 'Flower of Machángara,' Mercedes Castro, the one that sold her lover, Roberto Sanchez, to the King's men."

"What may she want here?" resumed the first speaker.

Mercedes had passed them and entered the doorway.

"Now she raises her veil to speak to that Caballero."

"How pale and conscience-stricken she looks. Perhaps she wants to atone for her treachery by begging for his life."

"Ah!" shrieked an old woman who kept a chicha-shop. "The witch! The viper! It is right enough to serve our Lord the King, and this rebellion was all wrong; but there is no excuse for that fair-faced snake. No honest Christian woman would sell her lover and the father of her child, rebel or no rebel. Her face should be scorched with henbane. The conceited little snake!"

In the meantime the subject of these remarks had accosted the Marquis of Solando, who was just about to leave the house, accompanied by some of Arana's officers, and followed by a retinue of servants. Mercedes had thrown herself down before him, and dropping her black shawl over her shoulders, disclosed a face so beautiful in its pale agony, that it enlisted the interest of the Marquis' Spanish companions, to whom this flower of the Sierra was unknown.

"What dost thou wish, my good woman?" said the Marquis.

"For the sake of God, and by all that is sacred to your Excellency, I beseech your Excellency to let me speak to the Royal Commissioner!"

"And why shouldst thou wish to speak to his Grace, my child?" inquired Solando with more kindness in his tone than usual; but it flattered him to patronize a beautiful young woman in the presence of the foreign officers.

"May it please your Excellency!" answered Mercedes still on her knees, "I want to implore him for mercy— mercy to one who is to be executed to-morrow."

"My poor girl! Thy errand will be fruitless. The Señora Sanchez is now with his Grace, and she will implore him in vain. His Grace is inclined to be merciful where he can, but it will be impossible in the case of that desperate young man."

"Oh, no! No! Señor Marquis. Do not say it will be impossible. Oh, let me see his Grace."

"And what wouldst thou say to the Commissioner? Hast thou ever spoken to persons of his quality and power?"

"No, your Excellency; but God will give me words to move his heart. I have prayed to the Virgin as no woman ever prayed to her. She will not abandon me in this solemn hour. And if I can not save his life, his Grace will at least permit me to see him before he dies." And here the poor girl broke into wild, hysteric sobs.

"I should think thou mightst get that permission without troubling his Grace."

"No, your Excellency; they have refused to admit me. I have besieged the doors of his prison. I have implored his guards on my knees to let me see him. It was all in vain. Without an order from his Grace, they said, I could not be permitted to see him. And see him I must, your Excellency, and should I pay for it with my life."

"Well," said the Marquis. "What say you, Caballeros? Shall we accede to the request of this young woman. I fear his Grace has been worried enough by applicants, and I should like to spare him the annoyance."

"If your Excellency will permit," said one of the young Spanish officers, "I shall take charge of this girl, and procure her the audience which she so fervently prays for. I am satisfied that the latter part of her request will be granted. Come Señorita!"

The officer led the way, and Mercedes followed him up stairs. The house was built in the most approved style of that period. An uncovered gallery, overlooking the courtyard below, ran along one side of the house. This was a sunny place in the forenoon, for which reason Pedro de Arana had sought it out, because the nights and mornings at Quito are cold, the interior of the houses is generally cold, and the Royal Commissioner was an old man, unaccustomed to the rarified and chilling atmosphere of the Sierra. There he sat in an easy-chair, resting against the balustrade, covered with a heavy cloak, and a poncho over his knees, warming himself in the pleasant rays of the bright sun of Quito. He was a queer-looking man of small stature, heavily built and very fleshy. His iron-gray hair was short and stood on end when he doffed the black velvet cap which now covered his head. His moustache was shorter than usual with Spanish noblemen, and curled upward, bringing into high relief the humorous and sometimes even Mephistophelian expression which played around his mouth, If Don Quixote had been published in those days, there would have been a great deal in Arana's appearance which might have reminded those who saw him, of Sancho Panza. He seemed to be a man of fifty although in reality he was older. He produced the impression of a cynic, yet when the occasion required it, he knew how to make a great show of reverence, and could talk like a preacher. He was not a man of learning, but of great shrewdness and sound common sense. The proverbial sayings, in which the Spanish language abounds, recurred to him almost continually, and gave force and terseness to what he said. He had received his mental and moral training in camps and barracks, and in the school of the Albas and such other men as Philip II selected for his service. Pedro de Arana seemed to be a jolly old soul, overflowing with good nature and the milk of human kindness, fond of good cheer and comfort, and still fonder of a good joke; yet he was not troubled with that sensibility which feels the pain it inflicts upon others, or shrinks from inflicting it. The sufferings of others had never disturbed his sleep, nor would it have spoiled his appetite for dinner to pronounce sentence of death on a rebel prisoner.

Mercedes did not see the dreadful personage at once. The officer led her to a covered gallery running at right angles from the gallery on which the old Commissioner sat. There her protector told her to sit down and to await his return. He would speak to his Grace for her. A few minutes elapsed before Mercedes dared to look around. At last she looked up and beheld a sickening spectacle which made her heart sink and her faintest hopes vanish. Roberto's mother, more dead than alive, her face covered with gastly pallor, her knees breaking, her dress torn and disordered, was led away almost insensible by Doña Catita and Mother Santos. Arrived at the head of the stair-case, she turned back toward where the Commander sat, and with uplifted hands folded in prayer, fell on her knees again, screaming: "Mercy! Mercy! For the love of God!"

One of her own attendants who had waited on the landing of the main stair-case, now came up, and with the aid of the other two women, lifted her from the stony floor and carried her down stairs into one of the servants' rooms, where they spoke, unavailingly, words of comfort, until the poor lady had gathered strength enough to repair to the prison of her son, whom she had obtained permission to see for a last farewell.

It had become a terrible certainty to Mercedes that her prayer would not be granted after the mother's prayer had been refused. And yet does not the human heart hope against hope, does it not cling even to the hope of hope, after all real hope is gone?

The young officer returned. His Excellency would speak to Mercedes. Her pretty face had secured her an audience, which for the Señora Sanchez only the influential exertion of the Marquis, an old friend of the family, had been able to obtain.

The Commander seemed to be in excellent spirits. The scene with the mother of his victim had not ruffled his composure. He was tasting a draught of sweetened *chicha* which the Señorita Dolores had sent to convince him that a very palatable drink could be made of the national beverage of the aborigines by artistic treatment and additions.

The old gentleman winked knowingly at the young officer as he approached with his protegé.

"By Santiago! That scapegrace Ramirez is always in luck," his Excellency was pleased to remark to the officer who stood at his side, holding the silver plate from which his commander had taken the goblet. "A beautiful face! Doña Inez of Ambato will be forgotten, now. 'Out of sight, out of mind.' 'Young heart, light heart!'"

The bystanders laughed dutifully at the pleasantry of their superior.

"Well, Ramirez," continued the old man. "We are ready to inspect your new flame. Caramba! This is a treasure of an inheritance. Accept our congratulations, if you are to be the heir, of which I have no doubt, judging from your past successes. 'To be born lucky is better than to be born rich.'"

In the meantime, the trembling subject of his Excellency's coarse jokes had thrown herself on her knees before the old man, and stammered: "Mercy, Señor, mercy!"

"Well! Well!" said Arana, pleased with the appearance of the girl, "this, then, is the pretty bait with which our friends entrapped the rebel chief. By Santiago! If I were not so old, I should have gone into that trap myself. We owe thee an important debt, my pretty American, for the service thou and thy house have rendered to the King's cause."

The first impulse of Mercedes was to deny the dreadful charge which weighed so heavily on her soul, although she was conscious of her innocence; but at that moment the thought flashed through her mind that Arana's mistaken belief might give her a claim on his mercy. Hence she said after a moment's reflection:

"On my knees, I thank your Excellency for these kind words, and if the service—my—my—mother has rendered, should really be considered important by your Excellency"—

. "Do not let us speak of your mother now, my little one. Thy mother has received her reward. It is the daughter to whom some acknowledgment is due. If thou wilt ask a favor which I have the power to grant, I will grant it. Speak out without fear, and be short about it. 'Long speeches will make the soup boil over.'"

"Yes, your Excellency. One word will express all that I pray for on this side of the grave. It is the life of Roberto Sanchez. Mercy, Señor, *misericordia!*"

The commander had taken a sip from the goblet he still held, and then handed it with a grimace to the officer behind his chair, saying: "With all due respect and admiration for our excellent hostess, the Señorita Dolores, I must say that this native drink is detestable. Of course we shall not tell her so, but bring me some Christian *aguardiente* to get this heathenish taste out of my mouth." And, turning to the girl, he continued: "Thou art a strange child! If thou didst not wish him to die, why didst thou entrap him? Jealousy, perhaps! I see! I see! The young man had played with others, and we became mad with jealousy, thirsting for revenge, and now we repent of it. O, women, women! They are all alike."

All the considerations of prudence to which Mercedes had forced herself to yield, broke down now, and before the Count had quite finished his speech, she exclaimed! "But I did not entrap him, your Excellency. I am innocent of all treachery!"

"There! there!" replied Arana. "Upon what ground, then, dost thou come before me to ask favors?"

"On the ground of mercy, Señor, in the name of God, and for the love of Jesus Christ. God is mercy, and he has placed the King over us, whose loyal servant I am. Why should not the King be merciful? God forgives us our sins; why should not the King forgive? Your Excellency stands in the King's place. Why should not your Excellency be merciful? What is one life to the King, who has been set to rule over millions? Who could prevail against the King's power? The King can afford to pardon those who err, as God in Heaven forgives us our trespasses."

"This girl talks remarkably well," said Arana, quite amused; "but we must impart a little religious instruction to her ignorant mind. Thou considerest not, my child, that the King can not change the hearts and minds of men. The King is not almighty. The King must punish where God might pardon. Mercy to the wicked is cruelty to the good. The lions and the tigers must be killed; they can not be tamed. The man whom thou lovest has committed almost every crime mortal man can commit. He has been a rebel and a traitor to his King, and an apostate to his God; he has committed murder after murder; he has been guilty of tyranny and robbery. To spare his life would be an encouragement to others to do as he has done. No, my child! God may pardon, but I must condemn him. Thank you, Olivarez," he added, as he took the glass of rum presented to him by an officer, and emptied it at one draught; "that's better than that Indian abomination."

CHAPTER II.

IN THE TOILS.

A SUITE of three rooms in the barracks was occupied by Juan del Puente and Idelfonso Coronel. These rooms had the view of the street, and doors leading to an arched corridor, running along a large, square court. The outside door to the third of these rooms, and its only window, had recently been walled up. This room was the prison of Roberto Sanchez. Whatever light and air it had, it received through a door inside, which led into the second room, and was always kept open. This was Juan del Puente's room, who thus kept his prisoner continually in sight. The third and outer room was the present habitation of Idelfonso Coronel. Sentinels were pacing the corridors, the court, and the streets outside. In addition to all these precautions, Sanchez was chained by the foot to a ring in the floor, the chain being long enough to enable him to lie down on a bed of straw, covered with sheepskins and a few *ponchos*. His wrists were in fetters connected by a chain, the shortness of which was a source of constant annoyance. In this prison he had languished since Arana's triumphal entrance in Quito. No one had been allowed to see him. Del Puente and Coronel were his only companions, with the exception of a

Spanish priest, whose visits had been permitted since the promulgation of the death-sentence.

On the day before the execution, however, Roberto's mother, as we already know—thanks to the intercession of the Marquis of Solando—had secured the privilege of being admitted to her son's prison. She was now with him, pressing him to her bosom in an agonized embrace. as if she could tear him away from the hateful flight of time, or stem the terrible escape of the sand which was irretrievably ebbing away from the hour-glass, steadily diminishing the short remainder of life.

"Señor Del Puente!" said Sanchez after he had extricated himself from her first embraces. "May I ask a favor of you. I have given you little or no trouble, and complied with all your regulations; and you might now do a little act of kindness to me."

"What is it, Señor Don Roberto?"

"Take off my handcuffs—take them off for a few minutes at least. I could not escape if I would, and, while you oblige me, I would not if I could."

"I regret to say, Señor Don Roberto, that I have no authority to do so."

"Authority! You are in command here, Don Juan. Your will is your authority, I dislike to remind you that you were my prisoner once—a very, very short time ago. I saved your life, Don Juan, which my comrades would have sacrificed, and I leave it to you to say whether I did not treat you as a Christian knight should treat a prisoner of war?"

"What you say, Señor Don Roberto, is true, and thousand thanks to your Grace for it. But your Grace must consider that you were your own master, while I am my master's servant. Your Grace *gave* orders instead of *receiving* them. I receive orders and must obey. If I were not afraid of committing high treason myself, I should like to say that if the King of Spain were not my master, but if I had the choice of a master, I could not wish a better one than your Grace. But the King of Spain *is* my master, and that's the end of it."

"But I ask a mere nothing, Señor Del Puente. Here is my mother, to whom I must bid a last, an eternal farewell. Let me clasp her to my breast but for a few seconds. I can not do it with these handcuffs on. Look at the shortness of this chain, and have pity on both of us. Nobody will know it, Señor Del Puente."

"Ah, Señor Don Roberto, should a soldier, a splendid soldier like your Grace, thus speak to a soldier like myself, acting under orders. Suppose your Grace, while in command, had given an order to one of your men. Would your Grace have him disregard it, on the supposition that his offense would not come to the knowledge of your Grace?"

"I shall not trouble you again," said Sanchez, turning away. "Come, Mother, let us sit down on this bed and let us speak of yourself, Mother. My account is easily settled, and I do not fear death. If I did fear it, I should not be where I am now. But I grieve for you, dear Mother. It is my only grief. To suffer death under some circumstances is not as hard a task as to suffer life. What will become of you, Mother?. They have confiscated our estates; they will drive you from our house in order to raze it to the ground. This thought, Mother, is more horrid to me than the cruel death which I must suffer to-morrow."

We shall drop the curtain over this painful scene. There is an end to all things, and where time is most precious, its flight is the swiftest.

The door between the room of Del Puente and the adjoining room of Corónel was closed, and a sentinel was placed before it. The time allotted for the visit of the Señora Sanchez had expired. She begged to return on the following morning, but Sanchez insisted that she should not. He also made her promise not to see him led out to his end, but to offer up prayers during his last hours on earth. Del Puente led her away. He opened the door for her and almost carried her to the room of Coronel. That worthy was out, but the attendants of the Señora awaited her. In the darkest corner of the room sat a woman dressed in deep mourning, covered with a black veil, and attended by a young Mestizo girl who played with a smiling babe which she held in her arms.

The Señora Sanchez was so overcome that for a long time she was unable to compose herself. Sinking into a chair, she buried her face in her hands, and wept until her sobs died away in a heart-rending moan. At last her attendants prevailed upon her to arouse herself, and to go. At the same time, Del Puente, who had strolled out into the court-yard, returned, and said to the woman in the corner, that he would now announce her to Don Roberto. Mercedes—for it was Mercedes—arose tremblingly, and stepped forward, waiting to be called in. Just then the eyes of Roberto's mother fell upon her, and recognized her in spite of her veil. The old lady at once pressed back her garments, as if to escape the polluting touch, and grasping the arm of one of her companions with her other hand, drew her away, exclaiming: "Hence! Hence! Let us not breathe the air poisoned by that viper, that vile, treacherous murderess."

These words stunned and nearly crushed poor Mercedes, and she sank back into the chair from which she had arisen.

"I will not see her!" said Roberto, after he had learned from Juan del Puente that Mercedes was in waiting.

"But she has an order from the Royal Commissioner allowing her to see your Grace!" rejoined the Spaniard.

"Allowing her to see me; yes. But has she an order compelling me to see her, Señor del Puente?"

The Spaniard seemed puzzled. "My orders are to let her in!"

"You may let her in, Señor del Puente, if I wish to see

her. The Royal Commissioner does not object to my seeing her. But I will not receive her, unless the Royal Commissioner compels me to undergo this additional punishment. Go, Señor del Puente! Do not torment your prisoner. You refused to take off these manacles for a moment, because you had no orders allowing it. Stand by your orders now. You have no orders to inflict a visitor on me, whom I refuse to admit. There comes my Reverend Father. Do not distract my thoughts now, Señor del Puente, but leave me with him."

Del Puente left, but after a little, returned again.

"That girl is distracted, your Grace. She swears she did not betray your Grace. She implores your Grace, by all that is sacred, to let her come in."

"Señor del Puente, must I be tormented during the few hours that are left to me of life. I have decided, and the moments are too precious to be wasted thus."

"Well, then, she begs that your Grace may at least see and bless the child."

"The child! Whose child? How do I know that it is my child? Shall I believe the woman who sold me? She must have betrayed me before, as she did afterward."

"My son! My son!" now interrupted the monk, who was no less a person than the Superior of La Merced. "Hast thou forgotten that Christ on the cross forgave his enemies? I do not find thee in the spirit in which I left thee on yesterday. Thou must forgive this girl!"

"I do. so, Reverend Father; I forgive her. It is hard, dreadfully hard to forgive her. When I think that victory was in my grasp; that but for her the Royal Commander would have been my prisoner; that I should have been King of the realm, the happy husband of a beautiful and lovely Princess, the possessor of untold wealth, the commander of an army of my own formation, and that even if I had failed in the end, my name would have lived forever; when I think that success, glory, happiness, greatness would have been mine, but for the viper who entrapped me into destruction—it is almost too hard to forgive."

"Think of thy Savior, my son. Time flies. The hour approaches; thou must appear before thy God."

"I know, Reverend Father, and I forgive—I forgive her."

"With all thy heart?"

"With all my heart, Father; but I can not see her. It would unsettle my mind; it would distract my thoughts; it would disturb my composure. I could not drink in your holy words as I wish to. I forgive her, and you may tell her so. Impose any penance upon me, Father, but do not compel me to see her. Anything but that! I will not, I can not, see her!"

An hour after these scenes, Juan del Puente stepped out into the court-yard and looked around for Ildefonso Coronel. Not seeing him anywhere, Del Puente asked one of the sentinels whither that worthy had gone. The soldier said that Señor Ildefonso had left word he would be back in a very short time to relieve the Señor Captain."

"Yes, indeed," thought Del Puente, "it is no pleasure to be a jailer. I long for a little fresh air and for a chat with Doña Panchita, after having been locked up all day."

At last Ildefonso returned, growling as usual.

"Where have you been, man?" asked Del Puente.

"Hang your impudence!" muttered his worthy comrade. "Am I to be a prisoner because we have to keep one?"

"I do not like to remind you, Ildefonso, of a fact which you seem to forget. Are you at all aware that I am your superior officer?"

"And why should you be? How came you to be my superior officer? By snatching from me what belonged to me. You are pushing and bold, while I am modest and retiring."

"I see! I see, Ildefonso, I am in your way again. If

it were not for me you would rise in the world. It is well. You shall not remain with me any longer. To-morrow 1 shall make application to the Commander to put you in charge of an independent post—to send you anywhere, so that you get away from me."

"Go to the devil, Del Puente!" interrupted the other, "you will never understand me. Here I have been hurrying back to relieve you; in fact, I have hardly been out. I hastened home to enable you to rush into the arms of Doña Panchita, and now you grumble and rail at my good will, and scold me for my readiness to sit here all alone with our prisoner until you get through with your lovemaking."

"Your good will! Your readiness! Let me tell you, once for all, Ildefonso Coronel, that I am tired, thoroughly tired, of your grumbling, your ingratitude, and your insubordination. I am in earnest, Ildefonso. Either you will now and forever realize your position as my subordinate, and act accordingly, or we shall part to-morrow. I shall give you a night to sleep over it. Do not say another word! I am not in a humor to listen. Adios!"

"His Grace is not in a humor to listen to Ildefonso Coronel," muttered that subordinate, as he entered his room. "His Grace is tired of me, thoroughly tired of my insubordination, his Grace was pleased to remark. Yes, yes, the swine-herd, the beggar, the hired assassin is getting tired of the ingratitude of those who made him. We shall see! There is a bull for this sin!* We shall see who will be the better and the richer man, when we return to Spain. Is the prisoner alone, sentinel?"

"No, Señor. His Reverence, the Father Superior, is with him."

"It is well!" And now Ildefonso entered Del Puente's

* A well-known Spanish proverb:- "*Contra este pecado hay una bula.*"

room, and closed the door behind him. Roberto and the monk were engaged in close conversation. "I hope that friar will go," thought Coronel, "before Del Puente comes back. I must prepare the young rebel. But now the goblet. I must fix that first. Ten drops will do to put a man into a death-like sleep, which will last ten hours. 'No power on earth,' the fellow said, 'will awake your man before the time is up. But,' said he, 'if you do not want him to awake at all, give him more. If you give him twenty drops, your man will sleep forever.' Now, let me see whether I understand it right. Ten drops I want in mine, for I do want to awake and to go back to glorious Spain, to enjoy this great good fortune, this unexpected windfall of luck. Ten drops for me, to avert suspicion. I shall be careful to count them, and shall not mix them before Del Puente has gone to sleep. But Del Puente's goblet must be fixed now. There it goes! One, two, three, five, seven, eight, nine, eleven, twelve—what a mistake! These drops rushed out before I could count them! H'm! what was it he said? He is tired of my impudence. I must not forget that I am his subordinate, or he will have me sent elsewhere! There drops another! Thirteen! Now, really, I did not mean that. It was not my intention. But I can not waste the precious liquor by throwing this out. There would not be enough left for the sentinels. He will not put up with my hatefulness any longer —the great man who allowed himself to be captured, like a monkey, by a handful of half-starved insurgents—will he not? But suppose I should not put up with him any longer? Suppose this were my turn, Juan del Puente— the turn of grumbling, ungrateful, impudent, incapable, envious, and insubordinate Ildefonso Coronel, who did all the hard work, and suffered all the heavy blows, while you reaped the honors and the emoluments. Fourteen, fifteen! No, Juan del Puente, I will not cheat the devil of his due. My conscience would not allow it. The devil must get thee in the end, and the sooner he gets thee the better it will be for all Christians. Sixteen, eighteen, twenty—and one over, for better assurance. It will be a good, sound sleep, Señor Captain. Thou wilt surely enjoy it. Now for the wine—Caramba! What elegant flavor! Here goes! Your very good health, Señor del Puente!"

CHAPTER III.

THE UNSEEN PROTECTRESS.

THE Count of Arana was an early riser. He took two or three naps during the day, but he rose before five in the morning in order to dispatch his civil business and correspondence, so as to be free to devote the rest of the day to military matters and to amusements. In this, as in everything else, he was pedantically systematic, and his civil and military dependents were compelled to accommodate themselves to his unreasonable hours.

The mail from Lima and the coast had arrived the evening before, and Arana's secretaries had spent half the night in digesting and abbreviating its contents so as to present a short summary of the principal points to their chief in the morning. Arana had risen earlier than usual this day, for he wished to hold himself in special readiness for the execution. He was now at work with his secretaries while sipping a cup of hot chocolate with a strong admixture of rum. Two or three wax candles burned on the table, dimming under the increasing daylight.

"There are several long communications with reference to the Señor Julio de Carrera," said one of the secretaries. "Society at Lima is in ecstasies over his martyrdom. The poets have sung his praises. Señor Odriozola, by special instruction of His Royal Highness, has collected copies of all their pieces, and he transmits them herewith to your Excellency."

"By Santiago! Not for me to read!" thundered the old man.

"No, most excellent Señor," replied the secretary, unable to suppress a smile, "but to cause them to be delivered to the young gentleman's relatives, whom it is His Highness' purpose to honor by this attention."

"Did the young gentleman have any relatives?"

"No, most excellent Señor, none but his uncle, who is dead."

"Do you know who his principal friends were, or at whose house he made his *tertulia*?" *

"He was a regular and constant visitor at this house, your Excellency."

"Well, then, we shall refer these papers to the Marquis. The Señorita Dolores will tell us what to do with them."

"The ladies at Lima are wearing Carrera-ribbons and Carrera-combs; and at the theater they will have his story written up for a tragedy. His Royal Highness, the Viceroy, is satisfied that our Master the King will reward Carrera's noble self-sacrifice by some special act of recognition, either to the gentlemen himself, if he should ever be found, or to his family. In the meantime, His Royal Highness requests your Excellency to make special exertions to ascertain what has become of Carrera, and if there should be no doubt of his death to honor his memory by some temporary monument, with a suitable inscription, until the royal pleasure can be ascertained."

"Well and good!" said Arana. "The instructions of His Highness must be complied with to the letter. I think it would be best to offer a reward for the discovery and identification of Carrera's remains or for a clue to this mystery. If anything can do it, it will be money. I find the

---

* His regular daily visits.

Americans are as fond of it as our people at home.—Ramirez!"

That officer, who had been standing in the door, now sprung forward.

"Let Juan del Puente come here at once. I want to instruct him, personally, as to his duties to-day. This is our first execution, and it must be made as impressive as possible. I would not, for anything in the world, have this business bunglingly done. You had better go for Del Puente yourself, Señor Ramirez, and on your way to and fro, see whether everything is in proper readiness. Examine the scaffold, if you please. I saw an execution once where they had not fastened the fellow's seat properly. It broke down under his weight, and the whole thing became ridiculous. We will have no break-downs to-day, gentlemen, no break-downs. We shall break a neck, but not a seat." And, as usual, the old gentleman graciously led the laughter over his own pleasantry.

"Proceed, Mr. Secretary!" said Arana, after Ramirez had left the room.

"The *Fiscal* of the court-martial reports five sentences of death and confiscation for your Excellency's confirmation."

"Five! What a folly. Could he not have made it four or six for the time being? I do not like odd numbers. They always leave a chance for the devil. When we shall have to hang you, Mr. Secretary, you may rest assured we shall give you a companion." And over this new pleasantry his Excellency laughed until his laughter changed into a coughing fit, and his cough terminated in an oath. "And who are they?"

"The Señores Garcia, father and son, the Señores Olmos, father and son, and old Pedro Perez, the lieutenant of Roberto Sanchez. Old Perez was too sick to make a defense."

"Not necessary. If he is very sick, we shall save him

the trouble of dying, by cutting off his head. We shall do the part of a doctor by him. Ha! ha! ha! ha! Hand me the sentences. I shall sign them now, but they must not be published until we have secured the gentlemen from the country. We can not catch flies with vinegar. That must be a stupid fish which would swallow the bait after having seen the hook under it. No, Señor, let us go slowly, but be sure. Skill is worth more than strength. Let these sentences be kept secret until the proper time has come. I wonder how well Señor Paredes has succeeded in overcoming the shyness of some of these gentlemen?"

"He said he expected to make a favorable report to your Excellency this morning."

"Well, why has he not come? Where is he? He knows I require punctuality. Feed a horse regularly and you will save half the fodder."

"Ah, but your Excellency began work half an hour earlier this morning than usual."

"That's so! I had forgotten. Well, let it pass. Do you think," he added, leaning forward over the table and reducing his voice to a whisper, "that that man would presume to keep up a clandestine correspondence with the authorities at Lima or Madrid, now that I have arrived to take charge of matters?"

"I do not know, your Excellency. In fact, I can not suspect that he would presume to do so, now that his, or rather the Marquis' commission, has been superseded by your Excellency's. And how could he do it without our being informed by the post-office authorities?"

"True enough! But he is a man of great resources and —I say so cheerfully and willingly—a man of good uses. But the egg must not attempt to be wiser than the hen. While I am on deck I will be the captain, and I shall tolerate no meddling with my affairs. Men who have rendered valuable services are apt to become conceited or overbearing, or to think they are indispensable, and that the world would come to a stand-still without them. They are mistaken, Mr. Secretary. The world will not come to a stand-still when they are gone. Time and tide will roll on, Mr. Secretary, when you and I shall be no more. But there comes our great man himself!"

"I kiss your Excellency's hands," said Paredes as he entered, "and beg your Excellency's pardon if I should be late."

"Not at all, friend Paredes. We began our work a little earlier than usual. What good news can our friend give us this morning?"

"I think, your Excellency, I shall soon succeed in obtaining a clue as to the hiding place of that ruffianly and brutal murderer, Juan Castro, the chief of the ragamuffins of Quito."

"Castro!-Castro!" repeated Arana. "Who is he?"

"He was the ringleader in the dastardly murder of my lamented and noble friend, the Count Valverde."

"Ah, yes! Now I recollect! We have offered a reward for his apprehension."

"Yes, most excellent Señor, a large reward has been offered. But Castro is a most desperate character, who swayed the rabble by the terror with which he inspired them. I have no doubt there is a strong disposition among his former associates to earn the reward; but they are afraid of him. He is as brave as he is wicked and murderous. The difficulty would be in taking him alive. He would not allow himself to be taken alive. And if those who intend to capture him should kill him during the struggle, they would have had their risk and trouble for nothing. If your Excellency should not consider it forward or presumptuous on my part, I would suggest that the reward be promised to those who bring him dead or alive."

"Señor Paredes," answered the Count, "is undoubtedly a very shrewd man, who desires to serve the interests of the King to the best of his ability. But as to how these interests may be served best, your Grace must allow me to be the judge. More than the death of the villain, we want the example of his execution. The bringing in of his dead body would terrify nobody. No, Señor; let him be dragged into a public square, and there receive his punishment in the presence of hundreds of his awe-stricken confederates. That is the way we administer justice in Spain. You gentlemen of America may have your own way to do things; but it is not the right way, as your past troubles and your past helplessness have shown."

Paredes bit his lip, and, with a prompt effort, concealed and suppressed his resentment. A native American gentleman, be he never so able and useful, was a nothing, a nobody, in the eyes of those haughty Spaniards, who came to devour the substance of the colonies. With all the tact and shrewdness of Paredes, he had not been able to ingratiate himself with the Royal Commissioner. Paredes had tried his best to win the old man's favor, but he had failed. Perhaps the very greatness and value of the services rendered by Manuel Paredes had earned for him the jealousy and ill-will of Arana.

"But does it not strike your Excellency," resumed the Creole, "that it might be better to have his dead body, than not to get him at all?"

"How would your Grace accomplish his death?"

"I thought," answered Paredes, somewhat embarrassed, "that some of his old confederates who know of his hiding-place, would be willing to sell and deliver him, if they could do it without danger to themselves."

"But does Colonel Paredes know that those men are really so disposed?"

"I think, I may be sure of it."

"Well, then, why not seize the men who are suspected of knowing his hiding-place, and *make* them talk? The boot and the thumbscrew would soon open their mouths.

We have appliances, Señor Paredes, which would make them very anxious to divulge what they know. Nothing like a little gentle persuasion. Ha! ha! ha! Just give us their names, friend Paredes, and I shall answer for their readiness to talk."

"I have had no direct overtures, your Excellency, but I have received many an indirect hint or message through third and fourth parties, that if a reward might be earned by bringing him in dead, his body would soon be forthcoming."

"Well, the next time that such hints and messages are brought to your Grace, you will do me the favor of ascertaining the sources from which they came, and"—

Arana's sentence was interrupted by a tumult outside. Wild exclamations, hurried steps, and clanking swords were heard in the hall and on the staircase, and Ramirez, followed by five or six officers, and an equal number of men, appeared in the door. A number of civilians headed by the Marquis of Solando, Juan de Londoño, Ponce de Leon and others, also crowded into the room.

"Well, Caballeros," exclaimed Arana. "What is the cause of this most extraordinary excitement?"

"I hardly dare," said Ramirez, advancing with a piece of paper in his hand. "I hardly dare to acquaint your Excellency with what has happened."

"Speak man! What is the matter?"

"*Roberto Sanchez has escaped!*"

Arana stared at the speaker as if he had not understood him. His eyes protruded from their sockets, and his hair, which always seemed to stand on end, straightened itself still more, if that was possible. Absolute silence prevailed in the room. The civilians who were present, hardly dared to draw their breaths, while the soldiers were living pictures of amazement and apprehension.

The silence was painful. It was at last broken by

Arana, who, with a violent curse, exclaimed: "What did you dare to tell me? Repeat it, Señor!"

Arana now rose from his chair, and bent forward, as if to assure himself that he had heard right.

"The prisoner, Roberto Sanchez, I am sorry to inform your Excellency"—

"To the dogs with your sorrow! Do you tell me he has escaped?"

"Yes, your Excellency!"

"By all the Saints of Heaven!" exclaimed the Commissioner, inadvertently throwing down and dashing to pieces the valuable cup from which he had sipped his chocolate, "this shall cost more heads than there were hairs on that cursed rebel's head."

And here the old man fell into another coughing fit, during which the company in the room stood silent and motionless. "Report, sir, why do you not report? What is it you are twisting in your hands?"

"The paper which was found in the empty cell this morning. It was stuck to the wall, with a nail in the center."

"Let me see," said Arana grabbing it with trembling hands. It took some time until he had sufficiently mastered his excitement, to adjust the paper to the light, and his age-worn eyesight, and not being much of a clerk, he read slowly, and in a stammering manner: "'Thus Toa Duchicela protects her friends.' A plague on that Indian witch! But where is Juan del Puente? His head shall fall for this. The miserable incompetent! First he allows himself to be captured by a handful of nobodies, and now he lets them steal his prisoner under his very nose."

"Juan del Puente's head, your Excellency, I am afraid, is past the danger of being lost. We found him in a death-like stupor, breathing but faintly. By this time he will probably be dead."

"Good for him. He does not deserve to live. And where was Ildefonso Coronel?"

"He was found on the floor of his room in the same condition, although breathing more freely. They did everything to arouse him, but it was impossible. They pinched him, burned him, cut him, but could not make him come to. The surgeons are now in charge of him."

"Were there no soldiers inside or outside?"

"Yes, most excellent Señor. There were two men inside, who were also found on the floor in a condition of unconsciousness, and whom the leeches are now endeavoring to revive. The sentinels outside report that a little after midnight, Señor del Puente passed them, giving the watchword and walking out on the street. As he did not come back, they thought he had gone to see a certain woman of doubtful repute, whom he was in the habit of visiting. But when he was found in his room this morning, it was also discovered that his hat, cloak, sword, boots, and spurs were gone. Hence, the man who left the barracks after midnight must have been the traitor, Sanchez, wrapped up in the cloak and under the hat of Juan del Puente."

"And how did he get the watchword?"

"We shall not be able to learn more of this mystery, unless one or more of the drugged soldiers can be restored. On one of the tables two bottles were found that must have held Xerez of excellent quality. A little of the wine had been left in one of them."

"Let there be a searching investigation. Let it be ascertained from whom this wine was obtained."

There was a commotion at the door. An officer entered with news.

"Well," said Arana; "What else must I hear, Señor Luzarraga?"

"Juan del Puente is dead, most excellent Señor; so are the two soldiers; but the physicians entertain hopes of restoring Ildefonso Coronel; he shows symptoms of recovery."

"Well, well," said Arana. "Del Puente was a brave man and a good soldier. May the Lord have mercy on his soul. If he was guilty of negligence, he paid for it with his life. But I think the cause of this escape was witchcraft, not negligence. At what time was the escape discovered?"

"Between five and six, your Excellency," continued Luzarraga. "The sentinels outside were relieved every two hours. The men inside had been supplanted by two orderlies, who were to remain with Captain Del Puente from midnight to day-break. When the day dawned and nobody came out, although *reveillé* had been beaten at five, I entered the room and discovered the hideous sight."

"And what has been done to secure the recapture of the traitor?"

"May it please your Excellency," answered Lieutenant Luzarraga, "I at once dispatched cavalry in every direction, with instructions to scour the by-roads and to search the mountain-passes. Every post inside and outside of the city was notified, and the whole country must now be swarming with our troopers. I did this on my own responsibility, and before my messenger could have reached your Excellency, so as not to lose a minute of precious time."

"You did right, Luzarraga. We shall put you in command of the barracks. Continue to send out your men; have the whole city searched; have every village searched. We must have him again. Go!"

The lieutenant and some of the soldiers left.

"Ah! I told you this morning, Mr. Secretary, that odd numbers would always leave a chance for the devil. We should have given Sanchez a companion in death." With these words, the old commander left his position behind the table, and joined the group of civilians in the center of the room. "And now, gentlemen, what is your opinion?

Have you any advice to offer in this most unfortunate emergency?"

"I think your Excellency's plan," answered Juan de Londoño submissively, "is the best and only one under the circumstances. Let the search be incessant, and especially let it be directed to the Indian villages."

"You are right, Señor Alcalde. And you, friend Ponce, what is your counsel?"

"With the permission of your Excellency, we shall employ the Municipality Guards to aid in the search, so as to make it general and effective."

"Many thanks! I shall accept your assistance. And you, Señor Paredes, has your Grace nothing to offer?"

This temptation was too strong to be overcome by considerations of prudence, and so Paredes answered, in his most obliging tones: "Your Excellency knows how these things are done in Spain, where they do them so much better. I could suggest only some clumsy American way which, as your Excellency has well said, would not be the right way. I caught the traitor once and delivered him into your Excellency's hands; but, owing to our Creole helplessness, I might not catch him again. Still my services are at your Excellency's command. Your Excellency may dispose of them at pleasure."

"We shall make use of them shortly, Señor Paredes," said Arana, stung to the quick, "to ferret out the parties who have been troubling your Grace with indirect hints or messages as to that arch-traitor, Juan Castro. For the present, gentlemen, we shall detain you but another moment. It is time to put an end to the carnival of Indian witchcraft in this kingdom. There is one witch especially, who, as I am informed, has played a most prominent part in the late disturbances—the witch, Mama Rucu. This dangerous person, it seems, has practiced her vile arts for years, with the connivance almost, of the authorities. It has been intimated to me that persons high in power were afraid of her, because she was supposed to know every body's secrets. It is certainly evident that she has been treated with most incomprehensible indulgence. Well, old Arana is not afraid. The witch does not know any of my secrets; for I have none except those of the King's service. I have concluded to have her arrested and put to trial. If she knows any secrets I am willing to have her divulge them. I am not interested in shielding the possessors of evil consciences. All I ask of you, gentlemen, is a guide to show my soldiers the way to her cottage. Señor Londoño, have the kindness to attend to this. And now, gentlemen, I wish you good morning. Ramirez! Have my horse in readiness. I am going to mount." And, without another word or nod, Arana turned his back on the company, and walked into the adjoining room.

CHAPTER IV.

NOS PATRIAM FUGIMUS.

WE must now turn back to the night preceding the scenes described in the last chapter. It was a dark and starless night, premonitory of the approaching rainy season. The clouds were hanging low, some layers resting on the very roofs of public buildings in the city. Now and then a streak of lightning relieved the darkness, and the rolling thunder was heard in the distance, but it did not rain. The stillness of Mount Pichincha was hardly broken by the murmur of voices around Mama Rucu's cottage. A number of Indians were there, and others were going and coming. They glided along like shadows of night, and their faces could not be recognized in the darkness. Only one group of them spoke, the one nearest the cottage; the others were silent, silent as the mountain solitude around them.

The Shyri Toa sat on the little stone bench, which had been occupied by Mama Rucu when she was first introduced to the reader. Before her knelt or stood the one to whom she gave audience at the time, while the others kept at a respectful distance, so as not to hear what their Queen had not intended for their ears. They were happy if they could hear but the musical murmur of their beloved sovereign's voice. Toa's dress was not different from those of the people around her; but on her head she wore the diadem with the emerald emblem of her ill-fated house. This was her only badge of royalty, and it appeared and disappeared as the lightning struggled with the dense darkness of the night.

"Rise, Mariano!" she said to an Indian who lay on the ground before her, pressing the hem of her garment to his lips.

"Oh, take me along Shyri, take me!" he answered without changing his attitude. "Do not leave thy most faithful servant behind."

"Poor boy! Hast thou considered the hardships, the freezing cold, the gnawing hunger, the drenching rains, the shelterless nights of the journey? Hast thou considered the sickening climate, the poisonous serpents, the fierce beasts of the tropical forests, whither I am bound. Child of the genial table lands, the Paradise of earth, house-servant of Viracocha gentlemen, thou art brought up and accustomed to ease and comfort; the tropical forests, along the great rivers, with their steaming heat and aching fevers are not for thee!"

"But thou wilt be there, Shyri, and whither thou goest I want to go. To die where thou art will be happiness. Oh, deny it not to thy faithful servant."

"Mariano!" said Toa sternly, and yet with kindness, "I must treat all my children alike. They would all follow me and depopulate the land of our fathers, which they leave behind. They would follow me by thousands, only to perish by thousands on the way. We have to pass an unhospitable wilderness, where nothing can be found to sustain life. We can not carry provisions for the thousands that would go with me. Hence I have determined that not more than five hundred shall go, and I have selected them from the factories, and the mines, and the fields; thou art a gentleman's body-servant, thy condition will be one of ease and comfort if compared to the cruel lot of thy brethren. Yet thy devotion has touched my heart, and if among the five hundred that are to go, thou canst find one who will stay for thee, I grant thee permission to take his place."

"Thanks, a thousand thanks, most gracious Shyri," answered the Indian Mariano, whom the reader has met before, as the servant of Carrera; and again fervently kissing the hem of her garment, he arose and hurried away.

Toa now clapped her hands, at which signal a dark figure emerged noiselessly from the cottage and placed itself before her, with its head and shoulders bent low.

"Call Santos!" she said. The dark figure disappeared, and immediately afterward an Indian woman knelt before her Queen.

"Santos!" Toa began, with great solemnity, "Granddaughter of Cozopangui, of the noblest blood of our race! Toa Duchicela has sent for thee to bid thee an everlasting farewell." With these words she gently placed her hands on the woman's head, drew it to her, and kissed her on the forehead, while Santos broke into sobs and tears.

"Be quiet, Mama Santos! Dry thy tears and compose thyself. Knowest thou not that thou must be the custodian of my revenge. I do not speak to thee as thy sovereign now. It is the woman Toa who speaks to the woman Santos. Toa speaks not to her subject Santos, but to Santos her friend. The revenge of my crushed heart I have left with thee."

BOOK V. THE VALUE OF LIFE. 355

"Oh, speak, Shyri!" asked the other, with the quickness of burning zeal. "Wilt thou let me use the sharp dagger of the Viracochas, which I might send with unerring certainty to her cold heart?"

"No, Santos!"

"Or wouldst thou let me use the never-failing poison which I have learned to distil from plants and fruits, the poison which leaves no mark or trace for the eye of suspicion?"

"No, Santos! I told thee what it shall be. Not death, but life shall be his punishment. Death is short, and then all is over. But there is a life which is worse than death, and that life shall be his. Use not a knife of iron or steel, but a knife that enters the heart and kills not; a knife that wounds and stabs day after day, year after year; a knife that draws no blood, and yet causes intense suffering. Let it be a poison that consumes not the body, but the mind, a poison which does not cause death, but misery and heartache, a poison which instead of giving rest takes it away. A rankling wound in the heart, the pangs of jealousy, love unrequited, bitter disappointment, blasted expectations, vain regrets, pride mortified, confidence betrayed, and endless humiliation; such a life as the years roll on without change, without relief, without hope, will be a punishment worse than a thousand deaths. And if he were to live an eternity, it would not be revenge enough for the heart-ache, the misery, the disappointment, the defeat, which he has brought upon me and my race. And in order to secure this punishment that wicked woman must live, Santos! Hearest thou, Santos! She must live! Hence, kill her not, granddaughter of Cozopangui, but watch over her, nurse her, protect her, until my revenge is complete."

"Rely on me, Shyri! Thy commands shall be fulfilled."

"Yes, Santos, and fulfill them intelligently. Use thy best judgment. Thou art of a wise family, and thy grandfather was one of the wisest men of his day. Use thy wisdom! Be vigilant! Let nothing escape thy attention! Arm thyself with the facts and circumstances which will nourish his suspicion, and use them slowly, cautiously, but continually, and with the irrepressible force of fate. And now, Santos, farewell! I must attend to others before I go, and the hours are fleeting. It is my last night in the capital of my fathers, and, alas! it will be so short!"

"Oh, gracious Shyri, life of my soul, let thy humble servant beg for a last favor on this side of the grave."

"What is it, Santos?"

"Let thy queenly lips once more press my loyal forehead, as they did before."

"Come into my arms, Santos!" said the Queen, unable to repress the bitter tears which had started to her eyes.

"May the great Pachacamac protect thee kindly until the last!" With these words, Toa kissed her on both cheeks and dismissed her.

The dark figure again approached and said: "Thy servant Uma is now ready to receive thy parting commands."

"Let him come!"

"I have everything in readiness, Shyri!" said Uma. "If we succeed, he will be free after midnight. Shall I bring him to thee?

"No, Uma; he must not lose a minute. Take him into the mountains, at once, on thy way to the coast. I have provided thee with gold to send him out of this unhappy country, and to protect him from want for the rest of his days. Tell him that Toa Duchicela will never forget him, and that of all the Viracochas on earth, he is the only one whom she will ever hold in grateful remembrance. Tell him that his mother and child will not be abandoned or forgotten. Tell him that he has wronged the woman Mercedes, who is innocent of his betrayal. Tell him that the Sun and the Moon will ever hear my prayers for his happiness."

"I shall, Shyri! Hualpa shall bring the tidings of our

success. If we fail, I shall myself be the bearer of the news."

"Go with him to the coast. Leave him not until he is safe, and when thou hast accomplished thy task, join me on the banks of the Napo, if thou wilt still link thy fortunes to mine. But if thou wilt no longer follow the fading star, the waning emerald, thou art free, Uma, to go whithersoever thy heart may tempt thee, and so much of my treasures as thy future wants shall require, shall be thine."

"Where Toa Duchicela is," answered Uma slowly and in measured tones, "there Uma will be. He will follow in her path. He will wander where she wanders; he will tarry where she tarries; and wherever she sleepeth, there will he wake and watch!"

"I thank thee, Uma! I knew thou wouldst be faithful to the last. Thy house and our house have stood together in the days of their greatness and prosperity. Their descendants will be together in exile and adversity. Farewell, Uma; we shall meet again."

"If I live, Shyri, I shall soon be with thee!"

With these words he departed, calm, dignified and imperturbable as ever. Toa looked after him until his form had disappeared in the darkness. Then she rested her elbow on her knee and her head on her hand, and sank into gloomy meditation. A darkness blacker than that of the starless night had settled upon her soul. "Thousands of hearts," she sighed, "will cling to me, and yet I am nothing to them but a powerless, shadowy Queen, who demands services and accepts sacrifices; thousands of these unfortunates would follow me through poverty and misery to an untimely death ; yet he, the one for whose love I yearned, the man upon whom I should have showered greatness, renown, and prosperity, has turned away from me. Those to whom I give nothing will die for me; he to whom I should have given everything will not even live for me."

"It is a just punishment, Shyri Toa," said a voice at her side.

"Punishment? For what, Prince Cundurazu?"

"For the levity and thoughtless selfishness with which thou didst subordinate thy sacred mission to the petty fancies and desires of a woman's heart."

"Cundurazu"—

"Raise not thy voice in anger, for I *will* speak, and thou shalt hear me in spite of thy frowns. My days are numbered on earth. I can not follow thee to the land of the savage. What little strength there is left to me I shall fully need to carry back this worn-out body to Purruhá, the land of my fathers. There where thy ancestors lived and died as well as mine, in the recesses of the mountain whose name I bear, my bones shall bleach. There, among inaccessible crags, never to be polluted by the invader's tread, this weary wanderer shall sleep the last sleep undisturbed by the dream and hope of my long life, that glorious hope which thou hast wrecked."

"I"—

"Yes, thou, Shyri Toa, thou! It is hard to bear the burden of defeat; but defeat self-inflicted, misery of one's own creation, failure by one's own dereliction, is the most galling of all defeats, miseries, and failures. I can not spare thee this misery, Shyri Toa. Thou hast sacrificed the cause of thy race, and I must hold up a mirror to thy soul in order to let thee see what thou hast done."

Toa hung her head and said nothing.

"Have I thy permission to proceed, daughter of Autachi, whom I saved from the bloody fangs of Rumiñagui—of Autachi, whom I hid and nursed and brought up to be thy father, Toa Duchicela?"

"Thou hast! I am a woman. I am heart-broken and crushed, Cundurazu! Proceed, then, and add what thou canst to the load of misery and disappointment by which I am oppressed."

"I can not spare thee for the wrong thou hast done to thy race. After thou hadst agreed to the great plan of Collohuaso and myself, thou shouldst have carried it out in earnest. Thou shouldst not have thrown thyself away on the first pretty face that struck thy fancy. A man of iron thou neededst, but a toy of wax captured thy idle fancy. Thou shouldst have consulted the welfare of thy race, the purposes of thy royal mission, and not the untried predilections of an inexperienced female heart. Thy choice fell on the weakest, instead of the strongest, the ficklest, instead of the steadiest of the Viracochas. Instead of choosing wisely, thou didst not choose at all. There were hundreds among whom thou mightst have chosen and who would have died for the glory, the honor, and the wealth thy hand might have bestowed. Why didst thou not winnow and separate the chaff from the grain? Why didst thou not test the metal of the man and approve him worthy of thy cause and favor, before, like a heedless girl, thou throwest the treasure of thy love at the feet of a fool, who would not stoop to pick it up?"

"It is cruel, Cundurazu, to upbraid me with the mistake I have made. Have I not suffered for it? And would I not have rectified it, if the gods had granted the opportunity?

"No, Toa Duchicela! Blame not the gods for the crime which lies at thine own door. Thou hadst the opportunity. The gods had kindly granted it; but thou, Toa Duchicela, unworthy granddaughter of Atahualpa, unworthy daughter of Autachi, wantonly throwest it away. The glorious opportunity was sacrificed, discarded, trampled upon by thee. The gods had sent the man of iron to the relief of our sinking cause. There was victory in his hand and loyalty in his heart. He came, and our despair was changed into gladness—the certainty of defeat into the certainty of victory. Hadst thou but let him alone! But no! Thy heedless, reckless, shameless interference, destroyed our last hope. Thou didst take it upon thyself to arrest his uplifted hand. He would have crushed the viper before it stung his unarmed heel, and laid him low, but for thy unwarranted interference. What made thee send that fatal warning to Manuel Paredes, the enemy of our race? But for this warning, that traitor would have died, and our noble Viracocha friend would have captured the chief of the foreigners, and, with one glorious blow, forever set us free. Thy interference shielded the traitor and sacrificed our deliverer. Hence, blame not the gods, Toa Duchicela; blame not the Sun and the Moon for thine own crime. It is thou that hast betrayed us; it is thou that hast sacrificed us, and upon thy guilty, giddy, self-indulgent head, be the curse of our race."

Toa remained silent, stunned and crushed.

"I know why thou didst commit this reckless crime. I can read thy shallow heart, and discern the motive of thy wanton act. It was revenge on thy fickle and faithless lover, which seemed to thee more important than the success of our great cause. Millions had to be sacrificed in order to punish one whose whole guilt was but thy own folly. The brave men whom thou hast doomed to the scaffold, the friends thou hast abandoned, thy own race and kingly office, which thou hast trifled away, will rise against thee, darkening the Sun with sorrow and drawing tears from the loving Moon. No woman on earth has ever sacrificed so much to gain so little—a lover's punishment, for which a knife, a dagger, a stone, might have sufficed."

A flash of lightning lit up the scene for a moment, and discovered Toa's face bathed in tears. Rolling thunder, reverberating from the mountains and culminating in a terrible clap, interrupted the fierce eloquence of Cundurazu. The old man's wrath has exhausted itself, and he sank into silent contemplation, and all was stillness and darkness again.

CHAPTER V.

THE COYA CISA.

TOA arose at last and walked into the hut, without saying a word. Cundurazu followed her. We are familiar with the interior of the cottage. Nothing had changed since our last visit. A curtain suspended across its only room still divided it in two compartments. The kettle with the Samarucu was still boiling over a fire of aromatic woods. Mama Rucu sat before it, stirring the precious liquid as of old, and filling the calabash from which she drank. Her back was turned to the door, as usual, yet she knew who had entered.

"Granddaughter," she said, without turning round, "the great Sun be praised! I am once more under the influence of the divine potion. For weeks and weeks it had lost its effect upon me. I feared I should die without a last taste of its blessings. But now it has come again. The veil is rent once more; the dim mists are lifted before me, and by the clear light of our Great Father, the Sun, I see as of old. The future is again clear to me. What the next hours, the next years, will bring I see it all. I see it all."

There was a moment of silence, during which Mama Rucu took another draught of the charmed liquid.

"Granddaughter," she resumed, after a while, "and thou, Cundurazu, the best, the truest, the only friend I have had, the Coya Cisa, the widow of Atahualpa, the mother of Autachi, the prophetess, whom our conquerors call Mama Rucu, has but six hours to live. Her long, weary pilgrimage at last approaches its end. She will go to her eternal resting-place by the side of her son Autachi, in the cave of Pichincha, the mountain which has sheltered her for the last sixty years. Six short hours and the Coya Cisa will be no more."

A deep sigh from Cundurazu responded to her sad announcement.

"In twelve hours from now the soldiers of the foreigner will appear at this cottage to seize Mama Rucu and drag her before the tribunal of our oppressors. They will not find her. They will be balked of their prey. Death will be kinder to Coya Cisa than the oppressors of her race. Six hours are left to me on earth. Great Pachacamac! I praise thy kindness. Thou hast given me a life longer than that of thousands, and thou givest me six hours of preparation when I needed but one. Prince Cundurazu, Great Curaca of Purruhá, listen to the dying words of Cisa."

"Coya! I am listening."

"I see them again before me—the happy days of my early youth. I see the blooming child once more whom they called Cisa. Is it possible that these pretty features should wither and harden, that the long and smooth black hair should turn grizzly and white, that these smiling eyes should change into fiercely rolling orbs of fire? Ah, but this dreadful change is only a picture of the more dreadful change which has come to our race. Our costly garments of alpaca have changed into beggarly rags; the golden ornaments of our nobles into iron chains; our palaces into prisons; our temples into the tombs of our happiness; our free-born children into beasts of burden; our warriors into slaves. The great men of our land are gone, all gone, with but one last exception—Prince Cundurazu, Curaca of Purruhá "—

"Who will soon follow in the footsteps of his betters."

"Curaca of Purruhá! Do I recognize thy noble features in that shrivelled and care-worn face, the features that first awoke the delicious sentiment of love in this now stony breast? Where is the heart that once beat so wildly at thy approach? It is here—it beats faintly, faintly; it will soon have ceased to beat."

Toa threw herself on a low stool near the door and buried her face it her hands. Cundurazu stood motionless with his white head hung upon his breast.

"For all thy love, Curaca, I thank thee. There was a time when we dreamed of happiness. It was a dream never verified—a hope never realized—a beautiful sunbeam on the icy páramo, a sunbeam that soon died away in mists, clouds, tempests, and snow. Alas, the day of our hope was so short, and the night of our misery was so long. To thee, Curaca, I once hoped to belong; but our dread Inca, the ill-fated son of the unfortunate Pacha, willed it otherwise. The Coya Cisa found favor in his blood-shot eyes; the Inca took me to his royal bed. Great was the honor he conferred on me; but I paid for it with a broken heart. And thou, noble Curaca, never ceasedst to love me and to mourn for what thou hadst lost. And when Rumiñagui, the villain, the tyrant, the usurper, was bent on my death because I carried an heir to Atahualpa under my heart, it was thou, Curaca, to whom I owed my rescue and deliverance. To thee I owed my life and that of Autachi, my son. Once more, Curaca, I'thank thee. I was a loyal wife to Atahualpa, the father of my royal child; but my heart remained faithful to thee, until the childish love for one man expanded to that great loving compassion for our groaning and bleeding race. But now, as I stand upon the brink of death, the old tenderness steals back into this dying bosom. I shall ask thee a last favor, Cundurazu."

"Speak, Coya."

"Thy hand has rescued me from death and given me a life of almost endless years. Let thy hand restore me to the silence of death, from which it snatched me sixty years ago."

"What shall I do, Coya?"

"Thou shalt put me into my mountain-chair. Thy faithful hand shall help to carry me to the cave of Pichincha. It shall place me on my last seat by the side of Autachi, my son. And when I have ceased to breathe, thy hand shall rest on my silent head, while thy lips utter the great prayer for the scions of the royal house of the Shyris. Doest thou remember the words of the prayer, Curaca of Purruhá?"

"I do, Coya."

"Then speak them for me when I am dead, and perform my funeral rites in the cave of Autachi. And now, thou must not harden thy heart in anger against the Shyri Toa. Thou hast done her injustice. Remember that it was our plan we persuaded her to adopt, not hers. It may be, after all, that I was mistaken in the interpretation of my visions. Now that the veil is again lifted, now that I can see more clearly than ever before, I am almost convinced that I was mistaken. See, Cundurazu, I dreamt of the union of two races, as in the days of the first Toa, the daughter of the last Shyri and of Duchicela, of Purruhá. Toa was to represent *our* race—a friendly Viracocha, the race of our conquerors. This was my mistake, not hers. Not by a union with a Viracocha, but by a union with one of the powerful chiefs in the country of the dense forests and the great rivers, where the Samarucu grows, my vision will be fulfilled. That union will give freedom to the Indian in the country of the rising sun beyond you mountain-range. There we shall be avenged on our oppressors. The rivers will run red with the blood of their men. The forests will resound with the shrieks of their women. The puma will crush the bones of their children. Their cities will be wiped from the face of the earth. The nights will be ablaze with the flames of their burning habitations. A great Indian confederation of freemen will accomplish this work of deliverance, and Toa will be their Queen."

"To reign over worthless tribes of naked savages!" sneered Cundurazu. "What is that to me? What is it to the suffering children of Purruhá, to the bleeding sons of Quito, to the enslaved nations of Otabalo and Caranqui? The savages beyond the mountain range are nothing to us. Their freedom will not lighten *our* hardships. Their independence will not break *our* chains. They are strangers to us, strangers in blood, in customs, and in allegiance. They never were united to us in bonds of common interest and fellowship. Divided from us by almost impassable mountains and deserts, they never partook of the blessings of our civilization. Savages they were, and savages they will remain, and Toa will be a Queen of naked barbarians, while she might have reigned over the land of her fathers, and over the descendants of our Viracocha conquerors, breaking the fetters and righting the wrongs of our race. What can those savages ever be to her? Her palace will be the four poles of a hut with a roof of palm-leaves. A hammock of twine will be her throne. Her garden will be the steaming forest with its serpents, wild beasts, and fevers. Her allies will be men who feast upon human flesh, and paint their unsightly faces and forms. She will be a stranger among strangers, who can be nothing to her polished mind. Separated from all the surroundings that were dear to her, she will pine away in the wilderness by the side of a brute, who will soon diseard her; she will die without honor, without glory, without benefit to herself and her own people, with the gnawing consciousness of what might have been, with that everlasting and regretful remembrance of what she has thrown away."

"It is well, Cundurazu," now interrupted Toa, rising from her stool with all the majesty of a Queen. "I shall not embitter thy few remaining days on earth by recriminations. I was young, and thou wast old. I was blinded by love, and thou hadst eyes. I was without the experience in which thou aboundedst. I was a silly, loving woman, and thou wast a wise old man. I was a Queen, and thou wast my councilor. I shall not reproach thee, Cundurazu. I shall be more generous to thee than thou hast been to me. It is true, I am going among savages. It is true, my life will be joyless and sad, even if I do succeed. It is true, I must bury the aspirations, the hopes, the dreams of my life, and content myself with a lot little above that of the animals of the forests I shall inhabit. But has thy cold and unloving heart died even to the feelings of revenge? Our plans—thy plans—have failed, and the past is irrevocable. I can not free our people, but I can avenge their wrongs upon so many of their oppressors. I can not punish them all for the crimes they have committed against us, but I can punish thousands of them. I am defeated and betrayed, but yet I may be revenged. This revenge, it is true, means self-sacrifice; but still it is revenge. When my aunt, Carmen Duchicela, had sent for masters to Lima, to instruct her rebellious niece in the mysteries of the new faith, they taught me the story of an ancient warrior, whose name I have forgotten. He had been made a prisoner by his enemies, who put out his eyes, and compelled him to play a musical instrument in the temple of a god who was not his God, to enliven their sacrificial feast. He was a man of almost incredible strength, who could work miracles by it. And when thousands of his enemies had assembled in the temple and on the roof of it, he seized the two pillars on which the edifice rested, and by the wondrous strength of his arms, broke them down and buried himself and his tormentors. Seest thou, Cundurazu! such will be my revenge. I am broken, and my life is hopeless, like that of the blind Hebrew warrior in the story. What is life to me now? But I can bring down the roof of the temple upon thousands of my enemies. What if I do perish—it will be in a glorious blaze of revenge."

"And, after all," she continued, after a pause, during

which nothing was heard but the bubbling of the water in Mama Rucu's caldron, "thou, Prince Cundurazu, wantedst me to be a Queen. To that purpose thou hadst trained and shaped my mind ever since my childhood. Thy wish shall be fulfilled. I shall be a Queen. And if I can not rule over our own race and the Viracochas of our land, I shall rule over painted savages. The Záparos and Jivaros are not entire strangers to our royal house. My great-grandfather conquered them. My grandfather kept them in obedience. The descendants of our *mitimaes* * are still among them. My reign may not be one of glory or greatness; it will not fulfill the great dream and purpose of my life; but I shall be a Queen, which is better than to be a wanderer without a home, or a prisoner in the hands of the Spaniards."

With these words, she walked to the fire, snatched a brand from it, and lit a taper, which stood on the table. She then disappeared behind the curtain, where she remained for the next fifteen minutes. Cundurazu took the seat which she had left, covered his head with his *capisayo*, and his face with his hands, and was soon lost in meditation. Mama Rucu, in the meantime, proceeded, with calm composure, with the preparations for the journey to her eternal resting-place. A large earthen jar, with a long neck of Indian workmanship, stood by the side of her fire, and into this vessel she slowly and carefully poured the liquid from the caldron, using her calabash instead of a ladle, and sipping from it from time to time. When the kettle had been emptied, she blew a little silver whistle, which hung from a string around her neck. The Fool, whom our readers will remember, answered her call.

"Take this kettle away, and give it to Mama Guantu, to keep it for my sake. Take it away and come back."

The Fool left, with a puzzled expression, and the old

---

* Colonists.

woman stirred the fire and then arose; but her strength gave way, and she fell back on her stool.

"My strength is going fast," she muttered. "My limbs refuse to obey my head; and yet this head," she added, striking her forehead, "is so clear, so clear!"

The Fool returned.

"Take these herbs, man, and throw them on the fire!"

The Fool looked at her in hesitation and amazement.

"Do as I tell thee. Nobody could use them to advantage after I am gone. And it is better our children should not know the future, than to behold the misery of centuries which is before them."

"But, Coya, how canst thou do without the Samarucu?"

"Look at this jar. It is full. It will do me for ages."

"The vessel of the dead?"

"It is filled and prepared. Thou shalt carry it to my *tola*.*"

The Fool burst into tears.

"No childishness, man! I have lived long enough. Do as I tell thee!"

Sobbing and moaning, the Fool took bundle after bundle of the dried herbs piled up along the wall, and threw them on the fire. With a sudden flash, the flames leaped up and strangely illumined the cottage, throwing ghastly shades on the features of the living mummy who had ordered this holocaust.

Toa now reappeared from behind the curtain.

"And our patient, Grandmother? Does he require nothing else?"

"Nothing at all. He will sleep until the soldiers come."

"Is he sure to recover?"

"He will surely recover. I have steeled his system against the poisons which the Viracocha medicine-men will give him."

---

* Mound over a tomb.

"Is he sure to live?"

"He is sure to live."

"For years?"

"For years; and I can tell thee more. Thou shalt see him again."

Toa started in terror. "Grandmother, what dost thou mean?"

"I mean what I have said. Thou shalt see him and speak to him once more."

"Where?"

"In the country of the great forests and rivers, over which thou shalt be Queen."

"And when?"

"On the day of his death."

CHAPTER VI.

TRUE TO HIS FAITH.

THE spirit of Mama Rucu had fled. Cundurazu had spoken the great prayer for the departed of the royal house, and a band of faithful Indians had embalmed her remains and placed them in a chair of state by the side of her son, Autachi, with the jar of Samarucu on her right. Toa had knelt in prayer and meditation before the ghastly skeleton of her father. She had knelt before the new throne of death occupied by her grandmother. There was now but one direct lineal descendant of the house of Shyri-Duchicela-Inca, and that one was about to bid an everlasting farewell to the land of her fathers. And there were mounds of gold and silver piled up around her in the cave of Autachi, and she was poor and miserable in the midst of all these riches. Full of love and of hopes, she had been here a few short months ago with the man of her choice, and now, alas! her heart was broken, and life was a bleak waste of despair.

When everything was finished, the funeral party left the cave as silently as they had entered it. The day had begun to dawn, as they emerged from the bowels of the earth. The darkness of a tempestuous night had given away to a cheerless morn—

"Man has another day to swell the past,
And bring him near to little but his last."

They had reached the place where the water of the mountain-stream could be turned off in order to facilitate the passage of a ravine through which the cave had to be reached. Toa swung herself on a protruding rock, and, leaping from stone to stone, followed the course of the ravine upward for a short distance, and then stopped, intently examining a rock against which the water dashed with great violence. Cundurazu followed her, in strange bewilderment, and watched her closely with an expression of mingled surprise and suspicion.

"If I order this rock to be removed," she said, after a pause, "the water will make itself a new bed, and wash away the entrances to the cave of Autachi, which would then be closed up forever."

"And why should it be closed up forever?"

"Why should it not be closed up forever? The hopes of our house are forever extinguished. Why should a royal tomb be maintained, when royalty itself is dead? Who should be buried here?"

"Thou, Toa Duchicela, when thou art gone. If thou art worthy of thy name and family, thou wilt make provision to be brought here and be entombed by the side of thy father when thou art dead."

"My remains will need to be disposed of according to the customs of the nation whose chief will be my future lord."

"But thou wilt have followers of thy own race even in

those forests. Some of them will be left when the time has come to bury Toa Duchicela according to the rites of her house, after bringing her back dead to the country of her fathers, over which, living, she might have reigned. Thou talkest wildly, Shyri Toa. Close up the entrances to the cave of Autachi? It would be sacrilege! Hast thou forgotten that that cave containeth the great treasure of Quito?"

Toa uttered a contemptuous laugh. "Paltry, miserable gold, worthless as dust or ashes. With all these millions I could not buy liberty for my people or happiness for my own poor heart. Let that rubbish perish! Let it be buried in the womb of the earth from which it came."

"Hadst thou thought less of thy own selfish heart, and more of the cause of thy people, that treasure would have done its great work, and wrought innumerable blessings, instead of lying idly around the crumbling shapes of death."

"Wilt thou renew thy bootless upbraiding? I will not listen to it again.. That rock shall be removed!"

"It shall not be removed!"

"And who will hinder it?"

"I, Cundurazu, Curaca of Purruhá, the next in dignity to thyself, Toa Duchicela—I, who will assume the reins of our secret government, and transmit it to him whom I shall deem worthy of it, in case of thy death, thy abdication, or thy forfeiture of the throne by an act of faithlessness to the cause of thy people. Thou dost not know me yet, Toa Duchicela. This old man may have failed in the great work of his life. He may be a visionary, as thy aunt Carmen, the apostate's daughter, calls him, but he clings to his belief or vision with unremitting tenacity, and will worship even the empty shadow of that belief, while a drop of red blood is left in his shriveling veins. This treasure is the great hope of our race."

"Has not the Coya Cisa foretold that centuries of hopeless misery will come? And did she ever err in any of her predictions?"

"Ah, but there will be a time, even after the lapse of centuries. My love for my race, is not a love for myself or those whom I have known on earth. I love my race in its unborn generations. To them, to our remotest posterity, let this treasure be handed down. Two families of this province will be the custodians of the secret, which the father will hand down to his first-born, from generation to generation. As the traditions of our past greatness and glory, the existence of this hidden treasure will be known to thousands; its precise location will be known to but two living beings at the time. But two shall always know it, until the time of deliverance comes; and if it never comes, yet this treasure shall be held as a secret trust for the holy purpose of breaking, or at least lightening the chains of our people. If thou wilt not defend it and protect it, Toa Duchicela, I will. Thou must order the murder of the man who saved thy grandmother and thy father, before thou wilt succeed in destroying the entrances to the cave of Autachi. Order my death, thou future Queen of painted savages! It is very questionable whether thy order will be obeyed by the men who are now behind thee."

Toa hung her head in silence. At last she broke into tears. "Oh, Cundurazu, the most cruel of all my friends, hadst thou but let me die when I was a child. Would, I had never known thee, and thou hadst never haunted me with that spectral phantom of a throne. The humblest hand-maiden of Carmen Duchicela is happier than this mockery of a Queen. Oh, Carmen, Carmen, why did I not listen to thy voice of warning while it was time?"

"Thus speaketh a woman, in whom those tears are natural, although they are unworthy of a Shyri Inca. Then thou wilt not order the death of Cundurazu or the destruction of the entrances of the cave?"

"I shall not, Cundurazu. Thou art right. Yon treasure

belongs to that royalty, which I resign by emigration. Let its secret be kept as thy wisdom shall direct. Art thou content?"

"I thank thee, Shyri Toa, for this last favor to the old man who could not bear to depart even a hair's breath from the belief of his lifetime, and the belief of his fathers. And now Shyri Toa, our ways do separate. Thou wilt go to the north and the east. I shall return to the south, the cradle of my family. This was our last meeting, Shyri Toa. Farewell!"

"And wilt thou thus turn thy face on me forever, without a last friendly word or token of love. Where is thy heart, Cundurazu? Have I ceased to be anything to thee?"

"The *Shyri* Toa was everything to me. The *woman* Toa can not be more to me than any other of the noble women of our race. Look at yon snow-peak, now kissed by the first rays of our great Sun. Even the kiss of the Sun-God does not melt that everlasting garment of ice and snow. I have outlived myself, Toa Duchicela, and to the common feelings of the human kind, this old heart has died—died—died."

And with these words, the old man walked away without looking back, and was soon lost behind a bend of the mountain.

Toa felt crushed, deserted, hopeless, alone. With Cundurazu, a part of her past self had gone. The glorious dream, which he had instilled into her mind, had vanished. No longer a Queen, she was but a woman now, and it is so unspeakably sad and wretched for a woman to be alone in the world, a stranger among strangers, with all the yearnings of her heart disappointed, with no future to look forward, and the past—a regret.

And as she looked down on the city of Quito at her feet, the peals of Christian bells ascended to her lonely station, arousing her from her lethargy, and reminding her that there was no rest for the fugitive and the wanderer.

CHAPTER VII.

OUT OF THE JAWS OF DEATH.

PAREDES had informed Dolores of the scene between himself and Arana. Dolores at once proceeded to patch up a peace between her friend and the Royal Commissioner. After dinner, on the very day of the disagreement, she began to labor with the Count in the interest of Manuel Paredes. Her task did not prove very difficult. The merits of Paredes should not be overlooked. The confiscation of the estates of the Sanchez, Olmos, Garcias, Perez, and other leaders of the rebellion would furnish ample means of doing justice to all the loyal servants of the King. At the same time Arana advised his amiable hostess to urge upon her protegé the propriety of moderation and modesty; for, after all, he had but performed his duty to his master, the King. It was true he had performed it fully and successfully; but was he not bound to perform it to the best of his ability? And although the King would graciously remember and appreciate such conduct, a subject acquired no rights or claims on his Majesty by doing a duty properly, the omission, neglect, or improper discharge of which would be considered criminal, and make the offender liable to punishment. The King *owed* nothing to Manuel Paredes; but if, in the fullness of his generosity, he should considerately bestow rewards on those who had served him best, it was his royal privilege, as it would certainly be his princely inclination, to do so. By these rules, he, the Count Arana, the Commissioner and Representative of the King, would be guided in the distribution of the confiscated *encomiendas* and estates. He admitted no debt to anybody, and he would tolerate no presumption; yet he entertained no prejudice or ill-feeling toward the Señor Paredes, and if the latter would leave his cause in the hands of his fair advocate, instead of resorting to personal reminders of most questionable propriety, his interests would be taken care of. Such was the language intended for, if not directly addressed to, the man whose unscrupulous boldness and wonderful skill had either saved the kingdoms of Peru and Quito to the crown of Spain, or at least averted the dangerous necessity of a long and costly war. He had saved the lives of the King's ministers, and delivered the master spirit of the rebellion into the hands of the King's representative; and now he was told that he had only performed a duty, the nonperformance of which would have been a crime. The puppets, Juan de Londoño, Pedro Guzman Ponce de Leon, and others whom he, Paredes, had manipulated and directed, were basking in the sunshine of commissarial favor, while he whose genius had shaped hopelessness into success and triumph was coldly ignored and neglected.

Dolores, by order of Arana, had received through her father all the Carrera papers that had been sent from Lima. She had retired with them to her room, and read the long and glowing eulogies in poetry and in prose with which the *literati* of Lima had celebrated his noble martyrdom. She also read the assurances of the deep interest which the Viceroy had taken in the young gentleman's fate, and the announcement that Carrera's heroism should be recognized and rewarded if he lived, and immortalized if he was dead. Had she caused his death? Perhaps she had! But had she intended his death? Certainly not. Could she have foreseen that such violence would be done to him, she would not have acted as she did. And yet why not? Had it not been her duty to do so? At the time of the crisis she had been acting under her father's commission. Was it not her duty, in order to save the royal cause, to sacrifice Carrera, if it was necessary, as her own brother was sacrificed, and as she should have sacrificed herself if the King's service had demanded it? The slaughter of Carrera was certainly to be deplored; and who had deplored it more profoundly than Dolores Solando? Many a sigh and many a tear, especially in the company of others, had she devoted to the memory of her ill-fated lover. But her conscience acquitted her of all guilt in his death. Had she profited by his sacrifice? Was she not the heaviest loser? No, Dolores Solando had nothing to reproach herself with in the death of Carrera, by which she had personally gained nothing, yet lost so much.

While she was still poring over the papers, a sudden confusion of voices arose in and around the house. The plaza in front of her window had filled with people, who crowded around the main entrance. Yet they were not tumultuous or clamorous, but spoke in subdued tones, with surprise and excited curiosity depicted on every face.

Dolores arose to ascertain the cause of the excitement, when Aunt Catita burst into the room.

"Oh, Doloritas! Doloritas!" exclaimed that lady, gasping for breath.

"What is it, Auntie, dear? What makes you look so pale and excited?"

"Doloritas, they have found him! They have brought him into the house!" With these words Doña Catita sank into a chair.

"Whom?" exclaimed Dolores, while her heart began to palpitate.

"Oh, how haggard and wan he looks! It is pitiful to see him."

"But you have not told me who it is. Is it Carrera?"

"Of course it is Carrera, risen from the dead, and the very picture of death."

Dolores stood thunderstruck. For an instant her usual presence of mind seemed to have deserted her.

"The soldiers," continued Aunt Catita, "who had been sent to arrest Mama Rucu, found him in her cottage. There he lay in a dark place behind a curtain, weak and insensible, and O! so thin and emaciated; he looks almost like a skeleton."

"And Mama Rucu?" asked Dolores, with a shudder.

"Could not be found anywhere. They searched the mountain, far and near, but she was gone."

"Where is Carrera?"

"Still in the doorway. They brought him in on a rough board covered with sheep-skins, and now they do not know what to do with him. Count Arana has gone out; the Marquis is not at home; Carrera's house is closed up, and without comforts or attendance, and so nobody knew what should be done, and this is the reason why I flew upstairs to hear your opinion, Doloritas."

"There is but one thing to be done under the circumstances," said Dolores with decision; "he must be brought upstairs and placed in the best room that we can give him. Our house is very crowded now, but I shall give him my own room as long as his condition demands it. You will allow me to share your room in the meantime? Let it be done at once, Auntie."

"But your father, Dolores, what will he say to this?"

"He will be delighted with it, I assure you. Let us lose no time where a human life may be at stake;" and thus saying, Dolores snatched up her shawl and rushed down stairs, followed by her aunt.

The soldiers had formed a barrier to keep back the multitude, which was pressing against the main entrance. A part of the rabble had pushed themselves in during the first rush, and filled the doorway and the lower part of the staircase, in order to obtain a better view of what was going on. The officers were just driving them out into the court-yard when Dolores came down. Another woman had quietly preceded her, and knelt at the head of the stretcher on which Carrera lay, holding up his head and arranging his covering. It was Mama Santos. The Fool, with his hands tied upon his back, stood between two soldiers who had him in charge. He looked the very picture of discomfiture and wretchedness.

Carrera's wounds had healed, but his shattered nerves had not yet recovered from the terrible shock on the day of the riot. His mind was still wandering. He had been delirious for weeks and months, after having been brought to Mama Rucu's cottage. Even after the fever had subsided, his consciousness returned only rarely and for short intervals, after which he relapsed into a sleep or torpor, which was diligently nursed by Mama Rucu's potions. What he saw or heard during his lucid intervals became irretrievably blended in his mind with his feverish dreams and the visions produced by the samarucu and other decoctions with which the Indian prophetess kept him alive. His eyes were open as Dolores approached him, but they rested on the Fool with a queer expression of astonishment and solicitude.

"Señor de Carrera—Don Julio!" exclaimed Dolores, kneeling at his side. "The Holy Virgin be praised that you are alive and with us!"

Carrera's eyes wandered toward her, but expressed no recognition. He stared at her for a moment, after which his looks sought out the Fool again.

"Do you know me, Don Julio? Dolores Solando—have you forgotten her?"

There was no answer, no ray of intellect in that pale and haggard face, shadowed over by long and tangled hair, and covered with a shaggy beard of disordered and irregular growth.

"He does not recognize me, the poor darling! His mind is wandering. Have him taken up stairs at once, Señor Ramirez! Let him be carried to my room, which I have given up to him until his condition shall allow his removal."

Carrera's face assumed an expression of uneasiness as they lifted him up. But when they started to carry him away, he uttered a piteous cry. His carriers halted, and Dolores bent over him, endeavoring to ascertain what had pained him. He returned no answer to her question, but when his carriers again attempted to move on, he anxiously raised his head and stretched out his right hand in the direction where the Fool stood, accompanying this gesture with a low moan. None of the bystanders could divine the cause of his agitation.

"He seems to be delirious," said Dolores after a pause. "Take him up stairs where he can be comfortable." But, as they carried him away, he uttered another cry, and then fell back insensible.

CHAPTER VIII.

DOUBTS AND DIFFICULTIES.

Since the events narrated in our last chapter, nine months have elapsed. They had been months of gloom and terror for Quito. Executions had followed executions. The two Olmos, father and son, the two Garcias, father and son, old Pedro Perez, and a number of other patricians, and a much larger number of plebeians had been garroted in the Plaza of Santa Clara, in the Plaza of Santo Domingo, and in the Square of *La Carniceria*. Still others had been sent to penal colonies on the river Napo. And yet the prisons were full of men who were awaiting their sentences, or the results of the appeals which, as a special favor, they had been allowed to make to the clemency of the Viceroy. Some of the finest houses of Quito had been razed to the ground, salt had been strewn, and stone tablets sunk on their sites, with inscriptions stating the crime and punishment of their former owners. Among the executions those of young Garcia and young Olmos were heart-rending in the extreme. Handsome, dashing, brave, and popular, they were the victims who were most bewailed. Hundreds of women witnessed the death of these young officers, and rent the air with sobs and shrieks. Several of the noblest matrons of the city had made great efforts to secure their pardon, but no such appeals could touch the stony heart of the Royal Commissioner, who knew no mercy. Rich and childless, he was not accessible to bribes to which those who had governed before, and those who came after him, hardly ever failed to succumb. It seemed as if he delighted in human suffering. He relished the preparations for an execution, and planned and superintended them personally in all their details. Only one man had escaped his wrath, but Arana vowed that no one else should; and the representative of King Philip had kept his word. There was no escape for those whom he had doomed. Many a head had to fall for the one that had eluded him. Many a sentence of death was inflicted instead of a lighter punishment, because that one man was beyond the reach of the Royal Commissioner.

It is needless to say that all efforts for the recapture of Sanchez had failed. He was never heard of again. Not even his tracks had been discovered. The whole country from the northern confines of the kingdom to the coast of Buenaventura, Guayaquil, Esmeraldas, and Tumbez, had been explored in every direction, but no trace could be found, no clue to the mystery of his escape could be obtained. The belief finally gained ground and was eagerly accepted and circulated by Arana and his party, that Sanchez must have perished miserably on the paramos, while crossing the mountain ranges, or that he must have found his death in the tropical forests and jungles at the base of the Cordillera.

Having crushed the rebellion, restored the legitimate authorities, and re-established order and quietude—the quiet of the graveyard—and being about to announce the distribution of rewards, and the division of the spoils of confiscation, Count Arana was anxious to return to Lima, and thence to Spain. At all events he was anxious to get away from Quito, where his life was threatened by the plots of those whose fathers, brothers, husbands, or other relations he had put to death, and still more by the revenge of those whom his confiscations had reduced to beggary. He was anxious to get away from the ingratitude and disappointment of those whom he was about to reward for the services they had rendered to the King's cause. They were sure to be disappointed. Disappointments and resentments had always followed the reassignment of *encomiendas*, and the distribution of confiscated estates in Peru. All wanted what but a few could get. And even what there was could not all be distributed, as the Viceroyal coffers had to be reimbursed for the funds which had been advanced to fit out Arana's expedition.

But the Royal Commissioner did not intend to leave the city of Quito without having graced, by his distinguished presence, the approaching nuptials of Julio de Carrera and Dolores Solando. The marriage was announced to take place immediately after the expiration of the year of mourning consecrated to the memory of the mother and brother of Dolores. The distinctions and honors which the King and Viceroy had graciously pleased to shower on Carrera were, thus far, known only to Count Arana, who intended to announce them as his wedding present, on the day preceding the marriage. Both courts had been exceedingly liberal, so much the more, as, in this case, liberality would not entail any expense on the treasury. Carrera, as the heir of his uncle, and the heir presumptive of the Marquis de Solando, would be the wealthiest gentleman of the old Kingdom of Quito, and perhaps the wealthiest of the whole Viceroyalty of Peru. No estates or donations were required to honor his martyrdom and loyal self-sacrifice.

The title of Countess would sound more bewitching to the ears of Dolores, than the announcement of an addition to her wordly possessions. Hence Carrera was to be made a Count, and should be authorized, by a royal *cedula*, to wear in his escutcheon an aloe, with the blades of which plant he had been so cruelly beaten by the infuriated mob. In addition to this the high and honorable dignity of Royal Standard-bearer should be conferred on him, and be inherited by his male descendants. He should be entitled to visit Spain, or any of her colonies, without first making application for special permission, as other subjects were required to do. The royal standard which he was to bear on all festive or warlike occasions, should be made in Spain by the artisans of the Court, consecrated by the Archbishop of Toledo, and sent to America by a special messenger, who should also bring the chain and cross which the King himself would transmit to Carrera. The Viceroy sent a magnificent sword, with belt and hangings of exquisite workmanship, such as had never been seen at Quito. The patents of these grants were in the hands of Arana, and their delivery should be made the occasion of great public ceremonies in the Cathedral and the Palace. These were honors enough to turn the head of any ordinary young gentleman, but Carrera bore them modestly and meekly, and with a vague and secret apprehension that something was wrong, with a consciousness of regret and suspicion lurking somewhere in the inmost recesses of his heart. He felt, at times, as if some calamity were impending, or as if something were to happen that would disturb his security or endanger his well-being. He could not account for these sensations, although in a measure he attributed them to the shock his nervous system had suffered. And in this, perhaps, he was right. The weakness and prostration following a long and serious illness, will often produce those unaccountable attacks of moral fear, startling us like sudden presentiments of evil. But Carrera's physical condition was not the only and not even the principal cause of these attacks, which he did not confide to anyone, and which he hardly confessed to himself. The image of Toa had not faded from his mind. She was continually in his thoughts. She had returned good for evil. He had deceived and rejected her, and she had saved his life. As to this he had no doubt. Without her orders he would not have been carried to Mama Rucu's cottage. He had seen Toa's face bent over him in his dreams, while he lay helpless on his couch. He had seen her in his lucid intervals, when he was awake. He did not know how she had come and how she went, but he knew that she was there. During none of these visits had she spoken to him. Her face was bent over him many a time, not in reproach or in anger, but in sadness and resignation. Her eyes, as they looked at him, steadily, watchfully, not in bitterness, yet unforgiving, had sunk deep into his heart, and there they were an ineffaceable remembrance, a mortifying problem, a worrying doubt, an ever-recurring regret, now speaking to his conscience in whispers hardly audible, then in tones of deep meaning, sorrow, and humiliation.

During his illness, he had contracted habits of solitude. He had learned to shrink within himself and to shun visitors. He had become fond of self-communion. There were so many things over which he wished to ponder; so many questions which he alone could ask, and which no one else could answer. How little those around us dream what a vast world expands within the hearts and minds of those of whom they believe to know so much, while in reality they know so little. That world of secret thoughts and feelings could hardly be translated into words; and even if it could be, would we not shrink from revealing it even to those that are near and dear to us, as from an act of profanation or sacrilege? No! However vast and wonderful, however lonely and inexplicable, however full of love, and of undefined yearnings, or of regrets and disappointments, of hopes and airy castles, or of doubts, wrecks, and ruins, of soaring lightness, or of heavy sadness, that hidden inner world may be, let it remain hidden and impenetrable to all but our own mental eye, which alone can discern and understand it, and realize its treasures and beauties, as well as its chasms and its miseries.

Now that Toa was forever gone from him, he began to wish that he had not lost her by his own unworthy conduct, ingratitude, and fickleness. She had shown herself so noble and so great, while he had shown himself so ignoble and so little. Grand, true and unselfish, she had appeared to him; small, false, and selfish, he must have appeared to her. She was a heroine, physically and morally, while his great act of physical bravery and self-sacrifice was, after all, but an act of moral cowardice. He felt that she must despise him, and yet he wished that she would not. What right had he to betray her? He had accepted her love. He had professed love to her. Had he acted in good faith? *He* had done the worst a man could do to a woman; *she* had rescued him from the jaws of death, and then flung him back contemptuously upon the world. He was too despicable for her revenge. This thought was humiliating in the extreme. He had destroyed the ambition of her life, and God alone knew what he had thrown away that might have come to him through her. His uncle had made him believe that the cause of the rebellion was hopeless from the beginning; and Dolores had told him that it was betrayed from the beginning, and experience had shown that both were right; yet when he considered how much the fierce energy of one earnest and determined man had been able to accomplish, and how Roberto Sanchez, if not entrapped, might still have saved the cause of the Revolution, Carrera fell into a course of thoughts which suddenly brought back to his mind the two memorable visions which Mama Rucu's potion had made him see in her cottage on the evening before his first meeting with Toa. Had he not beheld victory, and had not Toa appeared to him as his queenly bride? And had he not seen Sanchez at his side, fighting his battles? It was a vision only, but Mama Rucu's visions, like her prophecies, were but the announcements of things real which always came to pass. The attack of the mob on himself to force him to be their King, and the terrible treatment he endured at their hands—had he not seen it all, in its minutest details, months before it happened? Mama Rucu had promised to show him what would follow, if he took to the right, and what would befall him, if he took to the left. He had made his decision, and his vision was fulfilled accordingly. If the one was fulfilled, would not the other have been fulfilled just as well, if his decision had been different? It was all clear to him now, and he brooded and pondered over what he had lost.

But why should he brood and ponder—he, the most honored, the wealthiest, the most renowned, and the most envied gentleman of the old kingdom of Quito. The wildest dreams of his youth had not carried him to an eminence loftier than the one upon which he now stood. Out of all dangers, overwhelmed with honors and distinctions, and engaged to his first love, the most accomplished lady in America, what more could his heart desire? Yet Carrera was one of those characters who wear themselves out in longing and striving for the unattainable, and subject to the microscopic tests of the most searching and fault-finding criticism what they may or do possess. The moment the possession of Dolores had become an assured fact to him, the blindness of love had left him, and he began to observe, to study, to analyze her features, her ways, her character, and her conduct; to take notice of every one of her words, looks, gestures, and expressions, and to weigh them, not with the scales of an infatuated lover, but with the self-tormenting soberness of one who has rashly entered into an ill-considered engagement. Having made his choice of a wife, he longed to be free to choose. Love and desire had seized him first; doubt and distrust took hold of him afterward. With such men, the distant prospect of success will redouble the vigor of pursuit; the certainty of success will at once relax it, and even turn it into halting hesitation or regretful disappointment. The objections and undesirable features which prudent men will consider before entering into an engagement, men like Carrera, will not consider until after the engagement is made. But then these objections will strike them not only with their own force, but with the additional sting produced by the reproachful consciousness that it was imprudent and foolish to overlook them.

There were many things in Dolores which he had not noticed while he was a nightly visitor at her house, but which forced themselves upon his observation since he lived under the same roof with her—things which somewhat grated upon his finer feelings. But, most of all, he felt nettled by a certain tone of confidence in her intercourse with Paredes, which troubled, while it occupied, the mind of Carrera. It did not show itself in acts or words; not even in looks or anything that might have given room to comments. There was nothing improper in their behavior to each other; nothing that implied either familiarity or the cautious and generally suspicious avoidance of the semblance of familiarity; yet Carrera felt instinctively, as it were, that there was an understanding of some kind between the two, to which he was not a party. He had not betrayed this apprehension to Dolores, except once, when he hinted at it in a half-jocular, half-remonstrative way; but Dolores had answered him so skillfully, candidly, and submissively, that he felt disarmed, and even rebuked. "This man," she said, "has saved the life of my father,

Julio, for which he is entitled to my eternal gratitude; but if my treating him with that confidence to which his position as an old friend of the family and his great services to my father have entitled him, should displease you, I shall certainly be more distant to him hereafter, although I am not conscious of anything in words, conduct, or thought which might be considered in the least improper or unbecoming my dignity as a lady and as your future wife."

After this, Carrera did not dare to recur to the subject, but kept his observations to himself, jealously adding atom to atom, treasuring up in his memory every little trifling incident, gesture, or circumstance, and nursing in secret what his silent watchfulness had gathered.

He had resumed, as soon as he was strong enough to do so, those lonely walks of which he had been so fond even long before the great trials through which he had passed had made him older in mind and seriousness than he was in years. Very often he sought out that secluded mountain spot, where Toa had appeared to him first, and where he had been searching for hidden treasures with Valverde and Paredes. He sat for hours at the place where he had met Toa, Cundurazu, and Bellido on the night of their visit to the cave. A book was generally on his knee as he rested with his back against a rock; but his eyes were not on the printed characters, but stared vacantly into space. He roamed over the mountain in every direction, tracing every ravine and every watercourse to its beginning, and constantly expecting, yet dreading to see her once more, of whom his thoughts were full. On these occasions, the Fool was almost invariably his follower. He was not obtrusive, never spoke unless he was spoken to, and always kept at a respectful distance. Carrera had succeeded in dissuading Arana from subjecting the poor devil to an inquisition, and had taken him in his service for what little he could do. Carrera's old servant, Mariano, had disappeared while his master lay senseless in Mama Rucu's cottage. Nobody could tell what had become of him. Many Indian house-servants, field-laborers, and factory-workmen had disappeared at the same time. Their number was estimated at from six hundred to a thousand. Their tracks showed that they had betaken themselves to the eastern mountain range, which, as far as the wild and inhospitable nature of the *sierra* would permit, was searched in every direction by the men of the *Alguacil del campo*, whose office it was to catch fugitive Indians and Negroes, and to restore them to their owners. But it was impossible to discover the whereabouts of the missing Indians. Their flight was a heavy loss to their owners, considering the general impoverishment, which had been aggravated by the late disturbances and the introduction of a new and burdensome tax.

The Royal Commissioner seemed to have relented to Manuel Paredes. Dolores had the promise of the Count that the man who had saved her father's life should be properly taken care of in the final distribution of rewards. This promise, Paredes felt, could be relied on. He no longer feared that others would be unjustly and disproportionally preferred to him. But aside from this it was exceedingly mortifying to him to see that he had absolutely no influence with Count Arana, who systematically disregarded or rejected all suggestions or advice that came from Manuel Paredes, and left his requests almost invariably unattended to. This unfriendly disposition had been very disagreeable, if not alarming, in one respect, to Manuel Paredes. He had never been able to induce the Count to change the proclamation promising a reward for the capture of Juan Castro, by the addition of the words "dead or alive." Paredes had tried it on several occasions, until he became afraid that, by referring to it again, he might arouse a suspicion in the Commissioner's mind. And yet it was very important that Juan Castro should be dead when delivered to the authorities. He knew too much for the comfort of Manuel Paredes. Perhaps it was not probable that those in power would believe the slanderous inventions of the lying ruffian; still it would be exceedingly unpleasant, if not dangerous, to let those "inventions" become known, circulated about, and commented upon. Castro, if taken alive, would look upon Paredes as his protector; and if abandoned by him, the reckles ruffian might revenge himself by charging the responsibility of his own crimes upon his noble patron. It was out of the question to surrender Juan Castro alive. And yet his surrender depended upon Manuel Paredes, who not only knew the hiding-place of the villain, but, in fact, had helped him to get there. If it should ever become known that the chief of the murderers of Valverde had been protected and hidden by Manuel Paredes on territory belonging to one of his *haciendas*, he would be ruined. Under these circumstances, Paredes had no hope of extricating himself from this difficulty, other than the departure of Arana, after which the latter's successor in power, the new President of the Royal Audience, would probably be more accessible to well-meant suggestions and prudent advice.

Things had turned out quite differently from what Paredes had hoped and expected when he accepted the secret commission intrusted to him, under the King's seal, by the Marquis of Solando.

CHAPTER IX.

IN THE COUNTRY OF THE SAMARUCU.

ENDLESS are the forests along the many rivers forming the great fluvial system of the Amazons. On the left bank of one of these rivers, abounding in rapids and falls of both picturesqueness and danger, the *machete*,* which the Indian buys from the white *corregidors*, and their trading partners or agents, had cleared away the dense undergrowth of creepers and jungle for a considerable distance, so as to make the place available for the primitive habitations of the children of the wilderness. The virgin trees had risen to an immense height, and their entwined crowns of dense foliage afforded protection from the burning sun and the dense showers, which, on the eastern slope of the Cordillera, are of almost daily occurrence, impregnating the atmosphere with an annoying excess of moisture, destructive to garments as well as cereals.

On this secluded spot, situated, at a considerable distance, to the northeast of the Spanish settlements—Logroño, Mendoza and Sevilla de Oro—Toa had encamped with her followers, in order to give them a rest after the painful hardships of a long and dangerous march across the mountains, and of the equally trying descent into the lowlands, where esculents could again be found—tropical fruits, fish in the rivers, and birds and monkeys on the trees. For the time required to reach these lowlands, provisions had to be carried on the backs of Indians—the foot-paths, or tracks rather, which must serve instead of roads, being entirely impracticable for beasts of burden; and as a *greater number*

---

* Sword-knife.

of her people had followed Toa than she had intended and commanded, their supplies of provisions had not held out long enough, and, hence, privations had been the result, to which many of the fugitives had succumbed. The hardy children of the Sierra were accustomed to the colds and snows of the mountain-passes over which they had to climb, but not to the heat and fevers of the tropical lowlands, which broke their powers of endurance, weakened as they were by the hardships of the journey. In addition to those who had perished during the descent, many more died after their arrival in the hot forests, and others were now prostrate with dysenteries and fevers, and unable to proceed. Toa was unwilling to abandon them, and as her present task was not one which required precipitation or haste, she had commanded a halt, so as to give the sick time to recover, and to inure those that were well to a climate to which they were unaccustomed.

This was the sixth week of her encampment, during which time she had been a ministering angel to those who stood in need of nursing and kindness. The messengers of Quirruba, the Chief of the Jivaros, had met her as she descended the Cordillera, and had guided her to this place. They had brought her a hammock of twine as a present from their chief; they had also brought bows and arrows for the chase, and bows and other weapons for warfare, and poison in which to steep the points of deadly missiles.

Quirruba's men had helped to put up the encampment for Toa and her followers. The hut for the Queen rested on poles driven into the ground, with a roof of *bijao* leaves, and a flooring of wild cane. The hammock, swung from two of the poles, served her, as Cundurazu had predicted, for a throne, a chair of state, and a bed. Her followers camped under the low shelter of reeds and cane, supporting extemporized roofs of dried leaves and grasses. The modest wants of these people were easily satisfied, and if it had not been for the deadly climate which undermined their vital strength, they would have been happy in their escape from their cruel Spanish task-masters, and in the presence of their Queen. .

It was early in the forenoon. The ground was still wet, and the trees and bushes were dripping with the dews and showers of the night. Toa sat in her hammock. A number of her followers surrounded her in a semi-circle, and Quirruba's half-naked and painted messengers stood before her, four of them ready to return to their chief, while two of them were to remain to serve her as guides through the wilderness. The former were about to receive their parting orders, and to take leave of the Shyri-Inca.

"Take these presents to your great chief," said Toa, in the language of the Jivaros, which very few of her own followers understood, "and assure him of my friendship and regard. His enemies are my enemies. The foreigners who have invaded his country are the same that have oppressed my people. Tell him that I shall come to him, to concert with him the plans for the expulsion of the Viracochas from the country of the great rivers and forests. I shall visit the territories of other tribes and nations on my way. They must all unite for the common purpose."

"Yes, Shyri Toa; but my chief, the noble Quirruba, wishes thee to hasten thy journey to his country, for he is anxious to celebrate his nuptials with the great Queen whom he has loved for years."

"Tell him that on this point I must and shall inflexibly adhere to my determination. Among all the Indian nations, on both sides of the mountain range, there is but one man whom Toa will have for a husband. That man is your chief, Quirruba! But Toa has made a solemn vow to the great God Inti, the Sun, that she will be wedded to no man who is a subject to the invader. She will live in no country which tolerates the rule of the foreigner. On the day when our great plans have succeeded—on the day when the bearded oppressors of our nations are driven from the land that belongs to Quirruba and his allies—on the day when the Spanish towns in the heart of these glorious forests shall be wiped from the surface of the earth, and their inhabitants shall either be dead or in wild flight back to the table-lands on the other side of the Cordillera—on that day of retribution and revenge Toa will be the wife of Quirruba, but not before."

"It was the hope of my chief, great Shyri-Inca, that the marriage should take place upon thy arrival in his country, and that then, by your united efforts, the great work should be prosecuted to a happy conclusion."

"I have spoken. When Toa Duchicela has made a vow, but two things are possible—Toa Duchicela will either keep her vow, or she will die in the attempt to keep it. The Shyri Toa never breaks her word. She has devoted herself to the service of thy chief, Quirruba, and while life is left in her she will be true to him. She will work night and day to make him a great king. He shall be the chief of the united nations of the rivers and forests, and those nations shall be free from the yoke of the invader. Until then Quirruba must have patience. Now she knows but the love of the race to which we all belong, although we may be divided into many nations and tribes. But when our work is done she will know but one love, the love for the man who has accomplished it. Tell him all this, and bid him, in my name, to begin the work at once. Let him visit the tribes of the east and of the south, as I shall visit the tribes of the west and of the north. And now, go! May the Sun and the Moon guide your steps, and grant you a safe and welcome return."

The messengers threw themselves on the ground and pressed their faces against the earth, reverently kissing it before they arose to take their departure. Nearly all those that were well, accompanied them to the river to see them embark in two small canoes, which were rapidly borne away by the strong current, and were soon out of sight.

The messengers were not gone long when a shout arose at the other end of the encampment. Toa had adopted the European system of using a number of her available men for picket- and sentry-duty. These men were placed on knolls, rocks, or trees, from which they could command a view of the surrounding country. The shout had proceeded from one of these guards, and it was taken up by those that happened to be near the bank of the river. They had descried a long log with three men on it. It came floating down along the shore. One man piloted it with a pole, while the others waved their hats in token of recognition. In a few seconds the whole camp was astir. "It is Uma! It is Uma!" was the joyful cry which was repeated from mouth to mouth. And really it was Uma, who, bounding from the log with his two companions, was at once locked in the embrace of the fugitives, who received him with delirious joy, as a messenger from the dear old home which they had left behind. In triumph they conducted him to the hut of their Queen, before whom he prostrated himself, according to the custom of their fathers.

"Rise, Uma, trustiest of my servants. Toa bids thee welcome, thrice welcomè, to the country of the great rivers and forests."

Uma did not rise, but remained motionless.

"Why dost thou hide thy noble face? Why dost thou not rise to thy feet? Is it evil news thou bringest?"

"Yes, Shyri; but it is not my fault. My work was done well. But the Gods were against us."

"Sad news is no news to Toa Duchicela. She is not used to glad tidings. Speak! how is our Viracocha friend?"

"He is dead!"

"Dead!" repeated Toa, and sunk her head in silence. A pause followed, during which nothing was heard but a low wail from those around them, who were doubly affected when they saw the two tears which slowly trickled down the cheeks of their Queen.

But Toa was soon composed. Dashing the tears away, she roused herself and said : " Why should I weep for one man, a stranger, where thousands of our people have died. Yet he was a good man—the noblest, the truest, the best of the Viracocha race. Rise, Uma, and tell me how it happened."

"Everything had succeeded admirably. I met him as he walked out of the barracks, and led him to the mountain. We passed the Coya Cisa's cottage a few minutes after thou hadst left it. But our friend's feet were swollen from the chains he had worn, and his long imprisonment had made him weak and unable to undertake our arduous march that night. Thus we had to rest in one of the caves the remainder of the night and the whole of the next day. It was nearly dark when we skirted the dread cliffs of Rucu Pichincha, and descended into the wilderness on the other side. The storms howled, and the fogs enveloped us, so that I feared we should have to retrace our steps; but the great Moon was kind, and dispelled the threatening clouds, and lent us sufficient light to get over the most dangerous passes. It was a long and troublesome journey. Our friend was weak, and we had to rest so often that our supplies gave out, and we were left without provisions long before we had escaped from the Paramos. Often I thought, during those trying days, I should never behold thy Royal face again. One of my men succumbed to starvation and cold, and we placed him in a sheltered spot where the spirits of the mountain will shrivel up his flesh and preserve his skin from decay. O, that our Viracocha friend should have survived all these dangers and hardships to die at the very moment that would have perfected the success of his escape!"

"And how did he die?"

"I took him down the mountain range and through the forests to the coast of Esmeraldas. Thy messenger had arrived before us, and had communicated with the ships of the smugglers who trade with the people of those villages. Thy servant Hualpa, who knows the secret of the emerald mines, conducted the negotiations, and the captain of one of those vessels consented to take away our friend and carry him to some port outside of the dominions of Spain. For this service the captain was to receive two hats full of emeralds; one of them at once, and the second upon his return to the bay of Esmeraldas, with a letter from our friend informing thy servants of his arrival and landing at a port of safety. Everything had been arranged before we arrived. The ship had been in waiting for more than two days when we came. But this was our misfortune. The smugglers feared to tarry longer. The vessels of Arana had lately been cruising along the coast. The pirate captain was afraid of being chased, and insisted that the Señor Sanchez must embark on the very night of our arrival. It was a dark and stormy night. The rain poured down in torrents, and the sea went high. Still, the boat of the smugglers had plied easily between the vessel and the shore, and we dreamt of no danger. He embraced me long and tenderly before he stepped into the boat. He begged me to assure thee of his eternal gratitude. I helped him into the boat. By the light of our torches I saw the boat glide away. I heard his inspiriting voice come to me through storm and darkness; but all at once a big rolling wave struck the boat sideways, capsizing it—I saw it by the glare of the sheet-lightning—and our friend was lost. The two oarsmen, familiar with the element and its perils, saved themselves in the shallow water, and recovered even the boat, but the Señor Sanchez was lost. Thus it all came, Shyri Ton. I swear by the great Sun that it was not my fault."

"I know it, Uma, I know it. Thou hast done thy full

duty. And, perhaps," she added after a pause, "it was better for him to end thus, than to suffer the miseries and privations of exile among strangers, whose language even he would not have understood. Was his body recovered?"

"It was washed ashore a day or two afterward. We saved it from discovery, and gave it a secret burial. His sword, and an amulet which we found around his neck, Hualpa will send to the Señora Sanchez at Quito, as soon as it can safely be done."

"It is well! To-day we shall celebrate his obsequies here in the forest, and honor him, as we should have honored one of the great and brave men of our own race. And what news dost thou bring me from Purruhá and Quito?"

"I bring a message from Purruhá where I tarried to see thy grand-aunt, Carmen Duchicela. She begs thee to desist from a roaming life of wretchedness, as she calls it, and bids me to implore thee to come back to her."

"The kind and noble woman! Does she not consider that it would be certain death to harbor the outlaw and a traitress on whose head a prize is set by the Spanish Government?"

"She says nobody will know it. Her estates are large and exempt from surveillance. She has houses in the mountains, never visited by Viracochas, and wholly unknown to them. 'Let her come,' she said, 'and she will be safe. Toa knows that my Indians would die rather than betray her.'"

"And Cundurazu?"

"He staid with thy grandaunt, Carmen for nearly a week, after which he went to the mountains, and was not seen or heard of again. The Coya Carmen wanted him to remain, but he said his hour had come, and that he must go to sleep among the rocks where his great ancestor, whose name he bears, found everlasting rest and shelter."

"Gone to sleep among the rocks," said Toa, slowly, as if

speaking to herself, "and here I am in the wilderness of rivers and forests, and it is *his* work."

A pause followed, after which Toa said to her men: "Go, my children, and prepare a meal for Uma of what little there is left to us. He must be fatigued and hungry, having traveled so far and so long to join us. Stay with me, Uma, while they prepare thy simple repast. I have other questions to ask thee."

The men withdrew. Toa and Uma remained alone, but in full sight of the camp.

"And he?" asked Toa after a while.

"Is married to Dolores Solando!"

The Queen remained silent. No muscle in her face betrayed her emotion. Another pause followed, during which nothing was heard but the quiet bustle of the camp and the rustling of the wind in the trees above them.

"Didst thou see Santos?" asked Toa at last.

"I did, Shyri!"

"Well?"

"She is doing her work."

Toa's eyes lit up for a moment with an expression of triumphant fierceness.

"Successfully?" she asked.

"Yes, Shyri. This is what the granddaughter of Cozopangui said to thy servant, Uma: 'Tell the Shyri Toa that he who has wronged and betrayed her, now meets with his reward. His life is a waste, and every hour brings its pangs and its miseries.'"

BOOK VI.
THE WORTHLESSNESS OF LIFE.

Las ojas del arbol caidas
Juguetes del viento son.
Las ilusiones perdidas
Ai! son las ojas caidas
Del arbol del corazon.
ESPRONCEDA.

When shall I meet thee?
After long years.
How shall I greet thee?
In silence and tears.
BYRON.

BOOK VI.

THE WORTHLESSNESS OF LIFE.

CHAPTER I.

SEVEN YEARS LATER.

NEARLY seven years have elapsed since our story closed in the tropical forests on the eastern slope of the Cordillera. Seven years—a short span in the history of a nation, but, aye, a long and eventful time in an individual's life, of which it often forms the best or the worst part. Great and continuous are the changes which seven years must effect *around* the individual man; but infinitely greater are the changes and transformations which seven years will work *within* him; changes imperceptible to himself and others, and changes painfully or gladly present to his own mind, and regretfully or wonderingly noticed by those who are near to him; and, hence, should know him best. Near to him? Those that were near or nearest to him seven years ago, may be dead or absent, or, what is still worse, may be farthest away from him in thought and feeling, though bodily near. The ravages of death are heart-rending, but leave sweet memories behind, growing dearer to us who cherish them, the nearer the fatal hour draws to ourselves. But for those whom estrangement has alienated, sweetness generally turns into gall, friendship and love into coldness or bitterness, and regard into disparagement. And when two human beings thus estranged are chained together by bands from which there is no escape on this side of the grave; when the one, sick and hopeless at heart, disenchanted, disappointed, and perhaps betrayed, must toil on to the end of life's journey by the side of the other, to whom he has sacrificed the best part of his life, his aspirations, his hopes of happiness, his present and future, while that other does not appreciate, and probably not even understand, the sacrifice, and, if so, would not repay it with charity, much less with gratitude; when the friction of souls which have become unsympathetic, nay, repellant to each other, is made chafing by a thousand annoying circumstances, by the peevishness or unreasonableness of the one, and the sensitiveness or indignation of the other; by spite and selfishness on one side, and deep anguish, regret, suspicion, or mortification, on the other; when each leads his own life, incessantly conflicting with, and grating upon, that of the other; then what a change there will be, at the end of seven years, in the heart of the one who has suffered most during the secret but remorseless conflict—what a contrast between the morning so hopeful and bright, and the long, dark night of misery and despair.

The Plaza Mayor—the Great Square of the city—where we once beheld the bloody conflict between the assailants of the Palace and its heroic defenders, presents a lively scene. Drums are beating, and the bugles resound lustily. Two companies, made up of regulars, militia-men, and fresh recruits, are drilling in the Square, and a great number of ladies and gentlemen have assembled to look on. The Marquis of Solando, withered by age, and steadying his uncertain steps with a cane, but still full of stately pompousness, is engaged in conversation with the President of the Royal Audience, and some of his Ministers, surrounded by a number of civil and military officers and ecclesiastics. The bishop occupies one of the balconies of his palace, while the Alcaldes and some of their colleagues of the Cabildo, gaze at the scene from the windows of the Municipality Building. The rabble of Quito, always idle and fond of sights, has been attracted in great numbers, by the military pageant, but is kept at a respectful distance by the Municipal Guards. And the equatorial sky is so bright and beautiful, and the whole scene looks so gay and festive, that we are tempted to forget the dark side of the picture, and the suppressed sighs and groaning heartaches masked by smiling faces. The men who are now drilling amidst the acclamations of the multitude, have a long and tedious march before them, which, for months to come, will take them away from their homes and their families, and expose them, not only to the pernicious effects of a dreadful climate and innumerable hardships and privations, but also to the dangers of an apprehended insurrection or rebellion.

Taught by past experience, the Royal Audience will not again permit the seeds of rebellion to grow, owing to the absence of timely and energetic repression. Any attempt at disobedience must be crushed in the beginning, so as not to develop into an insurrection, and thus bring about a repetition of the disorders of seven years ago. Hence these preparations. Hence the pomp and circumstance of war, after seven long years of peaceful repose.

The new cloud had arisen on the eastern side of the Cordillera, in the Province of Macas, containing four extensive departments, and including the towns of Logroño, Sevilla de Oro, and Mendoza. The origin of the trouble was this: Philip II, the remorseless despot, had died at last. Philip III had succeeded him. The announcement of his coronation had been received in America, and in all the colonies and provinces great festivals were arranged to accompany the pompous ceremony—*Jura del Rey*—swearing fealty and obedience to the new King. The Governor of Macas, too, had issued his orders for the occasion, and, with the usual rapacity of the Spanish Pro-Consul, he planned to avail himself of this opportunity for his own enrichment. He had issued a proclamation imposing, under the misnomer of a *donation*, an enormous tax from which to defray the expenses of the festivals which were to be celebrated in each of the departments of his jurisdiction. This tax was to be made up chiefly by the owners of landed estates and mines, by the shop-keepers and artisans in the towns, and by the Caciques or Chiefs of Indian tribes. It had been announced, in this proclamation, that the Governor himself would visit the three principal cities of his domain, in order to receive the money and attend the festivals. His first visit was to be made to Logroño, a young town which, by its rapid progress and development, had surpassed many of its elder sisters throughout the Kingdom. Logroño and Sevilla de Oro, by the fame of their gold mines, had attracted settlers and adventurers from every part of Peru. For miles around these cities, the forests had been cleared away, and many public and private edifices of taste and comfort, as well as churches and convents, had arisen where, twenty or thirty years before, the solitude of the forest had not been disturbed by the encroaching advance of civilization.

The impudent rapacity of the Governor created general indignation. It was universally understood that not one-twentieth part of the money demanded by him would be needed and actually expended for the festivals. The settlers well knew that the latter formed but a miserable pretext, and that the real purpose of the Governor was his own enrichment. Under these circumstances, they would have rebelled against this imposition, even if the tax demanded had not exceeded their abilities. But in a new country, where the struggle of civilization against the exuberant forces of tropical nature had just begun, they needed whatever gold-dust or ready money they could accumulate. The royal fifth of the proceeds of their mines was in itself a great burden, which heavily weighed them down. The distance from the coast, from which they were separated by both chains of the Cordillera, and the wretched condition of the roads, had increased the prices of all imported commodities to an extent such as to reduce the profits of all domestic enterprises to a pitiable figure, and leave the settlers poor, in spite of the large quantities of gold which they dug from the mountains and washed from the streams. Hence, when the Governor's rapacious intentions became known, the old spirit of resistance, crushed under the iron heel of Arana, at once revived. Conferences were held at the principal haciendas, as well as in the towns, and a league was formed for mutual support and armed resistance. The Governor trembled when he heard of these movements. He had no military power with which to curb the spirit of sedition. The militia, which he might have called out, consisted of, and was commanded by, the very men whom it would have been his object to put down. He, therefore, concluded that discretion was the better part of valor, and assured the leading colonists, either personally or by messenger, that they had misunderstood his proclamation. He had not intended to require or exact anything of them. He had asked for a donation only. It was a mere request, with which they were at liberty to comply according to the best of their ability, or not at all. The minimum which his proclamation had named had been fixed merely with a view of informing the Indian Caciques how much they were expected to pay. To bring these Indians to a sense of duty, the Governor very cunningly represented, had been the principal object of his proclamation. The Indian inhabitants of these forests had not bent their necks to the Spanish yoke as meekly and profitably as the Indians of the table-lands. The Macas Indians still lived together in separate and independent tribes, which paid their tributes very irregularly, and furnished their quota of farm- and mine-laborers only with great reluctance. It was necessary to break their independent spirit, and get them more completely under subjection, by involving them in debt. To effect this had been his main object. He thought that if the Indian Caciques were unable or unwilling to pay the required amounts, they would furnish him with *peons* instead, who would be of great service to the colonists themselves. By these representations, grateful to the rapacity of his white subjects, the Governor soon succeeded in allaying their indignation and disarming their suspicions. If his rapacity was to be directed against the Indians only, and if it was to be gratified in such a manner as to increase the number of slaves in the colony, it was not at all objectionable to the Spanish cavaliers and their plebeian followers; and, instead of opposition, his scheme met with applause and encouragement.

But the perfidious Spaniard had only dissembled his resentment. It was not his intention to forgive those who had thwarted him and defied his authority. He intended to make them pay for their disobedience. Hence, he had secretly dispatched special messengers to the Royal Audience at Quito with letters in which he gave a most alarming account of the sentiment and disposition prevailing in his Provinces. The spirit of sedition, he said, was rife. The leading men of the four department had thrown off all restraint and obedience. A great number of the banished or fugitive rebels of 1592 had found asylums on the farms and in the mines of his government, and infected the others with a spirit of restlessness and disloyalty. Still he, the Governor, had no power to prevent mischief or to bring offenders to justice. He was without troops, and the militia would turn against him, should he be imprudent enough to call it out. It was almost impossible, his representation continued, to collect the King's fifth of the proceeds of the mines, without an armed force. The colonists were unwilling to pay any taxes or contributions. Even a moderate donation for which he had asked in order to defray the expenses of the festive ceremonies in honor of the accession of the new King, had been refused. Under these circumstances, the Governor concluded, the outbreak of a new rebellion would only be a question of time, unless the Audience should send a sufficient number of troops so as to enable him to restore the Royal authority.

And this was the meaning of the military pageant on the Great Square of Quito. The two companies which were drilling there under the bright and beautiful sky of Quito, were to be sent to the Governor of Macas to crush the spirit of sedition in the country of the "great rivers and forests," on the eastern side of the Andean Cordillera.

"And what officer," asked the Marquis of Solando of the President of the Audience, "will your Excellency designate for the command of this expedition?"

"We have not quite determined yet, my dear Marquis," answered the President, "whether to give the command to the senior captain, or whether to put both captains under a regimental officer, so as to avoid jealousies. To speak frankly," added the President, laying his hand on the shoulder of the Marquis, and whispering in his ear, "I should greatly prefer to put the expedition in charge of a commissioner with civil powers. I have a suspicion that there is something wrong in the administration of the government of Macas. The Governor's own doings may require looking into. Of course, we must make an imposing military display, and strike terror to the souls of the evil-minded, but I think a man of judgment and shrewdness, entrusted with both civil and military powers, would soon set matters to rights."

At this moment, a gentleman on horseback, in traveling dress, followed by a servant, and both men and horses bespattered with mud, galloped across the opposite end of the Plaza, as if he had just arrived in the city. For a moment he stopped to look at the military pageant, and then rode on.

"Was not that your son-in-law, my dear Marquis?" inquired the President.

"My eyes have become very dim," replied the old man. "I could not discern his face, but I should not wonder if it was the Count, for we expect him home to-day from his *hacienda* at Puembo, where he has been detained for over two weeks."

"He seems to be away from the city a great deal," continued the President with affected innocence.

"Undoubtedly, your Excellency; but, in addition to the care of the estates which he inherited from his uncle, I have to trouble him with the superintendence of my own *háciendas*, because I am old and decrepit; and your Excellency well knows that it will not do to leave the management of important interests entirely to mayordomos and other employés."

In the meantime, Carrera—for the horseman referred to by the President was Carrera—had ridden to the Plaza of San Francisco, and stopped at the house of his father-in-law, with whom he resided, the old gentleman having refused to allow his daughter to leave him. The servants, with whom Carrera always was a favorite, welcomed him gladly as he ascended the staircase and walked to the suite of rooms occupied by himself and Dolores. The hounds, little and big, jumped around and up to him in big bounds, barking with delight at their master's return; the parrots screeched, and one little perroquet joyfully flew on his shoulder and then perched on his finger, repeating without end the two words he could say: "*periquito—chiquitito.*" And the pet ape, which was fastened to a ring and a thong in the Court-yard, sent up a tremendous chatter. Every being—brute and human—in the house greeted the returning master, except the one who should have been first to welcome him. Carrera felt the cut, because he had notified his wife by letter of the day and hour of his return, and he knew that the letter had been placed in her hands.

Sullenly he threw himself on a sofa and allowed his servant to divest him of his spurs and leggings, and there was quite a pause before he could prevail upon himself to ask the question: "Where is the Señora?"

"She went out!" answered one of the servants.

"Out?" echoed Carrera in amazement, "with whom?"

"With the Señora Catita."

"Whither did they go?"

"To the Plaza Mayor, to join his Excellency, the Marquis, who is there, to see the soldiers drill. Your Grace might have met them. They went a short time ago."

Carrera bit his lips. Would she not even save appearances? Was it right, was it wife-like, was it lady-like to go out when she knew that he would return after a protracted absence, and when the servants knew that she know it?"

"Have we had any visitors to-day?" he asked after another pause, while brushing the dust out of his hair and beard.

The servants seemed embarrassed, and exchanged sly glances among themselves, but said nothing.

Carrera repeated the question.

"The Señora Ramirez was here," said Mama Santos.

"Ah, good! Is she well again?"

"Yes, your Grace."

"I am glad to hear it," continued Carrera, and then added, attempting the greatest possible display of indifference in the tone of his voice: "Has anybody else been here?"

"Yes, your Grace," answered Mama Santos. "The Señor Paredes!" And again the servants exchanged furtive glances, while Carrera winced inwardly, but said nothing.

When he had finished his toilette, he asked whether any letters or documents had come for him. They were brought, and he gave them a hasty perusal, after which he locked them in his desk. He then left the house to go to the Plaza. His wife had disgraced him before the servants by not waiting to receive him, and by not even leaving a message for him when she went; but he would not disgrace her and himself by not going to seek her on the Plaza, or whithersoever she had gone.

He did not have to go far, but met the party as they returned to the house—Dolores and her aunt, the Marquis, Juan de Londoño, Manuel Paredes, and two or three young gentlemen. Dolores stepped forward to meet her husband, and gave him a cold and formal embrace. She did not kiss him, but presented her cheek to him, which, for the sake of appearances, he touched with his lips with equal coldness. Much more cordial was the reception Aunt Catita gave him, and still heartier the embrace of the old Marquis, who was very fond of his son-in-law. The gentlemen, in their turn, approached to salute their returning friend, and none of them with more warmth and cordiality than Manuel Paredes. Carrera felt as if he were taking a viper to his bosom when he opened his arms to Paredes for the customary Spanish embrace.

The Marquis invited the whole party to stay with him for dinner, claiming to have received a fresh quantity of most excellent wine from Lima; and they all accepted, and tasted the wine, which was strong and fiery, and made them exceedingly merry, all except Carrera, who remained moody and apparently abstracted, saying little, but drinking a great deal. Yet, while he seemed to be lost in thought, and returned short and unconnected answers to questions asked of him, he was incessantly, but furtively, watching Paredes and Dolores, who felt that his eye was on them, and consequently conducted themselves with the greatest circumspection.

A much larger number of gentlemen called after dinner to pay their respects to Carrera. Ladies, too, came in to see Dolores, and the company's merriment increased as the afternoon wore on. Carrera longed to get away from them. He longed to be alone with his thoughts. But it was impossible for him to go. Most of the persons present had come expressly to call on him, and so he had to bear it and force a smile on his lips, and small talk out of his mouth, while his heart was sick and heavy. The merriment led to cards, as usual, and a monte-table was organized, which soon absorbed the attention of everybody. The excitement of the game afforded some relief to Carrera, and he played and drank in order to stun the grief within him. Once, he noticed, while the players were going to, and coming from, the refreshment table, that Paredes and Dolores met in the center of the room, and that something was said by her in an abrupt manner while passing Paredes—a something which hardly anybody could have heard or noticed, a something that Carrera could not hear; but he saw or imagined to see the knowing and responsive look of Paredes, and that was enough. The supposition that there must be an understanding between Paredes and Dolores recurred to the mind of her husband with irresistible power; and others, evidently, had noticed it likewise. Many a time he thought he had seen people, who sat or stood at a distance from the main table, look at the two when they happened to stand together, and then exchanged looks and whispers among themselves. What *did* they think? Did their looks and whispers really refer to his domestic relations? Had it gone thus far? Had he become an object of pity or ridicule? If he could only know it! And yet he could not ask; and, besides, people would not tell him their thoughts or acquaint him with rumors or reports discreditable to himself, even if he should ask them. Such a life was terrible. Even the certainty of his shame would have been less intolerable than these vexing, wearing, gnawing doubts and suspicions.

The company broke up in time to get to their homes before the sounding of the stay-bell, a regulation which we described in the beginning of our story. No conversation had as yet taken place between husband and wife. After the visitors had departed, Carrera sat awhile with the old gentleman, giving him the information he was anxious to obtain about the state of the crops, the condition of the herds, and other matters of interest to a landed proprietor.

At last the Marquis retired. Dolores escorted him to his room to see to his comforts, while Carrera withdrew to his part of the house. Soon afterward his wife joined him. And now the time most dreaded by those who are chained together in conjugal misery had returned, the time when they are alone together, unprotected by the presence of outsiders or the restraints of society.

CHAPTER II.

HUSBAND AND WIFE.

Dolores said nothing, but without looking at her husband, quietly began to divest herself of her shawl, combs, and jewelry. Carrera had caught her eye but once; but this was enough to satisfy him that she was ready and prepared for a conflict. What should have aroused her wrath, masked for the present by an air of studied indifference, Carrera was unable to tell. She had returned his caresses when he took leave of her to go to Puembo. A temporary peace had been restored before he left the city. What could have disturbed that peace again? If she had any ground of complaint against him, why did she not state it, so that it might either be removed, rectified, or explained? Why should two human lives be made miserable, when a few friendly words of understanding could set them right? His wife's frequent fits of sullen silence had been among the worst trials of his wretched married life. They had either pained him like a slow, gnawing toothache, or they had filled him with rage and indignation, which often made him lose his temper when he struggled hardest to maintain it.

Should he speak first? But what should he say? He had often rehearsed in his mind, while absent from Quito, how he would talk to her on certain irritating subjects, how he would reason with her, and through words of kindness and persuasion open a new way to her heart. But he could not attempt to deliver these fine speeches now, when she met him with cold defiance, when she showed hostility without cause, and when he knew that the very first words he spoke would be the opening of a battle which he dreaded, because such conflicts were so entirely repugnant to his whole nature, which excelled by its anxiety to please and to conciliate, and longed almost morbidly for that reciprocity of kindness and affection, which, of all others, life seemed to deny to him who needed it most. He knew that a battle was before him if he spoke, and yet how could he remain silent? His heart began to palpitate the very moment he attempted to speak. He knew his pent-up excitement would give a strange tone and quiver to his voice, which would mar his most conciliatory language. And thus it was, that several times he opened his mouth to speak, but hesitation weighed down his tongue and sealed his lips; his voice refused to give utterance to the words his mind had spoken.

Carrera had stood at his desk waiting for something that might relieve this state of painful suspense, but nothing came to his aid. He, therefore, concluded to forego all his prepared speeches and arguments, and to make an effort to disarm her by demonstrative kindness. It was peace he wanted more than anything. If he was not to be treated affectionately, he would, at least, strive for peace. He knew he would have to buy it by humiliation and self-abasement; but it was indispensable to his wounded heart. It was the best he could attain under any circumstances, and he would make one more honest effort to attain it.

Hence, he approached Dolores, as if nothing had happened, ready to ignore and forgive the slight of the morning, and attempted to draw her to his breast. But she pushed him away contemptuously, and went to the other end of the room, where she sat down and began to undo her hair.

"What is the matter?" he asked, with a superhuman effort at self-control.

No answer. He repeated his question, and again there was no answer. True to his resolution to secure peace at any price, he continued: "Why do you act thus, Doloritas? Must there always be discord and bitterness between us? Can we never live in peace and pleasantness like other married people?"

Still no answer. Slowly, but irresistibly, the anger and indignation of Carrera gained the ascendancy over his prudent and peaceful resolutions.

"You seem to be angry," he said, "that I have come back. You wanted me to stay away longer, perhaps entirely. You could not express your disappointment at my return more manifestly than by the reception you gave me this morning."

"Perhaps you are right," she said, after a pause.

Carrera was stunned. He was not prepared for such an admission. It surprised and mortified him. "Then your conduct this morning," he asked, "was intentional?"

"I must give you the flattering satisfaction to say that it was not, although it would have been just as well if it had been. I wanted to see the soldiers on the square, but I expected to be back before your arrival. Not that I think you deserve any such considerateness on my part, but I know what I owe to myself. I do not intend to disgrace you, and consequently myself, before the servants, as you disgrace me in the presence of other people."

"I?" asked Carrera, amazed.

"Yes, you!" answered Dolores, who, woman-like, disdained to remain on the defensive.

"Would you have the kindness to explain," said Carrera, with increasing irritation, "how I disgrace you in the presence of other people?"

"Of course what *you* do is right. It never strikes you that anybody else can have feelings. You are conscious only of your own whims and suspicions."

"Suspicions?"

"Yes, suspicions!" resumed Dolores, aggressively. "Your unfounded and insulting suspicions have made me an object of public talk and derision. The way you watch me in company is scandalous. Or do you think I do not notice what to almost everybody else has become an object of comment and ridicule? When Señor Paredes happens to be with us, your eyes are always on me. Your looks are never averted for an instant. Wherever I go, they follow me. You look at me as intently as if I were a wild beast, every motion of which must be watched. Do you think that this is pleasing to me? Are you so dull as not to perceive that your conduct must expose me to injurious talk? People must notice, and have noticed, that you are dreadfully suspicious of me. Will their idle curiosity content itself with this one fact? Most certainly not. They will go, and have gone, farther. They will reason thus: 'If the Count de Carrera is so suspicious of his wife, that he forgets himself in company, and disregards the considerations which are due to her and to others, he must have grounds for his suspicions, reasons for his jealousy. He would not make such a persistent and reckless display of it, if she had not given him cause.' This is the way people will talk. Hence, if discreditable reports concerning myself and the Señor Paredes should be set afloat, it is your conduct to which they owe their origin. Do you think I thank you for it. Indeed, not! I hate you for it!"

Carrera was dumbfounded. His presence of mind was gone. He did not know what to say. By this sweeping attack, she had changed his position from that of a husband who dreaded to be injured by his wife, to that of a culprit who had injured and disgraced her. As our best thoughts are after-thoughts, so Carrera could not, at this moment, recall any of the many circumstances, of greater or lesser importance, which he had laid up in his mind against his wife. She had taken him by surprise by broaching a subject boldly from which he himself had shrunk. Her tone and bearing were those of injured innocence. And perhaps she was innocent. It was clear that she did not love him, as he yearned to be loved. Yet hers was a cold nature in which love's roots could not strike very deep; but she was proud and ambitious, and her pride might have done for her what virtue alone would not have accomplished.

She perceived the advantage she had obtained, and determined to press it. "Once and for all, Julio, I tell you that I am weary and tired of your unreasonable conduct. I have borne with it as long as I could; I can not and will not bear with it any longer. If you have no regard for my feelings, you should understand, at least, that by persisting in your insulting ways, you will disgrace our whole house, and worst of all, yourself. Whatever change my feelings toward you may have undergone, I am your wife, Julio, and know my position as such. The Countess of Carrera will never disgrace herself, and her family. I know my duty as a wife. Do you know yours as a husband? You have vowed to protect me, but instead of protecting, you disgrace me." And with these words she covered her eyes with her handkerchief, and broke into a sob.

Carrera was nearly subdued. He groped for a reply, but neither the suitable words nor the suitable ideas presented themselves.

"I am sure," he said at last in an apologetic way, "that you greatly exaggerate, Doloritas. But even if some of your charges were true, they would only prove my love. There could not be jealousy without love."

"Ridiculous! I know better! I have seen the great men of our city, and know what their jealousy is made of. It is wounded self-love and nothing else. They can even be jealous of a woman whom they have discarded. You may have ceased to love me, you may even hate me, still I see you tortured by the suspicion that I might have given another that love which you have rejected."

"But how unjust you are, Dolores. You seem to forget that your conduct toward Paredes has not been as strictly guarded as I should have desired. His visits are incessant"—

"To my father and family, such as they were before I married you."

"No, Dolores. He comes to see you. He is admitted to our rooms during my absence."

"But never when I am alone," interrupted Dolores. "I have never received him here, unless Aunt Catita, Mama Santos, or some of the servants were in the room. Where is the human being who can say that I ever received him without witnesses? Where is the man or woman who can charge me with anything wrong or even improper? What have I done? Why should I be disgraced by false suspicions, and persecuted with insults by my own husband? No, Julio, what you are doing to me is hateful, and it is but too natural that I hate you for it, and repel your treacherous caresses."

She had nearly subdued him. He did not know what to say. But there is this great defect in the strategy of women, that when once on the war-path, they do not seem to know when to stop; and that they are disinclined to rest on their laurels after having achieved a victory. It should have been clear to her discerning mind that her husband had been completely worsted during the engagement, and that in the softness of his sensitive nature he was now most anxious to surrender. She should have accepted this surrender, because by doing so she would have completely re-established her ascendency. After having defeated and captured the enemy she should have abstained from torturing her prisoner. But this is a temptation which women of a shrewish or tyrannical disposition will hardly ever be able to resist. It is not enough to fell the enemy to the ground; he must also be scalped and mutilated so as to punish him for the resistance he had attempted. Hence when Carrera meekly pleaded for reconciliation, mutual forgiveness, and peace, she persisted in trampling upon what she supposed to be his helplessness, and in doing so she forgot that it is not the heavy weight, but the additional straw which breaks the back of the over-laden camel. Not by stabbing him to the quick, but by turning the knife around in the wound, she wrung from her husband that cry of anguish with which the agonized slave at last breaks his fetters, and escapes from his tormentor.

Carrera had ceased to argue, to reason, to remonstrate. He sued for the peace which she withheld. Her real or pretended implacability made him unspeakably miserable. Death was preferable to such a life. He said so, but was answered with a sneer. At last he said, slowly nodding his head, and speaking to himself, while his memory wandered back to the happy time when he was still free to choose: "And this is the woman to whom I have sacrificed so much!"

"Sacrificed what, Señor?" she exclaimed sharply. "Have you considered, in the selfishness of your heart, which was the side that made the heaviest sacrifice? You are probably thinking of that Indian witch and adventuress, with whom you carried on amorous, treasonable, and ungodly relations, which would have landed you on the scaffold, or in the prisons of the Holy Office—and rightfully so—if my hand and my father's position had not saved you. Your impudence, Julio, can only be excelled by your ingratitude. What have you sacrificed to me? Your head would have ornamented the gates of the city, if it had not been for me. I risked my reputation to warn you the night before the riot. I told you what was to come on the next morning. But you, like a fool, waited for it, instead of betaking yourself to a place of safety. And who nursed you day and night when they brought you, a living corpse, to this house? For the fabulous treasure of that witch, which would .have disappeared in your hands like a mockery, I have given you solid wealth. I have conferred honors and distinctions on your empty head, instead of a traitor's hood or the *San Benito* which you should have worn if I had not saved you, and made you what you are. And now you talk of sacrifices, because you were once favored by an Indian impostress and vagabond."

"Not another word?" said Carrera, arising from her side, at which he had seated himself while pleading for reconciliation and forbearance. "Do not insult the memory of one who was infinitely better, nobler, purer, and truer than you. I have discarded the pearl for the shell, the jewel for the base imitation, and I am now suffering the just punishment of my treachery and folly. A short life of happiness and glory by the side of Toa, the great, the good, and the true, and even if followed by death on the scaffold, would have been preferable, immensely preferable, to a long and wretched life of misery by the side of Dolores, the wicked, the cruel, and the false. I might have been a King if it had not been for you?"

"And why were you not?" she asked, rising from her chair likewise, and drawing herself up opposite to him, with her long and beautiful hair flowing over her shoulders, and her eyes sparkling with the fire of hate and fierceness, beautiful as Medusa, but still beautiful, even in her moral deformity. "And why were you not, you faint-hearted slave? Why were you a coward? Do you think that I esteem the wretch who is too pusillanimous to conquer glory and immortality? Give me a man! It is manhood I admire! But you, Julio, are a woman, and a slave. Had I been a man and in your place, I should have been a King, at whatever cost, and if it had been only for a day, with death at the end of it, yet I should have been a King."

Carrera did not know whether he was awake or whether he was dreaming. He stood listening, with his eyes riveted on her, like the bird charmed by a serpent, and long after she had ended he still stood looking at her, unable to recover from the amazement which had overwhelmed him. At last he began to wring his hands, and said, in a piteous, incredulous, and almost shrieking tone of voice: "Dolores, did I hear right? Did you—you—you say all this to me?"

"I think I spoke plainly enough!" she answered, walking away from him haughtily to the other end of the room. But Carrera followed her.

"Did you mean these words, Dolores, you, the very woman for whom I refused it all? Dolores, you who came to me to warn me, to plead with me not to succumb to the temptation, do you now reproach me with doing what you had implored me to do?"

"I did my duty to my King, to my father, and to you, whom I then looked upon as a friend. *I* was right in what I then said, and you acted most properly and prudently in following my advice. But did you act heroically? Did you act like a man? Did you act as a cavalier to the Indian Princess who pretended to love you, and perhaps did really love you, and to whom you must have given some pledges to encourage her in the advances she had made to you? Did you act in good faith to Roberto Sanchez, your best friend? He might have supplied what *you* lacked, courage, determination, energy, ambition. Your Toa was a Queen, and possessed a treasure which you say you saw with your own eyes. Public opinion was on your side; hundreds of armed men stood waiting and anxious to strike. Arana might have been crushed in the mountains. You certainly had chances enough in your favor, but you were too dull to see and too timid to seize them. I despise a coward!"

"Almighty God!" exclaimed Carrera, still wringing his

hands, "and this from the woman who asked me to act as I have acted, and for whose sake I did what I have done."

But now the reaction set in. Whatever there was manly and noble in his nature rebelled against her heartless cruelty. He snatched up some of his *ponchos*, and, turning to the door, he said: "I shall relieve you from the presence of a man whom you hate and despise. What I have suffered during the long years of our unhappy marriage, language is inadequate to express. But to-night you snapped the last chord that held you to my heart. It is over now. May God forgive you the life of wretchedness and misery which you have led me!"

With these words he left the room. The darkness into which he stepped, as he closed the door behind him, was almost impenetrable. The night was as black as the hopelessness of his wounded soul. Every thing was still in the house. Once it seemed to him as if a shadow flitted past him, but he was too preoccupied to take notice of anything but the wounds from which his heart was bleeding. He felt his way out of the corridor into the main hall. The inhabitants of the mansion were all asleep, and little they dreamed of the anguish of their future master, who groped for the door of the reception-room. He feared lest he should find it locked. Fortunately it was open. He entered noiselessly, closed the door behind him, and stumbled over chairs and stools until he reached a sofa, on which he threw himself, covering his limbs, cold and trembling from excitement, with the *ponchos* he had brought. Here he would pass the night, not sleep, for sleep had fled from him. He had tasted the bitterest fruits of the tree of knowledge. His eyes were open, fully open, at last, and his heart was dead.

CHAPTER III.

REVELATIONS.

He must have lain for about an hour, during which the tension of his nervous system, and with it his bold determination had given way to fresh doubts, hesitations, and fears. Was it not too bold a step, he meditated? Carrera was not a man of action, and he shrank from the difficulties and troubles with which the execution of his resolution was beset. He felt like one helpless in the toils. What would the old Marquis say? Would not he and Doña Catita and all their relations and friends beseech him with all their influence, remonstrances, prayers, and authority, in order to prevent the scandal of a separation? And what excuse could he give for it? By what facts could he justify so momentous a step? His complaints were matters of feeling which could not be made public, and would be considered trifles and partly imaginary, could they be made known. There was no marriage without its quarrels; and the Church, as well as the world, would require him to bear his cross with charity, and to forget and forgive. But need there be a declared separation? He might go back to one of his *haciendas*, and from that to another. The productiveness of the estates of his father-in-law, as well as of his own depended upon his personal superintendence and exertions, and the more time he devoted to them, the better they would prosper. But could he stay away from Quito continually? Would not Dolores and her family require him to spend at least a part of his time with them in order to save appearances? His frequent and prolonged absences had already been commented upon by the idle gossips of Quito. And yet, how could he return to a woman who had treated him with such unnatural hatred and cruelty; a woman who trampled upon his heart and delighted in his sufferings? Could she really be such a fiend? Was it possible for a human being to be so destitute of all affection and charity? No. It could not be. She had evidently been very excited; he had wronged and offended her concerning Paredes; if she was really innocent, she had just cause to be indignant, and in the proud consciousness of her innocence, stung to the quick by his insulting suspicions, she had gone further than she intended, saying things which she had not meant, and could not have meant. If this was so, she was, to a certain extent, excusable, while he was in the wrong. But, being in the wrong, it was his duty to put himself in the right. Yet, had he not done so? Had he not already apologized to her and implored her forgiveness? Should there be no end to his self-abasement? Perhaps, however, he had made no allowance for the fact that women could not make up a quarrel as easily as men. A man might fire up in one moment and cool down in the next. A woman could not do that; her excitement lasted longer; she required more time to calm herself, and again to become accessible to considerations of reason and charity. By this time, probably, she had cooled down and was sorry for what she had said. But why, then, did she not come to call him back? Because she expected him to come, he being the one whose jealous conduct had given the first offense. Yes; he would make one more effort. He would go back to her bed, and if she again repelled him, then let the chord be cut forever.

He was about to rise in order to carry out this resolution, when the thought struck him that by doing so he would completely sacrifice all control over her, and forever lose all the ascendency which he, as the husband, should maintain. This consideration started a new train of thoughts in his mind, and threw fresh doubts on the problem which he was debating with himself. Should he—

His brooding was interrupted by a creaking noise caused by the opening of the door. A white figure appeared on the threshold. Was it Dolores? Who else should it be? Yes, it must be his wife, who, having come to her senses, at last had left her bed to seek him and to restore the peace for which he longed. In spite of all his misery his heart leaped with joy at the approach of relief, and if it were only temporary relief, from the difficulties and troubles with which he was surrounded. But why had she not brought a light? How could she find him in this darkness? Suddenly it struck him that this was not the figure of Dolores. Dolores was one of the tallest women at Quito, while the female apparition which stood in the door seemed to be much smaller. His eyes had now become used to the darkness. The hall outside, too, had become a little lighter, as the storm-clouds had passed away which had made the night so black when he left his room. He could plainly discern now that it was not the figure of Dolores which stood on the threshold; and yet who could it be? Superstitious terrors seized him. He had never seen a ghost, but he had heard those who pretended to have seen ghosts in which he and everybody else believed. The hair of the figure in the door seemed to be the long and coarse hair of an Indian woman. Could it be Toa, who had died and now appeared to him in the hour of his worst misery to reproach him with his treachery and desertion? He had lifted himself up on his elbows, and gazed speechless at the white figure before him. The apparition stood motionless for a few seconds, and then advanced toward him. The cold perspiration broke from his forehead, and his heart beat audibly. He was brave in danger, but helpless in the face of what he supposed to be the supernatural.

Nearer and nearer the apparition drew, until Carrera uttered an involuntary and hardly audible exclamation of terror. At this the figure halted. Carrera had now sufficiently recovered himself to invoke the Divinity, the Virgin, and the saints in order to ward off the specter.

"Is it your Grace?" the figure said at last, and Carrera heaved a deep sigh of relief, as he recognized the low and musical voice of Mama Santos.

"What art thou doing here, Mamita?"

"I hope your Grace is not sick," continued the Indian, without taking notice of his question.

"Not in body, Mamita," he said, half dreamily, "but I am sick at heart."

"I know it, *amo*," she said. "I have known it for years."

"Yes, I remember," answered Carrera, peevishly, "and I remember thee, woman, and the poison I always drew from thee."

"From me, *amo?*"

"Yes, from thee! It was thou, I remember, from whom I received all the information that slowly but irresistibly drove the sharp and poisonous dagger of doubt and distrust into my heart. Whatever troubled my mind, and took away my rest and my peace, I learned from thee. I remember it all."

"Your Grace is unjust," replied Santos, "cruelly unjust to a faithful servant. I am a servant at this house. The Niña Dolores is my mistress, and your Gracci s my master. I belong to the conquered race. Obedience is my duty. When I am commanded, I must do as I am told. When I am questioned, I must answer. I volunteer no information, and I carry no tales. What your Grace has asked of me, is all that I have ever told."

"Yes, but didst thou tell me the truth? Were thy answers always what they should have been?"

No answer.

"Why dost thou remain silent?"

"I am the granddaughter of Cozopangui, the governor of Quito under Atahualpa and Rumiñagui. I came from a noble house undefiled by lies or treachery. But your Grace need not believe me. Your Grace asked, and I answered. Your Grace asked a great deal; I never answered much. Am I to be blamed because I said too much or too little?"

"Dost thou insinuate that there is more to be told? Am I to understand that there are things which were left unsaid by thee? Answer me! Tell me the truth for the love of God! I am harassed to death by uncertainty. It is certainty I want. Canst thou give it to me?"

Again there was no answer.

"Speak woman! Wilt thou drive me mad?"

"I am a servant in this house," said Santos with Indian indirectness and stoicism. "I have never refused to answer my master's questions."

"Well, why dost thou not tell me all? Dost thou not see that I am heart-broken and miserable?"

"I know it without seeing it. I knew that it would be so, long before your Grace came to this house as the husband of Niña Dolores."

Carrera now jumped to his feet, and seizing her by both arms, he shook her passionately. "What didst thou know before I came to this house? Speak, woman, or I shall murder thee!"

"Calm yourself, Master. The grand-daughter of Cozopangui will not yield to threats or violence. But when spoken to in kindness, she will promptly obey the commands of her Master, whom she honors, because of all the inmates of this house, he is the only one who has been kind to her race."

Carrera accepted this rebuke, which restored him to his senses. "Forgive me, Mamita! I did not mean any harm to thee. I was excited, and I am so miserable. Sit down by me, Mamita, and tell me all. How didst thou know before I came to this house that I would be miserable?"

There was a pause, during which Carrera waited patiently for an answer. At last the answer came: "Because the Niña Dolores never loved the man to whom she gave her hand in marriage."

"Art thou sure of it, Mamita?"

"I am."

"How dost thou know it?"

"Because I know that she loves another!"

"Who is that other?"

"Your Grace knows it as well as I."

"How dost thou know that she loves him?"

"Give me your hand, Master." With these words she seized his left hand, lifted it to the level of his head, and then pressed it back against the wall. "Here, *Amo*," she continued. "Pass your fingers over the tapestry! Press it! Do you find anything?"

"Yes, there is a depression, a hole."

"Just so, Master. It was made by the Niña Catita, in order to listen to the conversation of people in the reception-room, and to see what they were doing. I discovered it in the wardrobe, and used it myself on several occasions."

"Well, what didst thou hear or see?"

"I both heard and saw!"

"Speak!" said Carrera, although he dreaded to listen.

"I heard them on the night before the riot, at which your Grace was nearly killed by the rabble"—

"Well, and?"—

"They were quarreling. The Niña Dolores said that she would go to your house to prevail upon your Grace to reject the offer of the crown. He objected to her going. He said he would go himself, and mold you. She insisted that she would. He then became jealous, very jealous, and there was a quarrel. But finally they made it up."

"How?"

"She told him that she did not love you, and that she never would. They then embraced and kissed each other!"

"Enough! Enough! I will not listen to more. At least not now. If it is false, the cruelest of all deaths would not be sufficient punishment for thee. If it is true, it is too much for me at once. I can not bear it all at once. It is too terrible a betrayal to be believed. My head swims. I feel dizzy and faint. Leave me, Mamita, leave me now! I must be alone with my thoughts. Go! Go! Mamita! I shall see thee to-morrow, when I am strong enough to hear the rest."

"You will be sick, Master."

"No, I shall not; but I must be left alone."

"You will not betray me, *Amo*?"

"Upon the honor of a cavalier, I will not. But, now, go; for the love of the Virgin, go!"

CHAPTER IV.

RESOLUTION.

The weary hours of the long night seemed to be interminable to Carrera, as he lay on the sofa, praying to God and the Virgin to show him a way out of this dreadful labyrinth. He was ashamed to face Mama Santos again, the woman who had direct and positive evidence of his disgrace. He was ashamed of himself and of the ridiculous part he had played, with the whole society of Quito for an audience. What was his title, what were his honors, what was his wealth to him now—to him, a cuckold at whom the finger of scorn and contempt would be pointed, and behind whose back people would laugh and sneer, and indulge in vile jokes and ribaldry at his expense? Should he kill that villain Paredes? Perhaps he should. A "dagger of the mind" assumed distinct and bloody shape in Carrera's imagination. But would it not be reckless to take life upon such testimony as this? Accepting all that Mama Santos had said as true, the proof was still deficient. Dolores may have dallied with Paredes before she married Carrera. Paredes was known to be one of her earliest pretenders. Yet she may have come to the conclusion that he was not the man whom she would prefer to all others. Carrera's heroism and sufferings, together with his titles and distinctions, may have turned the scale in his favor. She may have allowed Paredes to take certain liberties before she became another man's wife, and yet this conduct, however improper, might not be incompatible with her subsequent loyalty to her husband. Of acts or circumstances from which the crime of adultery might have been inferred, he had no proof except the treatment he experienced at her hands. And yet, did not this very treatment support the presumption of her innocence? If she were really guilty, would she not fawn upon him and kill him with kindness, rather than lead him to suspect her of infidelity? But guilty or not, the life she led him was unbearable. Any rescue from it, and if by death, would be a welcome relief after the years of suffering through which he had passed. And, after all, had he not told Mama Santos to stop before she had concluded her statements? She evidently knew more than she had told; but he had refused to listen. There was more behind, but he had been too cowardly to hear the whole truth.

Day dawned at last and brought no consolation, no ray of light to the darkness of his heart. The servants began to bustle about the house, and would soon enter the reception-room. What would they think if they should find their master lying on a sofa, and covered with ponchos, thus displaying the fact that he had spent the night away from his wife? He hastily arose and returned to his room. He opened the door noiselessly and entered. Dolores was asleep. Carrera dressed himself and then took up his plumed hat, his sword, and cloak, and was just about to leave the room when he turned to cast a last look at his wife. Dolores was now awake. Her eyes were wide open, and looked at him with cold indifference. Carrera was about to put a barrier of separation between himself and her. He had not yet determined how to do it, but he was resolved that it should be done. Still he would give her a last chance to return to her conjugal duty. So he advanced one or two steps toward the bed, and said, still holding his hat, cloak, and sword: "Dolores! Have you nothing to say to me with reference to our disagreement of last night?" She stared at him for a moment and then said: "Nothing!"

"Nothing with reference to the future?"

"Nothing, except this: I am willing to save appearances, if you are. Do not act the fool before people, but behave like a reasonable being."

"Is this all you have to say—nothing more?"

"Nothing!"

"It is well!" Thus saying, Carrera left the room.

With his hat over his eyes and wrapped up in his cloak, he had descended the first steps of the main staircase, when something pulled him back by his cloak. It was Mama Santos. "One word, Master!" she said, descending with him to the landing. "I found this paper in the *sala* this morning. I do not know who dropped it or from whom it came!" Carrera took it, and read the following lines: "The President insists on my going, at least as far as Riobamba. I must leave to-morrow morning, and shall not see you for several weeks." Carrera turned pale, as he read the paper which, he doubted not, had been written by Paredes. And to whom had it been written? Clearly it could have been intended for nobody but Dolores.

"I thank thee, Mamita," he said, as he hurried down stairs. "It is well."

He hastened on without knowing whither. Incessantly haunted by perplexities, he did not know what course to take. What should he do? What could he do? Where was the road to escape? The morning was cold. The sun had not yet arisen. Carrera—shivering with chilliness and excitement—kept up a rapid walk, so as to produce at least a physical reaction. Suddenly he was startled by the beating of drums. He stopped and listened. A thought flashed through his mind. It made him listen almost with rapture to what sounded to him like notes of deliverance. At the same time, soldiers equipped for a journey came riding down from the barracks, preceded and followed by pack-mules with provisions and military stores. The road to escape was now open. There was his chance. Why had he not thought of this before? He would go and see the President of the Royal Audience as soon as he could be seen. His Excellency was not a very early riser, and Carrera could hardly restrain his impatience. He would have to wait two or three hours at least. There was no help for it. He would also have to get some breakfast, as he had eaten very little the evening before. But he did not intend to return home, before it was all done and irrevocable. He did not trust his own firmness. He knew but too well how easily he could be swayed and influenced. Hence, he would not go home for breakfast, nor would he go to the house of any of his friends where he might be molested and annoyed with questions, and compelled to talk when he preferred to be silent.

He, therefore, wended his way to the bridge of Machángara and across it to the now famous *tienda* of Doña Mariquita, the mother of Juan and Mercedes Castro. Doña Mariquita had not changed much in seven years. Her features had become a little sharper, her face a little stonier, and her hair a little whiter; but her neck was still unbent, her bearing as erect and her step as elastic as of old. Her circumstances had improved since the profitable night, when Roberto Sanchez was entrapped under her treacherous roof, and thence delivered a prisoner into the hands of Arana. But the payment of pressing debts, the restoration of her almost dilapidated house, and losses owing to ignorance and mismanagement, had greatly reduced the golden reward of the part which she had played in the plot. She was disappointed, too, in her daughter Mercedes. The worthy mother had hoped that Mercedes, in the course of time and events, would forget her dead lover, and console herself with a living successor, whose liberality would help to defray the expenses of the household. But in this Doña Mariquita was mistaken. Mercedes never forgot the lost Roberto, and never forgave herself for having been the innocent and unsuspecting cause of his shameful betrayal. Her life was devoted to God and to her child, a bright and energetic boy of seven years, the only link that connected his mother with the things of this earth. Aside from him she had neither eyes nor ears for the attractions and allurements of the world. The church was her only place of refuge. For whole hours she lay on her knees before some image of the blessed Virgin. The fasts she imposed upon herself, the pilgrimages she undertook, the number of masses she heard, the discipline to which she subjected herself, had made her a *beata* in the eyes of the multitude which at first had been inclined to judge her very harshly. But now everybody pitied the pale and angelic sufferer who quietly glided through the streets on her way to or from church or chapel, with her head bent low and her eyes seeking the ground, speaking to nobody unasked, yet when spoken to, having a polite and modest answer for everybody, which pleased and conciliated, while it precluded familiarity. If her boy was with her, her whole being was wrapt in him. He was her past, her present, and her future, in whom and for whom alone she lived. If her boy was not with her, her thoughts and hopes were in the other world, where some day, after this long and weary earthly suffering had ended, she would be reunited to her Roberto, who must know then, if he did not know it now, that she had not betrayed him in life, and that she was true and faithful to him until death. In the meantime she earnestly, fervently, and continually prayed for his release from purgatory; and what little money she was able to save was spent for masses for the peace and salvation of his soul. Time, that wears out everything could not deaden or diminish the intense love of that gentle creature for the dead hero who had rested in her arms when she dreamed that short dream of happiness—alas! so very short—which was followed by such a cruel and terrible awaking.

Doña Mariquita was in ecstasies to see such a great and distinguised personage in her humble *tienda* as the Count Julio de Carrera. She cringed before, and fawned upon, him, and flew about, as if on wings of lightning, to obey the commands and gratify the wishes of his Excellency. Such high honor had not been conferred on her lowly house since the great Count Arana had condescended to enter it, in order to look at the room in which Roberto Sanchez had been taken prisoner. Mercenary visions of frequent and profitable repetitions of Carrera's visit arose in the mind of Mariquita, who, in spite of seven years' experience, did not yet quite know her daughter. Count Carrera's unhapy domestic relations constituted a public secret. He was the richest man of the kingdom. Mercedes was still young and her beauty had increased instead of fading. Perhaps the Señor Count had come with a view to establish more intimate relations.

What else should he have come for? Mercedes, it is true, had proved strangely inaccessible and intractable thus far, but Carrera had been the best friend of Roberto Sanchez, a fact which was known to everybody and well-known to Mercedes. Perhaps she would look upon the confidential friend of her dead lover with more willingness than upon the other cavaliers who had endeavored to succeed him in her favors. It was so provoking that she was not at home. She had gone to mass with her boy; and she was such a religionist nowadays that there was no telling when she would return.

The prattling of Doña Mariquita was grating to Carrera; but it was preferable to what he might have had to endure elsewhere. Her loquacity relieved him of the necessity of saying anything in return. He listened to hardly one-half of what she said, and returned only short and unsuitable answers. But his moodiness did not discourage the worthy mother, who received it as evidence of his disappointment at not finding her daughter at home, for whose absence she continued to apologize, while assuring him of the probability of her immediate return. Even the breakfast Carrera had ordered was delayed so as to give Mercedes a chance to return, before the distinguished and promising visitor should take his departure.

Mariquita had conducted her guest to the best room of the house, apologizing for its dust and disorder on the ground of the early morning hour, and entirely ignoring the very great probability, if not certainty, that he would not have found it differently, had he called at any other time of the day. Carrera was greatly relieved when his hostess betook herself to the kitchen in order to give her personal superintendence and co-operation to the preparation of his breakfast. He took the paper which Mama Santos had given him out of his pocket and looked at it intently. He was not familiar enough with the handwriting of Paredes to be convinced that he was the writer. But he would soon know. If Paredes had really gone to Riobamba, there was no doubt that he had written the paper. And to whom could he have written it but to Dolores? He may have dropped it on the floor, while attempting to slip it into her hand. Or she may have dropped it inadvertently, before or after she had read it, thinking that she had put it in her pocket.

Carrera's perplexing thoughts were at last interrupted

by Doña Mariquita and her servant, who brought in his breakfast.

"There must be a great deal of travel and custom now, Doña Mariquita," he began, "on account of the sending of troops from here to Macas."

"O, yes, your Grace. I have been up before daybreak this morning, in order to attend to business."

"Did any person of note come by here this morning?"

"Yes, Señor Count, the Señor Manuel Paredes passed here this morning on his way to Riobamba, where he is to make arrangements for the collection of provisions and the impressment of Indian carriers for the expedition to Macas."

Carrera turned deathly pale and could hardly swallow the morsel he had in his mouth when he heard the prompt confirmation of his suspicions. Doña Mariquita, not noticing her guest's perturbation, continued: "His Mayordomo, Don Tomas, is now in my *tienda*. He accompanied the Señor Paredes as far as Turubamba, and has just come back. The Señor Paredes, he said, might have had the command of the Macas expedition, but declined it on the ground of the dreadful hardships of such a campaign. It is a fearful task to cross the Cordillera into the wilds on the other side, where the roads are so bad that half the time the travelers will have no use for their horses, but must wade through mud, swamps, or jungle. Besides, that country is said to be very sickly, full of fevers and insects, and so damp that the clothes will rot from the bodies of travelers. They say its mines are wonderfully rich in gold and emeralds; but the Señor Paredes has become so wealthy since half the estates of the Sanchez were allotted to him, that he need not expose his life in search of mines. But your Excellency does not eat. Have I failed to give satisfaction to your Excellency? This is the best breakfast we are able to get up here; but, of course, your Excellency is used to such splendid living that even our best must appear unpalatable to the Señor Count."

"Not at all, Doña Mariquita. Your breakfast is very good. But, to tell the truth, I am not well. I have not felt well for several weeks. It is rest more than nourishment I require. Would you have the kindness to let me rest here for about half an hour? I shall not put you to any further trouble."

Doña Mariquita was delighted. Carrera evidently wanted to wait for Mercedes. If that girl would only hurry home! Why must she stay away so long? The old woman placed a pillow on the sofa and then hurried to her shop, where she had a long conversation with her old friend and *compadre*, the Mayordomo of Manuel Paredes. When she returned to the room she discovered, to her great amazement, that her visitor was gone. He had left a gold piece on the table; but his breakfast had remained almost untouched.

CHAPTER V.

THE APPOINTMENT.

An hour later Count Carrera was in the august presence of the President of the Royal Audience.

"I have come," the former began, "to remind your Excellency of an old promise. I had fondly hoped that it would not become necessary for me to trouble your Excellency with a request for its fulfillment."

"I should have regretted very much if his Majesty's most loyal and most prominent subject in this kingdom, had never given me the opportunity to serve him."

"When, years ago, I had taken the liberty of appealing to your Excellency on behalf of the Señora Sanchez and others who had suffered on account of the Rebellion of

1592, your Excellency, while regretting the inability of the government to comply with my request, assured me of your Excellency's willingness and desire to grant anything that I should ever ask for myself. Thus far I have had no occasion to avail myself of your Excellency's kindness; but now the opportunity has arisen. I am ambitious to distinguish myself. I long for activity. I am dissatisfied with myself and restless for the want of something to do different from the routine of *hacienda* life. There is to be an expedition to Macas. Its commander has not yet been appointed, and I beg to offer myself for the position."

"You, my dear Count?" exclaimed the President, with unfeigned surprise. "You? Would you really exchange a life of luxury, of ease, and of pleasure, for the hardships, the annoyances, and the dangers of such a command?"

"I wish for nothing better, and I only hope your Excellency will grant my request."

"But do you know, *amigo*, that I have offered this position to a number of prominent gentlemen, both Spaniards and natives, by all of whom it has been declined?"

"Then my offer, I am delighted to hope, will relieve your Excellency of a serious embarrassment, provided, of course, your Excellency entertains no doubt as to my fitness for the task."

"Not the least, my dear Count; but I am too great a friend of your family to allow you to make such a self-sacrifice. What would the old Marquis say? It would kill him to lose you. He loves you like a real son. You are his main-stay. You are his factotum. He would be perfectly helpless without you. And your wife, the charming Señorita Dolores. She would be in despair if I should confer on you such a dangerous appointment."

"On the contrary, your Excellency, she is as desirous as I am that her husband should distinguish himself in some civil or military capacity."

"Yes, of course; but not such an appointment. The

chances would be nine to one against your return, in case there should be real trouble in Macas."

"I can only add that I would pay the expenses of my own equipment, that I should serve without compensation, and that I am ready to leave to-day, or whenever the troops may be ready to march."

"I could not think of it, Señor Count. Your wife would think that I must be a monster for thus depriving her of her husband."

"But whom would your Excellency appoint in case my own application should be unsuccessful?"

"Well, we might fall back on our first idea of making one of the two captains who will go the commander of the whole force. This will be the proper thing to do, in case a man of prominence and distinction can not be found."

"I do not know what degree of prominence and distinction your Excellency requires. Without immodesty I may claim that I am not without either. I was forced into prominence by the assault made upon me seven years ago; and I was subsequently distinguished by the favor of my gracious master, the King, which I have done so little to deserve. And herein lies my ambition. I wish to merit the honors which have been conferred upon me. I long to prove my patriotic zeal. If your Excellency will appoint me to this command, I shall not only pay my own expenses, as I have said, but I shall also contribute my share toward the payment of the costs of the expedition, by placing in your Excellency's hands, within an hour from now, a thousand ounces of gold, to be used solely and exclusively by your Excellency for the best service of the King in this matter."

This offer at once overcame the objections of the greedy Spaniard. In fact, he had waited for it. He would have conferred the appointment on Carrera for nothing, and been glad enough if the latter had accepted it; but when he saw how anxious Carrera was to obtain it, and how lavish he seemed to be with his money, the sly President held back on purpose, in order to bring about this very result. Having succeeded at last, he fell on Carrera's neck with affected pathos, and gave him a most fervent embrace, exclaiming: "Count, you are really a patriot. The King has no better subject in this realm. You deserve to be what you are, the first gentleman of the kingdom. God bless your loyal heart. Such a noble spirit of self-sacrifice recalls to my mind the palmiest days of classic Greece and Rome. As much as I regret," he added, releasing Carrera's neck and seizing both his hands, which he shook enthusiastically, "to yield to your patriotic request, I have no right, under the circumstances, to refuse it. You have made my consent an imperative duty, the fulfillment of which I owe to the King's service. You shall have the appointment. You are the bearer of the royal standard for the kingdom, and it is quite proper and just that this post should be assigned to you. Your commission will be made out at once. The instructions for the commander have long been prepared. I can hand them to you now."

"There is one additional favor I must ask of your excellency."

"Speak on!"

"My wife, as I have told your Excellency, desires me to go." This statement, Carrera thought, would be literally true, although not correct in the sense in which the President would naturally understand it. "Her ambition will soon reconcile her to my absence. But as to the old gentleman, my father-in-law, I fear your Excellency's apprehensions are well founded. I should not wish to hurt his feelings. Hence, I beg your Excellency not to let it be publicly known that I applied for this appointment myself. Let it be considered as having been tendered to me without a previous understanding."

"I comprehend! Rely on me, my dear Count. I not only understand, but appreciate your delicacy and considerateness, and honor you for it. Leave the old gentleman to me. I shall set you right as far as he is concerned."

Before an hour had elapsed the thousand ounces of gold were in the hands of the President of the Royal Audience, who immediately transferred them, not to the royal treasury, but to his own strong-box, from which they did not emerge until his Excellency's return to Spain several years afterward. There was no deduction made on account of Carrera's donation from the items of expense that were charged against the treasury in connection with the expedition.

A detachment of the two companies of which the expedition was to consist had left Quito on the day before Carrera's appointment. Another detachment had left the city that very morning. The remainder of the force received marching orders from him almost before the ink was dry with which his commission had been signed. Carrera himself determined to leave at once. When Dolores returned home from a round of visits to some of her lady-friends, she found her father, Aunt Catita, and all the servants in tears surrounding Carrera, who stood in the court-yard, booted and spurred and ready to mount, having delayed his departure to await the return of his wife.

Determined as he was, his courage nearly failed him when the decisive moment came. His face was ashy pale and his heart almost burst through his breast with wild palpitation when he stepped up to her and said, within the hearing of those around him, in a hurried tone so as to give her no time to recover from her surprise: "Dolores! The President of the Royal Audience has seen fit to appoint me commander of the expedition to Macas. Considering the favors I have received from my sovereign and his representatives, I had no right to deny myself to this call of duty. I have accepted the appointment."

"Julio!" she exclaimed, almost overcome with surprise, but whether it was secret joy or real amazement, that made her shiver and tremble, Carrera was unable to decide.

"I have accepted the appointment," he continued, "and it is of the utmost importance that I should leave at once. I have waited to say good-bye to you. You will soon hear from me by letter. *Adios*, Dolores!"

The customary embrace now followed. Both parties seemed to be deeply moved, while those around them were sobbing loud.

"What do you mean by this?" whispered Dolores, as she lay in his arms.

"You willed it so. It was your own doing," he replied in the same manner. "This morning you might have kept me. Now it is too late!"

"And what are your intentions?" she whispered, still in his arms and clinging to him for the benefit of those who witnessed the scene.

"This is an *adios* forever! Farewell, Dolores, forever!" was the whispered reply with which he released her.

He had walked two steps from her, when he suddenly turned back, and, taking her by the hand, led her away from the group. "This paper," he said in an undertone, handing her the lines of Paredes, "you must have lost, or it failed to reach you. I know the writer. and shall personally give him your answer at Riobamba. Farewell!"

A few seconds afterward he was on his horse, and dashed out of the doorway. He was followed by a mounted servant and by the Fool on foot, who would not allow himself to be left behind by his benefactor.

As Count Carrera appeared on the Plaza in front of the house he was received by about a dozen mounted soldiers and a much larger number of friends, who, having heard of his appointment and intended departure, had come to escort him beyond the city limits, a custom still prevailing in South America. Soldiers and cavaliers waved their hats to welcome him, and shouted: "*Viva el Señor Commandante!*"

Carrera waved his hat in return, and shouted "*Viva el Rey!*" ("Long live the King!")

Then with the old Spanish battle-cry, "Santiago! Santiago?' the cavalcade moved on.

CHAPTER VI.

AN OLD ACQUAINTANCE AND NEW DANGERS.

PAREDES, who traveled alone, had traveled fast, while Carrera could only advance by slow stages, if he wanted to provide for the comfort of the troops under his command. The result was that the former reached Riobamba in three days, while it took the latter thrice that time to get there. When he arrived, Paredes was already on his way back to Quito. He had left Riobamba as soon as he received the news, astounding to him, of Carrera's appointment to the command of the expedition. Paredes had more than one reason for avoiding a meeting with Carrera. The supplies and provisions which Paredes had been authorized to purchase for the maintenance of the expeditionary force during its march across the Cordillera, and down the uninhabited slopes on the other side, were miserably deficient, both in quantity and quality. Paredes had purchased the cheapest and the worst, for which the Government had been charged enormous prices, while its agent had to share the profits of this iniquitous transaction with the President of the Royal Audience. Most of the goods were found worthless on inspection, and Carrera had to make additional sacrifices out of his private means in order to provide for the absolute necessities of the men intrusted to his charge. To inform the Royal Audience of the rascalities of Paredes would have been not only useless, but dangerous to the informer. Though this was Carrera's first experience of official life, he had learned enough to know that the real guilt rested not with the criminal, but with those who, in case of a complaint, would be the indulgent judges of their accomplice. Moreover, against Paredes Carrera did not intend to invoke the sword of the law. It was his own sword which he hoped, some day, to steep in the blood of the villain.

In the meantime, however, the latter was safe and prosperous in Quito, where he enjoyed his steadily increasing wealth and the favor of his powerful patron, the President of the Audience, to whom Manuel Paredes was a much more grateful person than he had been to the Count Arana.

Paredes had returned in time slily to contribute his share to the judgment of condemnation which public opinion had determined to pass upon poor Carrera, who was absent, and hence, according to the French proverb, unquestionably in the wrong. His domestic difficulties had been made the subject of endless discussion in all the family circles of Quito, on the streets, and in the houses, by the patricians as well as the plebeians. It was generally asserted and believed that for years past he had treated his wife with insulting coldness and shameless indifference. He had passed most of his time away from her on his *haciendas* in the country, where he amused himself in the company of low-born characters and half-breed or Indian women. During the short intervals he spent with his wife, the most amiable, the most refined, and the most accomplished lady of Quito, he had tormented her with groundless jealousy and unfounded reproaches, invented probably as a blind for his own derelictions. He had nearly broken the heart of his aged father-in-law, who had loved him as fondly as if he had been his own son. He had applied for the command of the expedition to Macas for the only purpose of releasing himself from all restraint and freely indulging his low and immoral tastes. That he was unfit for the task he had undertaken, nobody doubted. He had never had any military experience, and should not have accepted a position for which different qualifications were required. There were at least a dozen men, tried and skilled soldiers, to whom the appointment should have been tendered in preference to Carrera, to whose inexperienced ambition their better claims had been sacrificed. Of course, it was not known, and would not have been believed, that the appointment had been tendered to all these men, and that for reasons of indolence and unwillingness, they had declined it. Falsehoods and slanders travel with the rapidity of the lightning, while the truth advances at a snail pace, ever unable to overtake them. It also became known that on the morning of his departure from Quito, Carrera had called at the house of Doña Mariquita Ycaza for no ostensible purpose, and had taken breakfast there. Why he should have gone there, instead of breakfasting at his own house, was entirely inexplicable, except on one hypothesis. Doña Mariquita had a very beautiful daughter, Mercedes Castro, whom Carrera probably had desired to take with him on his expedition to Macas. It would have been very easy for him to obtain the consent of a mother who was known to be mercenary, but her daughter had led such an exemplary and almost sainted life since the death of her seducer, Roberto Sanchez, that it was clear that she must have rejected Carrera's dishonorable proposals with indignant contempt.

Thus public opinion had worked itself to a high pitch of virtuous indignation against its absent victim, who was universally condemned, while everybody overflowed with sympathy and regard for Dolores, the injured and the crushed, and with pity for her venerable father, whose love and liberality had been rewarded with such unfeeling ingratitude. Carrera, who had always preferred solitude to idle gossip, and books to bull-baitings and cock-fights, and who was not in the habit of proclaiming his real or imaginary wrongs from the house-tops, remained without a defender in the elegant circles of the capital. It had become fashionable to denounce him, and thus, as usual, society pronounced its infallible judgment upon the merits of a case of which only one side had been heard. Those who knew him least were the fiercest in their condemnation, and those who lived in the most brittle glass houses threw the heaviest stones.

And now we must follow Carrera's expedition through the almost impenetrable forests on the eastern slope of the Andean Cordillera. We find it trudging and toiling along the wretched track, for it did not deserve the name of a road, from Sevilla de Oro to Logroño. Both cities have since disappeared from the face of the earth. Over the sites once occupied by them, the tropical forest has closed. Their names have become mere reminiscences in the blood-stained history of Peru.

Carrera had reached Sevilla de Oro after a long and arduous march across the Cordillera, and down the slopes, and through the forests. As usual, during such expeditions, he had lost a considerable number of his soldiers, and a still larger number of his Indian carriers. They had succumbed to the climate and died in the wilderness, where there were no human habitations to receive them, and no resources of any kind from which to draw food, shelter, or supplies.

On his arrival at Sevilla de Oro, Carrera learned that the governor had proceeded to Lograño, having left orders for the expeditionary force to join him there. At Logroño he was to receive the "donations" which he had demanded of the chiefs of the Indian tribes under his jurisdiction, as "voluntary contributions" toward defraying the expenses of the great festivals which he intended to celebrate in honor of the accession of Philip III. The white settlers of Logroño had evinced a most rebellious disposition—so the governor thought—and to them he wanted to pay his first military compliments, as soon as he had secured all the gold-dust he could extort from the Indians.

Carrera's men needed rest and recreation. Having toiled through the wilderness for weeks, they needed, first of all, the stimulus of human society. But the governor's orders were peremptory, and the causes for which Carrera, under his instructions, might have deposed and superseded him, were not yet clearly established. Nor would Carrera avail himself of his powers, before he had met the governor, and had heard his statement of the controversy. Hence, Carrera determined to leave those of his men who were too sick or exhausted to follow him, at Sevilla de Oro, while with the available remainder of his force he continued his march to Logroño. The remainder of his force! It consisted of about one-third of the men with whom he had marched from Riobamba. The climate of the forests was an insidious foe against whom even the loving and self-sacrificing care of Carrera was of no avail.

Two or three days had elapsed since his departure from Sevilla de Oro. His march was tedious and toilsome in the extreme. The roads were almost impassable—"roads for birds and not for men," as the Spanish proverb says—while the country seemed to be without inhabitants. For the last twenty-four hours the expedition had not met with a human soul, except painted savages, who shrunk away from the approaching troops and disappeared in the thickets. There were no *haciendas* to be found along the road after the first day's march from Sevilla de Oro. The stillness and loneliness of the primeval forest had become oppressive in the extreme. The rains, too, increased as the troops struck the heart of the forest, and it had become almost impossible for the soldiers to keep their weapons from rusting, and their powder dry.

Toward the close of their third day's march, when, according to the assurances of their guides, the steeples of

Logroño should soon be in sight, the foremost men of the van-guard discovered four or five men, who emerged from behind the bushes on the road-side and hailed the soldiers with frantic demonstrations of delight. The soldiers of the van rode up to them, and were soon joined by their chief, who had just returned from an inspection of his long and straggling line.

As the strangers climbed down from the steep hill-side to the left of the road, Carrera was struck by the appearance of one of them; for in spite of the hair and beards of these men, which had grown to an inordinate length, and in spite of their almost unearthly appearance of shagginess and dilapidation, he recognized the never-to-be-forgotten eyes of Juan Castro, in all their terrible fierceness.

"Keep your eye on these men!" he whispered to the soldier next to him. "Do not let them get away from us. I have my reasons!"

In the meantime the commander of the van had begun to question the strangers: "Who are you, and where do you come from?"

"For the love of God!" exclaimed Juan Castro, "Let us have something to eat. We are nearly dead with hunger."

"Where do you come from?" continued the officer, while some of the soldiers opened their saddle-bags to the intense joy of the strangers, who watched every motion of the men on horseback, with a fierce expression of greed, almost painful to behold.

"We have been hiding in the forest among the bushes, in ravines and hollow trees, for the last forty-eight hours, and have had nothing to eat for nearly three days."

"Why were you hiding?" resumed the officer; but he received no answer. The pieces of bread and smoked meat which the soldiers had taken from their saddle-bags, had created a contention among the strangers. In their struggle for the first morsel, two had fallen to the ground, and being too weak to rise to their feet, raised a piteous howl, while their luckier comrades devoured the pieces which they had been able to snatch with wolfish rapacity.

Some of the soldiers on foot had now overtaken the van, and supporting the strangers, who had sunk to the ground, strengthened them with a little *aguardiente*. But the poor wretches did not cease their wail until food had been given them.

The soldier first spoken to by Carrera, now said: "Your Excellency need not fear that these men will run away. They are more dead than alive."

"It is very strange!" answered Carrera, "Very strange! Jaramillo! proceed with your examination. They can speak while they eat."

The officer repeated his question: "Why were you hiding?"

"For fear of the Indians, Señor."

"The Indians?"

"Yes, your Grace, the Indian tribes have risen in rebellion, under the lead of the Jibaros. They have destroyed all the settlements in this neighborhood and murdered all the inhabitants."

"This is terrible news," said the officer, turning to Carrera, who now felt that it devolved upon himself to continue the examination. "Had you no time," he asked, "to take refuge in Logroño?"

"The Lord have mercy on our souls," answered one of the strangers. "There is nothing left of Logroño."

A general cry of amazement and horror followed this announcement, and the soldiers crowded anxiously around the newcomers, who continued to eat with unabated voracity, reckless as to the next moment, and indifferent to everything save the morsels of bread, which their eyes seemed to swallow faster than their mouths.

"Man! Thou art delirious!" said Carrera. "What dost thou mean?"

"It is true, your Lordship," said Castro. "Logroño has been destroyed. The Indians took it by surprise during the night. Not a soul has escaped."

"And the Governor?"

"His fate was terrible. They seized him and tied him to a bench. Then they melted the gold they had brought as their donation for the festivals, opened his mouth with a bone, and slowly poured the molten mass into his throat until he died."

There was a pause, during which Carrera and his men stood horror-struck, while Castro and his comrades continued to eat as if for dear life.

"Did you, men, live at Logroño?" asked Carrera, after a few seconds.

"No, Señor, we are outlaws," replied Castro, without reserve or fear, "fugitives from justice. I have no doubt your Excellency has recognized one of us by this time. We could not live in the towns, but had to establish our homes in the neighborhood of the frontier-posts, where we were secure, and could hide away in case of necessity. But a few days ago, while hunting in the woods, we saw the smoke of our burning cottage, and heard the yells of the savages, and we knew what it meant. Had we not been outlaws we should have fallen into the hands of the barbarians. But, having made the art of hiding the business of our lives, we knew how to skulk, and were more familiar with the forest than the Indians who had come from a distance. We had made a secret pathway between our cottage and the outskirts of Logroño, where we had friends, good friends, who often helped us. But for the Virgin's sake, give me another swallow of *aguardiente*. I feel like fainting."

His request was complied with, after which he fell to eating again.

"But if you did not live at Logroño," resumed Carrera, "how did you learn what had happened there?"

"I was just about to tell your Excellency," answered Castro. "We intended to go to Logroño. Outlaws as we were, we should have been welcomed as men who could fight. But the Indians were there before us and destroyed the place. There is nothing left of it but charred ruins and smouldering ashes. It was a slaughter without resistance. The beasts and birds of prey are now reveling on the corpses of the residents. When we reached the place where Logroño had stood, the Indians had gone, probably to Sevilla de Oro, and to this most fortunate circumstance I attribute our escape. We searched among the ruins but found nothing except corpses. At last we tried the ranch of one of our friends and found him helpless and wounded, but alive. The fiends had left him for dead, and he had crawled into the bushes. They had made him, and a great many others, witness the horrible death of the governor before they killed them. Our friend had learned, from the conversation of the Indians, that their rising was to be general throughout the government of Macas. They had conspired to rise, at the same time, everywhere, and to destroy all the towns. The chief of their confederation is *Quirruba*, the King of the Jivaros. But my friend heard them shout for Toa, the Shyri, who must also be in the plot."

Carrera felt a pang shoot through his breast, as if an arrow had pierced him. Toa here, and in arms against the Spaniards, and he in command against her! The vision in Mama Rucu's cottage again returned to his mind, to which it conveyed the terrible certainty that he should never leave these forests. He had felt, thought, and sometimes almost hoped that he would perish during this expedition; yet, when the dreadful certainty presented itself, it came like a stunning blow—stunning, because it had come so sudden and unexpected.

"What has become of your friend?" he asked, after a pause.

"He is dead!"

"Did you kill him?"

"What else should we do, your Excellency? The poor fellow could not go with us. Should we leave him to die a slow and lingering death, or to be found and tortured by the Indians? It was a Christian's duty to put him out of the world."

"You say the Indians have left the neighborhood of Logroño?"

"Yes, Señor!"

In the meantime the main body of Carrera's force had come up. The detention of the van had brought the whole expedition to a halt. The men who had listened to Castro communicated the news to those who were behind them, and in a short time it had penetrated to the rear, spreading dismay and demoralization as it went.

"Jaramillo!" said Carrera to the officer at his side, "if what these men report is true, we must turn back at once. We are too late to save anybody at Logroño; but we may still be able to come to the rescue of our friends at Sevilla de Oro or at Mendoza. And what do you intend to do?" he added, turning to Castro and his companions.

"For the love of God! Your Excellency will not leave us behind in the wilderness. Misericordia! Señor! Take us along, for the sake of the Holy Cross. We can fight, your Excellency, and we know the roads and the country."

"It would be but a just punishment of thy crimes, Juan Castro, to leave thee alone in the wilderness to the mercy of savages and wild beasts."

"I know, your Excellency, and I do not deny it. God is just, and my punishment will come. The innocent and the guilty will be punished alike. The chances are that we shall all perish. Your Excellency's command may be overwhelmed by the savages and we may all be killed. But let me die with your Excellency and with your men! Do not let me perish alone! Do not cast me out in the wilderness! Let me remain with my own race, with white men and Christians. If we escape I shall be in your Excellency's hands, and your Grace may deal with me according to my deserts; but, by all the saints in heaven, do not drive us away! On our knees we implore your Excellency for this mercy."

"How are we off for provisions, Jaramillo?" asked Carrera, without seeming to notice the outlaws who were kneeling before him.

"Very poorly, Señor Commander!" answered the officer spoken to. "As we expected to reach Logroño to-night, we had supplied ourselves for only three days."

"We shall have to kill our horses if we find nothing to eat," remarked Carrera. "Horses are of little or no use on these wretched roads." Then addressing himself to Castro, he added: "Juan Castro, if there is a man in the world who deserves to be hung to the first tree, thou art the man! If there is a man in the world who should order thee to be hung to the first tree, I am the man!"

"I know it! I know it! your Excellency!" groaned Castro.

"But, with the judgment of God impending over us all, I will not attempt to be thy judge. God has delivered thee into my hands. I shall reserve thee for the judgment of God. You may assign these men to such duty, Jaramillo, as they may best be fitted for. Perhaps we shall need them! And now let us turn back. The clearing which we observed about an hour ago will be a safe place to pass the night."

But there was to be no safe place for the men of Carrera to pass the coming night. The order to turn back had hardly been given, when the stillness of the forest was broken by the report of an arquebus, from what, until now, had been the rear of his line of march. At the same time the thickets along the road seemed to be alive with savages, with whose wild war-whoops the tropical forest suddenly resounded. A hail-storm of deadly arrows poured down upon Carrera's devoted band, which was at once thrown into confusion. It was one of those attacks from which flight is impossible, because the troops were surrounded on all sides. They could neither retreat nor advance. They were hemmed in, and helpless against an almost invisible foe. Their powder had become wet and nearly useless, in consequence of which their fire was weak, and did little or no execution.

At last, however, the elements came to their rescue. A terrible shower of rain, a perfect freshet, broke over their heads, and by compelling a temporary cessation of hostilities, afforded a respite for organization, and a breathing spell for consultation. Yet this rain was but a treacherous relief. It took away more than it gave. It made the soil so slippery for men and horses, that it became as difficult to move on as to maintain a firm foothold where they stood. The garments of the soldiers hung so heavily to their limbs, that they could hardly bear the weight of their arms and accoutrements. They could not reload their arquebuses for fear of spoiling what little powder had remained dry. And thus they stood like sheep in the shambles, helpless, hopeless, and suffering all the agonies of despair.

After an hour the clouds parted, and the rain ceased. It was now twilight, and swarms of mosquitoes ushered in the terrors of the approaching night. It was impossible to reach the clearing of which Carrera had spoken, as the men and horses stumbled and fell at nearly every other step, or stuck fast in the mire, while the arrows of the Indians harassed them incessantly. The sufferings of the disheartened band increased as night wore on, when fatigue, indescribable fatigue, and hunger were added to the terrors of the situation. It is under such circumstances that life loses its value and becomes a burden, and death is hailed as a relief, gladly welcomed by the hopeless sufferer.

CHAPTER VII.

THE LAST ENCAMPMENT.

AFTER days of fighting, marching, and fasting, the little band of fugitives, reduced to about one-third of those who had marched from Sevilla de Oro, reached an open knoll where they might rest from the fatigues of pushing through the jungle, and recover strength to plunge into the tropical forest again. Here they might be protected for a short breathing spell, from Indian ambuscades, and from the mosquitoes which were unbearable in the thickets. The clouds had cleared away, and some respite might be hoped from the drenching rains. The sun which had been hidden for several hopeless days, smiled upon the fugitives again, and promised to dry their shapeless clothes which rotted from their weary limbs. At the foot of the hill on which they now encamped, there was a mountain-stream sparkling with cool and limpid water.

They had dragged themselves to this beautiful spot, without hope. The instinct of self-preservation, the love of life, the expectation of escape had long since died out. Their comrades who had dropped down by the wayside or had been poisoned by the arrows of the invisible enemy, had welcomed death as the end of their intolerable sufferings. The preservation of life had become a matter of the utmost indifference. Death had lost its terrors for those poor, emaciated, foot-sore creatures, shaken with fevers, bleeding from suppurating wounds, and panting with physical exhaustion. Words are inadequate to describe the agonies of their march through the pathless forest, with its quagmires and lacerating creepers. The rest of the grave was infinitely preferable to such hardships. It was only the and property. The other detachment fell upon Carrera, as we have seen, and harassed him day and night, as he endeavored to cut his way through, in order to reach the shelter of the Cordillera, where he might put himself in communication with Riobamba. But his heroic resistance was of no avail. His advance was necessarily slow, and the distance which separated him from the mountain range so great, that he could not expect to reach it with his dying band of sufferers. Hence, if help did not come from somewhere, unexpected help, for which to hope was hoping against hope, the position which he now occupied on the open knoll would be his last stand, and his dream in Mama Rucu's cottage would be fulfilled here.

Carrera lay under the shelter of a rock and rested. He had not rested for many days, and it was so sweet to stretch his weary limbs once more. How delightful would be that eternal rest when all weariness was at an end! He occupied a position at some distance from his comrades. It was the post of danger, as it was nearer to the forest than any other place in the encampment. Carrera had reserved this post to himself, because he was, physically, in better condition than any of his companions. They had struggled between the extremes of intense hope and absolute despair, while he, no longer tormented by uncertainty, had resigned himself to the inevitable. He knew what was to come, and the sooner it came, the more welcome it should be.

His eye was on the forest ahead of him, which he scrutinized with close attention, so as to give the alarm in case of a fresh attack by the Indians. Many of his men were asleep. They had longed and prayed for an unbroken hour of sleep. It had come at last, and Carrera did what he could to secure them in the undisturbed enjoyment of that precious rest. There were some that could not sleep. They had nearly fallen asleep while marching, but now that there was an opportunity to sleep, sleep had fled, and they tossed restlessly on the ground. There were others who were delirious with fever, and would soon be raving maniacs. It was difficult to keep them quiet. But fortunately, or unfortunately, they were too weak to disturb the slumber of their luckier comrades.

The sun had set with the bright promise of a clear and rainless day. The rays of the moon were struggling with the twilight, and playing tenderly on grass, trees, and jungle. Although determined to remain awake and watch for his comrades, he was too exhausted to resist the overpowering temptation. Fatigue proved stronger than resolution. An irresistible drowsiness came over him, and soon he sank in that indefinable state of torpor on the dim border-line of sleep and waking, when everything becomes uncertain, when dreams seem to be realities and realities seem to be dreams.

He thought, or dreamed, he saw the Fool (who had deserted on the day of the first attack, and had not since been seen or heard from), bend over him to see whether his master was alive or dead, and then turn around and beckon to some one in the direction of the forest.

"Ingrate!" Carrera muttered in his waking dream. "Thou hast deserted thy benefactor. Wilt thou betray him now?"

"No, *Amo*," answered the Fool. "I bring help—rescue —salvation."

"There is no rescue for me," continued Carrera in the same tone of drowsy helplessness. "I must die in the wilderness."

During all this time Carrera had seen a figure, which after emerging from the forest, stealthily crawled toward him. It was an Indian, but not of the savage race of the Jivaros. Instinctively and unconsciously Carrera put his hand on his sword, while he muttered: "As long as it is but one man I will not awake my comrades." And he dreamt that he raised his sword and struck at the approaching enemy. But this certainly was a dream only, for his arm lay motionless, and his hand had not even closed around the hilt of his sword. Again he had become oblivious.

He was aroused by a whispered call. Some one bending over him, said: "*Amo! Amo!* Do you recognize me?"

He opened his eyes and recognized the face which was over him. "Mariano!" he said in token of recognition, but without surprise or astonishment. He was too benumbed and dreamy to wonder how Mariano had come here, and *where* he could have come from.

"Yes, *Amo*, it is Mariano, who has come to save you. Open your lips and drink this," and while the Fool lifted up Carrera's head, Mariano poured the contents of a bottle into his mouth. Carrera swallowed it eagerly. It warmed and strengthened his whole system. A delicious feeling of languor came over him, similar to what he had felt after the first draught of Samarucu in Mama Rucu's cottage.

"Now sleep, *Amo*, sleep without fear. There will be no attack to-night. After midnight the Shyri Toa will come to see you. Meet her down by the stream under the big trees. I shall imitate the chattering of a monkey, followed by the shrieking of a parrot. When you hear that, come down to see the Shyri. You will be as safe as in your house at Quito. No harm will befall you while she is near."

After Mariano had spoken, everything became hushed, all visions disappeared, and Carrera fell into a long and dreamless sleep. Was it to be his last sleep on earth?

CHAPTER. VIII.

FAREWELL.

Carrera felt like a new being when he awoke. His faintness was gone; his weary limbs were rested; even a feeling of bodily strength had returned to him. He arose without pain, and cast a look at his encampment. Nearly all the men slept with the exception of those whom the fever kept awake. Even the guards had fallen asleep at the other outposts. Should he allow these guards to sleep? Why not? There was to be no attack this night. Had he dreamed this or had somebody said it to him? Was it Mariano? Yes, he must have dreamed of Mariano, who had told him that after midnight he should see the Shyri Tou. And yet, this dream was so life-like and so real. Could it have been a dream merely? Carrera had swallowed the beverage which they had given him. He still had the taste of it in his mouth. · If it was a dream, it was the most vivid he had ever dreamed.

While thus pondering, he was startled by the chattering of a monkey, near one of the big trees down by the stream. That was to be the signal. If it was followed by the shriek of a-parrot, it was no dream, and he must go. And forsooth, the shriek of the parrot came. Sharp and shrill it broke through the stillness of the night. Now there was no doubt of it. It was a reality. He was called upon to face the woman who had loved him, and whom he had betrayed, and whom he had sacrificed for the woman who had not loved him, and by whom he had been betrayed. He went.

There, under the dark shade of the big trees, she stood awaiting his approach, dressed in a tunic of coarse and dark-brown *lienzo*, such as the Napo Indians wore, with her arms and feet bare, with no ornament but the gold-hoop with the emerald on her forehead. Against one of the trees she had leaned her lance and bow, and the shield of hard wood covered with hides, such as the Jivaro warriors used. The quiver for her arrows was strapped to her back. There she stood, her beautiful face still full of intellectuality, but with deeper traces of hardness, hopelessness, and severity. These harder and sharper lines his treachery had engraved upon her countenance. They were but faint indications of the destruction he had wrought in her heart. Of a princess once so exquisite in her sensibilities, and of such refinement of thought and feeling, his faithlessness had made a savage Jivaro warrior. He had disappointed her hopes, blasted her existence, and thwarted the great purpose of her life. His punishment was just. He had ruined her life; and his own life was ruined in return. He had driven her into the wilderness, and he was now lost in the wilderness himself. He had defeated her aspirations, and shipwrecked the cause of her people; and now he was in her hands, a helpless victim of those whom she commanded. It was just retribution.

In silence Toa awaited his approach. When he was near enough to distinguish her features, and behold those wonderful eyes again, that once had looked upon him so lovingly, and now looked on him with such sadness, not with reproach, but with regret and tenderness, he was completely unmanned, and prostrating himself at her feet, he broke into long and convulsive sobs, which shook his weak and emaciated body as the storm shakes the reed.

Toa was speechless with emotion. Her breast heaved heavily; and tears choked her utterance. But she was stronger than Carrera. She had not hungered, toiled, and suffered as he, and so she succeeded first in regaining her composure.

. "When we parted on Mt. Pichincha," she began, speaking slowly and sadly, "on our return from the cave to which I had conducted you, neither of us could have dreamed that such would be our next meeting."

Carrera continued to weep bitterly.

"You spoke words of love to me then, Julio. I have not forgotten them. Those words formed the short and sweet dream of my life. I am still grateful to him who spoke them."

"No, no! Toa, not thus!" exclaimed Carrera in the anguish of his heart. "Take that lance and pierce me. I will bless the stroke of death, if dealt by your hand. But do not speak kindly to me. Tell me that you hate me, and I shall bless you for it. Tell me that you despise me, as I deserve it! Spurn me! Curse me! Trample upon me! But do not speak in these tones of kindness! It is too terrible a punishment. It is the worst of all the agonies I have undergone."

"Rise, Julio!" she said, bending over him, "and do not waste the precious moments in idle regrets. What is done, is done, and can not be undone. The past can not be recalled. The tide of time can not be turned back. You would act differently if you had to do it again. I know you would, and have forgiven you."

"Mercy, Toa, mercy! You lacerate my heart."

"Would I not act differently myself, if the last seven years could be lived over again? What am I now? I shudder at what I have done! The blood of thousands is on my head. I have wiped the Spanish colonies along these rivers from the face of the earth. I have secured the independence of the native inhabitants of these forests. But in order to do it, I have shed blood like water. I have slaughtered men, women, and children. I have been a fury of death and destruction to these settlements, and among my victims is the only being whom I ever truly, fondly, passionately, madly loved! But no! This shall not be, Julio. I can save you, and I will save you. In the disguise of an Indian, you shall be led out of these forests by my trusted servant, Uma. You shall live and think of me."

"And my comrades, noble Shyri?" asked Carrera, still on the ground. "What is to become of them?"

"I can not save them," answered Toa, plaintively. "On the other side of the mountains, in my own dear home, I was an absolute Queen, and my will was law. But here among these savages even their rulers are slaves, the slaves of iron custom through which they can not break without destroying their own authority. The men under your command are doomed. They will either die in battle or as prisoners. It will be better for them to die sword in hand!"

"And is there no escape for them?" urged Carrera endeavoring to rise, while a sudden attack of faintness, brought on by the effect of violent emotion on his debilitated and broken constitution, caused him to fall back to the ground.

"You are weak!" sighed Toa. I have ordered fruit to be brought. It is there, behind you. Eat! There is enough of it for yourself and your men for one meal. It is all I can give you. A poor gift of wild fruits is the best and only repast the owner of Atahualpa's treasure can now give to the richest man of the Kingdom of Quito. What are our riches to us now?"

"And there is no hope for my men?"

"None!"

"Can we not force our way through?"

"You are surrounded by ten Indian tribes. And the victorious warriors of twenty Indian nations are between you and escape. Your firearms have become useless. You have no bows and arrows. Your men are starving. There is no hope for them. But let me save you, Julio. It is all I can do."

"Would I ever have deserved your love, and would I now deserve your esteem, if I should be base enough to abandon those poor creatures who are intrusted to my care? I must share the fate of my comrades. Behold!" he said, pointing to the few tattered rags still dangling from the flag-staff in his encampment, plainly discernible by the light of the moon. "There is the royal standard of which I am the bearer, distinguished and trusted by my King. How could I desert both flag and comrades for the purpose of saving my own miserable and wretched life, which is not worth saving. I did not come to these forests to save my life; I came to lose it. I recognize the place where we now are. I saw it in a dream in Mama Rucu's cottage, the night before I first spoke to you. All I then saw, has come to pass as I saw it; all except the end; and the end is near."

There was a long pause which was first broken by Toa: "Your refusal is what I dreaded. I knew you would refuse. It nearly drives me mad, that you will not let me save you; and yet, I can not but say that you are right."

"I thank you, Toa, I thank you!" he said, embracing her knees, and kissing the hem of her garment.

At this moment, the chattering of a monkey, followed by a parrot's shriek, was heard again.

"This is the signal that I am wanted," said Toa. "My savage allies must not discover that I have spoken to the enemy of their race. I must go."

With these words, she took his hands, lifted him up, and drew him into her arms. It was a moment of sharp and bitter anguish; this last moment of parting and of eternal separation, with all the regrets of the past and all the hopelessness of the future concentrated into one deathly pang of utter and absolute despair. It was doubtful which was the unhappier, he who was to die in the morning, or she who was doomed to live on.

"And when shall we be attacked again?" asked Carrera, as she turned to go.

"At sunrise!"

" Shall I see you during the last struggle ?"
" You shall!"

CHAPTER IX.

THE END.

The sun had arisen as bright and rosy as if it were to shine on nothing but happiness, and not on scenes of cruelty and carnage.

Carrera had led his men to the big trees down by the stream, where he delighted them with the discovery of the fruit which Toa had left for them. It was a banquet to the starving sufferers, after so many days of gnawing hunger. They felt refreshed and revived, and strong enough to carry those who had become too sick and weak to march, under the shelter of the big trees.

There, where his meeting with Toa had taken place, Carrera took his last stand. This position afforded the advantage of water to wash their wounds and to quench their thirst during the heat of a protracted contest. The trees, too, promised at least some protection from the arrows of the Indians, while the clearing into which the Spaniards could dash, when necessary, without exposing themselves to hidden dangers, would cover their rear.

Carrera had told his men that, from what he had observed during the night, he was sure of an attack after sunrise. The enemy had harassed and pursued them until their firearms had become useless. This calamity having come to pass, it was probable that the Jivaros would risk a hand-to-hand engagement. Hence he bade his men to kneel down and once more to recommend their souls to God, before whose throne the next moment might summon them to appear.

The men obeyed, and passed a few moments in silent prayer. It was their last.

With the rays of the rising sun transforming the dew-drops on trees and grass into so many glittering diamonds, the Indians had emerged from their hiding places in the forest, and threw themselves with piercing yells upon the Spanish position, darkening the air for a moment with a shower of arrows, and then advancing to a close encounter.

The contest was short.

The Spaniards, weakened by starvation and disease, were soon overpowered. They fell like sheaves under the scythe. Those that had not been killed, were reserved for the more cruel fate of prisoners.

In less than twenty minutes, they were all overpowered but one, and he the leader. He stood with his back to the tree under which Toa had awaited him the night before. Here he would die, after selling his life as dearly as he could. Many an Indian warrior had bitten the dust under the desperate strokes of the Christian knight. At last one of them, upon whom the others looked as their chief, came up and shouted : " Take him alive ! It is the Commander !"

A rush was made against him, but again his sword did terrible execution, and kept his assailants at a respectful distance. This last charge and repulse was followed by a moment of anxious suspense. Suddenly he heard his name called. "Julio !" a familiar voice had exclaimed, which seemed to come from the opposite tree. He looked up and saw Toa in its foremost branches, with an arrow drawn from the bow and aimed at his breast.

"God of mercy !" he shouted, opening his arms. " Speed it to my heart !"

The arrow flew as he spoke. It had reached its aim. "God bless the hand that sent it," muttered his dying lips, as he fell to the ground. His broken heart had ceased to beat. His troubled spirit was at rest.

www.ingramcontent.com/pod-product-compliance
Lightning Source LLC
Chambersburg PA
CBHW022108300426
44117CB00007B/629